D1433512

DICTIONARY
OF
FIRST NAMES

DICTIONARY
OF
FIRST NAMES

TIGER BOOKS INTERNATIONAL
LONDON

© Geddes & Grosset Ltd 1994

This edition published in 1994 by
Tiger Books International PLC, London

ISBN 1-85501-375-4

Printed and bound in Slovenia

Contents

Introduction

This volume is comprised of Professor Ernest Weekley's fascinating academic work *Jack and Jill*, a recognised authoritative text in the field of name derivation, and a substantial A–Z listing of first names, their meanings and origins.

This edition also contains a listing of Girls and Boys names and a comprehensive index to the Weekley text.

PREFACE
TO THE ORIGINAL EDITION

THIS book has been on the stocks for many years; in fact the keel was laid in the very distant past. Ten years of schoolmastering, followed by forty years with adult students of both sexes, not to mention many thousands of examination papers, have given me rather unusual opportunities for accumulating and considering Christian names. Three or four years ago I was about to start putting my collections into shape, when my friend Mr Eric Partridge told me that he was writing a dictionary of Christian names. I therefore decided to leave the field free to him and to turn for a time to something else. As Mr Partridge's book has appeared and reached a second edition, there seems no reason why my own, conceived on quite different lines, should not be offered to the limited public that is interested in such studies.

I owe much to my predecessors in the field, most of all to Charlotte M. Yonge, that accomplished woman whose literary and historical knowledge might be envied by many of our contemporary highbrows. Her *History of Christian Names*, first published in 1863, is invaluable from the historical point of view, but her attempt to cover the whole of European nomenclature makes it rather bewildering to read and her method of arrangement is not altogether happy. Etymologically it is weak, as it appeared at a time when comparative philology was still embryonic, nor does the second edition of 1884 show much advance in that respect.

For Old Testament names and the Puritan eccentricities I have relied chiefly on Bardsley's admirable *Curiosities of Puritan Nomenclature* (1888), an acquaintance with which might induce some authors of 'popular' books on names to shrink from rushing in where scholars fear to tread. For other 'oddities' of nomenclature I am deeply indebted to our indispensable Notes and Queries. For names of historical or literary interest I have frequently consulted the *Concise Dictionary of National Biography*, the *Century Dictionary of Names*, *Chambers' Biographical Dictionary* and Sir Paul Harvey's *Oxford Companion to English Literature*.

This book resembles my former efforts in that it is neither methodical nor 'scientific'. I have always preferred to follow, 'longo intervallo', the system of one of my literary idols, Montaigne, and, like Mme de Sévigné, 'je laisse trotter ma plume'. Sometimes, especially in dealing with the old Germanic names, I have given etymologies in the text, but these are generally put, as concisely as possible, in the glossarial index. For the meanings of Scriptural names I have relied almost exclusively on that amazing 'multum in parvo', *Helps to the Study of the Bible*, published by the Oxford University Press.

As this is a book on English names, I have only touched lightly on those that have come recently from abroad or from the 'Celtic fringe'. For the meanings of the latter I have had much help from Macbain's *Etymological Dictionary of the Gaelic* Language. As for the Welsh, it seemed wiser to imitate old Camden and 'sparingly touch them, or leave them to the learned of that nation'.

It is obvious that a book of this kind cannot contain all Christian names now in use. Those of Biblical origin, especially, are rather a job lot. Moreover, the constant occurrence of new and fantastic female names, such as the Aerielle whose marriage was recently recorded, is almost calculated to reduce a student to despair. I believe, however, that no genuine name in familiar use has been omitted.

I have to thank two learned friends for their assistance with the proofs. Sir Allen Mawer has made some valuable comments on Chapter II and the Rev EGJ. Forse, late Vicar of Southbourne, Hants, has read the whole text carefully and added notes, many of which are embodied in the Addenda and indicated by his initials.

I feel that, having announced *Something about Words* (1935) as a positively last appearance, I may be giving occasion for my small public to murmur a well-known line from Johnson. My excuse is that the leisure of retirement craves for some innocent amusement and that none appeals to me so much as the hunting down of words and names.

ERNEST WEEKLEY
RICHMOND, September 1939.

CHIEF SOURCES CONSULTED

Searle, W. G., Onomasticon Anglo-Saxonicum (Cambridge, 1897).

Björkman, E., Nordische Personennamen in England (Halle a. S., 1910).

John of Gaunt's Register, 1372-76 (London, 1911).

Camden, W., Remains concerning Britain (London, 1605, 7th ed., 1674).

Littleton, A., Latin-English Dictionary, containing "The most usual names of men and women rendred into Latine" (London, 1678).

Yonge, Charlotte M., History of Christian Names (2nd ed., London, 1884).

Bardsley, C. H., Curiosities of Puritan Nomenclature (London, 1888).

Dawson, L. H., A Book of the Saints (London, 1908).

Partridge, E., Name This Child (2nd ed., London, 1938).

Century Dictionary of Names (New York, 1895).

Chambers's Biographical Dictionary (Edinburgh, London, New York, 1929).

Concise Dictionary of National Biography (Oxford, 1930).

Harvey, Sir P., Oxford Companion to English Literature (2nd ed., Oxford, 1938).

Notes and Queries, passim.

The Times, Births, Deaths and Marriages.

'This is to be taken as a granted verity, that names among all nations and tongues are significative and not vain senseless sounds'

(Camden).

CHAPTER I

Introductory

AMONG the many *gaffes* perpetrated in the course of a long life I remember with special contrition the occasion on which, as a young schoolmaster, I asked a new boy of Jewish race and faith what was his 'Christian name'. This use of the word 'Christian' seems to be peculiar to English. In all other languages with which I am acquainted the equivalent means 'baptismal name', e.g. French. *nom de baptême,* Italian. *nome di battesimo,* Spanish. *nombre de bautismo,* German. *taufname (taufen,* to baptize). Hence it seems likely that 'Christian name' is a corruption of the obsolete 'Christened name'.

The name given at baptism is the only true name of the individual, the surname being merely a description, and not originally a fixed description, added to assist in identification. Change of surname is much more common than change of Christian name. The former can be effected by the mere insertion of an advertisement, but the latter is generally done by deed-poll. This formality, however, though often resorted to in order to avoid later complications as to identity, is not legally compulsory. Both names were changed informally in

the historic case of Mr Joshua Bug, who, by an
advertisement inserted in the Times of June
26, 1862, announced his intention of being
known in future as Mr Norfolk Howard.

Lord Halsbury, whose Laws of England was
published 1905-16, is explicit on the subject—
'The law prescribes no rules limiting a man's
liberty to change his name. He may assume
any name he pleases in addition to or substitution for his original name.' This controverts
Coke upon Littleton, published 1628-44, according to which the Christian name can be
changed at confirmation but, apart from this
licence, 'a man may have divers names at
divers times, but not divers Christian names'.
Burn's Ecclesiastical Law (1760) states that,
by a constitution of Archbishop Peckham, 'the
ministers shall take care not to permit wanton
names, which, being pronounced, do sound to
lasciviousness, to be given to children baptized, especially of the female sex: and if otherwise it be done, the name shall be changed by
the bishop at confirmation'. This change has
often been effected, though, in none of the
cases that I have noted, has there been any
suggestion of a 'sound of lasciviousness' in the
original name. According to a clergyman, writing to Notes and Queries, the Christian name
is sometimes changed at ordination. In Roman
Catholic countries an additional name, usu-

ally of saintly type, is often assumed at confirmation or on taking vows.

All races give a name to the new-born child and usually to the accompaniment of some sort of ceremony. With us the Christian name has now become a mere label, chosen for various motives and usually without any knowledge of its meaning. This was not the case in ancient times. Old Testament names and those of Greece and Rome are significant and the Biblical names especially have, as a rule, a meaning associated with the circumstances of the child's birth and family, or, as Camden puts it, 'upon future good hope conceived by parents of their children, in which you might see their first and principal wishes towards them'. Less sophisticated races than ours still give names which have some bearing on actuality or which express some hope or augury for the child's future. In some Red Indian tribes, the father, emerging from the wigwam in which the newcomer has made his appearance, chooses a name from the first object that catches his eye. It was thus that the Sioux chiefs Sitting Bull, Rain in the Face, Red Cloud and Spotted Tail were 'christened'.

Our own method of name-giving has undergone many changes in the last two centuries. Before that it was a simple matter, the child regularly receiving the name of a parent or ancestor, of a godfather or patron saint. In some noble families the same names for men persisted for centuries; a Douglas was Archibald or James as inevitably as his Border foe was a Henry Percy, and the great Robert Bruce was the eighth of that name, his ancestor Robert de Bruis[1] having come over with the Conqueror. Nowadays the choice is more often determined by the taste and fancy of the parents and the problem leads to discussions, sometimes approaching acrimony, before and after birth. 'And now', wrote a sprightly lady to the author on the birth of his youngest grandchild, 'I suppose the great name competition will begin'. The usual modern solution is a compromise in the form of a bunch of names.

This use of more than one Christian name is, for the great bulk of the population, comparatively modern. Its timid beginning can be traced back to the sixteenth century, but it was long a privilege of the more aristocratic and wealthy classes and, even among these, the use of a double name is very rare before the eighteen century, while that of a triple, quadruple, etc was almost unknown before the nineteenth What may be called 'fancy names' were also rare up to the early nineteenth century The great names in literature at that period were Walter Scott, Jane Austen, John

[1] Bruis was a castle near Cherbourg.

Keats, Robert Southey, William Wordsworth, etc with an occasional Percy Bysshe Shelley or Samuel Taylor Coleridge, bearing 'middle names' given for family reasons. Of the three Brontë sisters only one, Emily Jane, had a double name. Later in the century we find among the novelists Charles John Huffam Dickens and William Makepeace Thackeray as symptoms of the modern craze, but, at a much later date, examples of simplicity such as George Meredith and Thomas Hardy.

Nowadays the single name has become rare. A scrutiny any day of the Times obituary will show that at least eighty per cent of the persons whose deaths are recorded have two or more Christian names and that the exceptions are, more often than not, very aged people born before the new fashion prevailed. Frequently the 'middle name' is really a surname, inserted either for family reasons or because of its aristocratic or dignified sound.

There is no limit to the accumulation of names with which an unfortunate child can be burdened, but the record, at any rate for a girl, is probably held by Anna Bertha Cecilia Diana Emily Fanny Gertrude Hypatia Inez Jane Kate Louise Maud Nora Ophelia Quince Rebecca Starkey Teresa Ulysis Venus Winifred Xenophon Yetty Zeno Pepper, born at Liverpool in December 1880, while Thomas

Hill Joseph Napoleon Horatio Bonaparte Swindlehurst Nelson, living at Preston, Lancs, in 1876, is a good second. More economical of effort than the parents of Miss Pepper were those of Mr Alphabet Ayres, licensee of the King's Head, Prestwood, Bucks, who died in 1933. Such absurdities as the above occur much earlier, e.g. Bardsley quotes from church registers (1781 and 1804) the baptisms of Charles Caractacus Ostorius Maximilian Gustavus Adolphus, son of Charles Stone, and Zaphnaphpaaneah Isaiah Obededom Nicodemus Francis Edward, son of Henry and Sarah Clarke.

The bunches of names often conferred on royal princes and princesses have more justification, as these have usually some historical or genealogical significance, and the same applies to the old aristocracy, e.g. the Times of April 6, 1939, announced the death of Warner Francis John Plantagenet Hastings, fourteenth Earl of Huntingdon, succeeded by his son, Francis John Clarence Westenra Plantagenet Hastings. The Dukes of Buckingham have usually had such combinations of names as Richard Plantagenet Campbell Temple Nugent Brydges Chandos Grenville.

The practice of giving double names probably reached us from France, where it is very old, for we find King Philippe-Auguste[1] there in the twelfth. century. Even triple names are not uncommon in sixteenth century France. The immediate seventeenth century source of our double names was probably Scotland, which had such close associations with France. Nor is Charles I's French wife Henrietta-Maria to be absolved from a share in the responsibility, for her name was given to the daughter of the royalist Earl of Derby (executed in 1651). Like some other historic ladies, e.g. Maria-Theresa and Marie-Antoinette, she is generally referred to by her double name. The practice became intensified under the Georges, when the German influence was for a time very strong. In Germany the double Christian name had been in aristocratic use since the fifteenth century. George I was christened (in 1660) Georg Ludwig and most of the great German writers of the eighteenth century bore double or triple names, e.g. Christian Fürchtegott Gellert, Gotthold Ephraim Lessing, Johann Wolfgang Goethe, Johann Christoph Friedrich Schiller, etc Goldsmith derided the growing eighteenth century fashion, and perhaps also the German influence, when he gave a comic character the name Carolina Wilhelmina Amelia Skeggs, all

[1] The Auguste may, however, be a complimentary addition made by chroniclers.

three rather 'new-fangled' names which were popular in Germany. I fancy that the double name was at first, among the less endowed classes, especially given to girls: witness the innumerable Mary Annes and Sarah Janes of the earlier nineteenth century.

Camden tells us, in 1605, that 'Two names are rare in England; and I only remember now His Majesty (James I), who was named Charles James, as the prince his son Henry Frederic; and among private men Thomas Maria Wingfield and Sir Thomas Posthumus Hoby'. The first 'private man' is interesting as a parallel to the practice common in Roman Catholic countries of giving a female saint's name, usually that of the Blessed Virgin, by way of additional name to a boy, as in the case of Marie-Joseph Chénier, brother of the poet, and Victor-Marie Hugo. An earlier example is Voltaire's enemy, Élie-Catherine Fréron, whom he called frelon, hornet. Sometimes a female name alone was given, e.g. Anne de Montmorency, the famous Constable (d. 1567) whose godmother was Anne, Duchess of Brittany. A French authority, however, says that the name should be spelt Ann and regarded as the masculine of Anne. If this is correct, we have a parallel in the name of Enrico Caterino Davila, the Italian historian, who, says Charlotte Yonge, 'had the misfortune to have

Catherine de Médicis as godmother'. In the Wingfield family the first Maria was Edward Maria Wingfield, father of the man mentioned above, who was named from his godmother, Princess Mary, daughter of Henry VIII. The use of Posthumus or Posthuma, for a child born after its father's death, also belongs to this period and even in one case led to a triple name. Gulielma Maria Posthuma Springett is recorded on a tablet at Ringmer, Sussex. The date is 1640 and the example must be almost unique.

The practice of giving female names to boys either singly or in combination, continued sporadically through the eighteenth century. In army lists of the period occur Lucy Weston and Ann Gordon, along with Caroline Fred Scott, George Henrietta Kyffen and James Susanna Patton. Lord Anne Hamilton, third son of the fourth Duke of Hamilton, was named after Queen Anne. Edward Louisa Mann was the brother of Horace Walpole's friend, Sir Horace Mann. Caroline Robert Herbert, godson of Queen Caroline, was rector of Iden, Sussex, in 1786. Nowadays, except in the case of names given indifferently to boys and girls (Cecil, Evelyn, Hilary, Sidney, etc), female names are no longer given to boys, though we find isolated examples of their use as 'middle names', e.g. Francis Marion Crawford the American novelist.

In modern America the 'middle name' has become almost compulsory and most usually it is a surname, of which more anon. Among men born *c.*1800 we find Henry Wadsworth Longfellow, the two historians, William Hickling Prescott and John Lothrop Motley together with the soldier and President Ulysses Simpson Grant. Earlier than these is the sixth president John Quincy Adams, named from his birthplace in Norfolk County, Massachusetts. Then we have the essayists James Russell Lowell and Oliver Wendell Holmes, the novelist James Fenimore Cooper, and, in our own day President Thomas Woodrow Wilson, to mention only a few examples. In the case of many of these it is especially the 'middle name' by which the bearer is known and referred to, e.g. we usually speak of Russell Lowell, Fenimore Cooper, Woodrow Wilson, as of our own (Henry) Crabb Robinson, (James Henry) Leigh Hunt, (David) Lloyd George, (James) Ramsay MacDonald, (Giles) Lytton Strachey, (Henry) Rider Haggard, (William) Somerset Maugham, etc, almost as if they were hyphened surnames. The same tendency appears when the middle name, though not a surname, is more uncommon or ornamental than the first, e.g. (Arthur) Conan Doyle, (George) Bernard Shaw, (Enoch) Arnold

Bennett. When a surname stands alone as a Christian name, we seldom refer to its bearer without including it, e.g. Rudyard Kipling, Lascelles Abercrombie, Eden Phillpotts and, in America, Sinclair Lewis, Upton Sinclair. A curious example is Gouverneur Morris, US Minister in France, 1791-4, whose Diary has just been published in full. Gouverneur, which probably many people take for a title, was the maiden name of his mother, who was of Huguenot descent.

The surname as middle name is also found frequently for women, though less so than for men. In one issue of the Times I find Susie Watson B., Clara Markham L., Elizabeth Bannatyne L., Ada Shute R., Jane Peak R., and Mary Sinclair S., along with Arthur Wentworth B., Herbert Granville D. and a whole crowd of other male examples.

We will now go back to the beginnings of a practice unknown to other languages, viz. the giving of a surname as a baptismal name. It appears to date, timidly at first, from the early sixteenth century. Fuller is 'confident an instance can hardly be produced of a surname made Christian in England, save since the Reformation'.[1] The oldest historical example that occurs to me is Guildford Dudley, fourth son of the Duke of Northumberland and hus-

[1] I have seen this quoted, but have not been able to verify it.

band of Lady Jane Grey, with whom he was executed in 1554. It is curious that his own surname was probably the first to be taken into common baptismal use. Bardsley compares Dudley and Sidney in England with the much later Chauncey and Washington in America. Both Dudley and Sidney are included among *'The Most Usual Christian Names of Men'* by Littleton. His list also includes the much less common Denzil. This is a Cornish surname derived from a placename dubiously explained by Dexter[1] as meaning 'sunfort'. The popularity of Dudley was probably due to the importance of Queen Elizabeth's favourite, Robert Dudley, Earl of Leicester (d. 1588).

Camden says, 'In late years surnames have been given for Christian names among us and nowhere else in Christendom; although many dislike it, for that great inconvenience will ensue, nevertheless it seemeth to proceed from hearty goodwill and affection of the godfathers to shew their love or from a desire to continue and propagate their own names to succeeding ages, and is in no wise to be disliked, but rather approved in those which, matching with heirs general of worshipful ancient families, have given those names to their heirs, with a mindful and thankful regard of them'.

[1] *Cornish Names* (London, 1926).

A rare, but curious, practice is that of simply duplicating the family name. Readers of Tennyson will remember 'Sir Aylmer Aylmer, that almighty man, The county God, etc', and Sir Creswell Creswell (d. 1853) was a famous English judge. In Wales such combinations as Edward Edwards, Owen Owens, etc are common. Compare also the Italian Galileo Galilei and Browning's Fra Lippo Lippi.

Bardsley gives several early examples of children named from their mother's families, e.g. Onslowe Winch, son of Sir Humphrey Winch, Queen Elizabeth's Solicitor-General, Woodrove Foljambe (born in 1648), son of Peter Foljambe, the name in each case being the mother's 'maiden'. The Canterbury register for 1601 records the baptism of Tunstall, son of Mr William Scott, son-in-law to the worshipful Mr Tunstall, prebendary of this church. With these we may put what is perhaps the most famous name in world fiction, for Robinson Crusoe tells us that he was christened Robinson in 1632 from his mother's family name. The same method was used for female children, e.g. Essex, daughter of Lord Paget (d. 1639), and Mallet, daughter of the notorious Earl of Rochester, the mother's maiden name being Elizabeth Mallet. Essex, as a girl's name, has been in continuous use in the Cheke family since 1614. Many other seventeenth cen-

tury examples are given in various volumes of
Notes and Queries, but, generally speaking, this
practice soon died out so far as girls were concerned, while it persisted for boys. The occasional modern use of surnames for girls, e.g.
Sidney, Lesley, Shirley, etc, is a matter of
taste, not of genealogy, the vogue of the last
being chiefly due to Charlotte Brontë's novel
(1849).

Here are a few early examples of male Christian names from surnames: Chidiock[1]
Tichborne, one of the Babington conspirators,
was executed in 1586. In 1634 Sir Sanders
Duncombe obtained a monopoly for supplying
London with 'sedans', later called sedan
chairs. In 1643 the gallant Sir Bevil Grenville
fell at the battle of Lansdowne, near Bath
(Bevil-le is an old Cornish surname). Among
my books is the Relation of Sydnam
(Sydenham) Poyntz, an adventurer who
fought in the Thirty Years War and afterwards
on the side of the Parliament. His first experience of war was his capture, in Flanders, by his
godfather, Captain Sydenham. He had a brother
Newdigate Poyntz, no doubt named in the same
way. Wentworth Smith and Shackerley
Marmion were seventeenth century dramatists,
the latter s name being derived from the hamlet

---

[1] This surname occurs in John of Gaunt's Register. It is derived
from the Dorset village of Chideock.

of Shakerley, Lancs. In seventeenth century America we have Cotton Mather, the notorious witch-finder.

In the eighteenth century the practice becomes still more common. A famous example is Warren Hastings, though this may have been a revival of a once familiar Christian name, and another is Spencer Perceval, the Prime Minister who was assassinated by a madman in the lobby of the House of Commons (1812). At this period too it became very usual to give double surnames at baptism, e.g. the notorious Bamfylde Moore Carew, 'king of the gypsies'. Sir Eyre Coote, the famous Anglo-Indian soldier, was succeeded in one of his commands by Sir Galbraith Lowrie Cole. Early in the nineteenth century we have the poet Winthrop Mackworth Praed, who died untimely in 1839. Lord Halsbury was Hardinge Stanley Giffard. The vicar of Hampstead, when I was young, was Sherard Beaumont Burnaby. Our dismal contemporary literature is brightened by one satisfying humorist, Mr Pelham Grenville Wodehouse, D.Litt. Oxon. An example of a triple surname Christian name is that of the poet Coventry Kersey Dighton Patmore.

Up to the nineteenth century the use of surnames as Christian names was practically limited to the aristocracy. Now the position is reversed. The aristocracy tends to go back to

John and Henry, while the *bourgeoisie* and the proletariat adorn their sons with names of historic and noble ring. We have all known men called Clifford, Courtenay, D'Arcy, Dudley, Howard, Mortimer, Neville, Pelham, Russell, Seymour, Spencer, Stanley, Tracy, Travers, Vere, Willoughby, etc Sometimes national heroes such as Clive, Nelson and Rodney are thus honoured. A few of this class have become so stabilized as Christian names that their origin is no longer recognized. Percy, from the family name of the Dukes of Northumberland, originally de Percy, from a Norman village, had a tremendous vogue in the later nineteenth century. Out of eight boys who composed the top form when I was at school (*c.*1880) five bore this name, which is now regarded in America as a ludicrous appellation for the typical young Englishman. Along with Percy go Cecil, Sidney and Montague. Cecil, as a boy's name, is more often from the family name of the Salisburys (originally Welsh Seysil) than from the Latin Cæcilius; Sidney, hereditary with the Earls of Leicester, is the French St. Denis; and Montague, the family name of several peers, comes from one of many places in France called Montaigu, i.e. sharp hill.

Although Camden approves the legitimate use of the surname as Christian, he condemns

the practice of borrowing noble names haphaz-
ard—'Surnames of honourable and worshipful
families are given now to mean men's children
for Christian names'. An example of this is the
frequent early (16–17th centuries) occurrence of
Bulmer as a Christian name in the Darlington
district a compliment to a great landowning family of the region.

The surname as Christian name epidemic
rages still more furiously in America. From a
book called *What shall we name the baby?* it
would seem that the large majority of American Christian names are of surname origin,
e.g. those enumerated on one page alone are
Darton, David, Davin, Davis, Dean, Dearborn,
Dedrick, Delmar, Delwin, Dempster, Denby,
Denley, Dennet, Dennis, Denton, Derrick,
Derwin, Desmond, nearly all of which are surnames. Parenthetically it may be remarked
that many of the female names recorded in the
same book give proof of considerable inven-
tiveness, e.g., to take another page, Valentina,
Valerie, Valonia, Valora, Vanessa, Vania,
Vara, Vashti, Veda, Vedette, Vedis, Velda,
Veleda, Vera, Veradis, Verda, Verna, Vernita,
Veronica!

We have already noticed the seventeenth
century Cotton Mather in America. The original settlement being largely Puritan, it was
the Biblical name which chiefly prevailed up

to the Revolution (see ch. v). After that event the names of the fathers of the American constitution began to be freely used baptismally, so that we find Washington Irving, Jefferson Davis, Hamilton Fish and, in our own day, Franklin Roosevelt. Apart from these political celebrities there are some surnames of noted American families which are often used baptismally. One of the commonest is Chauncey, from an English-born Puritan who became President of Harvard in 1654. With this name we can compare that of Dwight, President of Yale in 1795, who gave a Christian name to Moody, the nineteenth century revivalist. The Winthrops have supplied America with many administrators, the first being John Winthrop, an Englishman appointed Governor of the Massachusetts Bay Colony in 1629. John Caldwell Calhoun (d. 1850) was one of the great triumvirate of American political orators.[1] James Otis (1725-83) was a distinguished patriot and orator. But why Wilbur? The only Wilbur of any celebrity known to me is the fictitious Rev Homer Wilbur who edited the 'Papers' of the equally fictitious Hosea Biglow.[2] Somewhat curious is the great Republic's predilection at the font for Duke and

---

[1] The others were Henry Clay and Daniel Webster.
[2] By Russell Lowell, 1848 and 1867.

Earl.

A curious practice, long disused, is that of giving identical names to two or more brothers or sisters. A well-known example is that of Sir John Paston (1442-79) of the famous Letters, who had a younger brother John. It is possible that this practice may have originated in the desire to be sure of an heir appropriately named in an age when families were prolific and mortality was heavy. Here are a few examples. In 1340 Gilbert de Hawkewood left bequests to his two sons, John senior and John junior, one of whom became later the famous condottiere. Richard de Merton (d. 1371) left as co-heiresses his two daughters, Agnes and Agnes. In Beddington Church (Surrey) is a medieval brass (1414) commemorating Philippa Carew and her thirteen brothers and sisters, four of the boys being named John. Twins were sometimes named identically, e.g. in the register of Rothwell (Yorks) is recorded, for 1547, the baptism of Joh'es et Joh'es fil' gemelli Joh'es Saywell, and in the following year that of female twins Johanna.[1] In 1612 one John Willes made bequests to 'my brother John Willes the elder and my brother John Willes the younger'. Thomas Gawdy, of

---

[1] Medieval Rolls and early registers almost invariably give names in latinized form. In this book they are usually, for practical convenience, modernized.

Harleston, Norfolk, had three families by three wives, the eldest son of each being named Thomas. All three of them became distinguished men of law in the seventeenth century and the youngest changed his name to Francis at confirmation. The following curiosity must be almost unique. Ralph Selby, of Twisell, Northants, who died in 1660, left two daughters named Elizabeth. Both married men named Selby. Frances Selby, daughter of the younger Elizabeth, married Captain Rowland Selby, who was killed in a duel in 1691, the widow subsequently marrying the victor!

From what is said above it is clear that our baptismal nomenclature has been considerably modified in the last two or three centuries. The Middle Ages had a comparatively small stock of Christian names and relied almost entirely on less than two dozen for each sex. If we look up, in the *Dictionary of National Biography*, a list of celebrities who died before *c*.1750, we shall find that ninety-nine per cent of them are furnished with single names and that John, William, Thomas, Richard, Robert and Henry recur almost monotonously among the men and Agnes, Alice, Cicely, Joan, Matilda (or Maud), Margaret, Elizabeth and the related Isabel among the women. The female names are, however, much more distributed.

John of Gaunt's Register[1] (1372) gives a good idea of the nomenclature of medieval England, containing, as it does, an account of the duke's dealings with relatives, friends, purveyors, employees, etc and tenants on his widely scattered estates. The index numbers about a thousand names. Of the men quite eighty per cent are John, William, Thomas, Richard or Robert.[2] After these a fair show is made by Henry, Roger, Walter, Hugh and Ralf, the Anglo-Saxon Edmund and the saints' names Nicholas and Philip. Christian and Payn (the pagan!) each occurs once, the latter surviving as a common surname. Altogether there are only between fifty and sixty male Christian names.

The women's names in the same record, twenty-two in number, are less bunched and none of them appears particularly favoured. They are, with normalized spelling, Agnes, Alexandra, Alice and Alison, Amy, Beatrice, Blanche, Constance, Denise, Elaine, Eliza-

---

[1] Published (1911) by the Camden Society.

[2] The prevalence of these names during the 'surname period' (*c.* 1066–1400) is shown by the immense number of their modern surname derivatives. At about the same date as John Gaunt, in the West Riding Poll-Tax of 1379, out of 219 men whose names occur in the first five pages, 175 are accounted for by the above five names, viz. John (75), William (41), Thomas (23), Robert (19), Richard (17).

beth, Emmot (pet form of Emma), Isabel, Joan and Janet, Katharine, Mabel, Margery, Mary, Matilda and Maud, Philippa, Sibyl. Here already we see the power of fashion, for Blanche and Constance were the names of John of Gaunt's two wives, Philippa that of his heroic mother. In the first five pages of the West Riding Poll-tax there are 168 women, with only 16 names among them. They are Joan (30), Alice (25), Agnes (21), Isabel (19), Cicely (18), Matilda (14), Margaret (11), Elena, i.e. Helen or Elaine (8), Elizabeth (6), Denise (4), Sibyl (4), Beatrice (3), Emma (2), Katharine (2), Eve (1).

It is rather curious to find Edward so rare at this period, for there had been two great kings of that name and the Black Prince had also made it illustrious. There do not seem to be any other Anglo-Saxon names in this Register. The fact is that, except for the two royal saints, Edmund and Edward, the Anglo-Saxon names had practically died out by the fourteenth century. Alfred, Edgar, etc are revivals. Although the age of Edward III was poor in Christian names, the king supplied our own times with one that had some recent vogue before it became slightly pretentious, when he created for his son Lionel the rather artificially named Dukedom of Clarence.[1] The title has not usually brought luck to its bearers, for Lionel died at thirty, Thomas, brother of Henry V, was killed in France, George, brother of Edward IV, ended in a 'butt of malmsey', and Albert Victor, elder brother of King George V, died in early manhood. It is not likely that it will ever be revived.

If we take a rather larger section of time, reaching from John of Gaunt's period to Cromwell's, we find that names are still far from numerous. The Bury Wills[2] (1370–1649) contain naturally some hundreds of names, but, limiting ourselves to the male testators, we find John (11), William (9), Richard and Robert (3), Edmund and Thomas (2), Adam, Andrew, Baldwin, Francis, Henry,[3] Giles, James, Nicholas and Roger (1 each). Of 98 'gallant squires of Kent' who, in 1588, subscribed money towards the country's defence, 56 are accounted for by John, Thomas and William.

Taking another stride forward, we note that the baptisms at North Meols, Lancs, from 1632 to 1713, of 2742 boys and 2532 girls involved the use of only fifty names for the former and forty-eight for the latter, but that

---

[1] Apparently from the medieval Latin *dux Clarensis*, from Clare, in Suffolk.

[2] Printed for the Camden Society in 1850.

[3] Spelt Herry. The usual medieval pronounciation of Henry was Harry; hence our innumerable Harrises and Harrisons and the Welsh Parrys. In Scotland the nasal seems to have been more often preserved, as witness the Hendersons.

among the boys eight names and among the girls nine names were given over a hundred times. For the boys John and Thomas actually suffice for about one third of the total number. Elizabeth, if Betty is included, comes first among the girls, followed by Anne.

Littleton's *Latin Dictionary* (1679) has as an appendix 'The most usual Christian names of men and women'. These lists, numbering 270 male and 126 female names (a few of them mere variants), would seem to contradict the evidence already given as to the comparative paucity of Christian names before what may be called the modern period. They are, however, largely artificial. They include a number of Scriptural names which were certainly 'not usual', except among fanatical Puritans, e.g. Abiathar, Ananias, Balthasar, Baruch, Eleazar, Ezekias (Hezekiah), Gamaliel, Gideon, Jude, Manasses, Nathan, Philemon, etc More familiar Scriptural names are given in their popular form, e.g. Barnaby, Jeremy, Toby, Zachary. Few Scriptural names other than the familiar Anne, Elizabeth, Mary, etc appear among the females, though the Puritan abstracts are there in force, viz. Charity, Faith, Fortune, Grace, Love, Mercy, Patience, Prudence, Temperance, along with the similar Greek names Althea, truth, Philadelphia, brotherly love, and Sofia, wisdom.

Littleton gives no Scotch or Irish names except Brigid, *vulgo* Bridget, but is rather strong on Welsh, e.g. Cadwallader, Caradoc, Enion, Evan, Griffith, Howel, Madoc, Meredith, Meric, Llewellyn, Morgan, Owen, Rhese (Rhys or Recs), Ybel and Ythel, along with Nesta (Agnes) and Gladuse.

Many Anglo-Saxon names, certainly not in general use in 1679, owe their inclusion to their historical or hagiological importance, e.g. Aldred (d. 1069), the last English Archbishop of York, Bede (d. 735), the 'venerable' historian and saint, Dunstan (d. 988), Archbishop, statesman and legendary baffler of Satan, Egbert (d. 839), traditional first 'King of all England', Grimbald (d. 903), abbot and saint, invited to England by Alfred and prominent in the mythical history of Oxford, Swithin or Swithun (d. 861), the 'wet' Bishop of Winchester, Thurstan, Archbishop of York (d. 1140), who disputed precedence with Canterbury and rallied the North for the Battle of the Standard (1138), Uchtred (d. 1016), an Earl of Northumbria who fought against Canute, Wulfstan (d. 1093), a bishop of Worcester and famous preacher, canonized in 1203 by Innocent III. Thurstan, like Grimbald, was a foreigner, but his name (Tustain) is usually given in its Anglo-Saxon form. Along with these goes Anselm, who was born at Aosta, but bears a Old

English name.

All of these may be still used occasionally as Christian names, e.g. we have Dunstan Cass in *Silas Marner*, Uchtred[1] is traditional in the Kay-Shuttleworth family and most of us have run against an Egbert or a Thurstan, but it is obvious that they have never been 'usual' names since Anglo-Saxon times.

The Old English female names include the historical Etheldreda, Emma and Gertrude (these two both really Continental), Frideswide, Mildred, Rosamund, Walburg or Warburg, Winifred. Some of these are saints—from St Etheldreda, popularly Audrey, Queen of Northumbria and Abbess of Ely (d. 679), we have the word *tawdry*.[2] St. Frideswide (d. *c.* 735) is the patron saint of Oxford. St. Walburg was abbess of Heidenheim and is accidentally associated with the witches' revels on the Brocken on *Walpurgisnacht*.[3] St. Winifred or Winefride, who appears to have been a Welsh saint with a name approximating to Guinevere and later confused with the Old English male name Winifrith, is commemorated in the famous well (Holywell, Flintshire), which really has curative powers.

---

[1] This unusual name is from old English. *uht*, creature, spirit,'weight', and *ræd*, counsel, wisdom, thus almost equivalent to Alfred.

[2] See my *Romance of Words*, p. 65.

[3] See my *Words and Names*, p. 18.

It is characteristic of changing fashions in girls' names that Charlotte Yonge should have written that ' Winifred is occasionally found in England, though usually through a Welsh connection '. St. Mildred (+ c. 700) was Abbess of Minster, Thanet. For Emma, Gertrude and Fair Rosamund, mistress of Henry II, see pp. 48, 54, 134.

Other pretty names in the list are Dowsabel, i.e. Dulcibella, and Roseclere. The death of an octogenarian Dulcibella was recorded in the Times of May 2. Two curious female names in Littleton are Douglas and Tace. The former is an early example of a girl being christened by a surname , Douglas Denny, born *c.* 1545, was the daughter of Sir Anthony Denny and the goddaughter of Lady Margaret Douglas. The Latin imperative Tace, be silent, is also mentioned by Camden as 'a fit name to admonish that sex of silence'. It long survived among Quakers as Tacye, Tacey. Another curious female name is Anchoret, but this is possibly an imitative spelling of the Welsh name Angharad, which occurs in the Mabinogion and was in English use in the Fourteenth century.

Littleton's inclusion of the surnames Denzil, Dudley and Sidney has already been noted. He also gives Grey and Talbot, but no Percy, Montague or Clarence! Some foreign names of

German origin seem to be dragged in for their historical interest, e.g. Conrad, the stock name of the Hohenstaufens, Ferdinand,[1] historical in both Spain and Germany, Maximilian,[2] Emperor of Germany (d. 1519), 'the last knight', Sigismund, the name of the German Emperor (d. 1437) who suppressed the Hussites and of several Kings of Poland. He even includes Ernest, a name certainly not usual in England before the time of the Georges. He explains Amias as from Amadeus, 'the name of some Dukes of Savoy', but this is doubtful, though Charlotte Yonge is of the same opinion. Fathers of the Church are represented by Chrysostom, Cyprian, Ignatius and Hierom (i.e. Jerome).

Two very curious male names in the list are Original and Vital. The former has nothing to do with sin.—'The name was given in the early part of the sixteenth century, in certain families of position, to the eldest son and heir, denoting that in him was carried on the original stock. The Bellamys of Lambcote Grange, Stainton, are a case in point. The eldest son for

[1] It had, however, reached England. Ferdinando Stanley was the fifth Earl of Derby (d. 1594).

[2] 'A new name, first devised by Frederic the third Emperour, who, doubting what name to give his son and heir, composed this name of two worthy Romans' names whom he most admired, Q. Fabius Maximus and Scipio Aemilianus, with hope that his son would imitate their vertues' (Camden).

three generations bore the name' (Bardsley). Vitalis was the name sometimes given to a child, when, owing to the condition of the mother, it was doubtful whether it would be born alive. Creatura was used in the same way.

In quoting Littleton I have modernized the often antiquated spelling, but forms such as Reynold and Pierce (Old French Pierres, nominative case of Pierre) show that Reginald and Peter were little used, the former in fact not at all, as is shown by the very common surnames Reynolds and Pearce, Pearson. No one has ever heard of Peter Plowman or Peterkin Warbeck!

It is clear that, if the eliminations above suggested were carried out, Littleton's list of Seventeenth century names would be greatly reduced and that the Christian names in general use in his day did not really number more than a few dozen for each sex.

One female name given in his list is of special etymological interest, viz. Orabilis, yielding to prayer. The name Orable or Orabella[1] is not uncommon in medieval records and survives in the surname Orbell. I regard it as the origin of Arabella, chiefly remembered for the

[1] For instance it occurs several times in the Hundred Rolls (1273). In the Testa de Neville, *temp*. Henry III–Edward I, it is already found as Arable.

unfortunate Arabella Stuart, who died a prisoner in the Tower in 1615, known in her own day as the Lady Arbell. Pope's Belinda, in the Rape of the Lock, was really Arabella Fermor. The name is old in Scotland, where it dates back to the thirteenth century. Another name of the same type as Orabilis was Amabilis, meet to be loved, which became Amabel and Mabel. By dissimilation of the labials, perhaps partly also by association with Anna, this became Annabel or Annabella (also found as Annaple) and I conjecture that Arabella was an amalgamation of this name with Orable. This seems to me more reasonable than any of the fantastic theories that have been put forward by amateurs, while Charlotte Yonge's proposal to identify Arabella with Arnhild is obviously out of the question.

We have already noticed some of the fashions in names that now prevail. Another is the tendency for English parents to select names that come from what the great Lord Salisbury rudely described as the 'Celtic fringe'. It would not be easy before the nineteenth century to find an English child baptized Kenneth or Maisie, Desmond or Kathleen, Morgan or Gladys. Until what may be called recent times no Englishman and few Lowland Scots were baptismally associated with what Cuddie Headrigg calls 'a' the Donalds and Duncans

and Dugalds that ever wore bottomless breeks
' (*Old Mortality*, Ch. 37). Along with this goes
the love of historic Scottish surnames, such as
Campbell, Douglas, Gordon, Leslie, Stewart,
etc, often given in families that have never
been further north than Hampstead. My own
uncles Wallace and Bruce were more legiti-
mately named, for their father was a Mac,
whose ancestor had left his native Perthshire
with some precipitation in the eighteenth century. Neither of those famous surnames, however, was originally Scottish. For de Bruis,
which Scotch patriotism transformed into 'the
Bruce'. Wallace means foreigner, 'Welshman'.

Just now there is a reaction in the direction
of the old simple names, such as John, Henry,
Richard, etc for boys, and Jane, Anne, Mary,
etc for girls, and those adorned with fancy
names (Algernon and Clarence, Arabella and
Evelina) often try to shed them. I know two
charming and gifted young ladies who have
adopted Bobbie and Jimmy in lieu of more ambitious and resonant vocables. At the same
time there is a preference for the full name
rather than the pet form. Elizabeth is now
Elizabeth, not Bess or Betty, and none of the
young Richards of my acquaintance answers
to the name of Dick. But the love of foreign
names for girls, such as Yvette, Delphine,
Renee, Georgette, etc, as also of high-sounding

names persists in some circles. In one issue of the Times Literary Supplement occurred Jolanda and Melina as the Christian names of lady novelists. The first is Hungarian and may be related to Iolanthe, the second suggests the Greek names for millet or the ash tree. One also remarks an occasional predilection for archaic or unusual spelling. I have recently noticed in the Times Mairi and Sibell as the names of noble ladies and Mae is not unrecorded. Bertie Wooster's Aunt Dahlia expressly warns him that 'no good can come of association with anything labelled Gwladys or Ysobel or Ethyl or Mabelle or Kathryn— but particularly Gwladys'.

Apart from exposing its bearer to the possible derision of the impolite, the unusual name lends itself, in some cases disastrously, to scribal errors. The popularity of the Faerie Queene gave Amias or Amyas, the 'squire of low degree', some vogue among the Elizabethans.[1] Amias Hext, who was entered at Winchester in 1607, appears in the Index of Scholars as Ananias Hext.

[1] It was, however, in use before Spenser's time. In addition to the fictitious Amyas Leigh, we find two historical Sir Amyas Paulets, the elder of whom died in 1538, while the younger was in charge of Mary Queen of Scots: and examples occur as early as the 13th. century. It cannot phonetically represent Amadeus, so I conjecture that it was affected by the fairly common medieval surname Amias, which is derived from Amiens. This is a Kentish name, now usually sorrupted to Ames or Amos.

CHAPTER II

Saxon and Norman and Dane are We

THE great majority of names in common use in England from the coming of Hengist and Horsa to the time of the Plantagenets were of Germanic origin, either (1) Anglo-Saxon, (2) ' Danish ', i.e. Old Norse, or (3) Frankish ', i.e. Old German, *via* Norman-French. In the twelfth century they began to feel the competition of the saints (Ch. III). These three Teutonic languages were cousins and the names which they contributed were largely made up of similar elements with slight differences in form and sound. Some of these elements were specially favoured by one contributor, e.g. our names derived from the god Thor, such as Thurstan come from Old Norse. *Aethel* or *Ethel,* noble, was very popular with the Anglo-Saxons, and *Hrod,* famous, as in Robert, Roger, with the Continental Germans.

The normal Germanic name was dithematic; i.e. it consisted of two significant elements linked together with nothing to show any grammatical relation between them. A simple example is Ethelbert, Old English Æthelbeorht noble bright. This corresponds to the Old German Adalberaht whence Adelbert, the ' apostle of Prussia ', martyred in 997, and

47

the modern German. Albrecht, which reached England as Albert with the prince Consort and 'bids fair to become one of the most frequent of our national names' (Charlotte Yonge), a good example of the danger of prophesying. These Germanic names correspond in formation and sense, though not in vocabulary, with Greek names, so that Ethelbert is practically equivalent to Aristophanes.[1]

Many of the Germanic elements thus used could be reversed, e.g. Hereweald, army rule, whence Harold, is identical with Wealdhere, rule army, whence Walter. Both are found in Old English, but Harold is chiefly from Norse or Danish and Walter came to us via France from Old German. The Germanic word for army, which we still have in Hereford, appears in some of the names given by the Roman historians to German kings, e.g. Tacitus has Chariovalda (Harold!) and Cæsar has Ariovistus.

It might be well here to give a list of the commonest elements found in Old English so far as they survive in modern names. They are *œlf*, elf, *œthal*, noble, *beald*, bold, *beorht*, bright, *beorn*, warrior, but, in Norse and German, bear, *burg*, castle, protection, *cyne*, royal, and *cynn*, kind, race (seldom to be distin-

[1] For a fuller account of Old English names see my *Surnames* (ch. 2).

guished from each other), *cuth*, known, famous, *ead*, bliss, prosperity, *eald*, old, *ecg*, edge, sword, *eofor*, boar, *folc*, people, tribe, *frith*, peace, *gar*, spear, *god*, god,[1] *heard*, hard, strong, *helm*, helmet, protection, *here*, army, *hyge*, mind, heart, courage, *leof*, dear, *mœr*, famous, *mund*, protection, *os*, divinity, *rœd*, counsel, wisdom, *regen*, counsel, wisdom, *rœfen*, raven, *ric*, powerful, noble, *theod*, people, tribe, *thryth*, strength, *thur*, Thor, *weald*, rule, power, *weard*, guard, keeping, *wig*, fight, *wil*, will, resolution, *win*, friend, *wulf*, wolf. A few others will be explained as they occur. Some of the above, e.g. *œthel, theod*, were used only initially, and others, e.g. *mund*, only finally, but many of them could occupy either position. These elements were, as a rule, already archaic in Old English, surviving only in names and in the poetic vocabulary

Besides the dithematic, we find a large number of shorter names, to which immense additions are being made by the researches of the Place-Name Society. Many of them are obvious nicknames and others are clearly contracted or abbreviated forms of dithematic names, e.g. we find Æbba for the feminine Ælfthryth and Cutha for Cuthwin and Cuthwulf. Among the early invaders we find

[1] Not God.

Ælle, King of Sussex, Ida, King of Bernicia. Harold's two brothers, who fell with him at Hastings, were the dithematic Leofwin, dear friend, and the monosyllabic Gyrth or Gurth, Old Norse. *gyrthr,* one girded (with the sword). Almost the most famous of Anglo-Saxon names is that of St. Bede or Bæda, still given to children by devout Catholics. Two of the Danish kings of England were Sveinn, lad, 'swain', and Knutr, knot, knob, etc, i.e. Sweyn and Canute, in connection with which it may be noted that the Norsemen were particularly fond of nicknames. My own opinion, *quantum valeat*, is that these shorter names, where they are not obvious nicknames or descriptions, such as Ceorl, churl, Hafoc, hawk, etc, are usually pet forms of the longer dithematic names.[1]

A number of Old English names survived for some centuries, especially among the peasantry, but, as they had lost significance and vitality, most of them died out, their modern popularity dating almost entirely from the Romantic revival. We know that such names were scorned by the nobility and that Henry I's Norman courtiers derided their King and his Scoto-English Queen Edith, granddaughter of Edmund Ironside, by calling them Goderic and Godiva, two familiar Old English names. That

[1] On the whole question see Redin, *Uncompounded Personal Names in Old English* (Uppsala, 1919).

is perhaps why Edith assumed the Norman name Maud or Matilda. Even so pretty a name as Audrey is still rustic in *As You Like It*. The persistence of a few such names through the Middle Ages was due to their royal or saintly associations, the two factors being combined in Edmund, the martyr king of East Anglia (d. 870), from whom Bury St. Edmunds takes its name, and Edward the Confessor (d. 1066). These are the only two Ed- names which occur with any frequency in medieval records. Edgar and Edwin are, I think, largely revivals, though both were names of saints and Edgar occurs in *King Lear*. It was Scott's use of Edgar for the Master of Ravenswood that popularized the name in Europe; Edwin was immortalized by Goldsmith in his sentimental Edwin and Angelina, for a long time stock names in Punch for a loving pair. The restoration to royal rank of Edward, only equalled as a king's name by Henry, was partly political. The Normans had always claimed that the Conqueror was the legitimate heir of Edward the Confessor and, in 1269, when Henry III, who had already named his son Edward, completed the Abbey, the Confessor's body was translated to Westminster and buried before the high altar.

The names of the two most famous pre-Conquest kings were hardly in use during the Middle Ages. Harold was a rare name in Anglo-Saxon times, being usually an importation from Scandinavia, where Harold Fairhair[1] had made it illustrious. Harold, son of Godwin, himself was 'half-Dane' (whence the name Haldane), his mother Gytha being the daughter of a viking named Thurkil Sprakaleg ('with the creaking legs'). Alfred reappeared with the revival of learning and the new interest in the country's past. It became very popular in the 18–19th centuries and travelled to France, where it named the two greatest poets of the Romantic school, Alfred de Vigny and Alfred de Musset. About the same time French borrowed Edouard and Edmond. Alfred was sometimes written Alvred and misread as Alured, a name once dear to the romantic. Ælfric, a much commoner Old English . name, did not survive, in spite of the fame of Alfric Grammaticus (c. 1000), a great figure in literature, but the cognate Old German. Alberic passed into French and reached England with Alberic de Ver as Aubrey, which 'hath been a most common name in the honourable family of Vere, Earls of Oxford' (Camden). Auberon or Oberon is a diminvitive of this name. Elves and fairies were rather formidable or malignant sprites before the time of Spenser and

---

[1] So called from his abundant locks, not because, like most Norwegians, he was a blonde.

Shakespeare and Alp is the modern German for nightmare. The same applies to Puck, who, in the Middle Ages, was Satan. Littleton gives Alberic and Alfric, but they were hardly in use. Another Alfname was borne by a famous saint, Alphege, a Norman perversion of Ælfheah, elf-high, to whom a London church is dedicated. He was Archbishop of Canterbury and was murdered by the Danes (1011).

About equal in frequency to the Ed- names were those beginning with Ethel, noble, exemplified by a number of English kings.[1] I have known an Ethelbert and Thomas Hardy wrote *The Hand of Ethelberta*. Ethelstan, in its more familiar form Athelstan, the famous victor of Brunanburh (937), is still in baptismal use. Corresponding to Ethelwulf we have the German Adolf, introduced here in the eighteenth century in the terrible form Adolphus. The latter is, however, already in Littleton, probably as a compliment to the great Gustavus.[2] That Ethelbert and Athelstan are artificial revivals is shown by their form. In the Middle Ages they would have been contracted. Compare Aylwin or Alwyn which represents the popular

[1] There was a tendency for such initial elements as Ed- and Ethel- to persist in one family.

[2] This name, never in real English use, but popular in France as Gustave, perhaps means 'god-staff', from Old Norse. *guth*, god. It was the middle name of Colonel Burnaby, who rode to Khiva.

pronunciation of Aethelwin, now revived as Ethelwin, and Aylmer or Aymer from Aethelmaer, which is also the origin of Elmer,[1] so popular in the United States. Aymer de Valence, Bishop of Winchester (d. 1260), is also called Aethelmaer. Aylward, i.e. Aethelweard, is also somctimes found. Several of the Ethel-names were feminine, the most famous being Etheldreda, of which the second element is Old English *thryth*, might. I have lately noted this name in the Times. Audrey represents its Norman-French contraction. Ethelburga, patroness of an ancient London church and of a Woodard school at Harrogate, is apparently obsolete. The shortened Ethel is, I think, comparatively modern. According to Charlotte Yonge it is 'sometimes set to stand alone as an independent name'.

A more famous name is that of St. Hilda, the Abbess of Whitby (d. 680), which is probably for Hildeburg. Names in *Hild-*, war, also one of the Valkyries, 'choosers of the slain', are very uncommon in Old English, and the recently revived Hildebrand is an importation from the Continent, where it was made famous by St. Hildebrand (d. 1085), who, as Pope Gregory VII, restored the power of the Papacy and made the Emperor Henry IV wait in the snow at Canossa. The female names Hildegund and

[1] It is included in Camden's list of names.

Hildegarde have also been revived recently,
the latter for the detective heroine of a series
of 'shockers'; both are Continental.
Hildegunde, of which both elements mean
'war', is equivalent to our Gunhilda, sister of
Sweyn, who was one of the victims of the massacre of St. Brice (1002); the second element of
Hildegarde means 'protection'. Another shortened name as famous as Hilda is Bertha, wife
of King Ethelbert of Kent, who welcomed St.
Augustine, but she was a Frankish princess,
the daughter of Charibert (Herbert), King of
Paris. The name was also borne by Berthe au
grand pied, mother of Charlemagne and heroine of an Old French epic.

The only other group of names which have
survived or been resuscitated from the Anglo-
Saxon period consists of those beginning with
Os-, divinity, which corresponds to the Old
Norse. As-, as in Asgard, home of the gods, and
the Old German. Ans-, as in Anselm. These
are Osbern or Osborn, more common as a surname, Osbert, Oswald, Osmond and the rarer
Oswy and Osric, and I suspect that Oscar,
which dates from Macpherson's Ossian (1760),
belongs to the same category, as Osgar, divinity spear, is well recorded in Old English. Of
these by far the most popular is Oswald, the
name of a canonized Archbishop of York (d.
992) who was the protégé of Dunstan and Odo.

From the Continent came, through Old French, Anselm, divine helmet, the name of the canonizcd Archbishop of Canterbury (d. 1109), and Ankettle, divine cauldron, which some families still affect. It is probable that some of our Os- names were adaptations of Old Norse. As- names, or they may have reached us circuitously through the Normans, e.g. William FitzOsbern was the close friend of the Conqueror. He led the right wing at Hastings and became Earl of Hereford. The same applies to the names in Thor-, viz. Thurstan and Thorold, both very popular in Normandy.

A spurious Old English name, borne by Little Lord Fauntleroy, is Cedric, Scott's mistake for Cerdic, which, though the name of the first king of Wessex (d. 534), is probably Celtic. The same is true of Rowena, legendary daughter of Hengist and heroine of Ivanhoe. Her name should be Germanic, but is actually from Old Welsh. It means 'long white hair'. Eric, an Old Norse name of doubtful meaning, has still, in spite of Farrar, a certain popularity. A variant of Aldred, old wisdom, is Eldred, the Christian name of Pottinger, the famous Anglo-Indian soldier and diplomatist (d. 1843). Both Aldred and Eldred may also be contractions of Aethelred. The feminine Aldyth is the Christian name of a contemporary novelist, apparently a revival of Old English Ealdgyth. It is also shortened to Alda.

Other Old English names revived in recent times are Egbert, Egmond, Hereward, used in the Wake family, and Herwald, the old form of Harold, borne, at the moment of writing, by a Cabinet minister. Herbrand, the name of the present Duke of Bedford, appears to be a fancy choice, as the hereditary names of the Russells are Francis and John. I have recently noticed Ragnar as the name of an English admiral. This name, chiefly adorned by the famous Ragnar Lodbrog ('shaggy breeches'), the half-legendary Viking who raided England in the eighth. century, normally became Rayner. Its first element is *regen*, as in Reginald, its second is *here*, army. Reginald and Raymond were chiefly French introductions, though the former is found also in Anglo-Saxon. As noted elsewhere, Reginald is an artificial form, the natural contraction appearing in the French Renaud and the Italian Rinaldo. Reginald or Rainald was chaplain to William the Conqueror. Reginald FitzUrse ('son of the bear') led the murderers of Becket and, according to a tradition, went to Ireland and translated his name into MacMahon. Owing to a fancied Latin origin, Rex is sometimes used as a pet form. Raymond, Old german. Ragimnund, wisdom protection, was hereditary with the Counts of Toulouse. It went out of fashion in

England after the Middle Ages, but was revived in the later nineteenth century.

This about exhausts the names surviving or restored from the Anglo-Saxon period, though, as we shall see, many Germanic names cognate with recorded Old English names were popularized by the Normans or later contributors. Some Old English names, now no longer used baptismally, survive as surnames, e.g. Godwin or Goodwin, Goldwin, Herrick, Old English Hereric, Kennard, Old English Cyneheard, and Maynard, Old English Maegenheard, might strong.

The coming of the Frenchmen revolutionized our Christian names. Those of Old English origin were almost restricted to the peasantry and replaced in higher circles by French names of Germanic or Biblical origin. The Frankish conquerors of Gaul not only changed the name of that country, but also the names of its inhabitants. Just as the Romans had expelled the Celtic names from Gaul, so the Franks expelled the Latin names. In the sixth century about half the names used in France were Germanic. By the tenth century these were supreme; but, as they no longer had a meaning for the now French-speaking conquerors, new formations and combinations became impossible and the namelist was consequently very restricted. Germanic names naturally reigned completely in Normandy, where the Viking conquerors, who had converted Neustria into the land of the 'Northmen', had brought their Scandinavian names with them. It was partly as a consequence of the paucity of existing names that, from the twelfth century onward, the use of Biblical and saints' names became much more common, and eventually the Germanic names were in France, except for a few favourites such as Charles, Louis, Henri, etc, almost squeezed out by those more approved by the Church, such as Pierre, Jean, Jacques, Simon, etc Under the Plantagenets these latter names, for which see Ch. III, made a new invasion of England.

The list of William I's chief friends and supporters given in Planche's *The Conqueror and his Companions comprises* 80 names.[1] Of these the favourites are William (15), Robert (9), Hugh (7), Raoul, i.e. Ralph (5), Richard (5), Roger (4), Geoffrey (3), Odo (3), Walter (3), Fulk (2), all Germanic. Other Germanic names occuring once only are Toustain, i.e. Thurstan, Amery, Baldwin, Drogo (Drew), Gilbert, Humfrey, Henry, Bernard and Hamo. The only Biblical names are Samson and John. Then we have the dubiously Latin Guy (Vitus) and Neil (Nigel) with variants Neal and Niel,

---

[1] I give them in their usual English form.

the Greek Eustace and the two Breton names Alan and Ivo[1] for which see Ch. VII.

For many years after the Conquest William was the favourite name,[22] but, in the long run, Church influence superseded it by John, the name of the Baptist and of the 'beloved disciple', and, after the canonization of Becket, Thomas ran it close. Then came Robert and Richard. William, will helmet, Robert, fame bright, and Richard, powerful strong, were purely German and there are scarcely any corresponding names in Old English, though Robert of Jumieges (d. 1052) became Archbishop of Canterbury under Edward the Confessor and did much to spread the Norman influence. William owed its popularity to the Conqueror, while both Robert and Richard

---

[1] For names in -o see pp. 44-5.

[2] Its amazing popularity among the Norman nobility is commented on by Montaigne—'Henry, duc de Normandie, fils de Henry second, roy d'Angleterre, faisant un festin en France, l'assemblée de la noblesse y fut si grande que, pour passe-temps s'estant divisée en bandes par la ressemblance des noms, en la première troupe, qui fut des Guillaumes, il se trouva cent dix chevaliers assis à table portans ce nom, sans mettre en conte (= compte) les simples gentils-hommes et serviteurs' (*Essais,* i, 46). After the Franco-Prussian war of 1870–1 Guillaume and Frederic, the names of the victorious King and Crown-Prince of Prussia, were ostracized in France. For the final victory of John in England we have the following evidence from Dr Workman's *John Wyclif* (1926).—'At the Blackfriars synod of 1382, which condemned Wyclif, twenty-five out of the sixty-six who took part were called John, while of the twelve Oxford doctors who in 1381 sat in judgment upon his theses, no fewer than nine bore this name.'

were favourite Norman names. Robert was the name of the Conqueror's father. Its German form Ruprecht came to England as Rupert with that remarkable man who led cavalry charges, commanded fleets in action, invented mezzotint engraving and made scientific discoveries (Prince Rupert's drops). Richard was the name of two famous Dukes of Normandy, viz. Richard the Fearless (d. 996) and his son Richard the Good (d. 1026), with whom it is natural to link their descendant, Richard Coeur-de-Lion. The evil repute of Richard III may have given it some sinister association, for Jane Austen tells us playfully that Catherine Morland's father was 'a very respectable man, though his name was Richard' (*Northanger Abbey*, Ch. I).

Roger, fame spear, was hereditary in the great Bigod family, Earls of Norfolk, and often figures in medieval epic. One thinks also of Sir Roger de Coverley and Roger Tichborne, the latter a name on everybody's lips soon after 1870. In modern times it has mostly been a rustic name , but is now once more in favour. Geoffrey, i.e. Godfrey, god peace, was, with Henry and Fulk, hereditary with the Counts of Anjou, whence our Plantagenets, and was made illustrious by Godefroy de Bouillon, leader of the first Crusade. It was the name of the luckless Prince Arthur's father and appears to have been much favoured by ecclesiastics during the Middle Ages. It is very popular just now. Walter has already been mentioned . Perhaps the best remembered among early bearers of this name is that Walter Tyrrel who is usually credited with having done his day's good deed on August 2, 1100.

Raoul, though it looks monosyllabic, is also a dithematic name; it is the Old French form of Radulf,[1] counsel wolf, i.e. Ralph or Ralf. It is quite distinct from Ranulf, raven wolf, and Randulf or Randolph, shield wolf, the latter of which was formerly pronounced Randle or Randall, as by Randle Cotgrave, whose great French Dictionary appeared in 1611, and Randall Davidson, late Archbishop of Canterbury. Ralf and Randolph are both originally Old Norse, but Ranulf, the name of William II's rapacious minister Flambard, reached France from Germany, the first element being probably Old German *hraban,* raven.

Amery is from the Old German Amalric, of which the first element, supposed to mean 'work' or 'energy', named the royal dynasty of the Amelings, who ruled the Ostrogoths. Amalric became by metathesis Almeric, still in English use, and gave the Old French Aimeri, famous in the epic story of Aimeri de Narbone, and the Italian Amerigo, perpetuated in a con-

[1] In Old French a dental disappears between two vowels.

tinent. It survives in our surnames Amery, Emery. Another Amal- name is the female Millicent, which has a rather complicated history. The Old German Amalswint, of which the second element means 'strong', became Old French Melisande, daughter of Baldwin II, King of Jerusalem (12th century). This came early to England as Melisent, now usually Millicent. The Old French form has been used by modern romantics, e.g. Maeterlinck. For another possible Amal name see Amelia. Baldwin, bold friend, hardly occurs in Anglo-Saxon. Its great popularity came from Flanders. Baldwin, son of Charles the Bald, became Count of Flanders in the ninth century and practically all his successors bore the same name, which became so popular in his province that Flanders was sometimes called Baldwin-land. It was also the name of four kings of Jerusalem and two Emperors of Constantinople. The first element of Gilbert, earlier Gislebert, is German *Geisel,* pledge, hostage, which would imply a youth or maiden of high birth. Its chief English representative is Gilbert of Sempringham, founder of the Gilbertine order, who died a centenarian in 1189 and was canonized in the next century by Innocent III. It was hereditary in the de Clare family. The Humfrey or Humphrey who accompanied the Conqueror was a de Bohun and the name became hereditary in that family, which acquired the Earldom of Hereford. The first element is probably Hun, which, though the name of a squat, dwarfish race, became in German legend equivalent to giant; the second means 'peace' (cf. Geoffrey). Very popular in the Middle Ages, as is shown by the surname Humphreys, it suffered a long eclipse,—'From being a noble and knightly name, Humphrey, as we barbarously spell it, came to be a peasant appellation, and is now almost disused' (Charlotte Yonge). It is now once more in the fashion. The related Humbert is of modern introduction from French.

The first element of German Heinrich, whence, *via* French Henri, our Henry, is variously interpreted as 'home'; (German *Heim*) and 'grove, hedge', i.e. 'defence' (poet. German *Hain*), the second, cognate with *rich* and Latin rex,[1] means 'ruling', 'powerful'. At one time it looked like becoming the most popular of European names, being borne by seven Kings or Emperors of Germany, starting with Henry the Fowler[2] (d. 936), by four Kings of Castile, four Kings of France[3] and eight of England, or,

1 Compare also the Celtic Dumnorix, Vercingetorix, etc

2 One of the ' authorities' I have consulted makes the really hair-raising statement that he was called Heinrich von der Vogelsweide [*sic*].

3 'Now thought unlucky in France: when as King Henry the Second was slain at tilt, King Henry the Third and Fourth stab'd by two villainous monsters of mankind' (Camden).

if we include the Cardinal of York, who called himself Henry IX after the death of his brother, the Young Pretender, by nine. It was hereditary in the Northumberland family. As already mentioned, it became Harry in England—

> Not Amurath an Amurath succeeds,
> But Harry, Harry.
> *(Henry IV, P + 2, v.2)*

so that Harriet corresponds to Henrietta, French Henriette, which is apparently a 15th or 16th century coinage. Although Beornheard, from *beorn,* warrior, is a common Old English name, the vogue of Bernard comes from Continental German, in which the first element means 'bear'. Its popularity was chiefly due to St. Bernard of Clairvaux (d. 1153), who preached the fourth crusade, perhaps also partly to Bernard de Cluny, who wrote, in Latin, the famous hymn, 'Jerusalem the Golden'.

Hugh and Fulk are examples of the shortening of names by omission of the second element. Hugh, mind, thought, is short for Hubert, and Fulk, folk, tribe, for some such name as Folkard,[1] people strong, equivalent in

---

[1] Surviving as a common surname in E. Anglia.

sense to the Greek Demosthenes. Hugh became a favourite name, largely owing to the two Lincoln saints, Great St. Hugh (d. 1200), the bishop who rebuilt a great part of the cathedral, where his shrine was much frequented, and Little St. Hugh, the child fabled to have been martyred by Jews in 1225 and invoked by the Prioress at the end of her Canterbury Tale. The full Hubert also had some currency, its most notable bearer being Hubert de Burgh, who refused to put out Arthur's eyes and anticipated some modern tricks by getting to windward of Eustace the Monk and blinding that pirate's men with powdered quicklime. St. Hubert, Bishop of Liege (d. 727), became the patron saint of hunters, owing to his conversion having been brought about by a stag that he was pursuing. Five Counts of Anjou were named Fulk, as were eleven of the Shropshire Fitzwarins. The most important English bearer of the name seems to be Fulk Greville, the poet and friend of Philip Sidney.— 'This name hath been usual in that ancient family of FitzWarin and in later times in that of the Grevils' (Camden). It still turns up occasionally.

Odo and Hamo illustrate the Germanic practice of adding -o to the shortened form of a name. Hugh also is generally booked as Hugo and then treated as Latin, with genitive

Hugonis. Odo is from the first syllable of some Germanic name in Od- or Ot-, corresponding to the Old English Ed-. There were several pre-Conquest Odos in England, but they were no doubt foreigners or named under foreign influences. The most famous of them is that Archbishop of Canterbury (d. 959) who separated King Edwy from his wife Elgiva (Aelfgifu, elf gift) and, according to tradition, branded the Queen's cheeks to destroy her fatal beauty. Another famous Odo is the warlike Bishop of Bayeux and Earl of Kent, the Conqueror's half-brother. The name is not extinct, e.g. Lord Odo Russell was a distinguished diplomatist in the nineteenth century. The German form is Otto, the name of several early Emperors, and Othello is its Italian diminutive. It had an Old French nominative form Otes, still given as current by Littleton , whence the surname of a very gallant gentleman. Hamo is the shortened form of Hammond, once a common Christian name, which is the Old Norse. Hamundr, perhaps corresponding to the rather rare Old English. Heahmund, high protection. A famous -o name is Rollo, the Viking who became the first Duke of Normandy. In Wace he is Rou, but he was originally Rolf, the contraction of an Old Norse name answering to the German Rudolf, fame wolf, a great Hapsburg name, with the same first element as Robert and Roger. A still earlier example is Hludio, used in the Historia Francorum of Gregory of Tours (6th century) for Chlodowig (Ludwig, Clovis, Louis). Such names, usually of German origin, are occasionally used in English, e.g. Waldo of the South African Farm[1] and Bruno, the companion of Lewis Carroll's Sylvie. Saint Bruno (d. 1101) was the founder of the Carthusian order.

This irruption of names from France after the Conquest resulted in an actual shortage of Christian names in England. The Old English name-system, with its almost unlimited variety in combining the chief elements and of forming shortened names, produced an endless list. The examples given by Searle[2] are being multiplied tenfold by the valuable researches of the Place-Name Society. Some of these names persisted, as already stated, among the peasantry, but gradually tended to die out as the humbler classes imitated their social superiors, who, as shown by John of Gaunt's Register , had only some fifty or sixty Christian names at their disposal, even when the Norman-French names were reinforced, as we shall see in Ch. III, by those taken from the New Testament and the Calendar of Saints. And such was the nature of our name-list until

[1] Also Ralph Waldo Emerson.
[2] In his *Onomasticon Anglo-Saxonicum* (Cambridge, 1897).

the Renaissance.

We will now deal with the rest of the Franco-Germanic names that came in with the Conqueror and with a few others. Theobald, people bold, is found in Old English, but its currency was French. Theobald, Archbishop of Canterbury (d. 1161), was generally known as Tedbald, and Littleton still spells it Tibald; cf. French Thibaut and Shakespeare's Tybalt. Of almost the same meaning is Theodoric, the famous King of the Ostrogoths, who lives on in German saga as Dietrich of Bern (i.e. Verona), and has lately, via the Dutch form, given the English Christian name Derek or Derrick. The Germanic *gar*, spear, is the first element of Gerald and Gerard, separate names which have been sometimes confused in the past. Our most famous Gerald is perhaps the twelfth century historian of Wales, Giraldus Cambrensis, but Maurice Fitzgerald, a companion of Strongbow in his expedition to Ireland (1168), was the ancestor of the turbulent Gerald Fitzgeralds, or Geraldins, who were Earls of Kildare for centuries. 'Lady Elizabeth Fitzgerald, a daughter of this house, was the lady who, in imitation of Beatrice and of Laura, was erected by Surrey into the heroine of his poetry, under the title of the Fair Geraldine, this leading to the adoption of this latter as one of the class of romantic Christian names' (Charlotte Yonge). The most famous Gerard is the Dutch Gerhard or Geert, who mistranslated his name into Erasmus[1]; another founded (c. 1100) the order of the Knights of the Hospital at Jerusalem. Gervase, of which the second element is probably Old Germanic. *hwas,* sharp, is also a 'spear' name. It was borne by two important monkish chroniclers of the Middle Ages, viz. Gervase of Canterbury and Gervase of Tilbury (both *c.* 1200).

Another Ger- name, though unconnected with spears, is Jermyn, an alteration of French Germain, which is the tribal Germanus turned into a Christian name (cf. Francis and Norman, the latter of which had become a personal name even before the Conquest). St. Germain, Bishop of Auxerre, won (429) the 'Hallelujah victory' at the head of his converted Bretons. He was a very popular French saint, his name being commemorated by 130 French villages, a Parisian boulevard and the church from which the tocsin was sounded for the massacre of St. Bartholomew (1572). Traditionally he visited St. Albans,

---

[1] A Greek name meaning 'beloved'. St. Erasmus, martyred under Diocletian, became at Naples St. Elmo, patron saint of sailors. Hence St. Elmo's fire, corposant. The best-known bearer of the name in England is Erasmus Darwin, grandfather of Charles Darwin and his forerunner in enunciating a theory of evolution.

where the new Verulamium Museum stands near the site of his chapel. Among the 'spear' names which are hardly found in Old English is Gertrude, spear might, originally a Valkyrie , but made famous by St. Gertrude, a famous German mystic (d. 1311). The second element of her name, corresponding to AS. *thryth* , was later associated with Old Germanic. *trut*, now *traut*, beloved, trusty.

We have already noted the 'bear' of Bernard, the 'raven' of Ranulf and the 'wolf' of Randolph, etc Other animal favourites in Germanic names are the eagle and the boar. A familiar 'eagle' name is Arnold, eagle rule, which came, through French, from Old Germanic. Aranwald. It gave a familiar surname, but dropped out of use as a Christian, to be revived in the latter nineteenth century. Much more popular in the Middle Ages was Arnulf, eagle wolf, the name of a famous nineth century Emperor. Arthur, of which so many interpretations have been given, seems to be simply the ON. Arnthor,[1] eagle Thor. Apart from the semi-mythical King of the Britons, the name is chiefly associated with Henry II's unlucky grandson. Its disuse in the Middle Ages may have been due to his tragic fate. It was revived

[1] *Erne*, Old English. *earn*, is still used poetically for eagle, as is also the cognate German *Aar*. Charlotte Yonge slips up badly when she describes the modern German *Adler,* noble eagle, as a 'mere contraction of the Lat. *aquila*'.

by Henry VII for his elder son, who as a boy was married to Katharine of Aragon and died at the age of sixteen. Its nineteenth century popularity was due to the Duke of Wellington, whose godson, Arthur Duke of Connaught, is still with us. Everard is the Old French form of German Eberhard, boar strong, the name of the first Duke of Wurtemberg (d. 1496), famous in German song and legend. Sir Everard Digby, who died with the other Guy Fawkes conspirators, gave his son the purely Old English name of Kenelm, ? royal helmet (St. Kenelm was a Mercian king, *c.* 800). It was perhaps as a compliment to Sir Kenelm Digby, one of the most eccentric and picturesque figures of the Stuart period, described by John Evelyn as an 'arrant mountebank', that Littleton included Kenelm among his 'most usual names', for he also gives Venice, i.e. Venetia, the name of Sir Kenelm's wife. According to Charlotte Yonge, this is adapted from a Welsh name, but see. Venetia is also the heroine of one of Disraeli's novels to which she gives her name.

Our only 'lion' name, except the later Lionel, is Leonard, the name of a noble at the court of Clovis who was converted and later canonized. It is of late formation, the lion being hardly known to the old Germans. St. Leonard was revered on the Continent and in England, especially as the friend of poor prisoners. I do not remember any famous English Leonard, but the Italian form of the name was borne by the greatest genius of thc Renaissance. Lionel was the name of the first Duke of Clarence , and Leo has given a name to thirteen Popes, starting with St. Leo the Great (d. 46I). The Spanish form Leon is now sometimes found in England. Leopold, which looks like a 'lion' name, is Old German Liutbold, people bold. It is found in several royal houses on the Continent, but was hardly an English name before Queen Victoria gave it to her fourth son as a compliment to her friend and adviser, Leopold I, King of the Belgians, 'Uncle Leopold'. The fame of Bertram,[1] bright raven, and Bertrand,[1] bright shield, belongs especially to France, with the troubadour Bertran de Born, friend of the Lion-Heart, and the heroic Bertrand du Guesclin, Constable of France (d. 1380). Another 'raven' name, now rare except as a surname, is Ingram, from Ing, the name of a Germanic deity, which, confused with *engel,* angel, gave the Old English name Ingelram. The source is, however, Continental; cf. French Enguerrand, of very frequent occurrence in Old French epic.

Two famous Germanic names which reached

[1] The names may be identical, but both origins seem to be exemplified in Old German.

us from the Continent, though they have nothing to do with the Norman invasion, are Alaric and Roderick. Alaric, Old German. Adalric, noble mighty, was that King of the Ostrogoths who sacked Rome in 410. It is in occasional modern use with us, and Alaric Watts, a friend of the Wordsworths, is usually credited with 'An Austrian army awfully arrayed'. Voltaire, after his rupture with Frederick the Great, nicknamed that verse-writing conqueror Alaric Cottin, from the poetaster derided by Molière in *Les Femmes Savantes*. Few names have spread further than Roderick, though it has never been popular in England. It represents Old German. Hrodric, with the first element as in Rudolf, but its fame begins in Spain with the last of the Visigoth kings, who disappeared in 711 after his overthrow by the Moors and whose second coming was long awaited, as was that of Frederick Barbarossa by the Germans. He has been sung by Southey and Scott. Rodrigo was also the name of the Cid. As Rurik it went with the Varangians to Russia. In Scotland we have Roderick Dhu and in Ireland Rory O'More.

Other later introductions, which are among the most widely diffused of all Germanic names, are Louis, Frederick and Charles. Louis, Old German Hludowig, famous ('loud') war, begins in France with Chlodowig, i.e.

Clovis[1] (d. 611). He was converted to Christianity largely by the persuasion of his wife Clotilde, whose Valkyrie name has kept the initial guttural. Louis was the name of eighteen kings of France, if we include the hapless little Dauphin, who died of ill-treatment after the butchery of his parents. The fame of St. Louis, i.e. Louis IX, who died on Crusade in 1270, decided its choice as the royal name of France. In England it became Lewis, often adopted in Wales for Llewellyn, and in Scotland sometimes Ludovic, the name of Quentin Durward's uncle. Lois, now a girl's name, is an old French variant spelling of Louis. In Théodore de Banville's *Gringoire* it is the name of Louis XI's goddaughter. It is possible that Aloysius and Héloïse also belong here, for the sixteenth century Saint Aloysius was Louis Gonzaga.

Frederick, the name of a series of Danish and German Electors, Kings and Emperors, is a comparatively modern importation, as can be seen by the absence of surnames formed from it. Its meaning is 'peace-powerful', the

[1] This historic form is still used in France. Clovis Hugues was a rather militant French publicist of the later 19th century. A little book of saints, from which I have got much useful information, tells us that 'the battle-cry of "Montjoie Saint-Denys" is said to have originated with Clovis, who shouted, "Mon Jou Saint-Denys", "My Jove shall be St. Denys" '. It would appear that the 'furious Frank' was as weak in Old French as he was in his own racial mythology!

first element being identical with the second of Wilfred. It passed into Old French as Frery or Ferry, 'which hath been now a long time a Christian name in the ancient family of Tilney, and lucky to their house, as they report' (Camden), but I doubt whether an example of the full name will be found before James I's eldest son, Henry Frederick. Frederick is, owing to the fame of Barbarossa and Frederick the Great, almost national in Germany, especially in Prussia. In England it has twice missed the throne, the second time by the death, in 1751, of Frederick Louis, father of George III.

In spite of the fame of Charlemagne, Charles, i.e. Karl, which is simply the German *Kerl*, fellow, man, cognate with *churl,* had no success in England before the Stuarts. In Sweden it named fifteen kings. 'It was from Charles the Bold (of Burgundy, killed at Nancy, 1477) that the name was transmitted to his great-grandson, soon known to Europe as Carlos of Spain, Karl V of Germany, Carolus Quintus of the Holy Roman Empire. He was the real name spreader from whom this became national in Spain, Denmark and even in Britain, for his renown impressed James I with the idea that this must be a fortunate name, when, in the hope of averting the unhappy doom that had pursued five James

Stuarts in succession, he called his sons Henry and Charles. The destiny of the Stuarts was not averted, but the fate of the 'royal martyr' made Charles the most popular of all appellations among the loyalists, so that, rare as it formerly was, it now disputes the ground with John, George and William as the most common of English names' (Charlotte Yonge). This was written in 1863 and the last statement is now far from being true. The Slavonic form Carol is sometimes used by us both for boys and girls, though in the latter case it is probably rather a shortened form of Caroline.

Feminines are formed from these names, as from most others. Louisa came chiefly through Germany, where the memory of Queen Luise of Prussia, mother of William I of Prussia and Germany, is venerated. The shortened Frieda is now popular for English girls, and Charles has given us through German Caroline, through French and German Charlotte and through Italian Carlotta. Charlotte is now decadent, its former popularity being largely due to the heroine of Goethe's *Sorrows of Young Werther* (1774) and to its frequent occurrence in the House of Hanover, but Caroline has lately had a revival.

The survival of a few Old English feminine names has already been noted. To these should be added Edith, Old English Eadgyth, an Ed- name with a mysterious second element[1] which seems to have been early associated with *gifu*, gift, e.g. Godwin's daughter Edith, wife of the Confessor, is often called Ediva (cf. Godiva, Old English Godgifu). An early Edith is the nineth century saint, Abbess of Wilton, daughter of King Edgar; the most famous is Edith Swanneck, mistress of King Harold. The simple Githa or Gytha also occurs as a Christian name. Harold's mother was Gytha and Canute and Harold each had a sister so-named, the latter marrying Vladimir of Novgorod. Another female name, long obsolete but once popular, is that of Friswid or Frideswide, AS. Frithswith, peace strong, its rarity in Anglo-Saxon being counterbalanced by the fame of the patron saint of Oxford. But, for some centuries after 1066, girls as well as boys generally received foreign names.

The first important female foreigner arrived in pre-Conquest days, when Emma, daughter of Richard the Fearless of Normandy, married first Ethelred the Unready and secondly Canute. The Confessor was her son by her first husband. The foreign character of her name is shown by her later assumption of the English Elgiva. Emma comes, *via* Imma, from Irma, short for some such name as Ermintrude, in which the first element is the name of a Ger-

[1] Its historical associations show it to be Norse.

manic deity and the second as in Gertrude. Both Ermintrude and Irma have lately been revived by fanciful parents. But the most important of the Norman female names was Matilda, wife of the Conqueror, and later inflicted on Henry I's English Edith. Although always 'booked' as Matilda, it often had quite a different pronunciation. The Old German Mahthild, of which the first element means 'might' and the second is Hild, became, by regular phonetic change, Old French Maheud, whence our Maud. Matilda, daughter of Henry I, who was dispossessed by Stephen and married Henry V of Germany, was known in her own day as the Empress Maud. She was also called, I know not why, Athelicia or Aaliz. This brings us to another important name, Alice, which came through French from Old German Adalgis, with an obscure second element. The archaic form Adalgisa is the name of a character in Bellini's opera Norma (1831). It was sometimes wrongly 'latinized' as Alexia, instead of Adelicia or Alicia, and is also found as Alix. Much more frequent in German is Adelheid, an abstract compound meaning nobility, from which we have Adelaide, an early nineteenth century importation. A shortened form of the Adal- names gave Adela, daughter of the Conqueror and mother of King Stephen, and this has been later lengthened into

Adeline, of which Aline is a contraction. Adèle is thus the French equivalent of our Ethel.

Both Camden and Littleton register a number of names, chiefly due to the Normans, which are now rarely found, except as surnames. Such are Amery or Emery, Drew, 'latinized' as Drogo, but probably representing Old French *dru,* friendly, trusty, of Teutonic origin, Goddard, god strong, Hammond, Harman, army man (cf. German Hermann), Harvey, army fight, Ingram , Lambert, Payn, Rayner, Warner, protect army (cf. German Werner), Warren, Old French Warin or Garin, very common in the epics, a shortening of one of the Old German names in *warin,* protection, together with the Hebrew Ellis (Elias) and its dim. Elliot, and the Old French Bennet, i.e. Benedict. Charlotte Yonge derives Harvey, earlier also Hervey, from a Breton name meaning 'bitter'. It may have been mixed up with such a name, but its Germanic origin, from the Old German Harwig, is clear. 'Every schoolboy' remembers Lambert Simnel and some others of these names are still occasionally used. Bennet Burleigh was a famous war correspondent of the nineteenth century, Harvey Goodwin was Bishop of Carlisle 1869–91, President Roosevelt has a son Elliot, and I know of an existing Ellis; the name of Sir (Norman Fenwick) Warren Fisher became familiar when the 'Fisher' succeeded the 'Bradbury', and, in the Massey family, the eldest son has been Hamon (Hamo or Hammond) since the Conquest.

A few names taken from heroes and heroines of old romance may conclude this chapter. The two great paladins of Old French national epic were Roland and Oliver. Roland has probably the same first element as Robert and Roger and means 'famous land'. It is thus equivalent to Lambert, Old German Landberaht, land bright. Italian turned it into Orlando, which is sometimes found in England, e.g. Orlando Gibbons, the composer (d. 1625). Another loan from Italian is Tasso's Tancred, not much used in England. It is Old German Dankhart, thought strong. There can be little doubt that Oliver was adapted from the famous Old Norse Olafr, with the nominative -r exceptionally retained. This name is very frequent in Old Norse records and was borne by that King of Norway (1005–30) who spread Christianity with the sword. He became a saint to whom some London churches are dedicated. Oliver naturally went out of fashion after the Restoration and has hardly yet recovered.

With these we may put Bevys of Hampton, a legendary hero whose connection with this country is uncertain. The name, which is uncommon, belonged to the unsatisfactory son of the Earl of Dorincourt. It was also conferred by Marmion on his charger. It appears to be simply the 'bull,' Old French Bueves being a common name in epic. The 'latinization' Bogo introduces a -g- with as little justification as in Drogo. Another name very common in Old French epic is Jocelyn, which we sometimes give also to girls. It came early to England and was much more used in the Middle Ages than now. Its origin is mysterious, but it seems to be a double diminutive, -el -in, of Josse or Joce, the name of a famous Breton saint, who is 'latinized' as Jodocus. This suggests the Greek *iodokos,* holding arrows, but is probably a contortion of some Celtic name.

From the Arthurian epics, we have, besides the King, Lancelot, Tristram, Perceval and Gawain, all of dubious origin. The fanciful etymologies propounded for Lancelot have no basis in fact. 'Some think it to be no ancient name, but forged by the writer of King Arthur's history for one of his doughty knights' (Camden), to which view I subscribe. Its use as a Christian name, is I think, comparatively modern, and I know no earlier example than Lancelot Andrewes, Bishop of Winchester (d. 1626), who stood first in the list of divines entrusted with the preparation of the *Authorized Version.* So also Gawain, 'a name devised by the author of King Arthur's table' (ibid.), whence the Scotch name Gavin. Tristram or Tristan has been associated with French *triste,* sad, because of the tragedy of his love. Camden tells us that 'the son of St. Lewis of France, born in the heavy sorrowful time of his father's imprisonment under the Saracens, was named Tristan in the same respect'. It is quite possibly a corruption of the Germanic Thurstan. Tristram, unlike Lancelot, was a fairly common name in the Middle Ages, which rather suggests that it was one belonging to the everyday list. It has, however, never had any real popularity. By a misunderstanding it was unfortunately given to the son of Mr Walter Shandy—'Of all the names in the universe he had the most unconquerable aversion for Tristram; he had the lowest and most contemptible opinion of it of anything in the world—thinking it could possibly produce nothing in *rerum natura,* but what was extremely mean and pitiful' (*Tristram Shandy,*). Perceval or Percival is the hero of two great medieval poems, one French, by Chrétien de Troyes, the other German, by Wolfram von Eschenbach. The name probably means 'pierce-vale'; compare the Old French names, Perceforest, Percevent, etc.

With Lancelot and Tristram go the two tragic queens. Guinevere is probably related to Winifred, the first part meaning 'fair' or 'white', as in Gwendolen. The whole name may mean 'white wave'. It had European celebrity and many variants, including the Italian Ginevra, the subject of Samuel Rogers's 'Mistletoe Bough' poem. Victor Hugo, in *Les Burgraves* (1843), rather inappropriately uses the old form Guanhamara for a Germanic sibyl. It persisted in Cornwall as Jennifer, which has now become fashionable, and I have lately met a modern instance of the Middle English contraction Gaynor—

> And Dame Gaynor, his queen,
> Was somewhat wanton I ween
> (Skelton.)

Genevieve, patron saint of Paris, is no doubt related, but cannot be identical. This is used by Coleridge in his poem *Love*.

The origin of Isold, also Iseult, Yseult, etc, is unknown. As Isolda it is quite common in medieval records. It had many variants, one of which, Izod, is still in use. On the other hand, Enid, wife of Geraint,[1] was unknown to the Middle Ages. It is a modern revival, chiefly due to Tennyson, who found in the Mabinogion this Arthurian 'patient Grizel', the heroine whom Chaucer took from Boccaccio for his Clerk's Tale. The name Grizel or Griseldis,

[1] There was a Cornish Saint Geraint and the name is still in use.

probably of Germanic origin, has always been especially popular in Scotland. It is found as Grisel, Grissel in Middle English. I conjecture that the modern Selda, Zelda are for Griselda. Vivian, used for both sexes, is only indirectly connected with the Vivien who led Merlin astray, for it is usually registered in the thirteenth century as Vivianus, a late Latin derivative from *vivus,* living. Here, as an 'Ancient British' name, may be mentioned Shakespeare's Imogen, the original form and meaning of which are quite unknown. It is perhaps the same as Geoffrey of Monmouth's Ignoge and Spenser's Inogene of Italy. Cassibelan, Caesar's Cassivelaunus, is mentioned more than once in *Cymbeline,* and Robert Burton, of the *Anatomy of Melancholy,* actually had a nephew of that name. With Imogen we may put Cordelia and Ophelia, two of Shakespeare's more unusual names which are still occasionally given in baptism. Cordelia is Geoffrey of Monmouth's Cordeilla, of Celtic origin and uncertain meaning. Ophelia, the name of the New England spinster, Miss Feely, who tried to civilize Topsy, in Uncle Tom's Cabin, is apparently from Greek *ophis,* a serpent.

With these names of legend and romance we may associate Marmaduke, not because its history can be traced, but simply for its heroic sound! It is well recorded in the north from the thirteenth century, but its origin is unknown,—'A name usual in the North, but most in former times in the noble families of Tweng, Lumley and Constable, and thought to be Valentinianus translated' (Camden). Perhaps it is, contrary to all phonetic theory, the Irish Meriaduc, a name known to have been introduced into Northern England by Vikings who had long sojourned in Ireland. Algernon, on the other hand, can be easily traced. It was originally a nickname, from Old French *gernon,* moustache or whisker. 'William de Albini, the second husband of Henry I's widow, Alix (Adela in the DNB.) of Louvain, wore moustachios, which the Normans called *gernons,* and thus his usual title was William als gernons; and as the common ancestor of the Howards and Percys, he left this epithet to them as a baptismal name. From the Percys it came to Algernon Sidney' (Charlotte Yonge).

CHAPTER III

The Saints

As already stated, the Old Germanic names which had filled France in pre-Conquest days began early in the Middle Ages to give way to those of the Saints, and our own nomenclature soon showed the same tendency. The belief in the protective powers of the canonized was very real to our medieval ancestors. Every child was put under the guardianship of the saint, male or female, on whose day the birth had occurred or of one regarded by the family with special reverence and affection. Even such stalwarts as William, Robert and Richard would hardly have survived so hardily, if they had not named saints as well as historical characters—'Le culte des saints répand sur tous les siécles du moyen âge son grand charme poétique. Les saints étaient partout: sculptés aux portes de la ville, ils regardlaient du côté de l'ennemi et veillaient sur la cité. Les façades de nos vieilles maisons ont souvent plus de saints qu'un rétable d'autel. Dans nos grandes villes gothiques, Paris, Rouen, Troyes, la rue avait un aspect surprenant. Non seulement chaque maison montrait aux passants sa galerie de saints, mais les enseignes qui se balanc,aient au vent multipliaient encore les saint Martin, les saint Georges, les saint Éloi' (Émile Male, *L'Art religieux au moyen age*). Up to the time of the Reformation the saints reigned supreme, and, after the Restoration, they quickly regained much of the ground that had been temporarily occupied by the Puritan eccentricities.

We find a few Anglo-Saxon saints on our list of names, but their baptismal use is, I fancy, comparatively modern and partly due to the Romantic revival. Such are Cuthbert, Wilfred and Boniface. The first died in 687 in an anchorite's cell at Lindisfarne, whence his body was translated in 1104 to Durham Cathedral. During World War I Cuthbert was applied, as a presumably affected name, to shirkers, but it was borne by one of the truest and simplest gentlemen who ever served the country, Cuthbert Collingwood, Nelson's brother-in-arms. Wilfred, the name of the Knight of Ivanhoe, is not noted by Littleton, and its popularity is modern. St. Wilfred was a rather militant churchman who was at various times Bishop of York and of Hexham. During his exile in Sussex he taught the South Saxons more enlightened methods of fishing! St. Winfrith, who assumed the Latin name of Boniface, was the apostle of Germany, where he became Bishop of Mainz and was slain by pagans in 705.

Some other Anglo-Saxon saints are mentioned earlier on. The one most dear to popular fancy and tradition is naturally Dunstan, who, while working at the anvil at Mayfield, Sussex, was tempted by Satan in the form of a fair damsel. The saint seized the tempter by the nose with his red-hot tongs, and the latter, covering several miles in one agonized leap, dipped his glowing proboscis in a forest pool and thus created the healthgiving waters of Tunbridge Wells.

Biblical names can hardly be said to have existed in Old English, and the great mass of the saints whose names began in post-Conquest times to be given to English children, gradually tending to prevail over the old Germanic names, came from abroad with the Norman churchmen. This can be seen in the dedications of our medieval churches, though those of Cornwall preserve the names of many obscure Celtic saints. The Church had no great love of Old Testament names except the canonized Elias (New Testament form of Elijah), from whom we have Ellis, but all the apostles and evangelists are well represented in the centuries following the Conquest, and John and Thomas joined the Germanic William in a kind of baptismal triumvirate. Thomas of Bayeux was made Archbishop of York in 1070 and was followed, in 1100, by another Thomas, his nephew; but the great popularity of the name in later centuries was due much more to St. Thomas of Canterbury (d. 1170), whose shrine was the most famous in Christendom, than to the doubting disciple. As already mentioned, Peter was generally introduced in a French form as Piers or Pierce, and his alternative name Simon was not distinguished from its Old Testament form Simeon. From Peter is derived the once common female name Petronilla (Pernel, Parnel). Petronella Scholastica was christened at Stottesden, Salop, in the seventeenth century, her second name being that of a saint who was St. Benedict's twin sister, and a lady named Petronel was married in June, 1939. The disappearance of Parnel may be due to the fact that it became synonymous with a wanton, especially a priest's concubine. In both French and English it was also applied to a chatterbox; hence our plant-name 'prattling parnel' for 'London pride.' *Péronnelle,* pert hussy, is used by Moliere in *Les Femmes Savantes* and he gave the name Pernelle to the dictatorial mother of Orgon in *Tartufe.*

Simon Peter's brother Andrew, adopted as the patron saint of Scotland, had a vogue which is reflected in the Scottish Andersons. In Stuart England it became a stock name for a serving-man, whence the Merry Andrew, the mountebank's assistant. The Hebrew Jacob was latinized as Jacobus, whence French Jacques,[1] and gave in a way puzzling to phoneticians the Spanish dialect Jaime, which appears in Chaucer—'I thanke yow by God and by Saint Jame' (B. 1545). In Gaelic James became Hamish, now sometimes given to English children, while Ireland spells it Seumas (Shamus). No apostolic name, except Peter and John, has been so widely spread in Europe. As patron saint of Spain, St. James the Great was one of the Seven Champions of Christendom. By some mysterious process Jack (northern Jock), from French Jacques, became recognized as a familiar equivalent of John. A French feminine derivative Jacqueline is sometimes used in English.

John, whether in honour of the Baptist or of the 'beloved disciple', was easily the favourite and finally it overhauled William which had reigned supreme for more than a century. It has spread everywhere; cf. French Jean, German Johann (whence Hans), Scottish Ian, Irish Shane, Welsh Evan, Spanish Juan, Italian Giovanni, Russian Ivan and even Basque Iban, whence the surname Ibanez. Equally popular was its feminine Joanna or Joan, on which Camden remarks, 'In latter years some

---

[1] The -s which is characteristic of French male names represents the nominative ending of the Latin or latinized forms.

of the better and nicer sort, misliking Joan, have mollified the name of Joan into Jane, as it may seem, for that Jane is never found in old records; and as some will, never before the time of King Henry the Eight'. The 'mislike' of Joan may have been due to its use as a stock name for a kitchen wench, Shakespeare's 'greasy Joan'. It is characteristic of the ups and downs of female names that Bardsley should have opined, just fifty years ago, that 'Joan is obsolete; Jane is showing signs of dissolution'. Jean is the Scotch form of Jane, as Jeames[1] is of James. Associated with John is Jordan, once very common as a Christian name and surviving as a common surname. Its adoption dates from the Crusades and seems to have been due to some mystical identification of the river with the Baptist. A medieval chronicler even refers to 'Jordan or Johan the Baptist'.

Our first important Matthew is the historian Matthew Paris (1259), who succeeded Roger of Wendover as chronicler of the monastery of St. Albans. It is often recorded in its Old French form Mahieu, whence our surname Mayhew. The great popularity of Philip was due less to the apostle, of whom little is known, than to Philip the Deacon, who converted Simon the Sorcerer and the Ethiopian eunuch (Acts viii).

---

[1] Immortalized by Thackeray, but recorded already in the reign of Elizabeth.

It was the name of several French and Spanish kings and also of two great Dukes of Burgundy. It was borne by the most attractive of the Elizabethans, but, during that period, naturally lost caste, as a result of the manæuvres of Philip II of Spain. Bartholomew was also curiously popular, as may be seen by the number of ancient churches dedicated to him. This may have been partly owing to his identification with Nathanael, the Israelrite without guile (*John i. 47*). Bartholomew also penetrated Scotland, where, by the mysterious consonant-shifting of Gaelic, it gave the name Macfarlane. Jude suffered by association with Judas and is of rare occurrence, nor is the alternative Thaddaeus used in England, though Thady, an alteration of an old Erse name, is common in Ireland. A name connected with the apostles is Alphaeus, father of James the Less. Sir Alphaeus Cleophas Morton was a nineteenth and twentieth century M P and I have had a student of the name. I have also met a Zebedee (father of James and John).

Mark was not very popular with us until recent times, perhaps owing to the association of the evangelist's Latin name with the unrelated Celtic name of Isold's husband. Its great home was Italy and especially Venice, where, says Charlotte Yonge, every fifth man bore the name (Marco) of the city's patron saint. Marco

Polo (d. 1324), the great medieval explorer, who knew Kubla Khan and travelled in China, was a Venetian. The Latin form Marcus came into use with us in the nineteenth century. Luke is usually recorded in the learned form Lucas, whence a common surname. An ingenious theory of early theologians identified Luke with Silas, the companion of Paul, the argument being based on the fact that Luke, for Lat. Lucanus, was derived from *lucus,* a grove, and Silas, for Silvanus, from *silva,* a wood. When we add Paul, Barnabas and Stephen, we have almost exhausted the New Testament male names which are found in common use before the Reformation.

Paul has spread all over Europe, but, in spite of the dedication of our metropolitan cathedral, has never been very popular in England. The vogue of Pauline, first in France and then in England, probably owes something to Corneille's only really feminine heroine (*in Polyeucte*), while the masculine form received some impetus in modern France from Bernardin de Saint-Pierre's rather sickly *Paul et Virginie* (1788). With Paulus, little, may be mentioned, rather out of place, his opposite Magnus, which, being understood as a proper name in the title of Carolus Magnus, became very popular in Scandinavia and was borne by kings of Denmark, Norway and Sweden. The

Vikings brought it to the Scottish isles; hence Magnus Troil in Scott's *Pirate*. Among New Testament names the protomartyr Stephen comes next to Peter, John and James in popularity. There were nine early Popes called Stephen, and it became hereditary for the Kings of Hungary, the first of whom (d. 1038) became the patron saint of the country. The name came to England with Estienne de Blois, our King Stephen. The original saint has his day on December 26th; hence 'Good King Wenceslas, etc.' Barnabas is commemorated in Barnaby bright, his day, June 11th, being the longest under the Old Style—

> This day the sonne is in his chiefest hight,
> With Barnaby the bright,
> > (Spenser, Epith. 265.)

Of the lesser New Testament characters Timothy had some slight popularity, but the rest were hardly used as Christian names before Puritan times. An example is Philemon, the name of a seventeenth century translator of the classics, Philemon Holland (d. 1637), who deserves to rank with Jacques Amyot. Of the female saints of the New Testament Anna or Anne is found only in the apocryphal gospel of St. James. For Elizabeth, canonized by the Eastern Church, see. Mary was not common in

the Middle Ages. After the Marian persecution
it lost caste, but came back with William and
Mary. Magdalene, variously spelt, is not un-
common in the Rolls, and was popular enough
to name a ship—'His barge y-cleped was the
Maudelayne' (Chaucer, *Prol. 410*). The modern
Madeleine is from French and the shortened
Magda is a recent importation from Germany.

Of non-Biblical saints the oldest in England
is Alban, the British protomartyr, who suffered at Verulam in 303. Then comes Augustine, missionary to the Anglo-Saxons and first
Archbishop of Canterbury (d. 604). Except for
St. Thomas of Canterbury, this country supplied little in the way of famous saints' names
after the Anglo-Saxon period.

In dealing with the post-Biblical saints it
seems natural to begin with the Doctors of the
Church, four of whom were recognized in the
Western and Eastern Churches: in the former
Ambrose, Augustine, Jerome and Gregory, in
the latter Athanasius, Basil, Gregory,
Nazianzen and Chrysostom. Ambrose, from
the great Archbishop of Milan (d. 397) who
'converted' Augustine and wrote against the
Arians, must have had a good deal of vogue in
England, for his name was already well estab-
lished as a surname by the thirteenth century.
It was evidently popular in the seventeenth
century, for Littleton includes Nam for

Ambrose among his *'Abbreviatures of English Christian Names.'* This inevitably suggests the poetaster Ambrose Philips (d. 1749), forgotten as a writer, but immortalized by his nickname Namby-Pamby. The Augustine who ranked as Doctor was not our Archbishop of Canterbury, but the much earlier Augustine of Hippo (d. 430), son of St. Monica, who, with the help of St. Ambrose, converted him from heretical opinions and debauched habits. Augustine was always pronounced Austen or Austin in English, as in the Austin (i.e. Augustine) Friars, whose name survives in a City street. His mother's name, Monica, of unknown origin and meaning, has become popular of late for girls. Jerome, i.e. Hieronymus, to whom we owe the Vulgate, the Latin version of the Bible, has never been a popular English name, though Bardsley (in his *Dictionary of Surnames*) is mistaken in thinking that, there are no early examples. Gregory, represented in both Churches, has named sixteen Popes, beginning with Gregory the Great (d. 604), the 'non Angli sed Angeli' punster. It has been a favourite, especially ecclesiastical, name all over Europe and has even been adopted by a great Scottish clan. Charlotte Yonge is being a little too 'Anglican', when she remarks, à propos of the Popes, that the name Gregory 'has been far less popular among those who own their sway than among the Eastern Christians, who are free from it'.

Of the Eastern Doctors Athanasius and Chrysostom, golden mouth, the nickname of John, Bishop of Constantinople (d. 407), have never been in English use, but Basil, the great foe of the Arians and friend of Athanasius, is well recorded in Middle English. The name is, naturally, very strong in the Eastern Church. Another saint especially associated with the Eastern Church is Cyril, not he of Alexandria who instigated the murder of Hypatia, but the ninth century 'Apostle of the Slavs' who is commemorated in the Cyrillic alphabet. His name, like that of Milton's friend Cyriack Skinner, is derived from Greek *Kyrios,* Lord. It is common in Russia, but comparatively modern in England. Among the enemies of Arianism was the fourth century Hilary. The name has always been used indifferently for girls and boys; indeed, in the early medieval records, the former predominate.

It was natural that parents or godparents should show a preference for those saints' names which were associated with picturesque incidents. Probably the three favourite male names of this type were Martin, Christopher and Nicolas. St. Martin (4th century), patron of innkeepers, is usually shown in art in the act of dividing his military cloak with a shivering beggar. He also supplied language with a new set of words *via* the *cappella* at Tours in which the sacred *cappa* was preserved. The name, probably derived from Mars, has been especially popular in France, where it enters into many proverbs and popular sayings. In England it has become a very common surname. Christopher, the Christ-bearer, is represented as a giant. His name was assumed when he carried the Christ-child, who explained that his weight was due to the sins of the whole world. The great favourite was Nicolas or Nicholas (4th century), patron saint of Russia and also of pawnbrokers, schoolchildren and thieves, ' St. Nicholas' clerks' (*Henry IV, Part 1,* ii. I), who later became Santa Claus. His legend almost consists of a succession of conjuring tricks, the only theological incident in it being the tradition that he ' socked' Arius on the jaw at the Council of Nicaea (325). The popularity of Christopher and Nicholas is shown by the familiar abbreviations Kit and Nick. The Greek name Nicolaus, victory people, is synonymous with Nicodemus, the only bearers of which, so far as my memory serves, were Mr Boffin, in *Our Mutual Friend*, and Midshipman Easy's father.

A later saint whose miraculous adventures made a strong appeal to popular fancy was St. Giles. The French name Gilles was, by ways familiar to the philologist, but mysterious to the layman, 'miserably disjoynted', as Camden says, from Greco-Latin Bgidius, a derivative of oegis, the shield of Zeus and Pallas. The Old French Vie de Saint-Gilles, dating from the twelfth century, tells of his adventures and is our earliest authority for many nautical terms. At one time looked on as bucolic, Giles is now again in favour. Another saint of exciting experiences is Antony or Anthony, the patron saint of Italy, formerly invoked against St. Anthony's fire, i.e. erysipelas. He was an Egyptian and is looked on as the founder of monastic asceticism (4th century). His 'temptations' have supplied material to many writers and painters. Even more popular in Italy is the medieval St. Antony of Padua (1231), a Franciscan of whom strange miracles are recorded. He is especially invoked for the recovery of lost objects. The name has been popular enough in England to develop a pet form Tony, which was formerly, like so many other familiar names, used for a simpleton; hence Goldsmith's choice of Tony Lumpkin in *She Stoops to Conquer*.

The fame of St. Antony of Padua suggests the mention of another medieval saint, the most loved of all, viz. St. Francis[1] of Assisi,

---

[1] His first name was Giovanni (John) and tradition says that Francesco was really a nickname conferred on him for his schoolboy proficiency in French!

who founded the Franciscan order, the Grey
Friars, in 1210, about the time that his friend
St. Dominic established the Black Friars. The
name, Fr. François, is simply the older form of
Français; compare German and Norman, or
the Romain borne by a contemporary French
writer. Francis does not seem to have been
adopted into English before Tudor times as a
male and female name, the latter now spelt
Frances. Its rapid spread was no doubt due to
that brilliant monarch Francis I of France.
Shakespeare has Francis for some of his humbler characters, male and female, and also
Francisco, in *Hamlet*, but its Tudor dignity is
represented by Bacon, Walsingham and
Drake. Two other really saintly saints bore the
same name, the gentle St. Francis of Sales (d.
1622) and the heroic St. Francis-Xavier, the
apostle to the East, who died off the coast of
China in 1552. Xavier is of Moorish origin and
identical with Giafar, of the *Arabian Nights*,
the great Haroun's vizier. In England it only
occurs in Catholic families. Another saint of
modern times, and one of the noblest of all, is
the benevolent St. Vincent de Paul (d. 1660),
friend of the poor, but the early appearance of
the name points to one of the Christian martyrs under Diocletian. With this name, Latin
vincells, victorious, compare Clement, merciful, the name of the saint who traditionally

succeeded St. Peter at Rome. It is of very early occurrence, along with a feminine form Clemence.

Going back to the early days of Christianity, we find that some of the great names, such as Cyprian, Eusebius, Ignatius and Polycarp, are hardly represented in England. Cyprian was the Christian name of a distinguished admiral some years ago, and one has heard of Ignatius Donnelly, of the Bacon 'cryptogram'. This name is much more popular abroad and Inigo Jones (d. 1652), a Catholic, is thought to have been given this Spanish name in honour of Loyola, Inigo (i.e. Ignatius) Lopez de Recalde, founder of the Jesuit order. Of a later date than the above fathers is Benedict, founder of the most learned and humane of the monastic orders. The popularity of Benedict in England, as evidenced by the surname Bennett, was partly due to a seventh century Anglo-Saxon saint who assumed this Latin name and did much for the cultivation of the liberal arts in this country. Very strange is the comparative rarity of George, our patron saint. It occurs occasionally in medieval records, but I do not remember any important early bearer of the name except George of Clarence, and his fame depends chiefly on the 'butt of malmsey'. The modern popularity of the name, which is Greek for husbandman, 'earth-worker', dates from the royal Georges.

Two more patron saints are Denis or Dennis and Patrick, France and Ireland. The former is traced to St. Dionysius, traditionally an Athenian sent from Rome to convert the Parisians and martyred at Montmartre in the third century. Both Denis and its feminine form Denise are common in medieval England. The story of St. Patrick is very vague and his chief exploit seems to have been the expulsion of snakes from Ireland. The name has never been really popular in England, but the feminine form Patricia has been in fashion lately.

To make a complete catalogue of the saints who have supplied us with Christian names would be wearisome; in fact it would almost cover all the names in this book, few of which have escaped canonization at some time or other. Moreover many of these names were not taken from the Calendar, but chosen in quite modern times for reasons other than their sanctity. It would, for instance, be difficult to find an early example in English of Victor, a name which passed from Savoy into France in the eighteenth century and reached us a little later. There are, however, three more who seem to call for special mention, viz. Valentine, Vitus and Sebastian. Valentine, from Latin *valens,* strong, was a Roman martyr of the third century. The origin of the practice connected with February 14th is variously explained. Perhaps Chaucer's theory is as good as any—

For this was on Seynt Valentynes day,
Whan every bryd (bird) cometh ther to chese his make.[1]

> *(Parliament of Fowls*, 309.)*

The feminine use of the name is comparatively modern and comes from France, where the masculine is Valentin.

The connection of Vitus with the dance (French *danse de St. Guy,* German *Veifstanz)* is also mysterious. Tradition makes him a Sicilian child martyred *c.* 300, but the name does not appear to be Latin. There is an unsupported theory that 'the heathen god Svantveit was changed by the Christian Slavs into Saint Vitus'. Anyhow it became Guy, a very popular name in the Middle Ages, in England associated especially with the semi-mythical hero Guy of Warwick—

I am not Samson, nor sir Guy, nor Colbrand, to mow them down before me

> *(Henry VIII* v. 3.)*

It has recovered from the temporary eclipse due to Guy Fawkes.

Sebastian, from Greek *sebastos*, used by the Byzantine Emperors for the synonymous

[1] Choose his mate.

Latin *augustus,* was a Roman soldier condemned under Diocletian to be shot to death
with arrows. His martyrdom has inspired
many painters. Another Christian soldier was
St. Maurice, commander of the 'Theban Le-
gion', put to death in Switzerland (286) with
all his men. The name was often spelt Morris.
Our earliest historical Maurice was William
I's Chancellor and Bishop of London who
started the building of St. Paul's.

The four great virgin saints of the early
church were Agnes, Barbara, Katharine and
Margaret. The first, a very popular medieval
name, is probably connected with Greek
agnos, pure, but was popularly associated with
the unrelated Latin *agnus,* a lamb, with which
St. Agnes, martyred under Diocletian, is often
represented in art. Keats and Tennyson have
both celebrated the Eve of St. Agnes, January
20th, when maidens who go through certain
ceremonies are granted a sight of their future
husbands. Its medieval pronunciation was
Annis, still found as a Christian name. The
Spanish form Inez is also used. St. Barbara
was a Greek maiden, martyred at the instiga-
tion of her own father, who, with the responsible officials, was then destroyed by a thunder-
bolt. Hence she is invoked against lightning
and is the patron saint of gunners. The name
is now very popular, but was originally more

Scotch than English, as in the famous old ballad of Barbara Allen. With Barbara, the savage, it seems natural to mention Ursula, the little bear, also very popular in recent years. She is a legendary saint, fabled to have come to Germany from Britain and to have been martyred at Cologne with her eleven thousand companions—"'Eleven thousand virgins!' cried Denys. "What babies German men must have been in days of yore!'" (*The Cloister and the Hearth*). There were many St. Katharines, from Greek *katharos,* pure, whence the French Catherine. The most famous is the half-mythical maiden of Alexandria who was torn to pieces on a spiked wheel. Her fame was greatly extended by the medieval Catarina of Siena (d. 1380), a statesmanlike saint who influenced Popes. The name, also spelt Catarina and Catalina (cf. Irish Kathleen), was already pretty popular in England in the thirteenth century. Few female names have such royal associations, e.g. three of Henry VIII's six wives, the Queens of Henry V and Charles II, two famous Empresses of Russia and the most formidable Queen of France, Catherine de Médicis. Less known than the legendary St. Margaret of Antioch is her Scotch namesake.

Other favourite female saints whose names became popular in the Middle Ages were Agatha, Cecilia, Dorothy, Helena and Lucy.

Agatha, Grcek for 'good', was a Sicilian girl
martyrcd at Rome under Decius. William the
Conqueror had a daughter of this name, which
was used all over Europe during the Middle
Ages, went out of English fashion later, but
was revived in the nineteenth century. Cecilia,
from the Cecilian *gens,* probably from Latin
coecus, blind, was a Roman virgin martyr of
the third century who became the patroness of
music. She is celebrated in one of the great
odes of English poetry—Dryden's *Alexander's
Feast,* or the *Power of Music.* It was pronounced Cicely and for some centuries was
among the most favoured names, its later de-
cline being no doubt due to the fact that it had
become synonymous with milkmaid—

When Tom came home from labour and Cis
    from milking rose.

Dorothea or Dorothy, gift of God, a saint martyred in Cappadocia under Diocletian, is synonymous with Theodora. It had no great medieval vogue, but was very popular in Tudor
times, as may be seen by its acquiring the pet
forms Doll, Dolly and Dot. Dora is also used as
a pet form of both Dorothy and Theodora.
Charlotte Yonge is mistaken in saying that
'under the House of Hanover, Dorothy fell into
disuse'. The contrary is the case, for Dorothea

has always been a favourite name in Germany and was chosen by Goethe for the typical German maiden to wed the typical German youth Hermann. The pet form Dora is also used in German. Dorothy is one of the few names that have not suffered from changing fashions. With Margaret it always keeps its place among the half-dozen favourites.

Many legends have gathered round St. Helena, mother of Constantine the Great and restorer of the shrines of Jerusalem. Her fame even reached ancient Britain, where she was believed to be the daughter of King Coel of Colchester, 'old King Cole', and Charlotte Yonge is perhaps right in regarding Elaine as the British form of the name, which is of unknown origin. She is called Elena in Cynewulf's account of the *Discovery of the True Cross*. In English it became Helen or Ellen, registered as Elena in the Rolls, and Aileen or Eileen in Irish. The fame of the saint has been helped by that of a sinner, the most beautiful woman of antiquity. It seems to be assumed by all writers on names that Eleanor or Elinor is the same name, which seems to me rather like Fluellen's identification of Macedon with Monmouth. It is true that Ellen and Nell stand for both names. I do not know the origin of Eleanor, which apparently first came to England with Eleanor (Alienor or Aenor) of Aquitaine, wife of Henry

II, but is more associated in the popular mind with Edward I's noble queen, Eleanor of Castile, who is commemorated in the Eleanor Crosses, the last of which was erected in the 'little village of Charing',[1] between London and Westminster. I should conjecture some connection with Greek *eleos,* pity, mercy. The Spanish form Leonore even suggests *leon,* lion. From it we have Leonora and Lenore and it has also contributed to Nora.

A saint's name that has lent itself to the formation of many fanciful derivatives is Lucy, martyred *c.* 300, Latin Lucia, feminine of Lucius, 'a name given first to those that were born when daylight first appeared' (Camden). We may compare Dawn, now sometimes given to baby girls. Lucy is not uncommon in the Middle Ages and King Stephen had a sister of that name who went down in the White Ship; but its great popularity belongs to the Stuart period, which also indulged in Lucetta, Lucilla, Lucinda, Lucasta. It was under the last name that Richard Lovelace celebrated his betrothed, Lucy Sacheverell, to whom is addressed one of the most glorious of English lyrics—'I could not love thee, dear, so much, Loved I not honour more'. Quite legendary is St. Veronica, whose veil retained the impress

---

[1] Which is accordingly derived by amateur etymologists from *chère reine!*

of Our Lord's face after she had wiped the sweat from it as he passed to Calvary. The name is traditionally explained as a barbarous hybrid from Latin and Greek, *verum icon*, ' true image', but is more probably a distortion of Berenice, a Macedonian form of Greek Pherenike, bringer of victory, the Bernice of *Acts xxv*. Like many other pretty female names, e.g. the Amaryllis of Theocritus, Ovid and Milton, Veronica has been applied to a genus of plants. Whether our modern Verena is from a legendary Egyptian saint or formed by modern fancy as a variation on Vera or Veronica I know not.

A few favourite saints, e.g. Clara, Irene and Teresa, do not belong to the early days of the Church. St. Clara was a disciple of St. Francis and foundress of an order the members of which were called *soeurs clarisses,* whence Richardson's Clarissa, though both this and Clarice were in use already in the seventeenth century. Clarinda is another variation on the same theme, perhaps suggested by Tasso's Clorinda, unwittingly slain by her lover Tancred. Clara itself is now generally replaced by the older Clare or the French Claire. St. Irene was the wife of John Comnenus, Emperor of the East (1118–43), but the popularity of the name owes less to the saint than to the Renaissance passion for Greek names. Much later comes St. Theresa or Teresa, a Spanish visionary of the sixteenth century, whose name, probably from Greek *theros,* summer, harvest, spread all over Europe after her canonization in 1621. It is thus a comparatively late name, assisted in its spread by the great Maria-Theresa, Empress of Austria (1740–80). It has always been especially favoured by Catholic families and has given the pet forms Tess and Tessa, both of which have named heroines of novels. Tracy was formerly used in the same way, but will not account for Mr Tracy Tupman, who certainly bore the name of a noble family of which an early representative assisted in the murder of Becket. With the above celebrities may be mentioned the less known German St. Hedwig (d. 1243), whose name became, via Old French, Avoice, whence our Avice or Avis, not uncommon in early Rolls as Avicia and lately restored to favour.

Of the three archangels only Michael and Gabriel are much used in England, though Raphael is well represented in Italy. Michael was generally introduced in its French form Michel, as shown by our common surname Mitchell. This is, however, a ' learned' form and French also had the 'popular' form Mihiel, as in St. Mihiel, a famous 'salient' on the Meuse. This is one origin of Miles—'Whereas the French contract Michael into Miel, some suppose our Miles comes from thence' (Camden). Butler, in *Hudibras*, rimes 'St. Michael's' with 'trials'. Gabriel is not uncommon in medieval Rolls and was sometimes reduced to Gable, as it was by some of Gabriel Oak's rustic friends in *Far from the Madding Crowd*. The only Raphael who occurs to me is the sixteenth century chronicler Holinshed. Angel itself is recorded as a man's name, but it was barred by the Puritans, who also held it 'not fit for Christian humility to call a man Gabriel or Michael, giving the names of angels to the sons of mortality' (Adams, *Meditations upon the Creed*). The feminine forms Angela, Angelica and Angelina are, I think, post-Reformation adoptions, although Angelica is in Ariosto. Seraphina and Seraphita also exist. With these we may put Christian, still both masculine and feminine in Scotland. As a female name it is elaborated into Christina, with pet forms Christy and Kirsty. The great home of the male name is Denmark, where we find a long succession of King Christians, starting in 1450 with Christian I, founder of the House of Oldenburg. In England both the masculine and feminine forms are at least as old as the thirteenth century. Christabel, immortalized by Coleridge, is a north-country name, probably modelled, like Claribel and Rosabel, on the favourite Isabel. One might almost include with the angel choir the popular medieval name Beatrix or Beatrice, which owes some of its popularity to Dante, as Laura does to Petrarch, but perhaps still more to Shakespeare.[1]

---

[1] Another name possibly from the same source is the Italian Bianca, i.e. Blanche (*Taming of the Shrew* and *Othello*).

CHAPTER IV

The Greeks and Romans

THE revival of learning was accompanied by a rather too enthusiastic importation of Greek and Roman names. Already in the sixteenth century Thomas Cartwright, a very fervent Puritan, attacked these names as 'savouring of paganism'. In the next century Camden wrote that 'succeeding ages (little regarding St. Chrysostome's admonition to the contrary) have recalled prophane names, so as now Diana, Cassandra, Hippolytus, Venus, Lais, names of unhappy disaster, are as rife somewhere as ever they were in Paganism. Albeit, in our late Reformation, some of good consideration have brought in Zachary, Malachy, Josias, etc, as better agreeing with our faith, but without contempt of countrey names (as I hope) which have both good and gracious significations'. By 'countrey names' he means the traditional William, Richard, Robert, etc, by which many Puritan ministers refused to baptize infants, though one of the more broadminded of them admitted that 'he knew Williams and Richards who, though they bore names not found in sacred story, but familiar to the country, were as gracious saints as any who bore names found in it'.

The sixteenth and seventeenth centuries saw what Captain Marryatt would call a 'triangular duel' in which the combatants were: (1) the old-established national names dealt with in Chapters II and III, (2) the Greek and Roman names popularized by the new learning, (3) the Old Testament names due to the Puritan Reformation. Towards the end of the seventeenth century things were still further complicated, so far as female names were concerned, by the fantastic borrowings and coinages of which some account is given in Chapters VI and VII.

Very few Greek names were adopted and then usually in a latinized form, e.g. Ulysses, now more favoured in America than here, and Hercules. The latter was common in Italy as Ercole and Sir Hercules Robinson, later Lord Rosmead (d. 1897), was a famous English colonial governor. The names of the gods and goddesses were generally avoided, though Jupiter and Juno were often given later on to negro slaves, as were also Pompey, Scipio, Chloe, 'Uncle Remus', etc A striking exception was Diana, made fashionable in France by Diane de Poitiers (d. 1566), whence it passed to England, eventually naming Scott's most delightful heroine. Venus also occurs sporadically in the seventeenth century, 'but for shame it is turned of some to Venice' (Camden). Selina, the name of the pious Countess of Huntingdon (d. 1791), is probably not connected with the moon goddess (Greek *selene,* moon), but with French Céline, a derivative of Celia. With Diana it seems fitting to mention Endymion, of whom I know only two examples, Endymion Porter (d. 1649), the royalist trusted by Charles I, and Disraeli's fictional Endymion Travers. Aurora, goddess of dawn, had some popularity in the nineteenth century, when we have Mrs Browning's Aurora Leigh and Byron's Aurora Raby. It was in much more general use in France, e.g. Aurore Dupin (George Sand) and Hervé Riel's 'belle Aurore'. Vesta, goddess of the hearth, is only known to me as the name of a brilliant lady comedian on the 'Halls'. Hermes does not seem to be represented, though we have the feminine derivatives Hermia and Hermione, the latter the beautiful daughter of Menelaus and Helena and rival of Andromache in the tragedy of that name by Euripides. It was Racine's successful adaptation that made the name current in France. Shakespeare had already introduced it into England. Neptune Huncks, a captain in Charles I's army, suggests that the use of such names was once more common, and in the eighteenth century a girl was christened at Stottesden, Salop, with the curious combination Asenath Minerva!

One name of Greek origin goes back to 1066, viz. Eustace, which was hereditary with the Counts of Boulogne, one of whom accompanied the Conqueror, perhaps eager to settle an old feud with the family of Godwin. St. Eustace, a Roman general under Trajan, was, like St. Hubert, converted by the stag he was hunting. It is uncertain whether the name comes from Greek *eustathes*, steadfast, or *eustachus,* rich in ears of corn. Here it may be convenient to mention the other Eu- names. Eugene, wellborn, the name of a fifth century saint, was made illustrious *c.* 1700 by Prince Eugene of Savoy, Marlborough's brother-in-arms. It seems, however, to have reached Britain in pre-Conquest days and there is legendary record of eight kings Eugenius of Scotland. The feminine form Eugenia was little used in England before the time of the Empress Eugénie, Napoleon III's Spanish wife. In America Gene is used as an independent name for both sexes.Eulalie, well-spoken, the saint and martyr whose tragedy is recorded in the oldest extant piece of French verse, is a name used by Poe in one of his lyrics. Euphemia, with the same meaning (cf. *euphemism),* was another saint of the same period, viz. the persecution under Diocletian. This name has been especially popular in Scotland; witness Effie Deans of *The Heart of Midlothian.* The latinized Evangeline was, I suppose, borrowed by Longfellow from French to describe a French maiden. Whether Evadne, wife of one of the Seven against Thebes and heroine of Beaumont and Fletcher's *Maid's Tragedy*, belongs here I know not. The name is, of course, Greek, but I have only come across it in a novel.[1] For Eunice, happy victory, see.

The most famous of Greek names, Alexander, helper of men, borne by Popes, Tsars and Kings of Scotland, is also the most definitely established in the Middle Ages. Its popularity was due to the Old French Roman d'Alexandre, to which France also owes the doubtful blessing of the metrical alexandrine. In Gaelic Alexander became Alastair or Alister, while Elshender, Scott's Black Dwarf, represents the Lowland pronunciation. The feminine form Alexandra, of which Alexandrina is a diminutive, had a great vogue in England after the arrival of the beautiful Danish princess who married Queen Victoria's son, but it was already well established here in the Middle Ages. The idea of 'helper' is contained also in Alexis, a Syrian saint, later associated with Byzantium and Rome, whose life is described in a famous Old French poem. This is now a French rather than an English

1 Sarah Grand, The Heavenly Twins (1893).

name, the feminine Alexia, which we find in old records, being a mistranslation of Alice.

Alexander's Roman 'opposite number' has never had the vogue in England that Jules has had in France, nor has Cæsar been used with us as in Italy. Julius has a Welsh form Iolo. The feminine Julia was the name of daughters both of the great Cæsar and of Augustus, but its English vogue belongs to Herrick. This vogue did not become intense in England till the eighteenth century and lasted into the middle nineteenth,[1] after which its popularity gradually declined, modern taste preferring the diminutive Juliet. The derivative Julian, borne by an ascetic saint whose prayers were believed to have brought about the death of his imperial namesake, not to mention that of a few Arian bishops, is now fairly common, but its feminine Juliana, popularly Gillian or Jill, was one of the favourite names of the Middle Ages. This is now rather rare, but was borne by Juliana Horatia Ewing, author of the delightful *Jackanapes*. It is possible that Jolyon, which I only know from Galsworthy's *Forsyte Saga*, is a variant of Julian, for Camden tells us that 'the old Englishmen in the North parts turned Julius into Joly and the unlearned scribes of that time may seem to have turned

[1] At that period almost the three favourite girls' names were Ada, Emma and Julia.

Julianus into Jolanus, for that name doth often occur in old evidences'.

A few Greek names will be found in other chapters of this book, especially among the saints. To these may be added Theodore[1] (equivalent to Dorothea), a seventh century Archbishop of Canterbury, and Demetrius, one of the great saints of the Eastern Church. The latter name is derived from Demeter, the Greek goddess of harvest, corresponding to the Roman Ceres. So far as Demetrius has been used in England, it has come, not from the Thessalonian saint, but from the silversmith who raised a riot at Ephesus (*Acts xix*) or from his namesake mentioned in the Third Epistle of St. John. It has always been a great Russian name, and Dmitri, son of Ivan the Terrible, who was murdered as a child, was later impersonated by a temporarily succcssful 'Lambert Simnel'. With Theodore may be mentioned Theophilus, the name of the Countess of Huntingdon's husband and of Colley Cibber's son. Less familiar Greek names crop up occasionally, e.g. I have known a Bion, named either from the bucolic poet or from the 'Greek Voltaire', and those versed in the annals of the stage will remember Dion Boucicault (d. 1890); but he was christened

[1] The Latin equivalent Deodatus was in use in the 17th century.

Dionysius. Milo, the strong man of Crotona, was adopted very early in French and is one of the commonest names in the *Chansons de Geste*. Its Old French nominative was Miles, which, as an English name, has an alternative origin.

Greek and Roman names, partly because suggestive of Republicanism, have always been more popular in France than in England. A prominent French statesman of our own time was Aristide Briand and one of the greatest of nineteenth century intellects was Hippolyte Taine. Possibly the father of Camille Desmoulins, the regicide, who died by the guillotine 'not too heroically' in 1794, already had republican ideas. The Belgian hussar who, in Thackeray's *Vanity Fair*, left Waterloo in some haste was called Regulus—'He had been born in revolutionary times' (Ch. 32). America also has a liking for the names of antiquity, such as Virgil, Homer, Jason, Leonidas, etc

Female names of Greek origin are more numerous. One, a Greek plant name, which I cannot trace beyond Kingsley's *Yeast*, is Argemone. In the opinion of the late George Saintsbury, Argemone Lavington is one of the five most charming girls in English fiction. It was to Althea that Lovelace wrote his immortal lyric—'Stone walls do not a prison make'.

Althaea, sound, healthy, was the mother of Meleager, her name being perhaps an allusion to the firebrand which she preserved to guard her son's life. Almost as beautiful as Lovelace's song is Herrick's To Anthea—'Bid me to live'. The name is coined from Greek *anthos*, a flower. Plenty more classical names are to be found in Herrick, and, as Edmund Gosse says, 'it is not possible to disentangle Silvia from Perilla, or Corinna from Anthea, though his Julia has more individuality'.

Silvia or Sylvia, from Latin *silva,* wood, has been a favourite name since Shakespeare's time. We have also the masculine Silvester and Silvanus. The former, a canonized Pope, is commemorated on December 31st, whence the German *Silvesterabend* for New Year's Eve, but the early popularity of the name in England, from the twelfth century onward, was perhaps rather due to Gerbert of Aquitaine, Pope Sylvester II, 'the greatest figure in the 10th-11th. centuries, reckoned a magician for his knowledge, inventor, mathematician, scholar' (Harvey). The existence of the not uncommon surname Sylvester (there are 36 in the London Telephone Directory) points to its early adoption as a Christian name. Silvanus, a rustic deity later identified with Pan and Faunus, has given French Sylvain, the name of one of the twins in George Sand's *La Petite*

Fadette, but I know no earlier example in England than Sylvanus Urban, a *rus in urbe* pseudonym adopted in 1731 by Edward Cave, founder of the Gentleman's Magazine, though the shorter form Silas is familiar enough. Urban, the town-dweller, has named many Popes, but has never had any vogue in England. Its opposite Peregrine, the wanderer, pilgrim, has been in English use since the thirteenth century. Peregrine Bertie, Lord Willoughby de Eresby, was born at Lower Wesel, Germany, in 1555, whither his parents had fled from the Marian persecution, the name being chosen '"for that he was given by the Lord to his pious parents in a strange land for the consolation of their exile", as says his baptismal register' (Charlotte Yonge).

To return to the Greek ladies, I have found an Anastasia, popularly Anstice, in fourteenth century London, and the name is probably much older. It had a pet form Stacey, still used in America. It is rather surprising to find Cassandra, daughter of Priam and derided prophetess of woe, well represented in our thirteenth century records. The explanation must be the popularity of the story of Troy, the subject of an epic of 30,000 lines written in Old French *c.* 1160 by Benoit de Sainte-More and dedicated to Queen Eleanor of England. It was familiar enough to be shortened into Cass or

Cassy and was the name of Jane Austen's sister. More recently it was borne by the late Lady Rosse. Corinna, one of Herrick's loves ('Corinna goes a-maying'), was a Greek poetess who once vanquished Pindar in a public competition, which determined Mme de Staël's choice of the name for the very idealized portrait she drew of herself in one of the dullest novels ever written. The Restoration vogue of the name was due to Ovid's *Corinna*. It was also applied by Dryden to his friend Elizabeth Thomas, poetaster and blackmailer. It is a diminutive of the Greek kore, maiden, whence presumably Cora, a name which the adventuress known as Cora Pearl preferred to her original Emma Elizabeth Crouch.

Cynthia and Delia, birthplace epithets of Artemis or Diana, the first from Mount Cynthus in the island of Delos, were sixteenth century favourites. Spenser, as Colin Clout, and Ben Jonson, in Cynthia's Revels, both gave the name to Queen Elizabeth, and Samuel Daniel, brother of 'Rosalind', published in 1592 a book of sonnets to Delia. It is odd to find Charlotte Yonge describing Cynthia as 'a name of girls in America'. Ismenia seems to have reached us, *via* French romance, from Ismene, sister of Antigone. Melissa, bee, was a nymph who, according to tradition, first taught the use of honey. Ariosto gave this name to the kindly fairy of Orlando Furioso. A name which met with much favour in the sixteenth century was that of Penelope, the virtuous wife of Ulysses. According to Charlotte Yonge it began in Ireland as a substitute for Fenella. The traditional etymology is from Greek *pene,* the thread on the shuttle, because of the ingenious device by which, after the 'presumed' death of Ulysses, she put off her suitors. This sounds rather like an etymology made to fit the case. Greek *penelops* is a kind of duck, and, in Camden's opinion, this 'most patient, true, constant and chaste wife' had her name from the fact that 'she carefully loved and fed those birds with purpure necks called Penelopes'. Zenobia, the famous third century Queen of Palmyra, who was defeated by Aurelian and brought captive to Rome, is the heroine of a tragedy (1711) by the elder Crébillon, which gave Zénobie some currency in France. It has never been much used in England. The face-value of the name is 'living by Zeus', but Charlotte Yonge points out, with much probability, that, being an Arabian princess, she was perhaps originally named Zeenab. According to the same authority the Greek Zoe, life, was first used by the Alexandrian Jews to render the Biblical Eve. There was a Roman saint of the name who was thrown into the Tiber in 280.

A common Christian name in Scotland is Æneas, adopted as equivalent to the native Angus, as Hector was for Eachan. Of the Roman Emperors Augustus is, perhaps owing to the meaning of the title conferred on Octavius by the Senate, easily the favourite, though the name has never been as popular with us as Auguste in France. It is of late introduction, and both the masculine and feminine forms, favourite names in Germany, really came in under the Georges. Constantine, on the other hand, is well recorded in the Middle Ages. It was the name of many Emperors, starting with Constantine the Great and ending with Constantine Palæologus, the last Emperor of Byzantium. The success of the name was no doubt due to the Church, which regarded Constantine as the great Roman protector of Christianity. The popularity of the Claudian *gens* is harder to explain. The masculine Claude has long been familiar in France and Shakespeare makes use both of Claudius and the Italian Claudio. The Welsh Gladys is supposed to represent an early adoption of Claudia. The French Claudine is sometimes now found in England, presumably under the inspiration of a rather naughty series of French novels. All these names are probably derived from Latin *claudus,* lame.

Adrian (or Hadrian) was one of the greatest

Emperors, but the early adoption of his name was chiefly due to St. Adrian, who became Archbishop of Canterbury in 668. I doubt whether the great lawgiver Justinian's name has ever been in real English use. It is true that it was the middle name of James J. Morier, author of that brilliant book *Hajji Baba* (1824), and the brothers Smith, parodying Crabbe with amazing cleverness in *Rejected Addresses*, tell us that—

John Richard William Alexander Dwyer
Was footman to Justinian Stubbs, Esquire.

The name is a derivative of *justus.* Compare Justin, popular in Ireland, where it commemorates St. Justin Martyr (d. 167), the earliest of the great Christian apologists. St. Justina of Padua is the heroine of a strangely Oriental legend. She is also honoured at Venice, because considered to have decided the issue of the naval battle of Lepanto (1571) where Don John of Austria destroyed the Turkish fleet. The Cornelian *gens,* perhaps from *cornu,* horn, has given us Cornelius, more popular in Ireland than here, and Cornelia. A St. Cornelius was Pope and martyr in the third century. From *aurum,* gold, we have Aurelia, mother of Julius Cæsar, and the Emperor Aurelian, conqueror of Zenobia, also Aurel and Auriol, all rather uncommon.

Of the great classical writers, Homer and Virgil are more popular in America than here, where the two favourites are Horace and Terence. The Italian form of Horace was used by Shakespeare in *Hamlet* and named our greatest national hero. I have only known one Horatio, and he was Nelson's great-nepllew, but it was also one of the names of Lord Kitchener. Terence is popular in Ireland, where, according to Charlotte Yonge, it was adopted for the native Turlough. I have also known of one solitary Ovid. Another Latin name, Lucius, would seem, from Sheridan's *Sir Lucius O'Trigger*, to be especially Irish. There have been Popes of the name, which was also that of the noblest figure in our Civil War, Lucius Cary, Lord Falkland, who, says Clarendon, 'Often after a deep silence and frequent sighs, would with a shrill and sad accent ingeminate the word Peace, Peace', despairing of which he threw away his life at the battle of Newbury (1643).

On the whole the feminine forms of Roman names seem to have been preferred, although we have no feminine for Rufus, the first name of the late Lord Reading. This is generally said to be the origin of Welsh Griffith, but this is doubtful.[1] From Aemilia, grandmother of the Gracchi, we have, through French, Emily, but

[1] See Förster, *Keltisches Wortgut im Englischen* (Halle, 1921).

the masculine form, popular in France after Rousseau's rather crazy treatise on education (1762), has never been in use in England. Amelia is an eighteenth century adaptation of the German Amalie, which has been affected by the Germanic element amal. The great republican hero Camillus, 'the second Romulus', is unrepresented among us, but Camilla, the fleet-footed votaress of Diana, was popular in the eighteenth century and gave a title to one of Fanny Burney's novels. Fabius survives only in the derivative Fabian, the name of a 3rd.-century canonized Pope. We have no Cælius, but, since As You Like It, Celia has been as popular as Rosalind; no Marcius or Marcellus, but Marcia and Marcella, all apparently derivatives of Marcus. Other examples are Albinia, Clelia, popularized by Madeleine de Scudéry and still found in Crabbe, Flavia, the Anthony Hope princess, Lelia, possibly from George Sand's *Lélie*, not to be confused with Byron's Arabic Leila, Lavinia, Lucretia, Sidonia, Virginia and the French Valérie. Then we have the abstract nouns Honor, with its derivatives Honoria and Honorine, and Victoria, the Roman personification of victory. The great Queen, at whom the uninstructed of our day incline to sneer, was christened Alexandrina Victoria, from her godfather, Alexander I of Russia, and her German mother respectively, so that the name is really of German introduction. Both Rex and Regina are occasionally selected by ambitious parents, but the latter usually becomes Queenie. Of late Gloria has been used by film actresses and millionaire heiresses. A favourite classical name just now is Doris, mother of the Nereids. It is really of Greek origin, but was a common name in Rome. In Germany it is used, like Dora, as a pet form of Dorothea. It is uncertain whether the Restoration Chloris is to be associated with the Greek goddess of flowers or with that daughter of Niobe who evaded the arrows of Apollo and ever after showed the pallor of her narrow escape. The adjective *chloros* means 'light green' or 'blooming' and also 'pale'.

Many readers will no doubt be able to supplement from friends and relatives the list of names occurring in this chapter. Oenone is the middle name of a distinguished Irish authoress and Lord Oxford and Asquith's granddaughter Cressida was married the day before the above was written. There is nothing to prevent a parent of classical taste giving to his offspring Latin or Greek names of learned length and thundering sound, following the example of Pisistratus Caxton's scholarly father (Lytton, *The Caxtons*) or of the agricultural Jasper Yellowley (Scott, *The Pirate*), who, inspired by his wife's dream, named his son Triptolemus, from the mythological inventor of the plough.

CHAPTER V

The Old Testament and the Puritans

Old Testament names are scarcely recorded in Old English and in the Middle Ages we find only a few. The commonest of these are Adam and Elias[1]. The others that occur with any frequency are mostly those of important characters, such as Abel, Samson, David, Solomon, Joseph and Benjamin. Of the patriarchs, Jacob owed what popularity he had to the fame of St. James by which the official Jacobus is usually to be rendered. Daniel was, perhaps because of his miraculous adventures, the favourite of the major prophets, but the minor prophets and the kings of Israel and Judah were almost neglected, along with what may be called the supers of Old Testament history. The Church, restricting itself to the Calendar of Saints, did not encourage the Old Testament names of the uncanonized. Among female names we find Eva or Eve and Sara(h), while Anna and Elizabeth also enjoyed some popularity, less due to Hannah, the mother of Samuel, and Elisheba the wife of Aaron, than

[1] Such names were usually given preferably in their Greek New Testament forms, e.g. Elias for Elijah, Jonas for Jonah, Jeremias for Jeremiah, and even Jeremy (Matt. ii.17) So also Anna for Hannah, Elizabeth for Elisheba. Lazarus is the Greek form of Eleazar.

to St. Anna, apocryphal mother of the Virgin
Mary, and Elizabeth, mother of the Baptist.
Adam was a favourite name among early ecclesiastics and theologians. The *Dictionary of
National Biography* enumerates fifteen of
these, from the twelfth to the fourteenth century, i.e. before the fixed surname period, the
best remembered being Adam Murimuth, i.e.
merry mouth (d. 1347), who spent some time
at Avignon, where he represented the University of Oxford and the Chapter of Canterbury.
His name is preserved in the Merry-Mouth inn
at Fifield, Oxon. There can be no doubt that
the vogue of Old Testament names largely de-
pended on the extent to which they were made
familiar by the religious drama of the Middle
Ages.

The Reformation brought about a complete
change. The Puritans presumably hated the
Devil, but they hated the saints still more.
They 'baptized their children by the names,
not of Christian saints, but of Hebrew patriarchs and warriors' (Macaulay). So, not only
the glorious company of the apostles and the
noble army of martyrs vanished from their nomenclature, but also most of the old Germanic
names discussed in Ch. II, for were not many
of these also tainted with sanctity? From the
New Testament they took a few of the more obscure names, not suspect of canonization, but,

as a rule, turned for their children's names to the Old Testament and the goodly fellowship of the prophets. This craze prevailed throughout Protestant countries, but nowhere so violently as in our own. Montaigne wrote: 'Ne dira pas la postérité que nostre Réformation d'aujourd'huy ait esté délicate et exacte de n'avoir pas seulement combatu les erreurs et les vices et rempli le monde de dévotion, d'humilité, d'obéissance, de paix et de toute espece de vertu, mais d'avoir passé jusqu'à combattre ces anciens noms de nos baptesmes, Charles, Loys, François, pour peupler le monde de Mathusalem, Ezechiel, Malachie, beaucoup mieux sentants de la foy?' (*Essais*, i. 46). This, like most sarcasms, is an exaggeration, at any rate so far as France is concerned, for the inrush of Old Testament names in that country bore no relation to the same mania in England. At Geneva, under the régime of Calvin, an ordinance of August 30th, 1546, decreed 'que l'on ne mette point de noms, sinon de l'Écriture', while 'les noms des idoles qui ont régné au pays' (i.e. the saints!) were especially forbidden; but in France, except for the temporary popularity of Isaac and a few other names, no great harm was done.

In England it was otherwise. The practice varied with the strength of Puritanism in different localities, but in some regions the revolution was complete. The beginnings of the movement in the middle of the sixteenth century were modest, only the more prominent of the Old Testament names being used. Of these Samuel was easily the favourite, a position which it has pretty well kept up to the present day. The choice is easily understood, for the child Samuel was asked of the Lord and dedicated to His service. It is dramatic irony that such a scoffer at Puritanism as Samuel Butler, author of *Hudibras*, should have borne the stock Puritan name.

A word here on the Divine element which enters into so many Old Testament names. This is either *El* or *Jah*[1] (*jo, je, iah*, etc) and may be initial or final, both being combined in Elijah and Joel. Thus Nathaniel, gift of God, has approximately the same meaning as Jonathan, gift of Jehovah, Michael is equivalent to Micaiah or Micah, Eliakim, God establishes, to Joachim (Jehoiakim), Hezekiah, Jehovah hath strengthened, to Ezekiel, God will strengthen.

This flood of Old Testament names undoubtedly coincided with the circulation of the Great or Cranmer's Bible (1539), later of other versions, such as the Geneva Bible, and finally of the Authorized Version (1611). Until quite recent times the Bible was read aloud daily in

[1] *Jah* is the proper name (Jehovah), *El* the common (God).

most English families, which thus became familiar with names seldom found among foreigners.

As already stated, at the beginning of the new fashion only great names or those associated with some special me aning at birth were adopted. The heroic name of David seems to have been avoided by the Puritans, no doubt because another David (d. *c*. 600) was the patron saint of Wales.[1] The name had so long been established in Great Britain that it had become, so to speak, non-Biblical. Moses, Aaron, Joshua and Gideon make their appearance along with the three patriarchs, Abraham, Isaac and Jacob, the two favourite names among the latter's sons being naturally Joseph and Benjamin, both of which were already well known to the Middle Ages, as is shown by our numerous Jessops and Bensons. In fact the medieval popularity of Joseph was chiefly due to St.Joseph of Arimathea and his mythical connection with Glastonbury and its 'Thorn'. Joseph's son Manasseh had obtained an early and inexplicable popularity, his name being even recorded in Domesday Book. Caleb was, perhaps because of his special privilege, a great favourite and has had some success in

[2] Hence the frequency in Wales of the surname Davi(e)s. In the Welsh Rugby team of Feb. 1939 five of the fifteen players were named Davies.

fiction, and Melchizedek, as a Puritan name, antedates Evan Harrington's father by some centuries. There was also a strong tendency to choose names of melancholy import, such as Ichabod (I Sam. iv. 21), Jeremiah, Job and Jonas, the last being the only minor prophet to appear among the early examples; and, as will be shown in Ch. IX, some Puritan parents expressed their feeling of abjectness by giving repulsive Scriptural names to their children.

Less important names were sometimes given in connection with the circumstances of birth. A son born to an exile at Strasburg in 1543 was christened Gershom—'For he said, I have been a stranger in a strange land' (Exod. ii. 22). Another, born just after his father's death, became Jabez,—'His mother called his name Jabez, saying, Because I bore him with sorrow' (I. Chron. iv. 9). In fact, the Puritans, saturated as they were with Biblical knowledge and the Hebrew spirit, reverted to Hebrew practice. When Rachel's youngest son was born, 'it came to pass, as her soul was in departing (for she died), that she called his name Benoni ("son of my sorrow"); but his father called him Benjamin ("son of the right hand")'. About the middle of the seventeenth century one John Cromwell compromised by giving his son the name Ben-Oni-Jamin.

But the English love of individuality was not

long satisfied with stock Biblical names. Parents began to ransack the genealogical chapters of the Old Testament in search of something hitherto unused. Jesse, David's father, has always been a fairly popular name, but it is difficult to see why anyone should wish to name a child from David's 'bossy' elder brother; yet we find Eliab on record, and Sir Eliab Harvey commanded the Téméraire at Trafalgar. Sometimes also the name was chosen by opening the family Bible at random, a kind of *Sortes Virgilianæ*. Others deliberately chose the sesquipedalian type of name. These absurdities have persisted almost into our own time, e.g. 'Mrs Mahershalalhashbaz Bradford was dwelling in Ringwood, Hampshire, in 1863' (Bardsley), and further examples will be found in Ch. IX. Even as late as the second half of the nineteenth century we find record of the ridiculous Talitha Cumi and the blasphemous Eli-lama-Sabachthani!

The result of this search for 'unused' names was such that the nomenclature of the later Puritans could be, with little exaggeration, thus described by the Cavalier poet, John Cleveland, 'Cromwell hath beat up his drums clean through the Old Testament. You may learn the genealogy of Our Saviour by the names in his regiment. The muster-master uses no other list than the first chapter of Matthew.' This Hebrew nomenclature prevailed completely in many parts of the country, its greater or less vogue depending largely on the views of the parson.—'There had been villages in Sussex and Kent, previous to Elizabeth's death, where the Presbyterian rector, by his personal influence at the time of baptism, had turned the new generation into a Hebrew colony. The same thing occurred in Yorkshire only half a century later... As for the twelve sons of Jacob, they could all have answered to their names in the dames' schools... On the village green, every prophet, from Isaiah to Malachi, might be seen of an evening playing leapfrog' (Bardsley).

The Old Testament names persisted, especially in the north. Only some fifty years ago Bardsley finds that 'If we look over the pages of the directories of West Yorkshire and East Lancashire and strike out the surnames, we could imagine we were consulting a recently inscribed register of Joppa or Jericho. Within the limits of ten leaves we have three Pharaohs, while as many Hephzibahs are to be found on one single page. Adah and Zillah Pickles, sisters, are milliners. Jehoiada Rhodes makes saws and Hariph Crawshaw keeps a farm. Vashni, from somewhere in the Chronicles, is rescued from oblivion by Vashni Wilkinson, coal merchant, who very likely goes to Barzillai Williamson for his joints. Jachin,[1] known to but a few as situated in the Book of Kings, is, in the person of Jachin Firth, a beer retailer, familiar to all his neighbours. Heber Holdsworth on one page is faced by Er Illingworth on the other. Asa and Joab are extremely popular, while Abner, Adna, Asahel, Erastus, Eunice, Benaiah, Aquila, Elihu and Philemon enjoy a fair amount of patronage. Shadrach, Meshach and Abednego, having been rescued from Chaldæan fire, have been deluged with baptismal water. How curious it is to contemplate such entries as Lemuel Wilson, Kelita Wilkinson, Shelah Haggas, Shadrach Newbold, Neriah Pearce, Jeduthun Jempson, Azariah Griffiths, Naphtali Matson, Philemon Jakes, Hamath Fell, Eleph Bisat, Malachi Ford or Shallum Richardson.'

It is probably an accident that Bardsley did not come across an Enoch in this list, though the name, in spite of its bearer's 'translation' (Gen. v. 24), does not appear to have had much popularity before the time of Tennyson's Enoch Arden. Another missing name is Hiram, so popular in America, the King of Tyre who supplied Solomon with building materials. I have never met the name Eli, but one of his sons, Phineas, is well recorded. The

---

[1] It was the name given by Solomon to one of the pillars of his Temple porch and means 'May He establish'.

pretty name Thyrza, which is the Biblical Tirzah, was long a rustic favourite.

The same state of things is reflected in George Eliot's Adam Bede. Adam's brother was Seth, his bibulous father was Thias (Matthias), the two objects of his love were Hetty, i.e. Hester or Esther, and Dinah, and the latter had aunts Judith and Rachel. In connection with Esther and Judith, another change of fashion may be noticed. Bardsley says, 'Esther is still popular in our villages, so is Susan. Hannah has her admirers, and only Judith may be said to be forgotten.' Judith, well known already in the Middle Ages, is now once more in full vogue. The name of her victim[1] was borne by Holofernes Hunt, perpetual curate of Liphook, Hants, in the seventeenth century, another example of Puritan abjectness.

To return to the male names, it is evident that half of the sons of Jacob have gone out of fashion, viz. Issachar, Zebulun, Dan, Naphtali, Gad and Asher. Yet Issachar Jupp is a character in Blackmore's *Cradock Nowell* and Zebulun Cunninghame was among the early emigrants to New England. We have already noticed one of Joseph's sons; the other, Ephraim, has been quite popular. Ephraim Chambers published in 1738 the *Cyclopaedia*

[1] See the book of Judith in the Apocrypha.

which inspired the great *French Encyclopédie*, and cricket enthusiasts of the author's age will remember that great Yorkshire batsman Ephraim Lockwood, with whom it seems natural to mention the Notts wicket-keeper Mordecai Sherwin. The most popular 'pro' of our time is so universally known as Patsy that he must almost have forgotten that he is really Elias.

If we turn to the minor prophets, everyone will think of 'Amos Cottle,—Phoebus! What a name!' Obadiah was sometimes used by Cavaliers as a stock name for a Roundhead, as Aminadab was for a Quaker, and Macaulay's Battle of Naseby is given as by Obadiah Bind-their-kings-in-chains-and-their-nobles-with-links-of-iron,[1] Sergeant in Ireton's regiment. A ribald song of about sixty years ago, 'The two Obadiahs', did not do it much good. Jonas, i.e. Jonah, as already noted, was rather a favourite. Micah was very suitably chosen by Conan Doyle for the son of an Ironside in his stirring tale *Micah Clarke*. Its older form Micaiah was familiar in the name of Micaiah Hill, a London examiner in mathematics when I was a young student. Nahum Tate, poetaster (d. 1715), and, with Brady, author of the Metrical Ver-

[1] A blunder of Macaulay's. He should have remembered what 'every schoolboy knows', viz. that the eccentricities of the Puritans did not go as far as surnames.

sion of the Psalms, came off once with 'As pants the hart for cooling streams'. Malachi, adopted in Irish for the native name[2] Maelseachlainn, named two kings and a famous saint. The other minor prophets, along with Nehemiah and Ezra, are found in Puritan use, but are now rare. Zachary, the name of Macaulay's father, is not from Zechariah, but from its New Testament form Zacharias, father of the Baptist.

Biblical place-names, such as Eden, Bethsaida, Canaan, were also used baptismally. Beulah (Is. lxii. 4) is still popular in America and Nazareth is recorded both for boys and girls. I know a lady called Mizpah, the name of the cairn which was to be a witness of the covenant between Laban and Jacob (Gen. xxxi), and Ebenezer, the stone set up by Samuel (I Sam. vii. 12) to commemorate the defeat of the Philistines, is well utilized as a name, its most famous bearer being Ebenezer Elliott, author of the Corn-Law Rhymes. Those who remember Besant and Rice's delightful Goklen Butterfly will think of that amusing American Gilead P. Beck. Perhaps the best-known bearer of such a name is Sharon Turner (d. 1847), a pioneer in the study of early English history. The plain of

[1] Charlotte Yonge gives many examples of such adoptions, e.g. Jeremy for Diarmaid.

Sharon was proverbial for its fertility.

The Puritans who exiled themselves to North America took the Old Testament names with them. The lists of emigrants, surnames apart, suggest the crossing of the Red Sea rather than that of the Atlantic.[1] In the States they persisted even more strongly than in rural England and they still name a large proportion of American fictional characters. Moreover, they so completely dominated the nomenclature of the settlers that they became, as it were, national and underwent that transformation into shortened forms which native English names had experienced centuries before. In England, except for such old established names as Dan, Sam, Joe and Ben, and a few modern examples, such as the familiar Ike, for Isaac, Old Testament names are gen-

---

[1] I cannot refrain from quoting once more the admirable Bardsley on these Old Testament names—'Among the passengers who went out to New England in James's and Charles's reigns will be found such names as Ebed-melech (I omit the surnames), Oziell, Ephraim, Ezechell (Ezekiel), Jeremy, Zachary, Noah, Enoch, Zebulon, Seth, Peleg, Gercyon (Gershom), Rachell, Lea (Leah), Calebb, Jonathan, Boaz, Esau, Pharaoh, Othniell, Mordecay, Obediah, Gamaliell, Esaias, Azarias, Elisha, Malachi, Jonadab, Joshua, Enecha (seemingly a feminine of Enoch) and Job. Occasionally an Epenetus or Nathaniell, or Epaphroditus, or Cornelius, or Feleaman (Philemon), or Theophilus, or Ananias is met with; but these are few and were evidently selected for their size, the temptation to poach on apostolic preserves being too great, when such big game was to be obtained. Besides, they were not in the calendar !'

erally used in full. In America we find Abe, Eben, Rube, stock name for a yokel, Jed, Jake, middle syllables like Zeke and Lish, and the New Testament Pete and Steve. The American humorist H.W. Shaw (d. 1885) wrote under the names Josh Billings and Uncle Ezek. It would be possible to make a very long list of prominent Americans who have borne Old Testament names: we will be satisfied with Noah Webster, the great lexicographer, Ira Sankey, the musical companion of Moody, the revivalist, who visited this country in 1873, and Elihu Burritt, the Learned Blacksmith (d. 1879). Ira was one of David's captains (2 Sam. xxiii. 26). Elihu (I Sam. i. I) was the grandfather of Elkanah, memorable for Dryden's enemy, Elkanah Settle. In American fiction the most out of the way Old Testament names are utilized. Edith Wharton wrote a novel called Ethan Frome, but all we know of Ethan is that he 'was less wise that Solomon' (I Kings, iv. 34). In *The Crisis*, by Winston Churchill, there is a character named Eliphalet, from one of David's numerous sons. Curiously popular in the States is the name of Cyrus, the Persian.

As already mentioned, the Puritans shunned the great New Testament names, which, belonging to saints, were regarded as unclean. Timothy, first bishop of Ephesus, was naturally suspect, and Titus, destroyer of Jerusalem, would be repugnant to enthusiasts for the Hebrew tradition. The most notorious Titus in our annals has not helped to popularize the name. Felix was not a Puritan name. It was taken, not from the Roman governor, but from one of many saints. From it we have the feminine Felicia, borne by that graceful poetess, Mrs Hemans. Either the Puritans or later prospectors made it their business to dig out the less familiar names. Aretas has only an occasional mention (2 Cor. xi. 22), but I find that Aretas Seton was Governor of the Leeward Isles in the early eighteenth century. Artemas (Titus iii. 12) was traditionally the first Bishop of Lystra. Artemas Ward (d. 1800) was an American general whose name was adopted, altered to Artemus, by the greatest of American humorists, Charles Farrar Browne (1834–67).

The effect of a man's religious convictions on the naming of his children can be seen in the case of John Bunyan, in his younger days an enemy of the Quakers. By his first wife he had Mary, John, Thomas and Elizabeth, all New Testament saints! By the time of his second marriage his anti-episcopal fervour had so far intensified that he went back to the Old Testament for Joseph and Sara.

The female Scriptural names, though often showing the same eccentricities as the male, e.g. I have come across an example of Aholibamah, wife of Esau, are on the whole more picturesque and interesting. According to an old rhyming description of names which this writer learnt from his mother—

Elizabeth is a peerless name, fit for a queen to wear,
In castle, cottage, hut or hall a name beyond compare.

It was not of course a popular Puritan choice, for, besides the New Testament Elizabeth, we have St. Elizabeth of Hungary (d. 1231), whose pathetic story was used for a tragedy by Charles Kingsley. But the fame of the great Queen, 'daughter of the Reformation', did something to counteract the hagiological taint and in modern times it has reigned next to Mary among female names. Its transformations are rather puzzling. In the Old Testament it is Elisheba. It has always been a favourite name in Europe. According to Charlotte Yonge, the first historical example is 'the Muscovite princess Elisavetta,[1] the object of the romantic love of that splendid poet and sea-king, Harold Hardrada of Norway, who sang nineteen songs of his own composition in her praise on his way to her from Constantinople and won her hand by feats of prowess'. No

[1] The New Testament Elizabeth was canonized in the eastern Church.

female name has so many variant or pet forms, e.g. Lizzie, Beth, Bess, Betsy, Betty, Libby, Elsie, Lisbeth, Elspeth, etc It was, even in the great Queen's time, often shortened into Eliza (compare French Élise), now often regarded, like Beth and Betty, as a separate name, and Dr. Johnson always called his wife Tetty. I fancy that 'good Queen Bess' is one of Scott's inventions, like his 'bluff King Hal', but Shakespeare was already familiar with this pet form.—'Come hither, Bess, and let me kiss my boy' (*3 Henry VI v. 7*), says Edward IV to his Queen (Elizabeth Woodville). When Elizabeth of Hainault married Philippe-Auguste of France, her name was contorted to Isabelle, which, as Isabella, soon became very popular in Spain. Charlotte Yonge is surely mistaken in saying that the name 'took no hold of the English taste: and it was only across the Scottish border that Isobel or Isbel, probably named from French allies, became popular'. According to Bardsley, Isabel long ran neck-and-neck with Matilda as a favourite girls' name and any scrutiny of medieval Rolls will confirm his opinion. In early occurrences the same person is sometimes indifferently Elizabeth and Isabel. Later on they were regarded as separate and Isabel prevailed almost completely over Elizabeth in the Middle Ages.

Among female names from the Old Testa-

ment there seems to have been a decided predilection, at least among the Puritans, for
those associated with the discomfiture of the
ungodly. With the song of Miriam (Ex. xv.)
over the drowned Egyptians we may compare
that of Deborah the prophetess (Judges v.) after the victory of Mount Tabor, with its special
mention of Jaël, 'blessed above women', who
had distinguished herself by driving a tent-
peg through the head of the sleeping Sisera,
after offering him hospitality. Miriam later became Mariamne or Marianne, wife of Herod I,
and Mary is its New Testament Greek form.
Deborah was in great favour with the Puritans
and Jaël Mainwaring was christened in 1613 .
Esther or Hester was a type of political wisdom, to be celebrated later by Racine, and
Thackeray may have been influenced in his
choice of Rebecca for Miss Sharp by some rec-
ollection of Rebekah's oriental artfulness ex-
erted on behalf of her favourite son. Rachel's
appropriation of her father's household gods is
another example. Even Ruth's approach to
Boaz showed a certain feminine sagacity. Nor
were the Puritans so uninterested in the more
scabrous episodes of Holy Writ and the Apocrypha as to shun the names of Bathsheba and
Susan(na), not to mention Dinah and Tamar .
The names of all three patriarchs' wives became popular, but Rachel, mother of Joseph

and Benjamin, was as much preferred to Leah as the ornamental Mary was in pre- and post-Puritan times to the domesticated Martha.

The Puritans took from the New Testament many girls' names, including that of the 'Puritan maiden, Priscilla'. She is generally coupled in Acts with her husband Aquila, a name also used by the Puritans. For Drusilla, wife of Felix. Of those two quarrelsome church-workers Euodias and Syntyche (Philip. iv. 2) only the former appears to have been favoured. Eunice, mother of Timothy, has kept her popularity, but, like Irene, is often mispronounced by modern tongues. Damaris had a great vogue in spite of her casual mention (Acts xvii. 34), and the same applies to Phoebe (Romans xvi. I) and Lydia (Acts xvi. I4), the latter of which escaped from the Puritans and became a fashionable eighteenth century name. Tabitha, 'which by interpretation is called Dorcas', was a prime favourite, the same woman being sometimes called indifferently by either name, and, while pre-Reformation parents naturally preferred Mary to Martha, the Puritans logically reversed the choice. In short, as Bardsley puts it, 'the great national names of Isabella, Matilda, Emma and Cecilia had been replaced, on Elizabeth's death, by Priscilla, Damaris, Dorcas and Phoebe,' the last named being, of course, 'Phebe, our sister, a servant of the Church', and not the heathen Diana or Artemis regarded as the sister of Phaebus.

A further result of Puritanism was the wholesale introduction of abstract nouns as names, sometimes given to boys[1] as well as girls. This was no new thing. From Greek we already had Alethea, truth, Sophia, wisdom, and Irene, peace. The Middle Ages had Constance, popularly pronounced Custance, Lætitia or Lettice, and all the virtues and vices were personified in the later medieval drama. But an immense number of new names of this type were introduced after the Reformation. I have already given from Littleton those in common use. It was the custom to baptize female triplets as Faith, Hope and Charity, and one remembers that Mr Pecksniff's two daughters were Charity and Mercy, Cherry and Merry. Spenser had already put Fidelia, Speranza and Charissa in the House of Holiness. Sir Thomas Carew, Speaker of the House of Commons in the seventeenth century, had a wife Temperance and four daughters, Patience, Temperance, Silence and Prudence. Patience is already the name of a gentlewoman in Shakespeare's *Henry VIII*, and Prudence is rather exceptional in having devel-

---

[1] Patience Warde was Lord Mayor of London in 1681 and the Rev Experience Mayhew died as late as 1758.

oped a pet form Prue, Steele's nickname for his second wife, for whom Patience would have been more suitable. Other recorded names of this type, some still in use, were Abstinence, Comfort, Confidence, Diligence, Felicity, Honor, Humiliation and Humility, Joy, Obedience, Perseverance, Remembrance, Repentance, Truth or Troth, Victory, along with such adjectives as Faithful, Godly, Gracious, Humble, etc The gloom which seems inseparable from Calvinism appears in the choice of such names as Wrath and Anger. Sometimes resort was had to the dead languages: Fiducia Lee's name is on a tablet in Ockley Church, Surrey, and the Greek Philadelphia, brotherly love, was in great favour.

Camden gives specimens of all the above types, as also of another type, hardly to be called a name, which reinforced them—' The new names Free-Gift, Reformation, Earth, Dust, Ashes, Delivery, More fruit, Tribulation, The Lord is near, More trial, Discipline, Joy again, From above, Acceptance, Thankful, Praise-God, Love-God and Live-well, which have lately been given by some to their children with no evil meaning, but upon some singular and precise conceit'.

A few of such names have been attached to people of some importance. Accepted Frewen (d. 1664) was Archbishop of York, Increase

Mather (d. 1723) was an eminent American divine and father of Cotton Mather, the witch-finder. Best known of all is Praise-God Barbon, the fanatic whose name is associated with the Barebones Parliament of 1653. His brother is said to have been baptized If-Christ-had-not-died-for-thee-thou-hadst-been-damned. This is probably an invention, but it appears to be certain that he was known to the ungodly as Damned Barbon.

The subject of these 'Pilgrim's Progress' names coined by the Puritans from Scriptural and moral phrases lies outside the scope of this book, so I will be satisfied with the following panel of seventeenthcentury Sussex jurymen, given as authentic by Mr Arthur Bryant in his England of Charles II.—'Accepted Trevor, Redeemed Compton, Faint-not Hewit, Standfast-on-high Stringer, Kill-sin Pimple, Be-faithful Joiner, Fly-debate Roberts, Fight-the-good-fight-of-faith White, More-fruit Fowler, Hope-for Bending, Weep-not Billing, Meek Beaver.' Such names and those taken from Scripture by the Puritans excited the derision of ungodly dramatists, who are fond of giving them to rascally and hypocritical characters. As early as Ben-Jonson we find Zeal-of-the-Land Busy in *Bartholomew Fair* and Tribulation Wholesome in *The Alchemist*. Nor does the possession of edifying names seem to

have given their bearers the hoped for immu-
nity from sin. Gamaliel Ratsey was a famous
highwayman, hanged in 1605, and Salvation
Yeo, according to his mother, 'swore terribly in
his speech'.

CHAPTER VI

The Growing List

As the preceding chapters show, our list of Christian names has, since the close of the Middle Ages, been constantly enlarged from various sources. The most considerable modern importation has been from Scotland. It is probable that the great popularity of Walter Scott is partly responsible for the nineteenth century invasion of England by Scottish Gaelic names. The most familiar of these are Angus, unique choice, Donald, world-ruler, 'much the same in meaning as Dumnorix, world king, Caesar's opponent among the Aedui' (Macbain), Dugald, dark stranger, i.e. Dane, as contrasted with Fingal,[1] fair stranger, i.e. Norwegian, Duncan, brown warrior (on the three Ds see Cuddie Headrigg), Ewen, probably, like the Welsh Owen,[2] borrowed from Greco-Latin Eugenius, Fergus, super-choice, Gilchrist, servant of Christ, now chiefly a surname, but formerly used to translate the Greek Christopher, Hector, a Greek name, upholder, the 'prop of Troy', adopted for the native Eachan, Kenneth, fair one, Malcolm,

[1] This was Oscar Wilde's second name.
[2] Among the 14th.-century citizens of London I find a man whose surname is spelt indifferently Ewayn, Iweyn and Oweyn.

157

tonsured servant of St. Columba, Murdoch, sea-warrior, partly akin to the Welsh Morgan, Roy, red, but probably connected by parents rather with Old French roy, king. To these may be added three Scottish saints, viz. Ninian, missionary to the southern Picts in the fifth century, Conan, seventh century bishop of Sodor and the name of one of Ossian's characters, and Mungo, patron saint of Glasgow, really the nickname, 'beloved', of St. Kentigern, who built his cathedral at Glasgow on ground that had been consecrated by St. Ninian. None of these names has had much vogue in England; indeed, outside fiction, the only Mungo one remembers is the African explorer, Mungo Park (d. 1806).

Not all Highland names are purely Gaelic. Scotland received a considerable contribution from the Vikings, including Ivor, for Ingwar, the name of the Danish chief who murdered St. Edmund, Ronald or Ranald, the Old Norse equivalent of Reginald, and Torquil, i.e. Thor's kettle, which was contracted in England to Thurkil and became very common in East Anglia, still the great home of the surnames Thirkle, Thurkell, Thurtle, etc Brenda, the name of one of Magnus Troil's daughters in Scott's Pirate, is probably a feminine from the Norse name Brand, flame, swordblade. Desmond, Esmond and Redmond were taken to Ireland by the Vikings. Archibald came from the Continental German Eorcenbald, precious bold, via Old French, and is found in Middle English, but it became especially a Scottish name, when, in the twelfth century, the head of the Campbells adopted it in replacement of Gillespie, bishop's servant, since when 'the heads of the house of Campbell have been Archibald to the Lowlands, to their own clan, Gillespie' (Charlotte Yonge). Douglas, Gordon and Lachlan are surnames of place-name origin, the first meaning dark water, the second from a Berwickshire village, and the third, from Old Norse, apparently meaning 'fjord-land'.

Several Scottish pet forms of girls' names have become popular of late. Maisie (also Mysie), for Margaret, is the heroine of the old ballad of Proud Maisie, May is used in Scotland both for Mary and Margaret and Jessie is said to be similarly used for Janet, which, like Jean, shows French influence. Thus Jessie is not necessarily for Jessica. This was in medieval England a Jewish name, identified with the Iscah or Yiskah of Genesis xi. 29. Since *The Merchant of Venice*, in which Jessica shows some of the Oriental sagacity already referred to, it has naturally been shunned by the Jews. Margery for Margaret is common in Middle English, but Marjorie is essentially

Scottish and Marjorie Bruce, daughter of the great Robert, became the ancestress of a new royal house, when she married, in 1315, Walter the High Steward (Scottish Stewart) of Scotland. A very interesting old Scottish name is the historic Devorgilla, mother of John Baliol and foundress of Balliol College, Oxford. A newspaper of March 30th, 1939, recorded the marriage of a Scotch lady named Dorviegelda[1] Malvina. The second name is that of Oscar's lady-love in Ossian and was probably invented by Macpherson. Muriel or Meriel, a common name in Middle English, is explained by Macbain as 'sea-white'. It occurs in Old Irish as Muirgheal as early as 851. Some of the older Gaelic names have been generally replaced by others more familiar, e.g. Devorgilla by Dorothy, Fionnaghal, fair-shouldered, whence the Fenella of Peveril of the Peak, by Flora, Una, famine, by Winny.

Of the Welsh male names enumerated by Littleton only Evan, Llewellyn, lion-like, Coleridge's Leoline in Christabel, and Morgan, sea-dweller, have had much vogue in England. Cradock, i.e. Caradoc, made by the Romans into Caractacus, is found occasionally.

Of late several Welsh girls' names have become popular, especially Gladys and Winifred. Others are Gwendolen, of frequent occurrence

[1] Probably misprinted.

in Welsh history and legend, Gwynneth, Eiluned and Myfanwy. One of the most famil- iar is the shortened Gwen, which represents Welsh gwyn, white, fair.

No true Irish male names seem to be in gen- eral use with us, but, beginning with Kathleen, i.e. Catherine, and Nora(h), for Honora or Eleanor, there has been a recent importation, especially of -een names, e.g. Doreen, explained by Charlotte Yonge as meaning sullen, but possibly a mere diminu- tive of Dora, Maureen, a diminutive of Mary, and Rosaleen in whom is personified Ireland, 'Dark Rosaleen', a reference to whom by Tim Healy once caused a back-bencher to ask his neighbour in a worried whisper, 'What did he say about Rosebery?' The legendary Deirdre has, owing to her appearance in dramas by Synge and Yeats, recently attained some popularity. In my paper today is a picture of two actresses, one named Deirdre and the other Karen, the latter a recent importation from Denmark. Sheila is the Irish form of Cecilia or Celia.

The names so far discussed are new importa- tions or resurrections, but there are a few Celtic names of ancient adoption and lineage. We have noticed among the Conqueror's com- panions an Alan and an Ivo, both from Brit- tany. Alan, of which Allen is a later variant, is rather mysterious. It is explained by Charlotte Yonge as 'harmony', apparently allied to Welsh alaw, tune.—'It came into England with Alan, Earl of Britain (Brittany), to whom the Conqueror gave the greatest part of Richmondshire, and hath been most common since that time in the Northern parts' (Camden). Of all Breton names Yves is the commonest. It is the Old French nominative of Yvain, identical with Evan and John, and famous in medieval epic as the Knight with the Lion. From it are derived the female names Yvette and Yvonne. The most notorious Ivo in England was Ivo Taillebois, probably a man of low origin (woodcutter), the villain of the Hereward saga. The name is not extinct, for the Hon. Ivo Bligh, afterwards Lord Darnley, was a member of the most famous of all Cambridge cricket teams (c. 1880). A St. Ivo of Brittany gave his name to St. Ives in Cornwall, but the St. Ives of Huntingdon was traditionally a Persian! Another great Breton name which came over with the Conqueror is Brian, said to mean 'strength'. Its most famous bearer is Brian Boru, King of Leinster, who fought against the Danes and was killed at Clontarf in 1014. Other Celtic names established far back in history are those of the two tragic queens Guinevere and Isold, which will be found in Ch. II.

Of late a few Russian names have come into
fashion, e.g. Ivan, i.e. John, and the female
Natalie, Olga, Sonia and Vera. The first is of
Latin origin and cognate with Noël, Olga is the
Scandinavian Helga, holy, Sonia is a diminutive of Sophia, and Vera, when not short for
Veronica, is the Slavonic *viera,* faith. The
present Archbishop of Canterbury has the
Italian name Cosmo, famous in the Medici
family and said to come from Greek *kosmos,*
order, and Byron named his unfortunate little
daughter Allegra, cheerful. Some parents turn
to Spanish, e.g. Dolores, lit. sorrows, i.e. the
seven sorrows of the Holy Virgin. A Spanish
name which has never had much currency in
England is Alphonso, introduced by the
Visigoths from Old German Hildefuns, fight
ready. It has been popular in France
(Lamartine, Daudet, etc). Alonzo is said to be
the same name, which one doubts. Isidore, gift
of Isis, scarcely used in England except by
Jews, owes its Spanish vogue to two national
saints, one of whom was Isidor of Seville, a
great word-hunter of the early seventh century. The German abbreviation Max, for
Maximilian, is now quite familiar in England.
Even the Red Indians are not altogether neglected, e.g. I have met a Canadian lady
named Wenonah, from the mother of
Hiawatha—

Fair Nokomis bore a daughter
And she called her name Wenonah,
As the first-born of her daughters
                    (*Hiawatha*, iii, 23).

Owing to this relentless hunt for ever new and attractive female names, the feminine list is now immensely longer than the masculine. Just as the garb of the human female is distinguished from that of the male by constant changes in shape, colour and ornamentation, so do female names show recurring changes of fashion and all sorts of more or less fantastic attempts at intensifying their attractiveness. Moreover, constant inroads are made by the female on male territory. In May, 1939, the Times recorded the death of a lady named Alfreda Ernestine Alberta, three masculine names feminized. The practice of adding -a to a male name, e.g. Ethelberta, Theobalda, Louisa, etc is very ancient. Camden gives, as formerly in use, 'Nicholea, Laurentia, Richarda, Guilielma, Wilmetta, drawn from the names of men, in which number we yet retain Philippa, Francisca, Joanna, etc.' In modern America we find Willa. Sometimes such names were adopted from a father or ancestor, sometimes no doubt in honour of the saint on whose day the baby was born.

Another ending is -ina or -ine, as in Katharine. Later names of this type are usually of Italian or French origin, e.g. Adelina, Ambrosine, Georgina (also Georgiana), Clementina, Josephine, Thomasine, whence the rustic Tamsin, and German Wilhelmina, whence Minna. Diminutives were formed in -otta, -otte, e.g. the Italian Carlotta or the French Charlotte, which became so popular in Germany. Another dim. suffix is -etta, -ette, as in Henrietta, Harriet, Georgette, and Shakespeare's Jaquenetta (*Love's Labour's Lost*). Such endings are attached also to female names, e.g. Ellaline, Floretta and Lizetta, both of which I have recently noted in the Times. As will be seen in Ch. VIII, -ot and -et were in English use as diminutive long before these comparatively modern formations.

The later Stuarts had rather a craze for names in -inda, such as Clarinda, Dorinda, Florinda, Melinda, perhaps suggested by Ariosto's Belinda, which in its turn was possibly due to the many German names in lind. Lovelace wrote a poem to Ellinda's Glove, Rhodolinda is the heroine of D'Avenant's *Albovine* (1629), Pope invented Zephalinda and Gay the comic Blouzelinda for a 'blowzy' wench. To the same period belongs the restoration of Latin forms, so that Cicely became Cecilia and Lettice was replaced by Letitia or

Lætitia. This love of artificially elaborate names is reflected in the characters of the Restoration dramistists, e.g. Vanbrugh's Amanda, Berinthia, Belinda, Hortensia, Aminta, Clarissa, Araminta, Corinna and Clarinda. He might have defended his Amanda by the example set by Shakespeare with his much more pleasing Perdita and Miranda, an example followed in our own day by the dramatist who created Candida, perhaps with a reminiscence of Voltaire's *Candide*.

Among made-up names none is prettier than Vanessa, coined by Swift for *Esther Vanhomrigh*. I know a lady of this name who is a collateral descendant of the Dean. To the same class probably belongs Pamela, apparently coined by Sidney in his *Arcadia*. Later it was adopted by Richardson for his virtuous servant girl (*Pamela or Virtue Rewarded*, 1740), 'designed to cultivate the principles of virtue and religion in both sexes', to which Fielding replied with his 'lewd and ungenerous' *Joseph Andrews*, the name of his hero being suggested by one of the patriarch's Egyptian experiences. Pamela, says Charlotte Yonge, is 'still not uncommon among the lower classes.' It has since become popular enough to achieve a pet form, Pam.

Swift translated his other Esther (Johnson), whose name comes from the Persian word for 'star', by the Latin Stella, which now has variants Estella and Estelle. Stella had already been used by Sidney for Penelope Devereux, for whom, as Astrophel, he wrote a sonnet sequence. It was as Astrophel, 'a gentle shepherd born in Arcady', that Spenser lamented his death, a fact perhaps remembered by Shelley, when he elegized Keats as Adonaïs. A less pleasing device than Stella is the 'sugary' Sacharissa, Waller's name for Lady Dorothy Sidney whom he wooed unsuccessfully. One is inclined to smile at the 'Ayrshire Ploughman' imitating these earlier writers by addressing Mrs Agnes Maclehose as Clarinda and signing himself Sylvander!

Much earlier than the Restoration eccentricities we have the fantastic collection of names to be found in the *Faerie Queene*, especially that part in which the poet gives us—

> A chronicle of Britain Kings
>   From Brute to Uther's rayne;
> And Rolls of Elfin Emperours
>   Till time of Gloriane.

Some of these were coined by Spenser, others culled from the old chroniclers and from Malory, of whom a lady novelist has lately written, 'I found the fighting parts dull, but the names were superb'. In France of the seventeenth century, the age of the endless romances spun by Madeleine de Scudéry and others, the use of highsounding names was a mania. Catherine de Vivonne, Marquise de Rambouillet, chose the anagram Arthenice, after seriously considering Carinthée and Éracinthe, and Moliere's two Précieuses ridicules, Madelon and Cathos (Katie), elected to be known as Polixene and Aminte. Aminta, from Tasso's *bergerie*, was a favourite at the Restoration period and was revived by Meredith in his Lord Ormont and his Aminta. The Marquise de Rambouillet's English contemporary and namesake, Katherine Philips, chose, instead of an anagram, the fanciful Orinda, to which her admirers prefixed the epithet 'Matchless'. This was perhaps suggested by Oriana, one of the names by which Elizabeth's courtiers called the Queen and the subject of one of Tennyson's early poems. At a later date we have Zélide, the name given to herself by that Dutch lady, Isabella van Serooskerken van Tuyll, who rejected Boswell's suit. Still later one of Byron's flames, Isabella Harvey, changed her name to Zorina Stanley.

From what has been said it is clear that girls' names are subject to ever fluctuating fashions, while boys' names remain much more stable. Many female names described by

Charlotte Yonge and Bardsley as unusual or almost obsolete are now restored to favour.[1] A striking example is Joyce, of which name Bardsley says, 'Joyce fought hard, but it was useless'. On the same page he says that 'Barbara is now of rarest use'. Joyce seems to have been for a time a Puritan name, coupled with Abigail and Charity in Cavalier skits. In older records it is latinized as Jocosa, which, if it represents 'joyous', is an etymological error, since the origin of French jo*yeux* is *gaudiosus*. Some seventy or eighty years ago innumerable girls were christened Ada, but I do not remember an Ada among my forty years' experience of students. No doubt it will come in again along with its contemporary favourites Emma and Julia. The same phenomenon is observed in France, where 'Le prénom est soumis à une singulière fluctuation de la mode qui pourrait caractériser chaque génération. Toute une série de prénoms disparaît un temps pour reparaître trente ou cinquante ans plus tard et meme apres des siecles, comme il arrive aujourd'hui avec la mode moyenâgeuse des prénoms féminins: Renée, Anne, Simonne, Yvonne, Odette, Huguette, Bérangère, etc Tel prénom qui semblait hier vieillot et rustique apparaît comme plein de distinction et de

[1] See, for instance, Cynthia, Ethel, Joan, Judith, Olive, Pamela, Winifred.

fraîcheur. Les hommes, qui ont le prénom plus simple et moins prétentieux que celui des femmes, ont recommencé depuis quelques années, à s'appeler de nouveau: Pierre, Jean, Jacques, Claude, etc.' (Lévy, *Le Manuel des Prénoms*).

CHAPTER Vll

Fancy Names

Besides the traditional names derived from Germanic, Celtic and the languages of the ancients, we now have a large number which may be called fancy names. Some of these fall under the heading 'animal, vegetable and mineral'. Others are connected with days and feasts, with names of places, and finally we have the numerals. Even in the Middle Ages pretty names for women began to be invented. Dulcibella, or Dowsabel (*Comedy of Errors*, iv. I) must be one of the earliest and the modern Dulcie and Douce are its abbreviations; cf. the Spanish Dulcinea, the name substituted by Don Quixote for Aldonza. Clarimond, borrowed from Old French Esclairmond, wife of the epic hero Huon de Bordeaux, is another ancient example. It occurs in the old tale of Valentine and Orson. Littleton gives Roseclere, which Charlotte Yonge couples with Rosalba and Rosabella or Rosabel, 'all arrant fancy names'. Claribel, 'the King's fair daughter', is in Shakespeare (*The Tempest* ii. I), Lilybelle has lately been recorded in the Times and Maribelle is the Christian name of an American lady novelist. I once had a housemaid named Donna, probably a muddled memory of her mother's reading, and Senora has also been used.

As was seen in Ch. II, the names of animals entered freely into the old Germanic names. The same is true of Biblical names, e.g. Deborah, bee, is synonymous with the Greek Melissa, Jonah means 'pigeon', Rachel is 'ewe' and Tabitha, gazelle, was translated by the Gr. Dorcas (Acts ix. 36), whence the Dorcas societies, which make garments for the poor. For Leo and Lionel. The modern craving for fancy names has apparently limited itself to the feathered section of the animal world. I have seen Dove as a woman's name on a country tombstone. Mavis, a dialect name for the thrush, of Old French origin, and Merle, the French name of the blackbird, are occasionally selected by imaginative parents.

Of flower names one of our oldest and most generally used is naturally Rose, starting with the Greek Rhoda, who answered the door to St. Peter (Acts xii). It is possible that it has also absorbed the once common Roese, Rohais, latinized as Rohesia, of Germanic origin and meaning 'nobility', with first element as in Robert. The Greeks had Narcissus and Hyacinthus, from the latter of which comes also the gem called a jacinth, but these names, despite the many St. Hyacinths, have never been naturalized in England, though Jacintha

is the heroine of Hoadly's *Suspicious Husband*
(1747). Chaucer's Prioress was 'cleped Mad-
ame Eglentyne', a name found also in Old
French epic, but it has not survived. The synonymous Italian Flordespina is in *Orlando
Furioso*. Still earlier is Blanchefleur, the heroine of an Old French romance of the twelfth
century. A very 'collective' flower name was
that of Field Flowers Goe, a nineteenth century Bishop of Melbourne, who was said to
have a brother named Spring Flowers. Rose or
Rosa has a number of derivatives, such as
Rosine, the heroine of *Le Barbier de Seville*,
Rosaline (*Love's Labour's Lost* and *Romeo and
Juliet*), Rosalie, the patron saint of Sicily, and
Rosalind. The latter name only accidentally
ends in lind, which is usually Old German
lind, snake, whence the *Lindwurm* or dragon
of German legend. It is a common ending in
German female names. Gerlind was the
wicked old queen in *Gudrun*, the great medi-
eval epic which companions the
Nibelungenlied; Ethelinda was a concubine of
Charlemagne. Belinda, from Ariosto, was
popular *c*. 1700 and named the heroine of *The
Rape of the Lock*. There are several modern
German names in -linde, but they are less
common than the abbreviated Linda, which is
sometimes used in England.

Rosalind is pre-Shakespeare. It was used by

Spenser, and apparently coined by him. In the *Shepherd's Calendar*, 'Rosalinde is a fained name, which, being well ordered, will bewray the verie name of his love and mistresse, whom by that name he coloureth'. The lady was Rosa Daniel, sister of the poet Samuel Daniel and wife of Florio, lexicographer and translator of Montaigne. Such anagrams were in fashion at the period, e.g. Joachim du Bellay wrote his *Olive* for Mlle de Viole and this may have suggested the device to his admirer and translator. The name was afterwards used by Lodge in his *Rosalynde or Euphues' Golden Legacy* (1590), from which Shakespeare took As You Like it. Rosamond, popularly connected with 'rose', is pretty certainly Old German Hrosmund, of which the first element means 'horse', a strange exotic beast to the old Teutons, as evidenced by the war-names Hengist and Horsa, stallion and mare. The earliest historical Rosamond figures in a very grim legend. She was the daughter of a king of the Gepidæ who was conquered by Alboin, king of the Lombards. The victor married the daughter and compelled her at a banquet to drink from her father's skull, in revenge for which she caused him to be assassinated at Verona in 573.

Rosemary is quite a recent adoption and belongs to the modern fancy for flower names, of which Poppy, not, I fancy, often really given at the font, is a recent symptom; Rosemary is not really a 'rose' name, but comes from Latin ros mar*inus,* sea dew, whence French *romarin.* Whether Primrose, occasionally used as a name, originally had anything to do with 'rose' is doubtful. Lily is also not easily explained. As given now, it is the name of a flower, but there do not seem to be any early examples, nor is the corresponding word used as a name in other European languages, though we have the very ancient parallel of Susan, lily, in Hebrew. In German Lilla and Lilli are pet forms of Elizabeth, e.g. the Lilli to whom some of Goethe's poems were written was Elizabeth Schönemann. Perhaps our Lily, apparently shortened from the earlier Lilian and the Scottish form Lilias, is ultimately a pet form of some once very common name such as Cecilia. Violet seems to be next to Rose and Lily in order of popularity. It is recorded by Charlotte Yonge in sixteenth century Scotland and Shakespeare gave us Viola. Whether the Old French Violante is connected seems doubtful, but this is probably the origin of the French Yolande and of Iolanthe. Ione, the heroine of *The Last Days of Pompeii*, seems to be formed from Greek *ion*, a violet. Jasmine or Jessamine also occurs, hence the Jessamy bride, Goldsmith's name for Miss Horneck. The more homely Daisy, sometimes given as an independent name, was originally and still is a pet equivalent of Margaret, the name *marguerite* having been transferred in Old French to the flower. Marguerite de Valois, la reine Margot, is said to have had a necklace composed of pearls cut into the shape of daisies. May is sometimes chosen by parents who regard it as a flower or month name and Iris is perhaps more often associated with the flower than with the Greek name for the rainbow or messenger of the Gods.

Flower names seem to be now on the down grade and the Daffodil and Orchid whom I have recently encountered in a shocker can hardly have representatives in real life. Mr Bernard Shaw's Begonia Brown seems too good to be true, nor can I quite swallow Bertie Wooster's Aunt Dahlia, though this name was also borne by Rhoda Fleming's sister. Picotee Chickerel, in *The Hand of Ethelberta*, also seems altogether too fanciful.

Meredith and Hardy had a decided penchant for out-of-the-way names. Besides Dahlia Fleming we find in Meredith (*The Amazing Marriage*) Carinthia Kirby, whose name is curiously like one of the Marquise de Rambouillet's throw-outs, but is apparently from the province of Carinthia (Karnten), in Austria, where she grew up. Hardy has the obsolete Old English Edred Fitzpiers (*The Woodlanders*) and Elfride Swancourt (*A Pair of Blue Eyes*), the unusual Felice Charmond (*The Woodlanders*), the classical Damon Wildeve (*The Return of the Native*) and Cytherea Graye (*Desperate Remedies*), the classical or Scriptural Festus Derriman (*The Trumpet Major*) and the almost obsolete Diggory Venn (*The Return of the Native*). The last name, borne by Hardcastle's servant in Goldsmith's *She Stoops to Conquer*, is derived by Charlotte Yonge from the old metrical romance of Sir D'Egaré, in which the apostrophe is a misprint, as *d'égaré* cannot mean anything. Possibly the name was *Desgaré*, an Anglo-French substitute for Old French *esgaré* (*égaré*), strayed, lost.

Along with flowers go other vegetable products. Phyllis, from the Greek for 'leaf', was the name of a Greek damsel who, disappointed in love, committed suicide and was transformed into a tree. At the Renaissance Phyllis became a stock name for a maiden, the 'neat-handed Phyllis' of *L'Allegro*. Later, with her lover Philander, she inspired many of the Stuart poets, who also introduced Phyllida. Daphne is Greek for 'laurel' or 'bay', into which the Arcadian nymph was transformed to save her from the pursuit of Apollo. Chloe, tender shoot, young verdure, is immortalized in the beautiful Greek story of Daphnis and Chloe, which became familiar to the moderns in the French version of *Jacques Amyot*. Sidney introduced the name into his *Arcadia* and it became a favourite with the later Stuart songwriters. Olive probably owes much more to the paladin Oliver than to the tree. In fact there can be little doubt that Olivia, heroine of *Twelfth Night* and daughter of the Vicar of Wakefield, was coined as a feminine to Oliver. The name was very popular in the eighteenth century, but we now prefer the simple Olive, 'a form that still survives in some parts of the country' (Charlotte Yonge), one more illustration of the fickleness of fashion. Then we have Hazel, Heather, Ivy, Lavender, Myrtle, etc, all I think of quite recent introduction. I should be inclined to include here Eveline, which, in the form Evelyn, is of late also given to boys. It is found as Aveline in Normandy long before the Conquest and this is still French for 'hazelnut'. It may, as Charlotte Yonge suggests, have had contact with some Irish name, but, as it is recorded in our twelfth century Pipe Rolls, this seems unlikely. It joined the -a names in the eighteenth century and gave a title to one of Fanny Burney's three novels—*Evelina*, *Cecilia*, *Camilla*. The vegetable class of name is being constantly augmented by the fancy of parents or writers. In a novel published in

May, 1939, the heroine's name is Dittany, from Greek dictamnon, a plant credited with magic powers, traditionally from Mount Dicte in Crete. The parents who, not long ago, christened a girl Thistle had perhaps in mind the national emblem of Scotland and its motto, 'Nemo me impune lacessit'.

If Laura and Lawrence are related to Latin *laurus,* laurel, the above names have an ancient precedent, but it is very doubtful if the Roman mind was capable of so much imagination, though we owe to it Flora, the goddess of flowers, also Florentia, whence Florence, and even Florentina. Flora is especially popular in Scotland where it was adopted as a substitute for an old Gaelic name. Its popularity was increased by Flora Macdonald, the heroine of the Forty-Five. Flor- names have always been popular in fanciful formations, e.g. Ariosto has Flordelis and Flordespina, Spenser has Florimel, Southey has Florinda and Stevenson the masculine Florizel, Prince of Bohemia.

Presumably the oldest jewel name in use is Margaret, pearl, famous in hagiology, history and romance. It appears early in England. Margaret, sister of Edgar Atheling, married Malcolm III of Scotland, where it became, owing to the saintly character of the queen, almost a national name. Pearl is, except for its solitary appearance in an alliterative poem of thc later fourteenth century, a modernism. Even more ancient than Margaret may be the Biblical Sapphira, unless it is the Greek form of Saphir (Micah, i. II). Esmeralda is old in Spanish, Esmeraude occurs in Old French epic, and there was even a St. Smaragdus, martyred under Diocletian. Diamanta is not uncommon in Middle English and still occurs as Diamond, but Beryl and Ruby are not, I think, to be found before the nineteenth century. A contributor to Notes and Queries furnishes the following list culled from contemporary registers— Amber, Amethyst, Coral,[1] Crystal, Diamond, Emerald, Jet, Onyx, Opal and Topazia.

Many good Catholics give to a child the name of the saint on whose day the birth takes place.[2] Somewhat akin to this practice is that of using more general chronological terms. Philippe-Auguste, if he was really so christened, probably received his second name because he was born on August 21st, 1165, and the same reasons may often have determined the choice of Augustus and Augusta. May is sometimes selected for a similar reason; April and June also occur, and possibly Julia is sometimes due to July birth. The other months

---

[1] Hence, I suppose, the French name Coralie, sometimes used in England.

[2] Even All Saints' Day, as in the case of that remarkable negro Toussaint Louverture, to whom Wordsworth dedicated a sonnet.

do not lend themselves melodiously to the purpose. Of feast-days Noël is obviously the most important and is sometimes rendered by the native Christmas. Easter is also found, but Pascal can hardly be regarded as established in English use. The name Bertha was sometimes given in connection with Epiphany, i.e. showing brightness, and the obsolete Tiffany represents the alternative Theophania, God-showing. Tiphaine was the wife of Bertrand du Guesclin. To the same class belongs the *Twelfth Night* Jasper, not a jewel name, but the equivalent of French Gaspard and German Kaspar, the name of one of the Wise Men, otherwise called the three Kings of Cologne. It is of Persian origin and means 'treasurer'. Loveday, a day appointed for the settlement of quarrels, is still used for girls. Pentecost was once common and still survives as a surname. Rather curiously Pentecost is the origin of the almost famous name Pankhurst. This comes from a spot near Chertsey, now Pankhurst, but formerly called, *c*. 1600, Pentecost, and owned in the fourteenth century by one John Pentecost.[1] Dominic is sometimes given to children born on a Sunday and other days of the week have in the past been inflicted on foundlings. Those who remember Walter Besant's excellent *All Sorts and Conditions of*

[1] *Place-Names of Surrey*

Men will recall the amusing history of Saturday Davenant.

Some parents like to associate their children's names with localities of which they are particularly fond. A well-known example is Rudyard Kipling, named from Rudyard Lake (Staffs). This practice can have quite graceful results. Florence Nightingale was born at Florence. The name, usually representing Latin Florentius or Florentia, was, however, in general medieval use for both girls and boys. Florence's elder sister Parthenope was born at Naples and received the older name of that city, which was taken from that of a siren. Her cousin, Mr L.H. Shore Nightingale, tells me that 'We knew the elder sister as Aunt Parthé, but her contemporaries called her Pop'. The daughter of the Earl of Huntingdon is Moorea, the name of her father's South Sea residence. Lady Clodagh Anson, daughter of the Marquis of Waterford, was christened from a small stream that crosses her father's estate. A peeress named Castalia died in April, 1939, the name being presumably that of the famous spring on Mount Parnassus.

The Romans set the example of numeral names, such as Quintus, 'false Sextus', etc Octavius was even the name of a Roman *gens* to which Augustus belonged before his adoption by Julius Caesar. Most of the ordinals have been used by us both for boys and girls at some time. It will be remembered that Dr Tertius Lydgate had the misfortune to marry Rosamond Vincy (see also Rom. xvi. 22). A few seem especially favoured, e.g. Septimus, given, I suppose, in triumph at having achieved the 'perfect number', and Octavia for girls. Quintus seems to have been the ordinal most used in Roman names and, like Octavius, it was applied to a *gens*. Through the intermediary of Quintinus, a third century missionary to Gaul, it named the French town of St. Quentin and also the most attractive of Scott's generally rather colourless young heroes. Double figures are seldom attained, but I have known a Decimus, there is an English lady of title named Decima, and in November, 1938, the Times recorded the death of a lady named Adele Theresa Undecima. The record appears to be held by the parents of Vicesimus Knox (d. 1821), remembered as the compiler of *Elegant Extracts*. Truly there were giants in those days! Less ambitious was a Virginian gentleman of the nineteenth century whose tenth child was christened Decimus Ultimus. He was apparently of the same mind as John Grimston, vicar of Lyminge, Kent (1581-1602), who named his tenth daughter Sufficient.

CHAPTER VIII

Pet Forms

If we look through a medieval roll of names, we find that the men are usually Ricardus, Henricus, etc, and the women Cecilia, Margareta, etc, i.e. everything is 'latinized', and we are not told how these people were familiarly called by their neighbours. Our surnames, however, when derived from Christian names, supply this information, e.g. when we find Dixon or Dickson by the side of Richardson and Hawkins for an earlier Halkins, we are sure that, already by the thirteenth century and probably much earlier, Ricardus was often known as Dick and Henricus as Hal, while Sisley and Meggitt give us a clue as to the medieval pronunciation of Cecilia and Margareta, which were also shortened into Cis or Sis and Meg. Moreover, even the pronunciation of the full name was often quite different from the 'spelling pronunciations' now used, e.g. Bernard was Barnard or Barnett, Everard was Everett, Hubert was Hubbard, Gervase was Jarvis, Gerard was Garrard or Garret, Magdalen, now replaced by the French form Madeleine, was Maudlin, Constance was Custance and Juliana was Gillian.

The simplest way of reducing a name is to shorten it to its first syllable, e.g. Val for Valentine, Mike or Mick for Michael, Cis for Cicely, Kate for Katherine and Theo for several names of Greek origin. This formation is particularly popular in America,[1] e.g. Cal(houn or vin), Ed, Al, Cy, and the rather distressing Doug, Gord, etc See also the Biblical examples on.

As a rule only familiar names are thus treated. The existence of Prue points to the early popularity of Prudence among the 'abstract' names. It is, in fact, as old as Chaucer (*Tale of Melibæus*). Littleton also gives Temp. Sometimes it is not possible to say what a shortened form stands for, e.g. I have known two Rays, one a Raymond, the other a Rachel. Kay, now the name of many girls in fact and fiction, is usually for Kathleen and Fay for Faith. Deb and Di suggest that Deborah and Diana were once much commoner than now. With Di for Diana cf. Vi for Violet. Pen, also given by Littleton, shows that Penelope had become really popular in the seventeenth century. Many such forms are now pretty well obsolete. Littleton gives, among his *'Abbreviatures of English Christian Names'*,

---

[1] Some of them are puzzling. Is Lew for Lewis or Lewellyn, and what is the origin of the female Lee? The only Lee I know of was christened Letitia.

Assy for Alice, Bab for Baptist, Cass for Cassandra, Fritz for Fridswid, Gib for Gilbert, Hab for Herbert, Ib for Isabel, Jug for Joan, Kit for Christian, Pris for Priscilla, Sib for Sebastian, Sil for Silvester, Taff for Theophilus, Tid and Tit for Theodore, Vin for Vincent.

Sometimes more than one syllable is taken, e.g. Alex or Alick for Alexander and Bartle for Bartlemy, popular form of Bartholomew. Of the latter I only remember that distinguish ed statesman Sir Bartle Frere, first High Commissioner for South Africa (1877), and, in fiction, Bartle Massey in *Adam Bede*. The middle syllable is preferred in Gus and Liz, or Littleton's Beck, now Becky, the final in Bert, Bell or Bella, which may be for Arabella or Isabel, Beth for Elizabeth, Gail for Abigail,[1] Lottie for Charlotte, Trix for Beatrix or Trissy for Beatrice, Truda for Gertrude. Littleton also gives Mun for Edmund, Sander for Alexander and Ekiel[2] for Ezekiel.

The practice of adding -ie, -(e)y was espe-

---

[1] Also Abbey, e.g. Miss Abbey Potterson of the Six Jolly Fellowship Porters, of whom 'some waterside heads harboured muddled notions that, because of her dignity and firmness, she was named after, and in some way related to, the Abbey at Westminster. But Abbey was only short for Abigail' (*Our Mutual Friend*, Ch. 6). A favourite Puritan name, Abigail later penetrated elsewhere. Its most famous bearer, Abigail Hill (Mrs Mashamj, was of aristocratic birth.

[2] In Russell Lowell's delightful *Courtin'* we have 'Zekiel and Huldy, i.e. Huldah.

cially common in the North and Scotland.
Hence Richie Moniplies in *The Fortunes of
Nigel*, Dandie Dinmont in *Guy Mannering*,
and Robbie Burns. Steenie, James I's name for
Buckingham, is for Stephen, his favourite appearing to the King to have 'the face of an angel' (Acts vi. 15). Here again one pet form may
stand for more than one name, e.g. Jerry for
Jeremy or Gerald, Teddy for Edward or
Theodore, Milly for Millicent or Amelia, or
may have alternate forms, e.g. the Sc. Effie or
Eppie for Euphemia. That one-time national
figure, Ally Sloper, appears to have been christened Alexander.

Most of the ways of playing variations on a
name can be illustrated by the history of
Margaret, which has almost as many derived
forms as Elizabeth. Mag, with diminutive
Maggie, shows our common disregard for the
consonant -r-, often quite mute in Southern
English. The same disappearance of a sound is
seen in Bab for Barbara, Biddy for Bridget,
Bat, once used, rather than Bart, for
Bartholomew, Kit for Christopher, Fanny for
Frances, Gatty for Gertrude, Matty for
Martha, and the once popular Frideswide had
a pet form Fiddy. In the Scottish Kirsty for
Christine or Christian, and Girzie for Grizel,
the latter is transposed. In Meg and the rather
crude Moggy we see the same disregard for the

original vowel that appears in Jem and Jim for James, or Jock for Jack. Other examples are Jenny and Jinny for Jane, Kitty for Katy, Gillian for Juliana, Larry for Lawrence. Margery and Marjorie show the substitution of a diminutive form for the full name, as well as a complete change in the sound of the consonant -g-, a change also found in the shortened Madge. They perhaps represent Old French margerie, used for 'pearl' in the early 'lapidaires'.

The French diminutive Margot is an example of a formation once much commoner in English; in fact, medieval Margarets are often listed as the 'latinized' Magota, i.e. Magot. We still have Annot, perhaps rather for the popular Agnes or Annis than for the much rarer Anna, but in early records we find Emmot for Emma, Ibbot and Tibbot for Isabel, Sissot for Cecilia, Tillot for Matilda, and Mary was almost replaced by Mariot.[1] This diminutive form was less frequently used for boys' names, e.g. Elliot, but Wilmot was used for both sexes. The ending -et was less common, but we find Marget and the modern Janet, Juliet, etc At a later date, as we have seen, these old diminutive suffixes were revived as the more elaborate -otta, -otte, -etta, -ette, for many fanciful formations. Of special interest is Hamlet, ear-

[1] The influence of these forms on modern surnames is obvious.

189

lier Hamnet, for Hamonet, diminutive of Hamon Shakespeare had a son Hamnet or Hamlet, named from his godfather, Hamnet Sadler. The disappearance of the name is in curious contrast with its former popularity. In an early number of Notes and Queries we read, 'The Rev Hamlet Marshall, D.D., died in the Close, Lincoln, in 1652. With him dwelt his nephew, Hamlet Joyce. He bequeaths legacies in his will to Hamlet Pickerin and Hamlet Duncalf, and his executor was his son, Hamlet Marshall.' Hamon is hereditary with the Cheshire Masseys and the ultimate identity of the various forms is shown by their records, e.g. Hamon de Massy, *temp*. Ed. III, Hamond Massey, *temp*. Henry IV, Hamlett or Hamnett Massy, 1566.

Other diminutive suffixes of Old French origin were -on and -in, as in Manon for Madeleine and Colin for Nicolas. From the former we have the feminines Alison and Marion. Alison is now considered specially Scotch, but it named the 'heroine' of Chaucer's Miller's Tale. Marion also became Marian, as in Maid Marian, and may have contributed to the later popularity of Mary Anne! Robin and Marion are the Old French Jack and Jill. We have also from -on the obsolete masculine Dickon—

Jocky[1] Of Norfolk, be not so bold,
    For Dickon thy master is bought and
sold.

(*Rich. III*, v. 3.)

The suffix -in survives only in the masculines Robin and Colin. The latter, usually from Nicolas, may have another origin in Scotland. These were both popularized so early that they became recognized as independent names and are 'booked' as such already in the twelfth century.

Margaret also gives us an example of the rhyming trick to which many pet forms are due. Meg becomes Peg, just as Molly becomes Polly and Matty becomes Patty. There were also an obsolete Padge for Madge and Pal for Mal, i.e. Mary. The name Greta, earlier also Gritty, exemplifies the formation of a pet form by taking the last part of a name. Compare the familiar German diminutive Gretchen.

Molly,[2] earlier Mally, for Mary, illustrates another tendency which believers in the inflexible laws of sound change might find it hard to explain, viz. the change of -r- to -l-, also exemplified in Sally for Sarah, Hal for Harry, Doll and Dolly for Dorothy. Further puzzles for

---

[1] John Howard, Duke of Norfolk, fell at Bosworth (1485).

[2] For the change of vowel cf. Moggy and the obsolete Vol, given by Littleton as an 'abbreviature' of Valentine.

the phonetician are Hetty for Hester, Sadie for
Sarah, Sukey for Susan, Ike for Isaac, Frank
for Francis, Geordie for George, Flossie for
Florence, and Hatty for Harriet. In Wat for
Walter and the obsolete Gib for Gilbert we
have the disappearance of -l-. In fact the -l- in
the full names is largely a restoration, as their
immediate source is Old French. The trick of
rhyming mentioned in connection with
Margaret has had curious results in the case of
our three chief R- names, Richard, Robert and
Roger. Richard must have been often pronounced Rickard, still a surname, which was
shortened into the archaic Rick, on which were
rhymed Dick and Hick. Robert went still further with Rob, Hob, Bob, Dob and Nob. Of
these Bob is the chief survivor, but Rob, or
Rab, is still current in Scotland, Hob became
the pet name of the goblin, Dob, with a diminutive ending, became generic for a horse, and, in
King John, Robert Faulconbridge is still called
Sir Nob by his brother the Bastard. Similarly
Roger gave Dodge and Hodge, the former surviving only as a surname (22 in the London
Telephone Directory; compare also Dodgson),
and the latter, since the sixteenth century and
probably much earlier, generic for a farmer or
clodhopper. Andrew gave, in Scotland, Dandie,
Edward and Edmund developed pet forms Ted
and Ned, the latter an example of that prefix-

ing of N_ which has given us Nan, lengthened into Nancy, for Ann, Nell for Ellen or Eleanor and Noll for Oliver, in addition to which we find in Littleton Nam for Ambrose, Nump for Humfrey and Nykin for Isaac. From the fact that he does not include Bill we may suppose this pet form of William to be rather modern.

Some examples of aphesis, i.e. loss of the first syllable, are mentioned elsewhere, e.g. Tony, Nora, with which compare Lena for Helena, Nessie for Agnes, Tilda and Tilly for Matilda. An interesting example is Mabel, 'still used among the northern peasantry' (Charlotte Yonge). This is shortened from Amabel, the lovable, and is itself shortened to Mab, the name of the Queen of the Fairies, but, in pre-Shakespearean times, a nightmare or grisly hag, e.g. Chaucer's Mably in the Friar's Tale.[1] Queen Mab may have been associated with an Irish fairy called Meave, but to derive her name thus, as Charlotte Yonge does, is fantastic. Amy may sometimes be short for Amabel, but usually represents the French Aimce. It was often latinized as Amicia, whence the once popular Amice, the name of Simon de Montfort's English mother. With it we may compare Esmé, used for both sexes, a sixteenth century Scotch borrowing from French. It is apparently the past partici-

[1] See my *Words Ancient and Modern*, s.v. *mop*.

ple of Old French esmer, to esteem.

There are a number of short female names which are very puzzling, though they do not seem to have offered any difficulty to some of my predecessors. One is Edna, explained by one 'authority' as 'Pleasure or delight (Hebrew). The name of the Garden of Eden is derived from the same word', a flight of etymological fancy rather beyond the powers of the present writer. The name seems to be quite modern and to have been made fashionable by Edna Lyall, whose novels enjoyed great popularity nearly half a century ago. Her name was Ada Ellen Bayley and I suspect she made up Edna. There is, however, record of an earlier Edina, which I should *guess* to be formed from Edwin, with the -w lost as in 'Ed'ard Cuttle, mariner'. The others are, in alphabetical order, Ada, Della, Eda, Ella, Ena, Etta, Ida, Ina, Lina, Lorna, Minna, Mona, Myra, Netta, Nina, Nita, Norma, Rita, Rona, Tina or Teena. I conjecture that Ada is short for Adela, Eda for Edith, Ella for Ellen, and Ida for Idonia, once a common name. Ena and Ina are more probably from names ending in -ena and -ina. Della seems to be purely fanciful. Etta may be for Esther or Henrietta, Lina for Adeline or Caroline, Netta for Agneta, Nita for the Spanish Juanita, Rita for the Italian Margherita, and the only Tina or Teena I have known was

christened Justina. The popularity of Lorna
dates from Blackmore's *Lorna Doone* (1869).
Mona may be for Monica, Myra for Miranda,
and Rona be formed from Ronald or from the
Celtic St. Ronan, but this is all guess-work. It
may be remarked that Mona is the old name of
Anglesey and Man and Rona is one of the Hebrides, so it is just possible that these names
are geographical; compare Islay, also one of
the Hebrides, the name of a Scottish lady
whose marriage was recorded in the Times for
July 18, 1939. Some of the above may be genuine old Celtic names, like Fiona, derived, I suppose, from Gaelic *fionn*, white. Nina is for
Nanine, a pet form in French of Anne, which
was the baptismal name of the famous Ninon
de l'Enclos (d. 1706). Norma dates from
Bellini's famous opera (1830). Minna came in
with Scott's Minna Troil in *The Pirate*. It is really a German name from Wilhelmina, perhaps with a reminiscence of the poetical
minne, love, whence the 'minnesingers.'
Minnie is not necessarily connected. It seems
to have been used first as a pet form of
Emmeline, diminutive of Emily, but the only
Minnie I know was christened Mina, this being the pet name of her aunt Jemima! When
we get to Bunty, Tottie and Wendy, it is time
to stop theorizing.

The fact is that female names, apart from

the relatively small group with a documented history, form an etymological labyrinth. The number is constantly being increased by new and fantastic formations and it would be possible to make a collection of such calculated to discourage anyone from writing on the subject. Moreover, most families have their own way of dealing with names in such a way that the results are philologically inexplicable. We know that Boz was an infantile attempt at Moses, Dickens's nickname for one of his brothers, and that Ouida was a similar mispronunciation of Louise (de la Ramée), but no one could guess that Bob, a name borne by a relative of mine for more than eighty years, was short for Libob, a childish shot at Elizabeth.

As already noted, formal records give us little information about the shortened, rhymed and contorted forms which usually replaced the full name in everyday medieval life, but we get a few clues from what popular verse has come down to us and an occasional hint from writers like Langland and Chaucer. In a political song of 1306 Robert Bruce is called King Hob; in Richard the Redeless, directed against Richard II, the king is addressed as Hick Heavyhead; in Chaucer the cook is called both Roger and Hodge. Gower's oft-quoted lines on Wat Tyler's Rebellion tell us who were regarded as Hoi Polloi in the fourteenth century—

Watte vocat, cui Thomme venit, neque
    Symme retardat,
Betteque (Bartholomew), Gibbe simul,
    Hykke venire jubent;
Colle (Nicolas) furit, quem Geffe juvat
    nocumenta parantes,
Cum quibus ad dampnum Wille coire vovet.
Grigge (Gregory) rapit, dum Dawe (David)
    strepit, comes est quibus Hobbe,
Lorkyn (Lawrence) et in medio non minor
    esse putat:
Hudde (?) ferit, quem Judde (Jordan) terit,
    dum Tebbe (Theobald) minatur,
Jakke domosque viros vellit et ense necat.

It will be noticed that the list does not include
an Old English name. Lorkin, usually Larkin,
is a diminutive formation now found only in
surnames, unless we regard Peterkin, of the
Coral Island, as a modern representative.
Such names were once in common use, e.g.
Jenkin and Malkin were general names for lad
and lass before the days of Jack and Jill, for
whom Tusser[1] has Jenkin and Gill. For the curious history of the feminine Malkin see my
Words Ancient and Modern.

Minsheu (1617) describes the rustics prac-
ising at the quintain as Jac and Tom, Dic,

---

[1] In his *Hundreth Good Points of Husbandrie* (1557).

Hob and Will, James I objects to criticisms of his government from Jack and Tom and Will and Dick, and Coriolanus (ii. 3) apostrophizes the Roman (!) plebs as Hob and Dick. This all suggests that this type of name had, up to *c.* 1600, a touch of contempt about it, at any rate for the male sex. The female forms had perhaps more dignity. It is true that Stephano sings—

The master, the swabber, the boatswain and I,
   The gunner, and his mate,
Loved Mall (Moll), Meg and Marian and Margery,
   But none of us cared for Kate
               (*Tempest* ii. 2.),

but Kate is used for Katharine by Hénry V, Henry VIII, and Petruchio, as Bess is by Edward IV for his wife Elizabeth. Still, an examination of all the Dolls, Molls, Nells, Nans, etc, who occur in Shakespeare and his contemporaries does not, on the whole, tend to edification. Moll, especially, had a shocking reputation which has lasted up to the present day, though Molly is now in great esteem. Jill also, now a favourite name for sprightly heroines, had a very sorry implication, the diminutive Jillet becoming 'jilt', once a much stronger term than now. Later in the seventeenth cen tury the use of these 'abbreviatures' seems to have become fashionable among the Cavaliers, perhaps in derision of the polysyllabic Old Testament names affected by their opponents. 'A poetical skit', says Bardsley, 'after running through a list of all the new-fangled names introduced by the fanatics, concludes—

They're just like the Gadaren's swine
   Which the devils did drive and bewitch:
An herd set on evill
Will run to the de-vill
   And his dam when their tailes do itch.
'Then let 'em run on!'
Says Ned, Tom and John.
'Aye! let 'em be hanged!' quoth Mun,
   'They're mine,' quoth Old Nick,
   'And take 'em,' says Dick,
'And welcome!' quoth worshipful Dun.

   'And God blesse King Charles!' quoth George,
   'And save him!' says Simon and Sill;
'Aye, aye', quoth Old Cole and each loyall soul,
   'And Amen and Amen!' cries Will.

In another ballad of the same period, similar views are expressed by Moll, Doll and Nan.

CHAPTER IX

Cruelty to Children

In an early number of Notes and Queries an inquirer would be 'glad to be informed as to what discretion the officiating clergyman has in reference to the names given in baptism. Can he positively refuse to give children such objectionable names as, e.g. Pontius Pilate, Judas Iscariot, Beelzebub, Cain, Esau, etc? I would also mention as an objectionable name, though for a different reason, Emanuel.'[1] The answer appears to be that the clergyman has no legal voice in the matter, though he would evidently try his powers of persuasion. 'A clerical friend of mine christened twins Cain and Abel, only the other day, much against his own wishes' (Bardsley). As we shall see in this chapter, unpleasing Scriptural names were, from motives of humility, sometimes given to children by the Puritans, but it is rather star-

[1] In connection with sacred names it may be noted that Jesus is used baptismally in Spanish, while Manuel and Manoel are common Spanish and Portuguese names. The present King of Italy is Victor Emmanuel. On the other hand Maria in Spain is sometimes replaced by (Maria de los) Dolores, (Maria de las) Mercedes, Concepcion and Asuncion. However, Sir Harry Smith's Spanish wife, who named a town in Natal, was christened Juana Maria de los Dolores. Dolores has a pet form Lola, now often given as an independent name. Its most notorious bearer was the adventuress Lola Montez, *alias* Maria Dolores Eliza Rosanna Gilbert (d. 1861).

tling to find Iscariot Buckley, a native of Staffordshire, bringing a charge of assault as recently as January, 1865. Perhaps his name had led to an altercation.

In Roman Catholic countries the officiating priest would certainly refuse to christen a child by an objectionable or ridiculous name; in fact, he would, I think, reject any not found in the Calendar of Saints. Even in a country so hostile to clerical domination as France, the choice of the names under which children may be registered at the local Mairie is somewhat restricted.[1] By enactments of the year 1803, 'Les noms en usage dans les différents calendriers et ceux des personnages connus de l'histoire ancienne pourront seuls être reçus comme prénoms sur les registres de l'état civil et il est interdit aux officiers publics d'en admettre aucun autre dans leurs actes'. This law is now, however, often more honoured in the breach than in the observance, though proud and inebriated fathers who attempt to inflict very fantastic names on their offspring are usually requested by the officials to call again when sober. Moreover, 'l'histoire ancienne' and 'connus' are rather vague terms, while 'les différents calendriers' might be taken to include the 'calendrier républicain',

[1] See Édouard Lévy, *Le Manuel des Prénoms* (Paris, 1922).

lyrically described by Michelet as 'le calendrier vrai où la nature elle-même, dans la langue charmante de ses fruits, de ses fleurs, dans les bienfaisantes révélations de ses noms maternels, nomme les phases de l'année,' but, in the opinion of M. Edmond-Biré, 'un ramassis de vulgarités et d'inepties.' At the moment of writing a bill is being drafted in Brazil empowering the authorities to refuse the registration of names 'susceptible to ridicule.'

In our country there seems to be no limit to baptismal cruelty. The conferring, already dealt with, of obscure and fantastic Old Testament names and the later Puritan eccentricities are early examples of this sadistic urge. Some of the ardent Puritans seem to have sought out the most repulsive Scriptural names for their unfortunate offspring. Ananias Warren was buried at St. Peter's, Cornhill, in 1603, and Ananias Jarratt was baptized at Stepney in 1621. In Bunhill Fields cemetery, the *campo santo* of nonconformity', lies Mrs Sapphira Lightmaker, who 'died in the Lorde' in 1704, aged 81 years.' Antipas Barnes was baptized at Stepney in 1633 and Increase Mather had a friend named Antipas Newman. One can only suppose that the parents of these two were so imbued with belief in original sin that they looked forward to their sons becoming adulterers and murderers, for the Antipas of Rev. ii. 13, who was canonized, would be considered 'untouchable'. Barabbas Bowery was buried at All Hallows, Barking, in 1713.

Among the least savoury stories of the Old Testament are those of Dinah (Gen. xxxiv.), Tamar (2 Sam. xiii.), and Bathsheba (2 Sam. xi.-xii), yet all three of them were popular with the Puritans and George Eliot gave the first to the saintly heroine of *Adam Bede*. One of the Ferrars of the famous Little Gidding community had a wife called Bathsheba. The name is still in rustic use, as it was for the heroine of *Far from the Madding Crowd*, and half a century ago the landlady of a riverside inn near Cambridge rejoiced in the almost perfect combination Bathsheba Gotobed.[1] It is to be hoped that those parents who selected Drusilla, the Jewish wife of Felix, had little acquaintance with the two very unedifying Roman ladies of the same name. Pharaoh occurs several times in the seventeenth century register of Repton (Derby) and is still found in the north.

A curious female name is Aphra (variously spelt), borne by the notorious playwright and political spy of Charles II's time. It was a common Puritan Christian name in seventeenth

---

[1] This quaint surname has been established in Cambridgeshire since the 13th century.

century Kent and means something like dust and ashes [1]—'Declare it not at Gath: in the house of Aphrah roll thyself in the dust' (Micah i. 10). Bardsley opines that Aphra Behn's 'father might have rolled himself several times in the dust, had he lived to read some of his daughter's writings.' Aphrah survived for some time as Affery, the name of Mrs Flintwinch in *Little Dorrit*.

Almost equally brutal is the piling up of obscure Old Testament names. I have already given an example on. At the beginning of the present century there lived in Norfolk a family of four—two brothers and two sisters, with the names Asenath Zaphnaphpaaneah Kezia Jemima Kerenhappuch,[2] Maher Shalal Hashbaz and Arphad Absalom Alexander Habakkuk William.

In Ch. VII some examples are given of more or less melodious names derived from or associated with localities. These have parallels in such classical names as Adrian from Adria, Sidonia from Sidon, in the Biblical surnames Iscariot, man of Kerioth, and Magdalen, woman of Magdala. Less fortunate was Brilliana, daughter (born *c.* 1600) of Sir

---

[1] The names of Job's daughters for three girls of a family were not infrequently used by rustics in quite recent times.

[2] Both Dust and Ashes were, according to Camden, in Puritan use as baptismal names.

Edward Conway, governor of 'the Brill' in Holland. An even worse case is that of Edward Littleton, Bengal President of the New East India Company in the seventeenth century, who christened his two daughters Jane Hugliana and Elizabeth Gangetica. Some unfortunate children have been absurdly named from battlefields such as Balaclava, Ladysmith and even Ypres. Of such are Alma and Maida, the latter a place in Calabria where Sir John Stuart defeated the French in 1806. These have survived because of their pleasant sound and Alma's pleasant Latin meaning. Alma was, however, according to Charlotte Yonge, an old Irish name long before Crimean days. It is used by Spenser, who may have picked it up in Ireland along with Una. To neither of these names did he attach their Celtic meaning, even if he knew it. Una was for him the 'one' true Church, opposed to Duessa, and Alma was the soul (Italian *alma*) opposed to Acrasia (Greek for incontinence).

Oceanus Hopkins was born at sea on the Mayflower in 1620, and Sea-born Egginton and Sea-Mercy Adams are to be found among early American settlers. Atlantic is also recorded. The parents of these children might have claimed the authority of Shakespeare—

My gentle babe Marina, whom,
For she was born at sea, I have named so,
(*Pericles*, iii. 3).

Children have been called Himalaya and
Orontes from the ships on which they were
born, and there is an authentic case of
Sou'wester, christened in January, 1880, at
Stone, near Dartford, and named after an uncle who was born at sea during a south-west-
erly gale.

Jack Mytton, the famous Shropshire squire,
named one of his children Euphrates from a
favourite racehorse, for which crime he was
justly rewarded by dying of delirium tremens
in a debtors' prison. Another squire, Somerset
this time, named his son Emorb, a reversal of
his own family name of Brome, and this has
been imitated in modern times by a lady called
Eleanor who has a daughter Ronaele. Perhaps
the worst of all outrages was perpetrated by
William Turton, a fervent disciple of Jenner,
who named his daughter Vaccina. Almost as
bad is Triandraphilia, conferred on a village
child at the suggestion of the vicar! It appears
to be a shot at the modern Greek word for
'rose'. In 1644 there lived at Baltonsborough,
Somerset, a woman named Misericordia-
Adulterina, probably a poor waif whom local
humour had thus baptized.

Akin to these eccentricities are the 'complementary' names inflicted on some children. Parents called Sharp sometimes regard Luke as particularly appropriate to a son, while the Carrolls naturally incline to Christmas. 'A former undergraduate of Harvard, named Spear, had the Christian names William Shake' (Bowditch);[1] there is record of a River Jordan, Paschal Lamb was rector of Ellington, Hunts, 1885–97, Sandylands Drinkwater was a London goldsmith c. 1750, and I have known of a female Woodbine Green. Charlotte Yonge remarks that 'the dainty[2] Tryphæna has only been revived in England by the Puritan taste'. It can still be pleasantly allied with a suitable surname, but some sixty years ago I met a lady thus christened who was afflicted with the surname Gibletts.

[1] Suffolk (U S A) *Surnames*, 1861.
[2] It is derived from Greek *tryphe,* daintiness, delicacy.

ADDENDA

Page 10. Denzil was famous, because Denzil Holles, baptized 1599, held the Speaker down in his chair in 1629 (E.G.J.F.).

p. 16. A two-syllable word, like 'film', Ur-rull (i.e. Earl) is, with Elmer, particularly popular in what might be termed the less sophisticated parts of the United States, such as Kansas. In these parts a peculiar custom is to hold 'husband-calling contests'. One has to hear a Kansas farmer's wife calling for her Earl or Elmer to appreciate the depths to which a so-called Christian name can sink (The Canadian Saturday Night).

p. 20. Balthasar is not Scriptural. See Index.

p. 24. Note the famous church of San Vitale in Ravenna. The Roman Calendar contains twelve saints called Vitalis (E.G.J.F.).

p. 26. The only thing that has kept girls' names from collapsing into sheer frivolity or worse has been the astonishing recrudescence of Ann and Jane (The Canadian Saturday Night).

p. 34. In all walks of life [in U S A] one encounters Elmers. Everywhere there are Elmers; the woods and the sky-scrapers alike are full of them (The Canadian Saturday Night).

One Ethelburga is living at Southbourne

and so is a Galfrida (E.G.J.F.). Galfrida is the 'latinized' feminine of Geoffrey.

p.35. Oswald was the canonized King of Northumbria (d. 642), the friend of St. Aidan. The other Oswalds are of less importance (E.G.J.F.).

My Cambridge tutor was Anchitel Boughey (E.G.J.F.).

p.36. Other Anglo-Saxon names of rare occurrence are Mervyn, Mærwine, famous friend, in which the -v- is due to Norman-French influence, Elswyth, the name of an American lady novelist, Æthelswith, noble strength, and Uffa, probably a shortening of an Old Norse name in Ulf-, wolf, borne by a nautical writer of our day.

p. 38. Samson was probably not Biblical in Normandy, but after the famous St. Samson or Sampson, Bishop of Dol, who died *c.*557 (E.G.J.F.).

p.52. Loïs is also Biblical. See 2 Tim. i.5 (E.G.J.F.).

p.57. Sir Allen Mawer regards the origin here given for Oliver as very dubious.

p. 63. Cuthbert Tunstall (1474-1559) was Master of the Rolls and a bishop.

p. 67. St. Bartholomew was flayed and is represented carrying his skin over his arm with a fine display of naked muscles. Hence he became a patron of hospitals, both in Rome and in London (E.G.J.F.).

p.84. The -bel names can hardly have been modelled on Old Testament names such as Jezebel and Mehetabel, as these were not in use early enough. Jezebel, unmarried, seems to have been quite ostracized, but Mehetabel, God benefits, was adopted by the Puritans and was long a favourite rustic name.

p. 111. Noah was not uncommon in the Middle Ages, a name no doubt often given in connection with religious drama. It was pronounced Noy, whence the surname Noyes. Of his three sons only Japhet has been much used, for Ham Peggotty is rather a freak name.

p. 132. Narcissus Marsh (1638-1713) was Archbishop of Armagh and an enthusiast for the old Irish language. He helped to found the Dublin Royal Society.

p. 138. Laurence or Lawrence should have been included among the major saints of Chapter III. He was martyred on a gridiron the outline of which is reproduced by the ground-plan of the Escorial at Madrid, built in fulfilment of a vow made by Philip II at the battle of St. Quentin (1557).

Probably not the liar 'Ananias', but the priest who baptized St. Paul. There are others in the New Testament; see Acts ix. 10 (E.G.J.F.).

More sympathetic to Puritan ideas would be

the high priest Ananias who ordered St. Paul
to be smitten on the mouth (Acts xxiii. 2).

As, however, the history of St. Antipas is so
obscure that his canonization may have escaped Puritan notice, it is possible that the
name was really given in honour of the 'faithful martyr'.

p. 159. Cf. Malta, Quebec and Woolwich
Bagnet in Bleak House (E.G.J.F.).

A-Z of first names

A

Aaron *masc* mountaineer, enlightener (*Hebrew*); a contracted dimunitive is **Arn**.

Abbie, Abby *fem* diminutive *forms* of **Abigail**, also used independently.

Abbott *masc* a surname, meaning father of the abbey, used as a first name (*Old English*).

Abe *masc* father (*Aramaic*); diminutive of **Abraham, Abram**.

Abel *masc* breath, fickleness, vanity (*Hebrew*).

Abelard *masc* nobly resolute (*Germanic*).

Abiathar *masc* father of plenty or excellence (*Hebrew*).

Aberah *fem* a variant form of **Averah**.

Abiel *masc* father of strength (*Hebrew*).

Abigail *fem* my father's joy (*Hebrew*); diminutive forms are **Abbie, Abby, Gail**.

Abihu *masc* to whom Jehovah is a father (*Hebrew*).

Abijah *masc* to whom Jehovah is a father (*Hebrew*); a diminutive form is **Bije**.

Abner *masc* father of light (*Hebrew*).

Abra *fem* mother of multitudes (*Hebrew*).

Abraham *masc* father of a multitude (*Hebrew*); diminutive forms are **Abe, Bram**.

Abram *masc* father of elevation (*Hebrew*); diminutive forms are **Abe, Bram**.

Absalom *masc* my father is peace (*Hebrew*).

Acacia *fem* the name of a plant, possibly meaning immortality and resurrection, used as a first name (*Greek*).

Acantha *fem* thorny, spiney (*Greek*).

Ace *masc* unity, unit (*Latin*).

Ackerley *masc* a surname,

meaning from the acre meadow, used as a first name (*Old English*).

Ackley *masc* a surname, meaning from the oak tree meadow, used as a first name (*Old English*).

Ada *fem* diminutive of **Adela** or names beginning with *Adal*, also used independently; a variant form of **Adah**.

Adabelle *fem* joyful and beautiful, a combination of **Ada** and **Belle**; variant forms are **Adabel, Adabela, Adabella**.

Adah *fem* ornament (*Hebrew*); a variant form is **Ada**.

Adair *masc* a Scottish form of **Edgar**.

Adalard *masc* noble and brave (*Germanic*).

Adalia *fem* an early Saxon tribal name whose origin is unknown (*Germanic*).

Adam *masc* man, earth man, red earth (*Hebrew*).

Adamina *fem* of Adam. (*Latin*);

Adar *fem* fire; as the name in the Jewish calendar for the twelfth month of the Biblical year and the sixth month of the civil year, it is

a name sometimes given to girls born in that period (*Hebrew*).

Addie *fem* diminutive of **Adelaide**.

Addie, Addy, Mina.

Addison *masc* a surname, meaning Adam's son, used as a first name (*Old English*).

Adela *fem* of noble birth; a princess (*Germanic*).

Adelaide *fem* of noble birth; a princess (*Germanic*); a diminutive form is **Addie**.

Adelbert *see* **Albert**.

Adèle, Adele *fem* the French form of Adela, now also used as an English form.

Adelheid *fem* noble kind (*Germanic*); a diminutive form is **Heidi**.

Adeline, Adelina *fem* of noble birth; a princess (*Germanic*); a diminutive form is **Aline**.

Adelphia *fem* sisterly, eternal friend of mankind (*Greek*); variant forms are **Adelfia, Adelpha**.

Adin *masc* sensual (*Hebrew*).

Adina *fem* voluptuous, ripe,

mature (*Hebrew*).

Adlai *masc* God is just (*Hebrew*).

Adler *masc* eagle, perceptive one (*Germanic*).

Adney *masc* island-dweller (*Old English*).

Adolf *masc* the German form of **Adolph**.

Adolph, Adolphus *masc* noble wolf; noble hero (*Germanic*); a diminutive form is **Dolph**.

Adolpha *fem* noble she-wolf, she who will give her life for her young, the *fem* form of Adolf (*Germanic*); variant forms are **Adolfa, Adolfina, Adolphina**.

Adolphe *masc* the French form of **Adolph**.

Adon, Adonai *masc* lord, a sacred word for God (*Hebrew*).

Adonia *fem* beautiful goddess of the resurrection; eternal renewal of youth (*Greek*).

Adoniram *masc* lord of height (*Hebrew*).

Adora *fem* adored and beloved gift (*Latin*).

Adorabella *fem* beautiful gift, a combination of **Adora** and **Bella**.

Adorna *fem* adorned with jewels (*Latin*).

Adrian *masc* of the Adriatic in Italy (*Latin*); a variant form is **Hadrian**.

Adrianne, Adrienne *fem* forms of **Adrian**.

Adriel *masc* from God's congregation (*Hebrew*).

Aefa *fem* a variant form of **Aoife**.

Aeneas *masc* commended (*Greek*); a variant form is **Eneas**.

Aethelbert *see* **Ethelbert**.

Aethelred *see* **Ethelred**.

Afonso *masc* the Portugese form of **Alphonso**.

Afra *fem* a variant form of **Aphra**.

Africa *fem* the name of the continent used as a first name.

Agatha *fem* good; kind (*Greek*); a diminutive form is **Aggie, Aggy.**

Agave *fem* illustrious, famous (*Greek*).

Aggie, Aggy *fem* diminutive forms of **Agatha, Agnes**.

Agnes *fem* chaste; pure (*Greek*); diminutive forms are **Aggie, Aggy, Agneta,**

Nessa, Nessie.

Agnès *fem* the French form of **Agnes**.

Agnese *fem* the Italian form of **Agnes**.

Agostino *masc* the Italian form of **Augustine**.

Agustín *masc* the Spanish form of **Augustine**.

Ahern *masc* horse lord, horse owner (*Irish Gaelic*).

Ahren *masc* eagle (*Germanic*).

Aidan *masc* fire, flame (*Irish Gaelic*); a variant form is **Edan**.

Aiken *masc* the Scottish form of **Atkin**, a surname meaning son of Adam, used as a first name (*Old English*).

Ailean *fem* Scots Gaelic form of **Alan**.

Aileen *fem* a variant form of **Eileen**.

Ailsa *fem* fairy (*Scots Gaelic*).

Aimée *fem* the French form of **Amy**.

Áine *fem* an Irish Gaelic form of **Anna**.

Ainsley *masc* a surname, meaning meadow of the respected one, used as a

first name (*Old English*).

Ainslie *masc* a Scottish form of **Ainsley**, used as a first name.

Aisleen, Aisling *fem* vision (*Irish Gaelic*).

Al *masc* diminutive of **Alan, Albert**, etc.

Alain *masc* the French form of **Alan**.

Alan *masc* meaning uncertain, possibly a hound (*Slavonic*), harmony (*Celtic*); variant forms are **Allan, Allen**.

Alana, Alanna, Alannah *fem* forms of **Alan**; a variant form is **Lana**.

Alard *masc* a variant form of **Allard**.

Alaric *masc* noble ruler; all-rich (*Germanic*).

Alarice *fem* of **Alaric** (*Germanic*); variant forms are **Alarica, Alarise**.

Alasdair, Alastair *masc* variant forms of **Alister**.

Alban *masc* white, or of Alba in Italy (*Latin*).

Albern *masc* noble warrior (*Old English*).

Albert *masc* all-bright; illustrious (*Germanic*); diminutive forms are **Al, Bert, Bertie**.

Alberta *fem* form of **Albert**.

Albin *see* **Alban**.

Albina *fem* white, very fair (*Latin*);.variant forms are **Albinia, Alvina, Aubina, Aubine**.

Albrecht *masc* a German form of **Albert**.

Alcina *fem* strong-minded one, from a legendary woman who could make gold from stardust (*Greek*).

Alcott *masc* the surname, meaning old cottage or hut, used as a first name (*Old English*).

Alcyone *fem* in Greek mythology a woman who drowned herself from grief at her husband's death and who was turned into a kingfisher; variant forms are **Halcyone, Halcyon**.

Alda *fem* wise and rich (*Germanic*); variant forms are **Eada, Elda**.

Alden *masc* a surname, meaning old or trustworthy friend, used as a first name (*Old English*).

Alder *masc* a surname, meaning alder tree, used as a first name (*Old English*); old, wise and rich (*Germanic*).

Aldis *masc* a surname, meaning old house, used as a first name (*Old English*); *fem* a diminutive of some names beginning with *Ald-*.

Aldo, Aldous *masc* old (*Germanic*).

Aldora *fem* of noble rank (*Old English*); variant forms are **Aelda, Aeldra**.

Aldrich *masc* a surname, meaning old, wise ruler, used as a first name (*Old English*).

Aldwin *see* **Alvin**.

Alec, Aleck *masc* diminutive *forms* of **Alexander**.

Aled *masc* the name of a river used as a first name (*Welsh*).

Aleria *fem* like an eagle (*Latin*).

Aleron *masc* eagle (*Latin*).

Alethea *fem* truth (*Greek*).

Alex *masc* diminutive of **Alexander**; *fem* diminutive of **Alexandra**, now both used independently; a variant form is **Alix**.

Alexa *fem* diminutive of **Alexandra**.

Alexander *masc* a helper of men (*Greek*); diminutive forms are **Alec, Alex, Alick, Lex, Sandy**.

Alexandra, Alexandrina
fem forms of **Alexander**;
diminutive forms are **Alex,
Alexa, Lexie, Lexy,
Sandie, Sandra, Sandy**.

Alexia *fem* form of **Alexis**.

Alexina *fem* form of **Alexander**.

Alexis *masc fem* help; defence (*Greek*).

Alf, Alfie *masc* diminutive
forms of **Alfred**.

Alfonsine *fem* form of **Alphonse** (*Germanic*); variant forms are **Alphonsina,
Alphonsine, Alphonza**.

Alfonso *masc* a Spanish
and Italian form of **Al-
phonso**.

Alford *masc* a surname,
meaning old ford, used as a
first name (*Old English*).

Alfred *masc* good or wise
counsellor (*Germanic*); diminutive forms are **Alf,
Alfie**.

Alfreda *fem* form of **Al-
fred**; diminutive forms are
Alfie, Allie; variant forms
are **Elfreda, Elfreida,
Elfrieda, Elfrida, Elva,
Elga, Freda**.

Alger *masc* elf spear (*Old
English*).

Algernon *masc* whiskered
(*Old French*); a diminutive

form is **Algie, Algy**.

Alice, Alicia *fem* of noble
birth; a princess (*Germanic*).—variant forms are
Alys, Alyssa.

Alick *masc* diminutive of
Alexander, now some-
times used independently.

Alida *fem* little bird; small
and lithe (*Latin*); a Hungarian form of **Adelaide**;
variant forms are **Aleda,
Aleta, Alita**; diminutive
forms are **Leda, Lita**.

Aliénor *fem* a French form
of **Eleanor**.

Alima *fem* learned in music
and dancing (*Arabic*).

Aline *fem* a contraction of
Adeline.

Alison *fem* diminutive of
Alice, now used entirely in
its own right; a variant
form is **Allison**; diminutive
forms are **Allie, Ally**; *masc*
son of Alice; son of a nobleman (*Old English*).

Alister *masc* the Scots
Gaelic form of **Alexander**;
variant forms are **Alas-
dair, Alastair**.

Alix *fem* a variant form of
Alex.

Allan, Allen *masc* variant
forms of **Alan**.

Allard *masc* noble and

brave (*Old English*); a variant form is **Alard,**

Allegra *fem* a word for cheerful or blithe used as a first name (*Italian*).

Allie, Ally *fem* diminutive of **Alice, Alison**.

Allison *fem* a variant form of **Alison**.

Allison, Al, Allie.

Alloula, Allula, Aloula.

Alma *fem* loving, nurturing (*Latin*).

Almira *fem* lofty; a princess (*Arabic*).

Almo *masc* noble and famous (*Old English*).

Aloha *fem* a word for welcome used as a first name (*Hawaiian*).

Alonso *masc* a Spanish form of **Alphonso**; a diminutive form is **Lonnie**.

Alonzo *see* **Alphonso**.

Aloysius *masc* a Latin form of **Lewis**.

Alpha *masc, fem* first one (*Greek*).

Alpheus *masc* exchange (*Hebrew*).

Alphonse *masc* the French form of **Alphonso**.

Alphonso, Alphonsus

masc all-ready; willing (*Old German*).

Alpin *masc* blond (*Scottish Gaelic*).

Alroy *masc* red-haired (*Scottish Gaelic*).

Alston *masc* a surname, meaning old stone, used as a first name (*Old English*).

Alta *fem* tall in spirit (*Latin*).

Althea *fem* a healer (*Greek*); a diminutive form is **Thea**.

Altman *masc* old, wise man (*Germanic*).

Alton *masc* a surname, meaning old stream or source, used as a first name (*Old English*).

Alula *fem* winged one (*Latin*); first (*Arabic*).

Alun *masc* the Welsh form of **Alan**.

Alura *fem* divine counsellor (*Old English*).

Alva *fem* white (*Latin*).

Alva *see* **Alban**.

Alvah *masc* exalted one (*Hebrew*).

Alvin, Alwin *masc* winning all (*Old English*).

Alvina, Alvine *fem* beloved

and noble friend (*Germanic*); a diminutive form is **Vina**.

Alys, Alyssa *fem* variant forms of **Alice, Alicia**.

Alyth *fem* a placename, meaning steep place, used as a first name.

Alzena *fem* woman, purveyor of charm and virtue (*Arabic*).

Amabel *fem* lovable (*Latin*); a diminutive form is **Mabel**.

Amadea *fem* form of **Amadeus**.

Amadeus *masc* lover of God (*Latin*).

Amado *masc* the Spanish form of **Amato**.

Amalia *fem* work (*Germanic*); an Italian and Greek form of **Amelia**.

Amanda *fem* worthy of love (*Latin*); diminutive forms are **Manda, Mandy**.

Amariah *masc* whom Jehovah promised (*Hebrew*).

Amasa *masc* a burden (*Hebrew*).

Amber *fem* the name of a gemstone used as a first name.

Ambert *masc* shining bright light (*Germanic*).

Ambrogio *masc* the Italian form of **Ambrose**.

Ambrose *masc* immortal (*Greek*).

Ambrosine *fem* form of Ambrose; variant forms are **Ambrosia, Ambrosina**.

Amédée *masc* the French form of **Amadeus**.

Amelia *fem* busy, energetic (*Germanic*); a diminutive form is **Millie**.

Amélie *fem* the French form of **Amelia**.

Amelinda *fem* beloved and pretty (*Spanish*); variant forms are **Amalinda, Amelinde**.

Amena *fem* honest, truthful (*Gaelic*).

Amerigo *masc* an Italian variant form of **Enrico**.

Amery *masc* a variant form of **Amory**.

Amethyst *fem* the name of the semi-precious gemstone used as a first name (*Greek*).

Aminta, Amintha, Aminthe *fem* protector, a shepherdess in Greek mythology (*Greek*).

Ammon *masc* hidden (*Egyptian*).

Amory *masc* famous ruler

(*Germanic*); variant forms
are **Amery, Emery, Emmery**.

Amos *masc* bearer of a burden (*Hebrew*).

Amy *fem* beloved (*Old French*).

Anastasia *fem* rising up, resurrection (*Greek*); diminutive forms are **Stacey, Stacy, Stacie, Stasia**.

Anastasius *masc* form of **Anastasia**.

Anatholia, Anatola *fem* forms of Anatole (*Greek*; a variant form is **Anatolia**.

Anatole *masc* from the East (*Greek*).

Anatolia *fem* a variant form of **Anatholia**.

Andie *masc* diminutive of **Andrew**.

André *masc* the French form of **Andrew**, becoming popular as an English-language form.

Andrea *fem* form of **Andreas** or **Andrew**; a variant form is **Andrina**; *masc* the Italian form of **Andrew**.

Andreas *masc* Greek, Latin, and German forms of **Andrew**.

Andrés *masc* the Spanish

form of **Andrew**.

Andrew *masc* strong; manly; courageous (*Greek*); diminutive forms are **Andie, Andy, Dandie, Drew**.

Andrina, Andrine *fem* variant forms of **Andrea**.

Aneirin, Aneurin *masc* noble, modest (*Welsh*); a diminutive form is **Nye**.

Anemone *fem* windflower, the name of the garden plant used as a first name (*Greek*).

Angel *fem* diminutive of **Angela** (*Greek*); *masc* form of **Angela**.

Angela, Angelina messenger (*Greek*).

Angelica *fem* lovely; angelic (*Greek*).

Angelo *masc* Italian form of **Angel**.

Angharad *fem* much loved (*Welsh*).

Angus *masc* excellent virtue (*Gaelic*); a diminutive form is **Gus**.

Anita *fem* Spanish diminutive of **Ann**, now used independently as an English-language form; a diminutive form is **Nita**.

Ann *fem* grace (*Hebrew*); a variant form is **Hannah**; a diminutive form is **Annie**.

Anna *fem* the Latin form of **Ann**.

Annabel, Annabelle, Annabella *fem* lovable (possibly from **Amabel**); diminutive forms are **Bella, Belle**.

Annan *masc* a Scottish placename, meaning water or waters, used as a first name (*Scottish Gaelic*).

Anne *fem* the French form of **Ann**.

Anneka *fem* a Dutch diminutive of **Anna**.

Annette *fem* a French diminutive of **Ann**, used as an English-language form.

Annika *fem* a Swedish diminutive of **Anna**.

Annis, Annice *fem* a medieval diminutive of **Agnes**.

Annona *fem* a variant form of **Anona**.

Annunciata *fem* Italian form of *nuntius*, bringer of news, i.e. the angel Gabriel, who delivered the announcement of the Virgin Mary's conception, a name often given to children born on 25 March, Lady Day (*Latin*).

Anona *fem* annual crops, hence the Roman goddess of crops (*Latin*); a variant form is **Annona**; diminutives are **Nonnie, Nona**.

Anora *fem* light, graceful (*Old English*).

Anscom *masc* one who dwells in a secret valley; a solitary person (*Old English*).

Anselm, Ansel *masc* a surname, meaning, god helmet, i.e. under the protection of God, used as a first name (*Germanic*).

Anselma *fem* form of **Anselm**; a variant form is **Arselma**.

Ansley *masc* a surname, meaning clearing with a hermitage or solitary dwelling, used as a first name (*Old English*).

Anson *masc* a surname, meaning son of Agnes or Anne, used as a first name (*Old English*).

Anstice *masc* a surname, meaning resurrected, used as a first name (*Greek*).

Anthea *fem* flowery (*Greek*).

Anthony *masc* a variant form of **Antony**; a diminutive form is **Tony**.

Antoine *masc* the French form of **Anthony**, now used independently as an English-language form; a variant form is **Antwan**.

Antoinette *fem* diminutive of **Antonia**, now used as an English-language form; a diminutive form is **Toinette**.

Anton *masc* a German form of **Antony**, now used as an English-language form.

Antonia *fem* form of **Antony**; diminutive forms are **Toni, Tonia, Tonie, Tony**.

Antonio *masc* the Italian and Spanish form of **Antony**.

Antony *masc* priceless; praiseworthy (*Latin*); a variant form is **Anthony**; a diminutive form is **Tony**.

Antwan *masc* a variant form of **Antoine**.

Anwell *masc* beloved (*Gaelic*).

Anwen *fem* very beautiful (*Welsh*).

Anyon *masc* anvil (*Gaelic*).

Aoife *fem* the Irish Gaelic form of **Eve**; a variant form is **Aefa**.

Aonghas *masc* Scots Gaelic form of **Angus**.

Aphra *fem* dust (*Hebrew*); woman from Carthage

(*Latin*).—a variant form is **Afra**.

April *fem* the name of the month, *Aprilis*, used as a personal name (*Latin*).

Ara *fem* spirit of revenge, and the goddess of destruction and vengeance (*Greek*).

Arabella, Arabela *fem* a fair altar (*Latin*); a woman (*Arabic*); diminutive forms are **Bella, Belle**.

Araminta *fem* beautiful, sweet-smelling flower (*Greek*); a diminutive form is **Minta**.

Archard *masc* sacred and powerful (*Germanic*).

Archer *masc* a surname, meaning professional or skilled bowman, used as a first name (*Old English*).

Archibald *masc* very bold; holy prince (*Germanic*); diminutive forms are **Archie, Archy**.

Ardath *fem* field of flowers (*Hebrew*); variant forms are **Aridatha, Ardatha**.

Ardal *masc* high valour (*Irish Gaelic*).

Ardella, Ardelle, Ardelis *fem* enthusiasm, warmth (*Hebrew*).

Arden *masc* a surname, meaning dwelling place or

gravel or eagle valley, used as a surname (*Old English*); burning, fiery (*Latin*).

Ardley *masc* from the domestic meadow (*Old English*).

Ardolph *masc* home-loving wolf rover (*Old English*).

Areta, Aretha *fem* excellently virtuous (*Greek*); variant forms are **Aretta, Arette, Aretas**.

Argenta, Argente, Argente *fem* silver or silvery coloured (*Latin*).

Aretta, Arette *fem* variant forms of **Areta**.

Argus *masc* all-seeing, watchful one, from Argus Panoptes, a character from Greek mythology with a hundred eyes all over his body (*Greek*).

Argyle, Argyll *masc* the Scottish placename, meaning land or district of the Gaels, used as a first name (*Scots Gaelic*).

Aria *fem* the Italian word for beautiful melody, from *aer*, 'breeze' (*Latin*), used as a first name.

Ariadne *fem* very holy (*Greek*).

Arianna *fem* an Italian form of **Ariadne**.

Arianne *fem* a French form of **Ariadne**.

Aric *masc* sacred ruler (*Old English*); diminutive forms are **Rick, Rickie, Ricky**.

Ariel *masc* God's lion (*Hebrew*).

Ariella, Arielle *fem* forms of Ariel (*Hebrew*).

Aries *masc* the ram, the sign of the Zodiac for 21 March to 19 April (*Latin*).

Arlen *masc* pledge (*Irish Gaelic*).

Arlene *fem* form of **Arlen**; a variant form of **Charlene, Marlene**; variant forms are **Arleen, Arlena, Arlina, Arline, Arlyne**.

Arlie, Arley, Arly *masc* a surname, meaning eagle wood, used as a first name (*Old English*).

Armand *masc* a French form of **Herman**.

Armel *masc* stone prince or chief (*Breton Gaelic*).

Armelle *fem* form of Armel.

Armilla *fem* bracelet (*Latin*).

Armin *masc* military man (*Germanic*).

Armina, Armine *fem* forms of **Armin**; variant

forms are **Erminie, Erminia**.

Armstrong *masc* a surname, meaning strong in the arm, used as a first name (*Old English*).

Arn *masc* diminutive of **Arnold, Arnulf**; a contraction of **Aaron**.

Arnalda *fem* form of **Arnold** (*Germanic*).

Arnall *masc* a surname variant form of **Arnold** used as a first name (*Germanic*).

Arnaud, Arnaut *masc* French forms of **Arnold**.

Arnatt, Arnett *masc* surname variant forms of **Arnold** used as first names.

Arne *masc* eagle (*Old Norse*); a diminutive form is **Arnie**.

Arno *masc* a diminutive of **Arnold, Arnulf**.

Arnold *masc* strong as an eagle (*Germanic*); eagle meadow (*Old English*); diminutive forms are **Arn, Arnie, Arno, Arny**.

Arnott *masc* a surname variant form of **Arnold** used as a first name.

Arnulf *masc* eagle wolf (*Germanic*); diminutives are **Arn, Arno**.

Arphad *masc* a variant form of **Arvad**.

Arselma *fem* a variant form of **Anselma**.

Artemas *masc* form of **Artemis** (*Greek*).

Artemis *fem* the name of the virgin Greek goddess of hunting and the moon, the derivation of which is unknown. The Roman equivalent is Diana.

Arthur *masc* eagle Thor (*Celtic*); a diminutive form is **Art**.

Arturo *masc* the Italian and Spanish forms of **Arthur**.

Arundel *masc* the English placename, meaning a valley where nettles grow, used as a first name (*Old English*).

Arva *fem* ploughed land, pasture (*Latin*).

Arvad *masc* wanderer (*Hebrew*); a variant form is **Arpad**.

Arval, Arvel *masc* greatly lamented (*Latin*).

Arvid *masc* eagle wood (*Norse*).

Arvin *masc* people's friend (*Germanic*).

Arwel *masc* meaning uncertain (*Welsh*).

Arwenna *fem* form of **Arwyn**.

Arwyn *masc* muse (*Welsh*); a variant form is **Awen**.

Asa *masc* healer, physician (*Hebrew*).

Asahel *masc* made of God (*Hebrew*).

Asaph *masc* a collector (*Hebrew*).

Ascot, Ascott *masc* an English placename and surname, meaning eastern cottages, used as a first name (*Old English*).

Ashburn *masc* a surname, meaning stream where the ash trees grow, used as a first name (*Old English*).

Ashby *masc* an English placename, meaning ash-tree farmstead, used as a first name (*Old English*).

Asher *masc* happy, fortunate (*Hebrew*).

Ashford *masc* an English placename, meaning ford by a clump of ash trees, used as a first name (*Old English*).

Ashley, Ashleigh *masc*, *fem* the surname, meaning ash wood or glade, used as a first name (*Old English*).

Ashlin *masc* ash-surrounded pool (*Old English*).

Ashton *masc* an English placename, meaning ash-tree farmstead, used as a first name (*Old English*).

Ashur *masc* martial, war-like (*Semitic*).

Asphodel *fem* a daffodil-like plant, the origin of whose name is obscure, used as a first name (*Greek*).

Astra *fem* diminutive of **Astrid**.

Astrid *fem* fair god (*Norse*); a diminutive is **Astra**.

Atalanta, Atalante *fem* the name of a mythological character who agreed to marry the man who could outrun her (*Greek*); a variant form is **Atlanta**.

Atalya *fem* guardian (*Spanish*).

Athanasius *masc* immortal (*Greek*).

Athena, Ahthene, Athenée *fem* in Greek mythology, the goddess of wisdom. Her Roman counterpart is Minerva (*Greek*).

Atherton *masc* a surname, meaning noble army's place, used as a first name (*Old English*).

Athol, Atholl *masc* a placename and surname, meaning new Ireland, used as a first name (*Scots Gaelic*).

Atlante *fem* a variant form of **Atalanta**.

Atlee, Atley, Atley *masc* a surname, meaning at the wood or clearing, used as a first name (*Old English*).

Atwater, Atwatter *masc* a surname, meaning by the water, used as a first name (*Old English*).

Atwell *masc* a surname, meaning at the spring or well of, used as a first name (*Old English*).

Auberon *masc* noble bear (*Germanic*); a variant form is **Oberon**; a diminutive form is **Bron**.

Aubin *masc* a surname, meaning blond one, used as a first name (*French*).

Aubrey *masc* ruler of spirits (*Germanic*).

Audrey *fem* noble might (*Old English*).

August *masc* the Polish and German form of **Augustus**; the eighth month of the year, named after the Roman emperor **Augustus**, used as a first name.

Augusta *fem* form of **Augustus**; diminutive forms are **Gussie, Gusta**.

Auguste *masc* the French form of **Augustus**.

Augustin *masc* the German and French forms of **Augustine**.

Augustine *masc* belonging to **Augustus** (*Latin*); a diminutive form is **Gus**.

Augustus *masc* exalted; imperial (*Latin*); a diminutive form is **Gus**.

Aura, Aure, Aurea *fem* breath of air (*Latin*); a variant form is **Auria**.

Aurelia *fem* form of **Aurelius**.

Aurelius *masc* golden (*Latin*).

Auria *fem* a variant form of **Aura**.

Aurora *fem* morning redness; fresh; brilliant (*Latin*).

Austin *masc* a contraction of **Augustine**.

Autumn *fem* the name of the season, the origin of which is uncertain, used as a first name.

Ava *fem* origin uncertain, perhaps a Germanic diminutive of names beginning *Av*.

Avera *fem* transgressor (*Hebrew*); a variant form is **Aberah**.

Averil, Averill *fem* English forms of **Avril**.

Avery *masc* a surname, derived from **Alfred**, used as a surname (*Old English*).

Avice, Avis *fem* possibly bird (*Latin*).

Avril *fem* the French form of **April**.

Awen *masc* a variant form of **Arwyn**.

Axel *masc* father of peace (*Germanic*).

Axton *masc* stone of the sword fighter (*Old English*).

Aylmer *masc* a surname, meaning noble and famous, used as a first name (*Old English*).

Aylward *masc* a surname, meaning noble guardian, used as a first name (*Old English*).

Azaliea, Azalia, Azalee *fem* variant forms of the name of the azalea plant, supposed to prefer dry earth, used as a first name.

Azaria *fem* form of **Azarias**.

Azarias *masc* helped by God (*Hebrew*).

Azura, Azure *fem* blue as the sky (*French*).

B

Bab, Babs *fem* diminutive forms of **Barbara**.

Bailey, Baillie *masc* a surname, meaning bailiff or steward, used as a first name (*Old French*); a variant form is **Bayley**.

Bainbridge *masc* a surname, meaning bridge over a short river, used as a surname (*Old English*).

Baird *masc* a Scottish surname, meaning minstrel or bard, used as a first name (*Celtic*); a variant form is **Bard**.

Baldemar *masc* bold and famous prince (*Germanic*).

Baldovin *masc* the Italian form of **Baldwin**.

Baldric, Baldrick *masc* a surname, meaning princely or bold ruler, used as a first name (*Germanic*); a variant form is **Baudric**.

Baldwin *masc* bold friend (*Germanic*).

Balfour *masc* a surname from a Scottish placename, meaning village with pasture, used as a first name (*Scots Gaelic*).

Ballard *masc* a surname, meaning bald, used as a first name (*Old English, Old French*).

Balthasar, Balthazar *masc* Baal defend the king (*Babylonian*).

Bambi *fem* a variant form of the word for *bambino*, child (*Italian*).

Bancroft *masc* a surname, meaning bean place, used as a first name (*Old English*).

Baptist *masc* a baptiser, purifier (*Greek*).

Baptista *fem* form of **Baptist**.

Baptiste *masc* a French form of **Baptist**.

Barbara, Barbra *fem* foreign, strange (*Greek*); diminutive forms are **Bab, Babs, Barbie**.

Barclay *masc* a surname, meaning birch wood, used

as a first name (*Old English*); variant forms are **Berkeley, Berkley**.

Bard *masc* a variant form of **Baird**; a diminutive form of **Bardolph**.

Bardolph *masc* bright wolf (*Germanic*).

Barlow *masc* a surname, meaning barley hill or barley clearing, used as a first name (*Old English*).

Barnaby, Barnabas *masc* son of consolation and exhortation (*Hebrew*); a diminutive form is **Barney**.

Barnard *masc* a variant form of **Bernard**; a diminutive form is **Barney**.

Barnet, Barnett *masc* a surname, meaning land cleared by burning, used as a first name (*Old English*).

Barnum *masc* a surname, meaning homestead of a warrior, used as a first name (*Old English*).

Baron *masc* the lowest rank of the peerage used as a first name (*Old French*); a variant form is **Barron**.

Barratt, Barrett *masc* a surname, meaning commerce or trouble or strife, used as a first name (*Old French*).

Barron *masc* a variant form of **Baron**.

Barry *masc* spear (*Irish Gaelic*).

Bart *masc* a diminutive form of **Bartholomew, Bartley, Barton, Bartram**.

Barthold *masc* variant form of **Berthold**.

Bartholomew *masc* a warlike son (*Hebrew*); diminutive forms are **Bart, Bat**.

Bartley *masc* a surname, meaning a birch wood or clearing, used as a first name (*Old English*); a diminutive form is **Bart**.

Barton *masc* the surname, meaning farm or farmyard, used as a first name (*Old English*); a diminutive form is **Bart**.

Bartram *masc* a variant form of **Bertram**.

Barzillai *masc* man of iron (*Hebrew*).

Basil *masc* kingly; royal (*Greek*).

Basile *masc* the French form of Basil.

Basilia *fem* form of **Basil**.

Basilio *masc* the Italian and Spanish form of **Basil**.

Bat *masc* a diminutive form of **Bartholomew**.

Bathilda *fem* battle commander (*Germanic*).

Bathilde *fem* the French form of **Bathilda**.

Bathsheba *fem* daughter of plenty (*Hebrew*).

Batiste *masc* the French form of **Baptist**.

Battista *masc* the Italian form of **Baptist**.

Baudouin *masc* the French form of **Baldwin**.

Baudric *masc* a variant form of **Baldric**.

Bautista *masc* the Spanish form of **Baptist**.

Baxter *masc* a surname, meaning baker, used as a first name (*Old English*).

Bayley *masc* a variant form of **Bailey**.

Bea *fem* a diminutive form of **Beatrice, Beatrix**.

Beal, Beale, Beall *masc* a surname variant form of **Beau** used as a first name (*French*).

Beaman *masc* bee keeper (*Old English*); a variant form of **Beaumont** (*French*).

Beata *fem* blessed, divine

one (*Latin*); a diminutive form is **Bea**.

Beatrice, Beatrix *fem* woman who blesses (*Latin*); diminutive forms are **Bea, Beatie, Beaty, Bee, Trix, Trixie**.

Beau *masc* handsome (*French*); a diminutive form of **Beaufort, Beamont**.

Beaufort *masc* a surname, meaning beautiful stronghold, used as a first name (*French*); a diminutive form is **Beau**.

Beaumont *masc* a surname, meaning beautiful hill, used as a first name (*French*); a diminutive form is **Beau**.

Beavan, Beaven *masc* variant forms of **Bevan**.

Beckie, Becky *fem* diminutive forms of **Rebecca**.

Beda *fem* maid of war (*Old English*).

Bee *fem* a diminutive form of **Beatrice**.

Belinda *fem* a name used by Sir John Vanburgh in his play *The Provok'd Wife*, its origin is uncertain, possibly beautiful woman (*Italian*).

Bella, Belle *fem* beautiful (*French, Italian*); diminu-

tive forms of **Annabel,
Arabella, Isabella**.

Bellamy *masc* a surname,
meaning handsome friend,
used as a first name (*Old
French*).

Ben *masc* a diminutive
form of **Benedict, Ben-
jamin**, also used independently.

Bena *fem* wise one (*Hebrew*).

Benedetto *masc* the Italian form of **Benedict**.

Benedict, Benedick *masc*
blessed (*Latin*); *also* **Bennet**; diminutives are **Ben,
Bennie, Benny**.

Benedicta *fem* form of
Benedict; a contracted
form is **Benita**; a diminutive form is **Dixie**.

Benedikt *masc* the German form of **Benedict**.

Beniamino *masc* the Italian form of **Benjamin**.

Benita *fem* form of **Benito**;
a contracted form of **Benedicta**.

Benito *masc* a Spanish
form of **Benedict**.

Benjamin *masc* son of the
right hand (*Hebrew*); diminutive forms are **Ben,
Benjie, Bennie, Benny**.

Benjie *masc* a diminutive
form of **Benjamin**.

Bennet *masc* a variant
form of **Benedict**.

Bennie, Benny *masc* a
diminutive form of **Benedict, Benjamin**.

Benoît *masc* the French
form of **Benedict**.

Benson *masc* a surname,
meaning son of **Ben**, used
as a first name.

Bentley *masc* a surname
from a Yorkshire pla-
cename, meaning woodland
clearing where bent-grass
grows, used as a first
name(*Old English*).

Beppe, Beppo *masc* a diminutive form of
Giuseppe, occasionally
used independently.

Berenice *fem* bringing victory (*Greek*); *also* **Bernice**.

Berkeley, Berkley *masc*
variant forms of **Barclay**.

Bernadette *fem* form of
Bernard.

Bernard *masc* strong or
hardy bear (*Germanic*);
also **Barnard**; diminutive
forms are **Barney, Bernie**.

Bernardin *masc* a French
form of **Bernard**.

Bernardino *masc* an Italian diminutive form of **Bernard**.

Bernardo *masc* a Spanish and Italian form of **Bernard**.

Bernhard, Bernhardt *masc* a German form of **Bernard**.

Bernice *fem* a variant form of **Berenice**.

Bernie *masc* a diminutive form of **Bernard**.

Bert *masc* diminutive forms of **Albert, Bertram, Egbert, Gilbert**, etc..

Berta *fem* a German, Italian and Spanish form of **Bertha**.

Bertha *fem* bright; beautiful; famous (*Germanic*); a diminutive form is **Bertie**.

Berthe *fem* the French form of **Bertha**.

Berthilda, Berthilde, Bertilda, Bertilde *fem* shining maid of war (*Old English*).

Berthold *masc* bright ruler (*Germanic*); variant forms are **Barthold, Bertold, Berthoud**; diminutive forms are **Bert, Bertie**.

Bertie *masc* diminutive forms of **Albert, Bertram, Egbert, Gilbert, Herbert**,

etc; *fem* a diminutive form of **Bertha**.

Bertold, Berthoud *masc* variant forms of **Berthold**.

Bertram *masc* bright; fair; illustrious (*Germanic*); a variant form is **Bartram**; diminutive forms are **Bert, Bertie**.

Bertrand *masc* the French form of **Bertram**.

Beryl *fem* jewel (*Greek*), the name of the gemstone used as a first name.

Bess, Bessie *fem* diminutive forms of **Elizabeth**.

Beth *fem* a diminutive form of **Elizabeth, Bethany**, now used independently.

Bethan *fem* a Welsh diminutive form of **Elizabeth-Ann** also used independently.

Bethany *fem* a placename near Jerusalem, the home of Lazarus in the New Testament and meaning house of poverty, used as a first name (*Aramaic*).

Betsy, Bette, Bettina, Betty *fem* diminutive forms of **Elizabeth**.

Beulah *fem* married (*Hebrew*).

Bevan *masc* a surname, meaning son of **Evan**, used

as a first name (*Welsh*); variant forms are **Beavan, Beaven, Bevin**.

Beverley, Beverly *fem masc* a placename, meaning beaver stream, used as a first name (*Old English*); a diminutive form is **Bev**.

Bevin *masc* a surname, meaning drink wine, used as a first name; a variant form of Bevan.

Bevis *masc* bull (*French*).

Bianca *fem* the Italian form of **Blanch**, now also used independently as an English-language form.

Biddy *fem* a diminutive form of **Bridget.**

Bije *masc* a diminutive form of **Abijah**.

Bill *masc* a diminutive form of **William**.

Billie *masc* a diminutive form of **William**; *fem* a diminutive form of **Wilhelmina**.

Bina, Binah, Bine *fem* bee (*Hebrew*).

Bing *masc* a surname, meaning a hollow, used as a first name (*Germanic*).

Binnie *fem* a diminutive form of **Sabina**.

Birch *masc* a surname,

from the birch tree, used as a first name (*Old English*); a variant form is **Birk**.

Birgit *fem* the Swedish form of **Bridget**; a diminutive form is **Britt**.

Birk *masc* a variant form of **Birch**.

Bishop *masc* a surname, meaning one who worked in a bishop's household, used as a first name (*Old English*).

Björn *masc* bear (*Old Norse*).

Black *masc* a surname, meaning dark-complexioned or dark-haired, used as a first name (*Old English*); a variant form is **Blake**.

Blair *masc* a placename and surname, meaning a plain, used as a first name (*Scottish Gaelic*).

Blaise *masc* sprouting forth (*French*).

Blake *masc* a variant form of Black; alternatively, pale or fair-complexioned (*Old English*).

Blanca *fem* the Spanish form of **Blanch**.

Blanche *fem* white (*Germanic*).

Bleddyn *masc* wolf

(*Welsh*).

Bliss *masc, fem* a surname, meaning happiness or joy, used as a first name (*Old English*).

Blodwen *fem* white flower (*Welsh*).

Blossom *fem* like a flower (*Old English*).

Blyth, Blythe *masc, fem* a surname, meaning cheerful and gentle, used as a first name (*Old English*).

Boas, Boaz *masc* fleetness (*Hebrew*).

Bob, Bobbie, Bobby *masc* diminutive forms of **Robert**.

Bonar *masc* a surname, meaning gentle, kind, courteous, used as a first name (*French*); variant forms are **Bonnar, Bonner**.

Boniface *masc* doer of good (*Latin*).

Bonita *fem* pretty (*Spanish*); good (*Latin*); a diminutive form is **Bonnie**.

Bonnar, Bonner *masc* variant forms of **Bonar**.

Bonnie *fem* pretty (*Scots English*); a diminutive form of **Bonita**.

Booth *masc* a surname, meaning hut or shed, used

as a first name (*Old Norse*).

Boris *masc* small (*Russian*).

Botolf, Botolph *masc* herald wolf (*Old English*).

Bourn, Bourne *masc* variant forms of **Burn**.

Bowen *masc* a surname, meaning son of Owen, used as a first name (*Welsh*).

Bowie *masc* a surname, meaning yellow-haired, used as a first name (*Scots Gaelic*).

Boyce *masc* a surname, meaning a wood, used as a first name (*Old French*).

Boyd *masc* a surname, meaning light-haired, used as a first name (*Scots Gaelic*).

Boyne *masc* the name of an Irish river, meaning white cow, used as a first name (*Irish Gaelic*).

Brad *masc* a diminutive form of **Bradley**, now used independently.

Bradford *masc* a placename and surname, meaning place at the broad ford, used as a first name (*Old English*).

Bradley *masc* a surname, meaning broad clearing or broad wood, used as a first

name (*Old English*); a diminutive form is **Brad**.

Brady *masc* a surname, of
unknown meaning, used as
a first name (*Irish Gaelic*).

Braham *masc* a surname,
meaning house or meadow
with broom bushes, used as
a first name.

Bram *masc* a diminutive
form of **Abram, Abraham**.

Bramwell *masc* a surname, meaning from the
bramble spring, used as a
first name (*Old English*).

Bran *masc* raven (*Gaelic*).

Brand *masc* firebrand (*Old
English*).

Brandon *masc* a surname,
meaning broom-covered
hill, used as a first name
(*Old English*); a variant
form of **Brendan**.

Branwen *fem* raven-haired
beauty (*Welsh*); a variant
form of **Bronwen**.

Brenda *fem* a brand or
sword (*Old Norse*).

Brendan *masc* prince (*Celtic*); a variant form is **Brandon**.

Brenna *fem* raven-haired
beauty (*Irish Gaelic*).

Brent *masc* a surname,
meaning a steep place,

used as a first name (*Old
English*).

Bret, Brett *masc* a Breton
(*Old French*).

Brewster *masc* a surname,
meaning brewer, used as a
first name (*Old English*).

Brian *masc* strong (*Celtic*);
a variant form is **Bryan**.

Brice *masc* a surname, of
unknown meaning, used as
a first name (*Celtic*); a variant form is **Bryce**.

Bridget *fem* goddess of fire
(*Celtic*); a variant form is
Brigid; diminutive forms
are **Biddy, Bridie**.

Brigham *masc* a surname,
meaning homestead by a
bridge, used as a first name
(*Old English*).

Brigid *fem* a variant form
of **Bridget**.

Brigide *fem* a Spanish,
Italian, and French form of
Brid-get.

Brigitte *fem* a French form
of **Bridget**.

Briony *fem* a variant form
of **Bryony**.

Britt *fem* a diminutive form
of **Birgit**, now used independently.

Brittany *fem* the anglicized
name of a French region,

meaning land of the fig-
ured, or tattooed folk, used
as a first name.

Brock *masc* a surname,
meaning badger, used as a
first name (*Old English*).

Broderic, Broderick *masc*
a surname, meaning son of
Roderick, used as a first
name (*Welsh*); brother
(*Scots Gaelic*).

Brodie, Brody *masc* a surname, meaning ditch, used
as a first name (*Scots Gaelic*).

Bron *masc* a diminutive
form of **Auberon, Oberon**.

Bronwen *fem* white breast
(*Welsh*); variant forms are
Bronwyn, Branwen.

Brook, Brooke *masc, fem*
a surname, meaning
stream, used as a first
name; a variant form is
Brooks.

Brooks *masc* a variant
form of Brook.

Bruce *masc* a surname,
meaning unknown, used as
a first name (*Old French*).

Brunella fem form of Bruno.

Brunhilda, Brunhilde
fem warrior maid (*Germanic*).

Bruno *masc* brown (*Germanic*).

Bryan *masc* a variant form
of **Brian**.

Bryce *masc* a variant form
of **Brice**.

Bryn *masc* hill (*Welsh*).

Brynmor *fem* large hill
(*Welsh*).

Bryony *fem* the name of a
climbing plant used as a
first name (*Greek*); a variant form is **Briony**.

Buck *masc* stag; he-goat; a
lively young man (*Old English*).

Buckley *masc* a surname,
meaning stag or he-goat
meadow, used as a first
name (*Old English*).

Budd, Buddy *masc* the
informal term for a friend
or brother used as a first
name (*Old English*).

Buena *fem* good (*Spanish*).

Bunty *fem* a diminutive
meaning lamb, now used as
a first name (*English*).

Buona *fem* good (*Italian*).

Burchard *masc* a variant
form of **Burkhard**.

Burdon *masc* a surname,
meaning castle on a hill or
valley with a cowshed, used
as a first name (*Old English*).

Burford *masc* a surname,

meaning ford by a castle, used as a first name (*Old English*).

Burgess *masc* a surname, meaning citizen or inhabitant of a borough, used as a first name (*Old French*).

Burk, Burke *masc* a surname, meaning fort or manor, used as a first name (*Old French*).

Burkhard *masc* strong as a castle (*Germanic*); a variant form is **Burchard**.

Burl *masc* cup bearer (*Old English*).

Burley *masc* dweller in the castle by the meadow (*Old English*); a diminutive form is **Burleigh**.

Burn, Burne *masc* a surname, meaning brook or stream, used as a first name (*Old English*); variant forms are **Bourn,**

Bourne, Byrne.

Burnett *masc* a surname, meaning brown-complexioned or brown-haired, used as a first name (*Old French*).

Burt *masc* a diminutive form of **Burton**, now used independently.

Burton *masc* a surname, meaning farmstead of a fortified placed, used as a first name (*Old English*); diminutive forms are **Burt**.

Buster *masc* an informal term of address for a boy or young man, now used as a first name (*English*).

Byrne *masc* a variant form of **Burn**.

Byron *masc* a surname, meaning at the cowsheds, used as a first name (*Old English*).

C

Caddie *fem* a diminutive form of **Carol, Carola, Carole, Caroline, Carolyn**.

Caddick, Caddock *masc* a surname, meaning decrepit or epileptic, used as a first name (*Old French*).

Cadell *masc* a surname, meaning battle spirit, used as a first name (*Welsh*).

Cadence *fem* rhythmic (*Latin*).

Cadenza *fem* the Italian form of **Cadence**.

Cadmus *masc* man from the east; in Greek mythology a Phoenician prince who founded Thebes with five warriors he had created (*Greek*).

Cadwallader *masc* battle arranger (*Welsh*).

Caesar *masc* long-haired; the Roman title of emperor used as a first name (*Latin*).

Cain *masc* possession; the Biblical character who

killed his brother Abel (*Hebrew*).

Cáit *fem* the Irish Gaelic form of Kate.

Caitlín, Caitrín *fem* Irish Gaelic forms of **Katherine**.

Cal *fem* a diminutive form of **Calandra, Calantha**.

Calandra *fem* lark(*Greek*); diminutive forms are **Cal, Callie, Cally**.

Calandre *fem* the French form of **Calandra**.

Calandria *fem* the Spanish form of **Calandra**.

Calantha *fem* beautiful blossom (*Greek*); diminutive forms are **Cal, Callie, Cally**.

Calanthe *fem* the French form of **Calantha**.

Calder *masc* a placename and surname, meaning hard or rapid water, used as a first name (*Celtic*).

Caldwell *masc* a surname, meaning cold spring or stream, used as a first

name (*Old English*).

Caleb *masc* a dog (*Hebrew*); a diminutive form is **Cale**.

Caledonia *fem* the Roman name for Scotland used as a first name (*Latin*).

Caley *masc* thin, slender (*Irish Gaelic*); diminutive form of **Calum**.

Calhoun *masc* a surname, meaning from the forest, used as a first name (*Irish Gaelic*).

Calla *fem* beautiful (*Greek*).

Callie *fem* a diminutive form of **Calandra, Calantha**.

Calliope *fem* lovely voice; the muse of poetry (*Greek*).

Callisto *masc* most fair or good (*Greek*).

Callista *fem* form of **Callisto**.

Cally *fem* a diminutive form of **Calandra, Calantha**; *masc* diminutive form of **Calum**.

Calum, Callum *masc* the Scots Gaelic form of *Columba*, the Latin for dove; a diminutive form of **Malcolm**; diminutive forms are **Cally, Caley**.

Calumina *fem* form of **Calum**.

Calvert *masc* a surname, meaning calf herd, used as a first name (*Old English*).

Calvin *masc* little bald one (*Latin*).

Calvina *fem* form of **Calvin**.

Calvino *masc* and Italian and Spanish forms of **Calvin**.

Calypso *fem* concealer; in Greek mythology, the sea nymph who held Odysseus captive for seven years (*Greek*).a variant form is **Kalypso**.

Cameron *masc* a surname, meaning hook nose, used as a first name (*Scots Gaelic*).

Camila *fem* the Spanish form of **Camilla**.

Camilla *fem* votaress, attendant at a sacrifice (*Latin*).

Camille *masc, fem* the French form of **Camilla**.

Campbell *masc* a surname, meaning crooked mouth, used as a first name (*Scots Gaelic*).

Candie *fem* a diminutive form of **Candice, Candida**.

Candice, Candace *fem* meaning uncertain, possibly brilliantly white or pure and virtuous, the name of an Ethiopian queen (*Latin*); **Candie, Candy**.

Candida *fem* shining white (*Latin*); diminutive forms are **Candie, Candy**.

Candy *fem* a diminutive form of **Candice, Candida**; a name used in its own right, from candy, the American English word for a sweet.

Canice *masc* handsome or fair one (*Irish Gaelic*).

Canute *masc* knot (*Old Norse*), the name of a Danish king of England (1016–35); variant forms are **Cnut, Knut**.

Cara *fem* friend (*Irish Gaelic*); dear, darling (*Italian*); a variant form is **Carina**.

Caradoc, Caradog *masc* beloved (*Welsh*); a variant form is **Cradoc**.

Cardew *masc* a surname meaning black fort, used as a first name (*Welsh*).

Carey *masc* a surname, meaning castle dweller (*Welsh*) or son of the dark one (*Irish Gaelic*), used as a first name; a variant form of **Cary**.

Caridad *fem* the Spanish form of **Charity**.

Carina *fem* a variant form of **Cara**.

Carissa *fem* dear one (*Latin*).

Carl *masc* an anglicized German and Swedish form of **Charles**; a diminutive form of **Carlton, Carlin, Carlisle, Carlo, Carlos**.

Carla *fem* form of **Carl**; a variant form is **Carlin**; diminutive forms are **Carlie, Carley, Carly**.

Carleton *masc* a variant form of **Carlton**.

Carlie *fem* a diminutive form of **Carla, Carlin**.

Carlin *fem* a variant form of **Carla**; diminutive forms are **Carlie, Carley, Carly**.

Carlo *masc* the Italian form of **Charles**.

Carlos *masc* the Spanish form of **Charles**.

Carlotta *fem* the Italian form of **Charlotte**.

Carlton *masc* a placename and surname, meaning farm of the churls—a rank of peasant, used as a first name (*Old English*).variant forms are **Carleton, Charlton, Charleton**; a diminutive form is **Carl**.

Carly *fem* a diminutive form of **Carla, Carlin**, now used independently.

Carmel *fem* garden (*Hebrew*).

Carmela *fem* a Spanish and the Italian forms of **Carmel**.

Carmelita *fem* a Spanish diminutive form of **Carmel**.

Carmen *fem* a Spanish form of **Carmel**.

Carmichael *masc* a Scottish placename and surname, meaning fort of **Michael**, used as a first name (*Celtic*).

Carnation *fem* the name of a flour, meaning flesh colour, used as a first name (*Latin/French*).

Carol *masc* a shortened form of *Carolus*, the Latin form of **Charles**; *fem* a shortened form of **Caroline**; diminutive forms are **Caro, Carrie, Caddie**.

Carola *fem* a variant form of **Caroline**; diminutive forms are **Carrie, Caro, Caddie**.

Carole *fem* the French form of **Carol**; a contracted form of **Caroline**; diminutive forms are **Caro, Carrie, Caddie**.

Carolina *fem* the Italian and Spanish forms of **Caroline**.

Caroline, Carolyn *fem* form of *Carolus*, the Latin form of **Charles**; diminutive forms are **Caro, Carrie, Caddie**.

Carr *masc* a placename and surname, meaning overgrown marshy ground, used as a first name (*Old Norse*); variant forms are **Karr, Kerr**.

Carrie *fem* a diminutive form of **Carol, Carola, Carole, Caroline, Carolyn**.

Carrick *masc* a placename, meaning rock, used as a first name (*Gaelic*).

Carroll *masc* a surname, of uncertain meaning—possibly hacking, used as a first name (*Irish Gaelic*).

Carson *masc* a surname, of uncertain meaning but possibly marsh dweller (*Old English*), used as a first name.

Carter *masc* a surname, meaning a driver or maker of cars (*Old English*) or son of Arthur (*Scots Gaelic*), used as a first name.

Carver *masc* great rock (*Cornish Gaelic*); a surname, meaning sculptor, used as a first name (*Old English*).

Carwyn *masc* blessed love (*Welsh*).

Cary *masc* a surname, meaning pleasant stream, used as a first name (*Celtic*); a variant form is **Carey**.

Carys *fem* love (Welsh).

Casey *masc fem* an Irish surname, meaning vigilant, used as a first name; a placename, Cayce in Kentucky, where the hero Casey Jones was born, used as a first name; *fem* a variant form of **Cassie** used independently.

Cashel *masc* a placename, meaning circular stone fort, used as a first name (*Irish Gaelic*).

Casimir *masc* the English form of **Kasimir**.

Caspar, Casper *masc* the Dutch form of **Jasper**, now also used as an English-language form.

Cass *fem* a diminutive form of **Cassandra**; *masc* a diminutive form of **Cassidy**, **Cassius**.

Cassandra *fem* she who inflames with love (*Greek*); in Greek mythology, a princess whose prophecies of doom were not believed; diminutive forms are **Cass**, **Cassie**.

Cassidy *masc* a surname, meaning clever, used as a first name (*Irish Gaelic*); a diminutive form is **Cass**.

Cassie *fem* a diminutive form of **Cassandra**.

Cassian, Cassius *masc* a Roman family name, of uncertain meaning—possibly empty, used as a first name (*Latin*); a diminutive form is **Cass**.

Castor *masc* beaver (*Greek*).

Catalina *fem* the Spanish form of **Katherine**.

Caterina *fem* the Italian form of **Katherine**.

Cathal *masc* battle ruler (*Irish Gaelic*).

Catharina, Catharine, Caterina *fem* variant forms of **Catherine**.

Catherine *fem* the French form of **Katherine**, now used as an English-language form; diminutive forms are **Cath, Cathie, Cathy**.

Cato *masc* a Roman family name, meaning wise one, used as a first name (*Latin*).

Catrin *fem* the Welsh form of **Katherine**.

Catriona *fem* the Scots Gaelic form of **Katherine**.

Cavan *masc* a placename, meaning hollow with a grassy hill, used as a first name (*Irish Gaelic*); a variant form is **Kavan**.

Cecil *masc* dim-sighted (*Latin*).

Cecile *fem* the French form of **Cecily, Cecilia**.

Cécile *masc* the French form of **Cecil**.

Cecily, Cecilia *fem* forms of **Cecil**; diminutive forms are **Celia, Cis, Cissie, Cissy**; a variant form is **Cicely**.

Cedric *masc* a name adapted by Sir Walter Scott for a character in *Ivanhoe* from the Saxon *Cerdic*, the first king of Wessex.

Ceinwen beautiful and blessed (*Welsh*).

Celandine *fem* the name of either of two unrelated flowering plants, meaning swallow, used as a first name (*Greek*).

Celeste, Celestine *fem* heavenly (*Latin*).

Celia *fem* heavenly (*Latin*); dimin of **Cecilia**.

Cemlyn *masc* a placename, meaning bending lake, used as a first name.

Cendrillon *fem* from the ashes, the fairytale heroine (*French*); the anglicized form is **Cinderella**.

Cephas *masc* a stone (*Aramaic*).

Ceri *masc* love (*Welsh*).

Cerian *fem* diminutive form of **Ceri**.

Cerys *fem* love (*Welsh*).

César *masc* the French form of **Caesar**.

Cesare *masc* the Italian form of **Caesar**.

Chad *masc* meaning uncertain—possibly warlike, bellicose (*Old English*).

Chaim *masc* a variant form of **Hyam**.

Chance *masc* the abstract noun for the quality of good fortune used as a first name (*Old French*); a variant form is **Chauncey**.

Chancellor *masc* a surname, meaning counsellor or secretary, used as a first name (*Old French*).

Chancey *masc* a variant form of **Chauncey**.

Chandler *masc* a surname, meaning maker or seller of

candles, used as a first name (*Old French*).

Chandra *fem* moon brighter than the stars (*Sanskrit*).

Chanel *fem* the surname of the French couturier and perfumier, Coco Chanel, used as a first name.

Chapman *masc* a surname, meaning merchant, used as a first name (*Old English*).

Charis *fem* grace (*Greek*).

Charity *fem* the abstract noun for the quality of tolerance or generosity used as a personal name (*Old French*).

Charlene *fem* a relatively modern diminutive form of **Charles**.

Charles *masc* strong; manly; noble-spirited (*Germanic*); a diminutive form is **Charlie, Charley**.

Charlie, Charley *masc, fem* diminutive forms of **Charles, Charlotte**.

Charlotte *fem* form of **Charles** (*Germanic*); diminutive forms are **Charlie, Charley, Lottie**.

Charlton, Charleton *masc* variant forms of **Carlton**.

Charmaine *fem* a diminutive form of the abstract

noun for the quality of pleasing or attracting people used as a first name; a variant form of **Charmian**.

Charmian *fem* little delight (*Greek*); a modern variant form is **Charmaine**.

Chase *masc* a surname, meaning hunter, used as a first name (*Old French*).

Chauncey, Chaunce *masc* a surname, of uncertain meaning—possibly chancellor, used as a first name (*Old French*); variant forms are **Chance, Chancey**.

Chelsea *fem* a placename, meaning chalk landing place, used as a first name (*Old English*).

Cher, Chérie *fem* dear, darling (*French*).

Cherry *fem* the name of the fruit used as a first name; a form of **Chérie**; a variant is **Cheryl**.

Cheryl *fem* a variant form of **Cherry**; a combining form of **Cherry** and **Beryl**; a variant form is **Sheryl**.

Chester *masc* a placename, meaning Roman fortified camp, used as a first name (*Old English*).

Chiara *fem* the Italian form of **Clara**.

Chilton *masc* a placename and surname, meaning children's farm, used as a first name (*Old English*).

Chiquita *fem* little one (*Spanish*).

Chloë, Chloe *fem* a green herb; a young shoot (*Greek*).

Chloris *fem* green (*Greek*).

Chris *masc fem* a diminutive form of **Christian, Christine, Christopher**.

Chrissie *fem* a diminutive form of **Christiana, Christine**.

Christabel *fem* a combination of **Christine** and **Bella** made by Samuel Taylor Coleridge for a poem of this name.

Christian *masc, fem* belonging to Christ; a believer in Christ (*Latin*); diminutive forms are **Chris, Christie, Christy**.

Christiana *fem* form of Christian; a variant form is **Christina**.

Christie *masc* a surname, meaning Christian, used as a first name; a diminutive form of **Christian, Christopher**; *fem* a diminutive form of **Christian, Christine**; a variant form is **Christy**.

Christina *fem* a variant form of **Christiana**.

Christine *fem* a French form of **Christina**, now used as an English-language form; diminutive forms are **Chris, Chrissie, Christie, Christy, Teenie, Tina**.

Christmas *masc* festival of Christ (*Old English*).

Christoph *masc* the German form of **Christopher**.

Christopher *masc* bearing Christ (*Greek*); diminutive forms are **Chris, Christie, Christy, Kester, Kit**.

Christy *masc fem* a variant form of **Christie**.

Chrystal *fem* a variant form of **Crystal**.

Churchill *masc* a placename and surname, meaning church on a hill, used as a first name (*Old English*).

Cian *masc* ancient (*Irish Gaelic*); anglicized forms are **Kean, Keane**.

Ciara *fem* form of **Ciarán**.

Ciarán *masc* small and black (*Irish Gaelic*); the anglicized form is **Kieran**.

Cicely *fem* a variant form of **Cecilia**.

Cilla *fem* a diminutive form of **Priscilla** (*French*).

Cinderella *fem* the anglicized form of **Cendrillon**, the fairytale heroine; diminutive forms are **Cindie, Cindy, Ella**.

Cindy *fem* a diminuntive form of **Cinderella, Cynthia, Lucinda**, now often used independently.

Cinzia *fem* the Italian form of **Cynthia**.

Claiborne *masc* a variant form of **Clayborne**; a diminutive form is **Clay**.

Claire *fem* the French form of **Clara**, now used widely as an English form.

Clara *fem* bright, illustrous (*Latin*); a variant form is **Clare**; a diminutive form is **Clarrie**.

Clarabel, Clarabella, Clarabelle *fem* a combination of **Clara** and **Bella** or **Belle**, meaning bright, shining beauty (*Latin/French*); a variant form is **Claribel**.

Clare *fem* a variant form of **Clara**; *fem, masc* a surname, meaning or bright, shining, used as a first name (*Latin*).

Clarence *masc* bright, shining (*Latin*); a diminu-

tive form is **Clarrie**.

Claribel *fem* a variant form of **Clarabel**.

Clarice *fem* fame (*Latin*); a variant form of **Clara**; a variant form is **Clarissa**.

Clarinda *fem* a combination of **Clara** and **Belinda** or **Lucinda**.

Clarissa *fem* a variant form of **Clarice**.

Clark, Clarke *masc* a surname, meaning cleric, scholar or clerk, used as a first name (*Old French*).

Clarrie *fem* a diminutive form of **Clara**; *masc* a diminutive form of **Clarence**.

Claud *masc* the English form of **Claudius**.

Claude *masc* the French form of **Claud**; *fem* the French form of **Claudia**.

Claudia *fem* form of **Claud**.

Claudio *masc* the Italian and Spanish form of **Claud**.

Claudius *masc* lame (*Latin*); the Dutch and German forms of **Claud**.

Claus *masc* a variant form of **Klaus**.

Clay *masc* a surname,

meaning a dweller in a
place with clay soil, used as
a first name (*Old English*);
a diminutive form of **Claiborne, Clayborne, Clay-
ton**.

Clayborne *masc* a surname, meaning a dweller in
a place with clay soil by a
brook, used as a first name
(*Old English*); a variant
form is Claiborne; a diminutive form is **Clay**.

Clayton *masc* a placename
and surname, meaning
place in or with good clay,
used as a first name (*Old
English*); a diminutive form
is **Clay**.

Clem *fem* a diminutive
form of **Clematis, Clem-
ence, Clemency, Clemen-
tine, Clementina**; *masc* a
diminutive form of **Clement**.

Clematis *fem* climbing
plant (*Greek*), the name of
a climbing plant with
white, blue or purple flowers used as a first name;
diminutive forms are
Clem, Clemmie.

Clemency *fem* the abstract
noun for the quality of tem-
pering justice with mercy
used as a first name (*Latin*); a variant form is
Clemence; diminutive
forms are **Clem, Clemmie**.

Clement *masc* mild-tem-
pered, merciful (*Latin*); a
diminutive form is **Clem**.

Clementine, Clementina
fem forms of **Clement**;
diminutive forms are
Clem, Clemmie.

Cleo *fem* a short form of
Cleopatra, used independently.

Cleopatra *fem* father's
glory (*Greek*); a diminutive
form is **Cleo**.

Cleveland *masc* a placename, meaning land of
hills, used as a first name
(*Old English*).

Cliantha *fem* glory flower
(*Greek*); a diminutive form
is **Clia**.

Cliff *masc* a diminutive
form of **Clifford**, now used
independently.

Clifford *masc* a surname,
meaning ford at a cliff,
used as a first name (*Old
English*); a diminutive form
is **Cliff**.

Clifton *masc* a placename,
meaning place on a cliff,
used as a first name (*Old
English*).

Clint *masc* a diminutive
form of Clinton, now used
independently.

Clinton *masc* a placename

and surname, meaning
settlement on a hill, used
as a first name; a diminutive form is **Clint**.

Clio *fem* glory (*Greek*).

Clive *masc* a surname,
meaning at the cliff, used
as a first name (*Old English*).

Clorinda *fem* a combination of **Chloris** and **Belinda** or **Lucinda**.

Clothilde, Clotilde *fem*
famous fighting woman
(*Germanic*).

Clover *fem* the name of a
flowering plant used as a
first name (*English*).

Clovis *masc* warrior (*Germanic*).

Clyde *masc* the name of a
Scottish river, meaning
cleansing one, used as a
first name.

Cnut *masc* a variant form
of **Canute**.

Cody *masc* a surname used
as a first name.

Colby *masc* From the dark
country (*Norse*).

Col *masc* a diminutive form
of **Colman, Columba**.

Cole *masc* a diminutive
form of **Coleman, Col-
man, Nicholas**; a sur-

name, meaning swarthy or
coal-black, used as a first
name (*Old English*).

Coleman *masc* a surname,
meaning swarthy man or
servant of Nicholas, used
as a surname (*Old Eng-
lish*).

Colette *fem* a diminutive
form of **Nicole**, now used
independently; a variant
form is **Collette**.

Colin *masc* a diminutive
form of **Nicholas**, long
used independently.

Colleen *fem* the Irish word
for a girl used as a first
name.

Collette *fem* a variant form
of **Colette**.

Collier, Collyer *masc* a
surname, meaning charcoal
seller or buirner, used as a
first name (*Old English*); a
variant form is **Colyer**.

Colm *masc* dove (*Irish
Gaelic/Latin*)

Colman, Colmán *masc*
keeper of doves (*Irish Gael-
ic/Latin*); diminutive forms
are **Col, Cole**.

Colombe *masc, fem* the
French form of Columba.

Columba *masc, fem* dove
(*Latin*); a diminutive form
is **Coly**.

Columbine *fem* little dove; the name of a flowering plant used as a first name (*Latin*).

Colyer *masc* a variant form of **Collier**.

Comfort *fem* the abstract noun for the state of well-being or bringer of solace used as a first name, in the Puritan tradition (*Latin/French*).

Comyn *masc* bent (*Irish Gaelic*).

Con *masc* a diminutive form of **Conan, Connall, Connor, Conrad**; *fem* a diminutive form of **Constance**, etc.

Conan, Cónán *masc* little hound (*Irish Gaelic*); a diminutive form is **Con**.

Concepcion *fem* beginning, conception, a reference to the Immaculate Conception of the Virgin Mary (*Spanish*); diminutive forms are **Concha, Conchita**.

Concepta *fem* the Latin form of **Concetta**.

Concetta *fem* conceptive, a reference to the Virgin Mary and the Immaculate Conception (*Italian*).

Concha, Conchita *fem* diminutive forms of **Con-**

cepción.

Conn *masc* chief (*Celtic*).

Connall *masc* courageous (*Irish and Scots Gaelic*).

Connor *masc* high desire or will (*Irish Gaelic*).

Conrad *masc* able counsellor (*Germanic*); a diminutive form is **Con**.

Conroy *masc* wise (*Gaelic*).

Consolata *fem* consoling, a reference to the Virgin Mary (*Italian*).

Consolation *fem* the abstract noun for the act of consoling or the state of solace used as a first name in the Puritan tradition.

Constance *fem* form of **Constant**; diminutive forms are **Con, Connie**; a variant form is **Constanta**.

Constant *masc* firm; faithful (*Latin*); a diminutive form is **Con**.

Constanta *fem* a variant form of **Constance**.

Constantine *masc* resolute; firm (*Latin*).

Constanza *fem* the Italian and Spanish forms of **Constance**.

Consuela *fem* consolation, a reference to the Virgin Mary (*Spanish*).

Consuelo *masc* consolation, a reference to the Virgin Mary (*Spanish*).

Conway *masc* a surname, of uncertain meaning—possibly yellow hound or head-smashing, used as a first name (*Irish Gaelic*); high or holy water (*Welsh*).

Cooper *masc* a surname, meaning barrel maker, used as a first name (*Old English*); a diminutive form is **Coop**.

Cora *fem* maiden (*Greek*).

Corabella, Corabelle *fem* beautiful maiden, a combination of **Cora** and **Bella**.

Coral *fem* the name of the pink marine jewel material used as a first name.

Coralie *fem* the French form of **Coral**.

Corazón *fem* (sacred) heart (*Spanish*).

Corbet, Corbett *masc* a surname, meaning raven, black-haired or raucousness, used as a first name (*Old French*).

Corcoran *masc* a surname, meaning red- or purple-faced, used as a first name (*Irish Gaelic*).

Cordelia *fem* warm-hearted (*Latin*).

Corey *masc* a surname, meaning god peace, used as a first name (*Irish Gaelic*).

Corinna, Corinne *fem* variant forms of **Cora**.

Cormac, Cormack, Cormick *masc* charioteer (*Irish Gaelic*).

Cornelia *fem* form of **Cornelius**.

Cornelius *masc* origin uncertain, possibly horn-like, a Roman family name; a variant form is **Cornell**.

Cornell *masc* a surname, meaning Cornwall or a hill where corn is sold, used as a first name; a variant form of **Cornelius**.

Corona *fem* crown (*Latin*).

Corrado *masc* the Italian form of **Conrad**.

Corwin *masc* friend of the heart (*Old French*)

Cosima *fem* form of **Cosmo**.

Cosimo *masc* an Italian form of **Cosmo**.

Cosmo *masc* order, beauty (*Greek*).

Costanza *fem* an Italian form of **Constance**.

Courtney *masc, fem* a surname, meaning short nose, used as a first name (*Old*

French).

Cradoc *masc* a variant form of **Caradoc**.

Craig *masc* a surname meaning crag, used as a first name (*Scots Gaelic*).

Cranley *masc* a surname, meaning crane clearing, spring or meadow, used as a first name (*Old English*).

Crawford *masc* a placename and surname, meaning ford of the crows, used as a first name (*Old English*).

Creighton *masc* a surname, meaning rock or cliff place (*Old Welsh, Old English*) or border settlement (*Scots Gaelic*), used as a first name (*Old English*).

Crépin *masc* the French form of **Crispin**.

Cressida *fem* gold (*Greek*); a contracted form is **Cressa**.

Crispin, Crispian *masc* having curly hair (*Latin*).

Crispus *masc* the German form of **Crispin**.

Cristal *fem* a variant form of **Crystal**.

Cristiano *masc* the Italian and Spanish form of **Christian**.

Cristina *fem* the Italian, Portuguese and Spanish form of **Christina**.

Cristóbal *masc* the Spanish form of **Christopher**.

Cristoforo *masc* the Italian form of **Christopher**.

Cromwell *masc* a placename and surname, meaning winding spring, used as a first name.

Crosbie, Crosby *masc* a placename and surname, meaning farm or village with crosses, used as a first name (*Old Norse*).

Crystal *fem* the name of a very clear brilliant glass used as a first name; variant forms are **Cristal, Chrystal**.

Cullan, Cullen *masc* a surname, meaning Cologne, used as a first name (*Old French*); a placename, meaning at the back of the river, used as a first name (*Scots Gaelic*).

Culley *masc* a surname, meaning woodland, used as a first name (*Scots Gaelic*).

Curran *masc* a surname, of uncertain meaning—possibly resolute hero, used as a first name (*Irish Gaelic*).

Curt *masc* a variant form of **Kurt**; a diminutive form of **Curtis**.

Curtis *masc* a surname, meaning courteous, educated, used as a first name (*Old French*); a diminutive form is **Curt**.

Cuthbert *masc* famous bright (*Old English*).

Cy *masc* a diminutive form of **Cyrus**.

Cynthia *fem* belonging to Mount Cynthus (*Greek*); diminutive forms are **Cindie, Cindy**.

Cyprian *masc* from Cyprus, the Mediterranean island (*Greek*).

Cyrano *masc* from Cyrene, an ancient city of North Africa (*Greek*).

Cyrene, Cyrena *fem* from Cyrene, an ancient city of North Africa; in Greek mythology, a water nymph loved by Apollo (*Greek*); a

variant form is **Kyrena**.

Cyril *masc* lordly (*Greek*).

Cyrill *masc* the German form of **Cyril**.

Cyrille *masc* the French form of Cyril; *fem* form of Cyril (*French*).

Cyrillus *masc* the Danish, Dutch and Swedish forms of **Cyril**.

Cyrus *masc* the sun (*Persian*); a diminutive form is **Cy**.

Cytherea *fem* from Cythera, an island off the southern coast of the Peloponnese, in Greek mythology, home of a cult of Aphrodite (*Greek*).

Cythereia *fem* from Cytherea, in Greek mythology, an alternative name for Aphrodite.

D

Daffodil *fem* the name of the spring plant that yields bright yellow flowers used as a first name (*Dutch/Latin*); a diminutive form is **Daffy**.

Dafydd *masc* a Welsh form of **David**.

Dag *masc* day (*Norse*).

Dagan *masc* earth, the name of an earth god of the Assyrians and Babylonians (*Semitic*).

Dagmar *fem* bright day (*Norse*).

Dahlia *fem* the name of the plant with brightly coloured flowers, named after the Swedish botanist Anders Dahl (dale), used as a first name.

Dai *masc* a Welsh diminutive form of David, formerly a name in its own right, meaning shining.

Daisy *fem* the name of the plant; the day's eye (*Old English*).

Dale *masc fem* a surname, meaning valley, used as a first name (*Old English*).

Daley *masc, fem* a surname, meaning assembly, used as a first name (*Irish Gaelic*); a variant form is **Daly**.

Dalilah, Dalila *fem* variant forms of **Delilah**.

Dallas *masc* a surname, meaning meadow resting place (*Scots Gaelic*) or dale house (*Old English*), used as a first name.

Dalton *masc* a surname, meaning dale farm, used as a first name (*Old English*).

Daly *masc, fem* a variant of **Daley**.

Dalziel *masc* a placename and surname, meaning field of the sungleam, used as a first name (*Scots Gaelic*).

Damian *masc* the French form of **Damon**.

Damiano *masc* the Italian form of **Damon**.

Damien *masc* taming

(*Greek*).

Damon *masc* conqueror (*Greek*).

Dan *masc* a diminutive form of **Danby, Daniel**.

Dana *masc, fem* a surname, of uncertain meaning—possibly Danish, used as a first name (*Old English*); *fem* form of **Dan, Daniel**.

Danaë *fem* in Greek mythology, the mother of Perseus by Zeus, who came to her as shower of gold while she was in prison; diminutive forms are **Dannie, Danny**.

Danby *masc* a placename and surname, meaning Danes' settlement, used as a first name (*Old Norse*); a diminutive form is **Dan**.

Dandie *masc* a Scottish diminutive form of **Andrew**.

Dane *masc* a surname, meaning valley, used as a first name (*Old English*).

Daniel *masc* God is my judge (*Hebrew*); diminutive forms are **Dan, Dannie, Danny**.

Danielle *fem* form of **Daniel**; *masc* the Italian form of **Daniel**.

Dannie, Danny *masc* diminutives of **Danby, Daniel**; *fem* diminutives of **Danaë, Danielle**.

Dante *masc* steadfast (*Latin/Italian*).

Daphne *fem* laurel (*Greek*).

Dara *fem* charity (*Hebrew*); *masc* oak (*Irish Gaelic*).

Darby *masc* a variant form of Derby, a surname meaning a village where deer are seen, used as a surname (*Old Norse*); a diminutive form of **Dermot, Diarmid** (*Irish Gaelic*).

Darcie *fem* form of **Darcy**.

Darcy, D'Arcy *masc* a surname, meaning fortress, used as a first name (*Old French*).

Darell *masc* a variant form of **Darrell**.

Daria *fem* form of **Darius**.

Darien *masc* a South American placename used as a first name.

Dario *masc* the Italian form of **Darius**.

Darius *masc* preserver (*Persian*).

Darlene, Darleen *fem* the endearment 'darling' combined with a suffix to form a first name (*Old English*).

Darnell *masc* a surname,

meaning hidden nook, used as a first name (*Old English*).

Darrell, Darrel *masc* from a surname, meaning from Airelle in Normandy, used as a first name; variant forms are **Darell, Darryl, Daryl**.

Darrelle *fem* form of Darrell (*French*).

Darren, Darin *masc* a surname, of unknown origin, used as a first name.

Darryl a variant form of **Darrell**, also used as a girl's name.

Darton *masc* a surname, meaning deer enclosure or forest, used as a first name (*Old English*).

Daryl a variant form of **Darrell**, also used as a girl's name.

David *masc* beloved (*Hebrew*); diminutive forms are **Dave, Davie, Davy**.

Davidde *masc* the Italian form of David.

Davide *masc* the French form of **David**.

Davie *masc* a diminutive form of **David**.

Davin *masc* a variant form of **Devin**.

Davina *fem* form of **David**.

Davis *masc* David's son (*Old English*).

Davy *masc* a diminutive form of **David**.

Dawn *fem* the name of the first part of the day used as a personal name (*English*).

Dean *masc* a surname, meaning one who lives in a valley (*Old English*) or serving as a dean (*Old French*), used as a first name; the anglicized form of **Dino**.

Deana, Deane *fem* forms of Dean; variant forms are **Dena, Dene**.

Deanna *fem* a variant form of **Diana**.

Dearborn *masc* a surname, meaning deer brook, used as a first name (*Old English*).

Deborah, Debra *fem* bee (*Hebrew*); diminutive forms are **Deb, Debbie, Debby**.

Decima *fem* form of Decimus.

Decimus *masc* tenth (*Latin*).

Declan *masc* the name, of unknown meaning, of a 5th-century Irish saint (*Irish Gaelic*).

Dedrick *masc* people's ruler (*Germanic*).

Dee *fem* a diminutive form of names beginning with D.

Deinol *masc* charming (*Welsh*).

Deirdre *fem* meaning uncertain, possibly sorrowful (*Irish Gaelic*).

Delfine *fem* a variant form of **Delphine**.

Delia *fem* woman of Delos (*Greek*).

Delicia *fem* great delight (*Latin*).

Delight *fem* the abstract noun for great pleasure, satisfaction or joy used as a first name (*Old French*).

Delilah, Delila *fem* meaning uncertain, possibly delicate (*Hebrew*); a variant forms are **Dalila, Dalilah**; a diminutive form is **Lila**.

Dell *masc* a surname, meaning one who lives in a hollow, used as a first name; a diminutive form of **Delmar**, etc.

Delma *fem* form of **Delmar**; a diminutive form of **Fidelma**.

Delmar *masc* of the sea (*Latin*).

Delores *fem* a variant form of **Dolores**.

Delphine *fem* dolphin (*Latin*); a variant form is **Delfine**.

Delwyn, Delwin *masc* neat and blessed (*Welsh*).

Delyth *fem* pretty (*Welsh*).

Demetria *fem* form of **Demeter**.

Demetre *masc* the French form of **Demetrius**.

Demetrio *masc* the Italian form of **Demetrius**.

Demetrius *masc* belonging to Demeter, goddess of the harvest, earth mother (*Greek*).

Dempsey *masc* a surname, meaning proud descendant, used as a first name (*Gaelic*).

Dempster *masc* a surname, meaning judge, used as a first name, formerly a feminine one (*Old English*).

Den *masc* diminutive form of **Denis, Dennis, Denison, Denley, Denman, Dennison, Denton, Denver, Denzel, Denzell, Denzil**.

Dena, Dene *fem* variant forms of **Deana**.

Denby *masc* a surname, meaning Danish settle-

ment, used as a first name
(*Norse*).

Denice *fem* a variant form
of **Denise**.

Denis, Dennis *masc* belonging to Dionysus, the
god of wine (*Greek*).

Denise *fem* form of **Denis**;
a variant form is **Denice**.

Denison *masc* a variant
form of **Dennison**.

Denley *masc* a surname,
meaning wood or clearing
in a valley, used as a first
name (*Old English*).

Denman *masc* a surname,
meaning dweller in a val-
ley, used as a first name
(*Old English*).

Dennison *masc* son of Dennis (*Old English*); variant
forms are **Denison, Tennison, Tennyson**.

Denton *masc* a surname,
meaning valley place, used
as a first name (*Old English*).

Denver *masc* a surname,
meaning Danes' crossing,
used as a first name (*Old
English*).

Denzel, Denzell, Denzil
masc a surname, meaning
stronghold, used as a first
name (*Celtic*).

Deon *masc* a variant form
of **Dion**.

Derek, *masc* an English
form of **Theoderic**; variant
forms are **Derrick, Der-
rik**; a diminutive form is
Derry.

Dermot *masc* the anglicized form of **Diarmaid**; a
diminutive form is **Derry**.

Derrick, Derrik *masc* variant forms of **Derek**; a diminutive form is **Derry**.

Derry *masc* the anglicized
form of a placename, meaning oak wood, used as a
first name (*Irish Gaelic*); a
diminutive form of **Derek,
Derrick, Derrik, Dermot**.

Derwent *masc* a pla-
cename and surname,
meaning river that flows
through oak woods, used as
a first name (*Old English*).

Desdemona *fem* ill-fated
(*Greek*), the name given by
Shakespeare to the wife of
Othello.

Desirée *fem* longed for
(*French*).

Desmond *masc* a varient
form of **Esmond** (*Germanic*).

Deverell, Deverill *masc* a
surname, meaning fertile
river bank, used as a first
name (*Celtic*).

Devin, Devinn *masc* a surname, meaning poet, used as a first name (*Irish Gaelic*); a variant form is **Davin**.

Devlin *masc* fiercely brave (*Irish Gaelic*).

Devon *masc* the name of the English county, meaning deep ones, used as a first name (*Celtic*)

Devona *fem* form of **Devon**.

Dewey *masc* a Celtic form of **David**.

Dewi *masc* a Welsh form of **David**.

De Witt *masc* fair-haired (*Flemish*).

Dexter *masc* a surname, meaning (woman) dyer, used as a first name (*Old English*).

Di *fem* a diminutive form of **Diana, Diane, Dianne, Dina, Dinah**.

Diamond *masc* the name of the gem, meaning the hardest iron or steel, used as a first name (*Latin*).

Diana *fem* goddess (*Latin*); a diminutive form is **Di**.

Diane, Dianne *fem* French forms of **Diana**.

Diarmaid *masc* free of

envy (*Irish Gaelic*); a variant form is **Diarmuid**; the anglized form is **Dermot**.

Diarmid *masc* the Scottish Gaelic form of **Diarmaid**.

Diarmuid *masc* a variant form of **Diarmaid**.

Dick, Dickie, Dickon *masc* diminutive forms of **Richard.**

Dickson *masc* a surname, meaning son of Richard, used as a first name (*Old English*); a variant form is **Dixon**.

Dicky *masc* a diminutive form of **Richard**.

Dido *fem* teacher (*Greek*), in Greek mythology a princess from Tyre who founded Carthage and became its queen.

Diego *masc* a Spanish form of **James**.

Dietrich *masc* the German form of **Derek**; a diminutive form is Till.

Digby *masc* a surname, meaning settlement at a ditch, used as a first name (*Old Norse*).

Dillon *masc* a surname of uncertain meaning, possibly destroyer, used as a first name (*Germanic/Irish Gaelic*).

Dilys *fem* sure, genuine
(*Welsh*); a diminutive form
is **Dilly**.

Dina *fem* form of **Dino**; a
variant form of **Dinah**.

Dinah *fem* vindicated (*He-brew*); a variant form is
Dina; a diminutive form is
Di.

Dino *masc* a diminutive
ending, indicating little,
now used independently
(*Italian*).

Dion *masc* a shortened
form of Dionysus, the god
of wine (*Greek*); a variant
form is **Deon**.

Dione, Dionne *fem* daugh-ter of heaven and earth
(*Greek*), in Greek mytholo-gy the earliest consort of
Zeus and mother of Aphro-dite.

Dirk *masc* the Dutch form
of **Derek**; a diminutive
form of **Theodoric**.

Dixie *fem* a diminutive
form of Benedicta.

Dixon *masc* a variant form
of **Dickson**.

Dodie, Dodo *fem* diminu-tive forms of **Dorothy**.

Dolan *masc* a variant form
of **Doolan**.

Dolina *fem* a Scottish di-minutive form of **Donalda**.

Dolly *fem* a diminutive
form of **Dorothy**.

Dolores *fem* sorrows
(*Spanish*); a variant form is
Delores; diminutive forms
are **Lola, Lolita**.

Dolph *masc* a diminutive
form of **Adolph**.

Domenico *masc* the Italian
form of **Dominic**.

Domingo *masc* the Spanish
form of **Dominic**.

Dominic, Dominick *masc*
belonging to the lord (*Lat-in*); a diminutive form is
Dom.

Dominique *masc* the
French form of **Dominic**,
now used in English as a
girl's name.

Don *masc* a diminutive
form of **Donal, Donald,
Donall**.

Dónal *masc* an Irish Gaelic
form of **Donald**.

Donal *masc* anglicized
forms of **Dónal**; a variant
form is **Donall**; diminutive
forms are **Don, Donnie,
Donny**.

Donald *masc* proud chief
(*Scots Gaelic*); diminutive
forms are **Don, Donnie,
Donny**.

Donalda *fem* form. of **Don-ald**.

Donall *masc* a variant form of **Donal**.

Donata *fem* form of **Donato**.

Donato *masc* gift of God (*Latin*).

Donna *fem* lady (*Italian*).

Donnie, Donny *masc* diminutive forms of **Donal, Donald, Donall**.

Doolan *masc* a surname, meaning black defiance, used as a first name (*Irish Gaelic*); a variant form is **Dolan**.

Dora *fem* a diminutive form of **Dorothea, Theodora**, etc, now used independently; diminutive forms are **Dorrie, Dorry**.

Doran *masc* a surname, meaning stranger or exile, used as a first name (*Irish Gaelic*).

Dorcas *fem* a gazelle (*Greek*).

Doreen *fem* an Irish variant form of **Dora**.

Dorian *masc* Dorian man, one of a Hellenic people who invaded Greece in the 2nd century BC (*Greek*); its use as a first name was probably invented by Oscar Wilde for his novel, *The Picture of Dorian Gray*.

Dorinda *fem* lovely gift (*Greek*); diminutive forms are **Dorrie, Dorry**.

Doris *fem* Dorian woman, one of a Hellenic people who invaded Greece in the 2nd century BC (*Greek*); diminutive forms are **Dorrie, Dorry**.

Dorothea *fem* a German form of **Dorothea**; a diminutive form is **Thea**.

Dorothée *fem* a French form of **Dorothea**.

Dorothy *fem* the gift of God (*Greek*); diminutive forms are **Dodie, Dodo, Dolly, Dot**.

Dorrie, Dorry *fem* diminutive forms of **Dora, Dorinda, Doris**.

Dorward *masc* a variant form of **Durward**.

Dougal, Dougall *masc* black stranger (*Gaelic*); variant forms are **Dugal, Dugald**; diminutive forms are **Doug, Dougie, Duggie**.

Douglas *masc fem* a placename, meaning black water, used as a first name (*Scots Gaelic*); diminutive forms are **Doug, Dougie, Duggie**.

Dow *masc* a surname, meaning black or black-haired, used as a first name (*Scots Gaelic*).

Doyle *masc* an Irish Gaelic form of **Dougal**.

D'Oyley *masc* a surname, meaning from Ouilly—rich land, used as a first name (*Old French*).

Drake *masc* a surname, meaning dragon or standard bearer, used as a first name (*Old English*).

Drew *masc* a diminutive form of **Andrew**; a surname, meaning trusty (*Germanic*) or lover (*Old French*) used as a first name.

Driscoll, Driscol *masc* a surname, meaning interpreter, used as a first name (*Irish Gaelic*).

Druce *masc* a surname, meaning from Eure or Rieux in France (*Old French*), or sturdy lover, used as a first name (*Celtic*).

Drummond *masc* a surname, meaning ridge, used as a first name.

Drury *masc* a surname, meaning dear one, used as a first name (*Old French*).

Drusilla *fem* with dewy eyes (*Latin*).

Dryden *masc* a surname, meaning dry valley, used as a first name (*Old English*).

Duane *masc* dark (*Irish Gaelic*); variant forms are **Dwane, Dwayne**.

Dudley *masc* a placename, meaning Dudda's clearing, used as a first name (*Old English*).

Duff *masc* a surname, meaning black- or dark-complexioned, used as a first name (*Scots Gaelic*).

Dugal, Dugald *masc* variant forms of **Dougal**; a diminutive form is **Duggie**.

Duggie *masc* a diminutive form of **Dougal, Dougald, Douglas, Dugal, Dugald**.

Duke *masc* the title of an English aristocrat used as a first name; a diminutive form of **Marmaduke**.

Dulcie *fem* a diminutive form of **Dulcibella**, meaning sweet beautiful (*Latin*).

Duncan *masc* brown chief (*Gaelic*); a diminutive form is **Dunc**.

Dunlop *masc* a surname, meaning muddy hill, used as a first name (*Scots Gaelic*).

Dunn, Dunne *masc* a surname, meaning dark-skinned, used as a first name (*Old English*).

Dunstan *masc* brown hill stone (*Old English*).

Durand, Durant *masc* a surname, meaning enduring or obstinate, used as a first name (*Old French*).

Durward *masc* a surname, meaning doorkeeper or gatekeeper, used as a first name (*Old English*); a variant form is **Dorward**.

Durwin *masc* Dear friend *Old English*); a diminutive form is **Durwyn**.

Dustin *masc* a surname, of uncertain meaning—possibly of Dionysus, used as a first name.

Dwane, Dwayne *masc* variant forms of **Duane**.

Dwight *masc* a surname, meaning Thor's stone, used as a first name (*Old Norse*).

Dyan *fem* a variant form of **Diane**.

Dyfan *masc* ruler (*Welsh*).

Dylan *masc* sea (*Welsh*).

Dymphna *fem* little fawn (*Irish Gaelic*).

E

Eachan, Eachann, Eacheann *masc* horse (*Scots Gaelic*).

Eamon, Eamonn *masc* an Irish Gaelic form of **Edmund**.

Éanna bird (*Irish Gaelic*); an anglicized form is **Enda**.

Earl, Earle *masc* an English title, meaning nobleman, used as a first name (*Old English*); a variant form is **Erle**.

Earlene, Earline *fem* form of **Earl**; variant forms are **Erlene, Erline**; diminutive forms are **Earlie, Earley**.

Eartha *fem* of the earth (*Old English*); a variant form is **Ertha**.

Easter *fem* the name of the Christian festival, used as a first name.

Eaton ma*sc* a surname, meaning river or island farm, used as a first name (*Old English*).

Ebba *fem* wild boar (*Germanic*); an Old English form of **Eve**.

Eben *masc* stone (*Hebrew*); a diminutive form is **Eb**.

Ebenezer *masc* stone of help (*Hebrew*); diminutive forms are **Eb, Eben**.

Eberhard, Ebert *masc* German forms of **Everard**.

Ebony *fem* the name of the dark hard wood used as a first name.

Echo *fem* the name for the physical phenomenon of the reflection of sound or other radiation used as a first name; in Greek mythology it is the name of the nymph who pined away for love of Narcissus.

Ed *masc* a diminutive form of **Edbert, Edgar, Edmund, Edward, Edwin**.

Eda *fem* prosperity, happiness (*Old English*).

Edan *masc* a Scottish form of **Aidan**.

Edana *fem* form of **Edan**.

Edbert *masc* prosperous; bright (*Old English*).

Eddie, Eddy *masc* diminutive forms of **Edbert, Edgar, Edmund, Edward, Edwin**.

Edel *masc* noble (*Germanic*).

Edelmar *masc* noble, famous (*Old English*)

Eden *masc* pleasantness (*Hebrew*); a surname, meaning blessed helmet, used as a first name.

Edgar *masc* prosperity spear (*Old English*); diminutive forms are **Ed, Eddie, Eddy, Ned, Neddie, Neddy**.

Edie *fem* a diminutive form of **Edina, Edith, Edwina**.

Edina *fem* a Scottish variant form of **Edwina**.

Edith *fem* prosperity strife (*Old English*); variant forms are **Edyth, Edythe**; diminutive forms are **Edie, Edy**.

Edlyn *fem* noble maid (*Old English*).

Edmond *masc* the French form of **Edmund**.

Edmonda *fem* form of Edmund (*Old English*).

Edmund *masc* prosperity defender (*Old English*).

Edna *fem* pleasure (*Hebrew*).

Edoardo *masc* an Italian form of **Edward**.

Édouard *masc* the French form of **Edward**.

Edrea *fem* form of **Edric**.

Edric *masc* wealthy ruler (*Old English*).

Edryd *masc* restoration (*Welsh*).

Edsel *masc* noble (*Germanic*).

Eduardo *masc* the Italian and Spanish form of **Edward**.

Edwald *masc* prosperous ruler (*Old English*).

Edward *masc* guardian of happiness (*Old English*); diminutive forms are **Ed, Eddie, Eddy, Ned, Ted, Teddy**.

Edwardina *fem* form of **Edward**.

Edwige *fem* the French form of **Hedwig**.

Edwin *masc* prosperity friend (*Old English*).

Edwina *fem* form of **Edwin**; a variant form is **Edina**.

Edy *fem* a diminutive form of **Edith**.

Edyth, Edythe *fem* variant forms of **Edith**.

Effie *fem* a diminutive form of **Euphemia**.

Egan *masc* a surname, meaning son of Hugh, used as a first name (*Irish Gaelic*).

Egbert *masc* sword bright (*Germanic*).

Egberta *fem* form of Egbert (*Old English*).

Egidio *masc* the Italian and Spanish form of **Giles**.

Eglantine *fem* an alternative name for the wild rose, meaning sharp, keen, used as a first name (*Old French*).

Ehren *masc* Honourable one (*Germanic*).

Eileen *fem* the Irish form of **Helen**; a variant form is **Aileen**.

Eilidh *fem* a Scots Gaelic form of **Helen**.

Eilir *masc* butterfly (*Welsh*).

Einar *masc* single warrior (*Old Norse*).

Eira *fem* snow (*Welsh*).

Eirlys *fem* snowdrop

(*Welsh*).

Eithne *fem* kernel (*Irish Gaelic*); anglicized forms are **Ena, Ethna**.

Elaine *fem* a French form of **Helen**.

Elder *masc* a surname, meaning senior, elder, used as a first name (*Old English*).

Eldon *masc* a surname, meaning Ella's hill, used as a first name (*Old English*).

Eldora *fem* a shortened form of El Dorado, meaning the land of gold, used as a first name (*Spanish*).

Eldred *masc* terrible (*Old English*).

Eldrida *fem* form.of **Eldrid**.

Eldrid, Eldridge *masc* wise adviser (*Old English*).

Eleanor, Eleanore *fem* variant forms of **Helen**; a variant form is **Elinor**; diminutive forms are **Ella, Nell, Nora**.

Eleanora *fem* the Italian form of **Eleanor**.

Eleazer *masc* a variant form of **Eliezer**..

Electra *fem* brilliant (*Greek*).

Elen *fem* angel, nymph

(*Welsh*).

Elena *fem* the Italian and Spanish form of **Helen**.

Eleonora *fem* the Italian form of **Eleanor**.

Eleonore *fem* the German form of **Eleanor**.

Eléonore *fem* a French form of **Leonora**.

Elfed *masc* autumn (*Welsh*).

Elfleda *fem* noble beauty (*Old English*).

Elfreda *fem* elf strength (*Old English*).

Elga *fem* holy (*Old Norse*); a variant form of **Olga**.

Elgan *masc* bright circle (*Welsh*).

Eli *masc* a diminutive form of **Elias, Elijah, Eliezer**; a variant form is **Ely**.

Elias *masc* a variant form of **Elijah**; a diminutive form is **Eli**.

Eliezer *masc* my God is help (*Hebrew*); a variant form is **Eleazar**.

Elihu *masc* he is my God (*Hebrew*).

Elijah *masc* Jehovah is my God (*Hebrew*); a diminutive form is **Lije**.

Elin *fem* a Welsh diminutive form of **Elinor**; a Welsh variant form of **Helen**.

Elinor *fem* a variant form of **Eleanor**.

Eliot *masc* a variant form of **Elliot**.

Elis *masc* a Welsh form of **Elias**.

Elisa *fem* an Italian diminutive form of **Elisabetta**.

Elisabeth *fem* a French and German form of **Elizabeth**.

Elisabetta *fem* an Italian form of **Elizabeth**.

Élise *fem* a French diminutive form of **Elisabeth**.

Elisha *masc* God is salvation (*Hebrew*).

Elizabeth *fem* worshiper of God; consecrated to God (*Hebrew*); diminutive forms are **Bess, Bet, Beth, Betsy, Betty, Eliza, Elsa, Elsie, Libby, Lisa, Liza, Lisbeth, Liz**.

Ella *fem* a diminutive form of **Cinderella, Eleanor, Isabella**.

Ellen *fem* a variant form of **Helen**.

Ellice *fem* form of **Elias, Ellis**.

Ellie *fem* a diminutive form of **Alice**.

Elliot, Elliot *masc* a surname, from a French diminutive form of Elias, used as a first name.

Ellis *masc* a surname, a Middle English form of **Elias**, used as a first name.

Ellison *masc* a surname, meaning son of Elias, used as a first name (*Old English*).

Elma *fem* a diminutive form of **Wilhelmina**; a contracted form of **Elizabeth Mary**.

Elmer *masc* noble; excellent (*Germanic*)

Elmo *masc* amiable (*Greek*).

Elmore *masc* a surname, meaning river bank with elms, used as a first name (*Old English*).

Éloise, Eloisa *fem* sound, whole (*Germanic*); a variant form is **Héloïse**.

Elroy *masc* a variant form of **Leroy**.

Elsa *fem* a diminutive form of **Alison, Alice, Elizabeth**.

Elsie *fem* a diminutive form of **Alice, Alison, Elizabeth, Elspeth**.

Elspeth, Elspet *fem* Scottish forms of **Elizabeth**; diminutive forms are **Elsie, Elspie**.

Elton *masc* a surname, meaning settlement of Ella, used as a first name (*Old English*).

Eluned *fem* idol (*Welsh*).

Elva *fem* friend of the elf (*Old English*); a variant form is **Elvina**.

Elvey *masc* a surname, meaning elf gift, used as a first name (*Old English*); a variant form is **Elvy**.

Elvin *masc* a surname, meaning elf or noble friend, used as a first name (*Old English*); a variant form is **Elwin**.

Elvina *fem* a variant form of **Elva**.

Elvira *fem* white (*Latin*).

Elvis *masc* wise one (*Norse*).

Elvy *masc* a variant form of **Elvey**.

Elwin *masc* a variant form of **Elvin**; white brow (*Welsh*); a variant form is **Elwyn**.

Emanuel *masc* God with us (*Hebrew*); a variant form is **Immanuel**; a diminutive form is **Manny**.

Emeline *fem* a variant form of **Amelia**; a diminutive form of **Emma**; a variant form is **Emmeline**.

Emerald *fem* the name of the green gemstone used as a first name.

Emery *masc* a variant form of **Amory**.

Emil *masc* of a noble Roman family the origin of whose name, *Aemilius*, is uncertain.

Émile *masc* the French form of **Emil**.

Emilia *fem* the Italian form of **Emily**.

Emilie *fem* the German form of **Emily**.

Émilie *fem* the French form of **Emily**.

Emilio *masc* the Italian, Spanish and Portuguese form of **Emil**.

Emily *fem* of a noble Roman family the origin of whose name, *Aemilius*, is uncertain.

Emlyn *masc* origin uncertain, possibly from **Emil** (*Welsh*).

Emma *fem* whole, universal (*Germanic*); diminutive forms are **Emm, Emmie**.

Emmeline *fem* a variant

form of **Emeline**.

Emery *masc* a variant form of **Amory**.

Emmet, Emmett, Emmot, Emmott *masc* a surname, from a diminutive form of Emma, used as a first name.

Emory *masc* a variant form of **Amory**.

Emrys *masc* a Welsh form of **Ambrose**.

Emyr *masc* a Welsh form of **Honorius**.

Ena *fem* an anglicized form of **Eithne**.

Enda *fem* an anglicized form of **Éanna**.

Eneas *masc* a variant form of **Aeneas**.

Enée *masc* the French form of **Aeneas**.

Enfys *fem* rainbow (*Welsh*).

Engelbert *masc* bright angel (*Germanic*).

Engelberta, Engelbertha, Engelberthe *fem* forms of **Engelbert**.

Enid *fem* meaning uncertain, possibly woodlark(*Welsh*).

Ennis *masc* chief one (*Gaelic*).

Enoch *masc* dedication (*Hebrew*).

Enos *masc* man (*Hebrew*).

Enrica *fem* the Italian form of **Henrietta**.

Enrichetta *fem* the Italian form of **Henrietta**.

Enrico *masc* the Italian form of **Henry**.

Enrique *masc* the Spanish form of **Henry**.

Enriqueta *fem* the Spanish form of **Henrietta**.

Eoghan *masc* an Irish Gaelic form of **Eugene**.

Eoin *masc* an Irish form of **John**.

Ephraim *masc* fruitful (*Hebrew*); a diminutive form is **Eph**.

Eranthe *fem* flower of spring (*Greek*).

Erasmus *masc* lovely; worthy of love (*Greek*); a diminutive form is **Ras, Rasmus**.

Erastus *masc* beloved (*Greek*); diminutive forms are **Ras, Rastus**.

Ercole *masc* the Italian form of **Hercules**.

Erda *fem* of the earth (*Germanic*).

Eric *masc* rich; brave; powerful (*Old English*); a variant form is **Erik**.

Erica *fem* form of **Eric**; a variant form is **Erika**.

Erich *masc* the German form of **Eric**.

Erik *masc* a variant form of **Eric**.

Erika *fem* a variant form of **Erica**.

Erin *fem* the poetic name for Ireland used as a first name.

Erland *masc* stranger (*Old Norse*).

Erle *masc* a variant form of **Earl**.

Erlene, Erline *fem* variant forms of **Earlene, Erline**; diminutive forms are **Erlie, Erley**.

Erma *fem* warrior maid (*Germanic*).

Ern *masc* a diminutive form of **Ernest**.

Erna *fem* a diminutive form of **Ernesta, Ernestine**.

Ernest *masc* earnestness (*Germanic*); diminutive forms are **Ern, Ernie**.

Ernesta *fem* form of **Ernest**; a diminutive form is **Erna**.

Ernestine *fem* form of **Ernest**; diminutive forms are **Erna, Tina**.

Ernesto *masc* the Italian and Spanish forms of **Ernest**.

Ernst *masc* the German form of **Ernest**.

Erskine *masc* a placename and surname, meaning projecting height, used as a first name (*Scots Gaelic*).

Erwin *masc* friend of honour (*Germanic*); a surname, meaning wild-boar friend (*French*), used as a first name; a variant form is **Orwin**.

Eryl *masc* watcher (*Welsh*).

Esau *masc* hairy (*Hebrew*).

Esmé *masc, fem* beloved (*French*).

Esmeralda *fem* a Spanish form of **Emerald**.

Esmond *masc* divine protection (*Old English*).

Esta *fem* a variant form of **Esther**.

Este *masc* Man from the East (*Italian*).

Estéban *masc* the Spanish form of **Stephen**.

Estelle, Estella *fem* variant forms of **Stella**.

Ester *fem* the Italian and Spanish forms of **Esther**.

Esther *fem* the planet Venus (*Persian*); a variant form is **Esta**; diminutive forms are **Ess, Essie, Tess, Tessie**.

Estrella *fem* the Spanish form of **Estelle**.

Ethan *masc* firm (*Hebrew*).

Ethel *fem* noble; of noble birth (*Old English*).

Ethna *fem* an anglicized form of **Eithne**.

Etienne *masc* the French form of **Stephen**.

Etta, Ettie *fem* diminutive forms of **Henrietta**.

Ettore *masc* the Italian form of **Hector**.

Euan *masc* a variant form of **Ewan**.

Eudora *fem* good gift (*Greek*).

Eufemia *fem* the Italian and Spanish form of **Euphemia**.

Eugen *masc* the German form of **Eugene**.

Eugene *masc* well-born; noble (*Greek*); a diminutive form is **Gene**.

Eugène *masc* the French form of **Eugene**.

Eugenia *fem* form of **Eugene**; diminutive forms are **Ena, Gene**.

Eugénie *fem* the French form of **Eugenia**.

Eulalie*fem* fair speech (*Greek*).

Eunice *fem* good victory (*Greek*).

Euphemia *fem* of good report (*Greek*); diminutive forms are **Fay, Effie, Phamie, Phemie**.

Eurig, Euros *masc* gold (*Welsh*).

Eusebio *masc* pious (*Greek*).

Eustace *masc* rich (*Greek*); diminutive forms are **Stacey, Stacy**.

Eustache *masc* the French form of **Eustace**.

Eustachio *masc* the Italian form of **Eustace**.

Eustacia *fem* form of **Eustace**; diminutive forms are **Stacey, Stacie, Stacy**.

Eustaquio *masc* the Spanish form of **Eustace**.

Eva *fem* the German, Italian, and Spanish forms of **Eve**.

Evadne *fem* of uncertain meaning, possibly highborn (*Greek*).

Evan *masc* young warrior (*Celtic*).

Evangeline *fem* of the Gospel (*Greek*).

Eve *fem* life (*Hebrew*); diminutive forms are **Evie, Evelina, Eveline, Eveleen**.

Eveline *fem* a diminutive form of **Eva, Eve**.

Evelyn *masc fem* the English surname used as a first name.

Everard *masc* strong boar (*Germanic*).

Everley *masc* Field of the wild boar (*Old English*).

Evita *fem* Spanish diminutive form of **Eva**.

Evodia *fem* good journey (*Greek*).

Ewan, Ewen *masc* Irish and Scots Gaelic forms of **Owen**; a Scottish form of **Eugene**; a variant form is **Euan**.

Ewart *masc* an Old French variant of **Edward**; a surname, meaning herd of ewes used as a surname(*Old English*).

Ezekiel *masc* strength of God (*Hebrew*); a diminutive form is **Zeke**.

Ezra *masc* help (*Hebrew*).

F

Fabia *fem* form of **Fabio**; a variant form is **Fabiola**.

Fabian *masc* the anglicized form of the Roman family name *Fabianus*, derived from *Fabius*, from *faba*, bean (*Latin*).

Fabián *masc* the Spanish form of **Fabian**.

Fabiano *masc* the Italian form of **Fabian**.

Fabien *masc* the French form of **Fabian**.

Fabienne *fem* form of **Fabien**.

Fabio *masc* the Italian form of the Roman family name *Fabius*, from *faba*, bean.

Fabiola *fem* a variant form of **Fabia**.

Faber, Fabre *masc* a surname, meaning smith, used as a first name (*Latin*).

Fabrice *masc* the French form of the Roman family *Fabricius*, from *faber*, smith.

Fabrizio *masc* the Italian form of **Fabrice**.

Fairfax *masc* the surname, meaning lovely hair, used as a first name (*Old English*).

Fairley, Fairlie *masc* a surname, meaning clearing with ferns, used as a first name (*Old English*).

Faith *fem* the quality of belief or fidelity used as a first name.

Fanchon *fem* a diminutive form of **Françoise**.

Fane *masc* a surname, meaning glad or eager, used as a first name (*Old English*).

Fanny *fem* a diminutive form of **Frances**, also used independently.

Farnall, Farnell *masc* a surname, meaning fern hill, used as a first name(*Old English*); variant forms are **Fernald, Fernall**.

Farquhar *masc* dear man

275

(Scots Gaelic).

Farr *masc* a surname, meaning bull, used as a first name *(Old English).*

Farrell *masc* warrior *(Irish Gaelic).*

Faustina, Faustine *fem* lucky *(Latin).*

Fatima *fem* the name of the daughter of Mohammed *(Semitic)*; of Fatima in Portugal *(Portuguese).*

Favor, Favour *fem* an abstract noun, meaning good will or an act of good will, from *favere*, to protect, used as a first name *(Latin).*

Fawn *fem* the name for a young deer or a light greyish-brown colour used as a first name *(Old French).*

Fay, Faye *fem* faith or fairy *(Old French)*; a diminutive form of **Euphemia**.

Federico *masc* an Italian and Spanish form of **Frederick**.

Felice *masc* the Italian form of **Felix**.

Felicia *fem* form of **Felix**.

Felicidad *fem* the Spanish form of **Felicia**.

Felicie *fem* the Italian form of **Felicia**.

Felicity *fem* happiness *(Latin).*

Felipe *masc* the Spanish form of **Philip**.

Felix *masc* happy *(Latin).*

Felton *masc* a placename and surname, meaning place in a field, used as a first name *(Old English).*

Fenella *fem* an anglicized form of **Fionnuala**.

Fenton *masc* a placename and surname, meaning a place in marshland or fens, used as a first name *(Old English).*

Ferdinand *masc* peace bold *(Germanic)*; diminutive forms are **Ferd, Ferdy**.

Ferdinando *masc* an Italian form of **Ferdinand**.

Fergal *masc* man of strength *(Irish Gaelic)*; diminutive forms are **Fergie, Fergy**.

Fergie *masc* a diminutive form of **Fergal, Fergus, Ferguson**; *fem* a diminutive form of **Ferguson** as a surname; a variant form is **Fergy**.

Fergus *masc* vigorous man *(Irish/Scots Gaelic)*; diminutive forms are **Fergie, Fergy**.

Ferguson, Fergusson
masc a surname, meaning
son of Fergus, used as a
first name; diminutive
forms are **Fergie, Fergy**.

Fergy *masc*, *fem* a variant
form of **Fergie**.

Fern *fem* the name of the
plant used as a first name
(*Old English*).

Fernald, Fernall *masc*
variant forms of **Farnall,
Farnell**.

Fernand *masc* a French
form of **Ferdinand**.

Fernanda *fem* form of
Ferdnand.

Fernando *masc* a Spanish
form of **Ferdinand**.

Ffion *fem* foxglove (*Welsh*).

Fid *fem* a diminutive form
of **Fidelia, Fidelis**.

Fidel *masc* a Spanish form
of **Fidelis**.

Fidèle *masc* a French form
of **Fidelis**.

Fidelia *fem* a variant form
of **Fidelis**; a diminutive
form is **Fid**.

Fidelio *masc* an Italian
form of **Fidelis**.

Fidelis *masc*, *fem* faithful
(*Latin*); a *fem* variant form
is **Fidelia**; a diminutive
form is **Fid**.

Fidelma *fem* faithful Mary
(*Latin/Irish Gaelic*); a diminutive form is **Delma**.

Fielding *masc* a surname,
meaning dweller in a field,
used as a first name (*Old
English*).

Fifi *fem* a French diminutive form of **Josephine**.

Filippo *masc* the Italian
form of **Philip**.

Filippa *fem* the Italian
form of **Philippa**.

Findlay *masc* a variant
form of **Finlay**.

Fingal *masc* white stranger
(*Scots Gaelic*).

Finlay, Finley *masc* fair
warrior or calf (*Scots Gaelic*); a variant form is **Findlay**.

Finn *masc* fair, white (*Irish
Gaelic*); a variant form is
Fionn.

Finola *fem* a variant form
of **Fionnuala**.

Fiona *fem* white, fair (*Scots
Gaelic*).

Fionn *masc* a variant form
of **Finn**.

Fionnuala *fem* white
shoulder (*Irish Gaelic*); a
diminutive form is **Nuala**,
also used independently.

Fiske *masc* a surname,

meaning fish, used as a first name (*Old English*).

Fitch *masc* a surname, meaning point, used as a first name (*Old English*).

Fitz *masc* son (*Old French*); a diminutive form of names beginning with Fitz-.

Fitzgerald *masc* a surname, meaning son of Gerald, used as a first name (*Old French*); a diminutive form is **Fitz**.

Fitzhugh *masc* a surname, meaning son of Hugh, used as a first name (*Old French*); a diminutive form is **Fitz**.

Fitzpatrick *masc* a surname, meaning son of Patrick, used as a first name (*Old French*); a diminutive form is **Fitz**.

Fitzroy *masc* a surname, meaning (illegitimate) son of the king, used as a first name (*Old French*); a diminutive form is **Fitz**.

Flann *masc* red-haired (*Irish Gaelic*).

Flanna *fem* form of **Flann**.

Flannan *masc* red-complexioned (*Irish Gaelic*).

Flavia *fem* yellow-haired, golden (*Latin*).

Flavian, Flavius *masc*

forms of Flavia.

Fleming *masc* a surname, meaning man from Flanders, used as a first name (*Old French*).

Fletcher *masc* a surname meaning arrow-maker, used as a first name (*Old French*).

Fleur *fem* a flower (*French*).

Fleurette *fem* little flower (*French*).

Flinn *masc* a variant form of **Flynn**.

Flint *masc* stream, brook (*Old English*).

Flo *fem* a diminutive form of **Flora, Florence**.

Flora *fem* flowers; the Roman goddess of flowers (*Latin*); diminutive forms are **Flo, Florrie, Flossie**.

Florence *fem* blooming; flourishing (*Latin*); diminutive forms are **Flo, Florrie, Flossie, Floy**.

Florian *masc* flowering, blooming (*Latin*).

Florrie, Flossie *fem* diminutive forms of **Flora, Florence**.

Flower *fem* the English word for a bloom or blossom used as a first name.

Floy *fem* a diminutive form of **Flora, Florence**.

Floyd *masc* a variant form of the surname Lloyd used as a first name.

Flynn *masc* a surname, meaning son of the red-haired one, used as a first name (*Scots Gaelic*); a variant form is **Flinn**.

Forbes *masc* a placename and surname, meaning fields or district, used as a first name (*Scots Gaelic*).

Ford *masc* the English word for a crossing place of a river used as a first name (*Old English*).

Forrest, Forrestt *masc* a surname, meaning forest, used as a first name (*Old French*).

Forrester, Forster *masc* a surname, meaning forester, used as a first name (*Old French*).

Fortune *fem* the word for wealth, fate or chance used as a first name (*Latin*); a variant form is **Fortuna**.

Foster *masc* a surname, meaning forester or cutler (*Old French*) or foster parent (*Old English*), used as a first name.

Fra *masc* a diminutive form of **Francis**.

Fraine *masc* a variant form of **Frayn**.

Fran *fem* a diminutive form of **Frances**.

Franca *fem* a diminutive form of **Francesca**.

Frances *fem* form of **Francis**; diminutive forms are **Fanny, Fran, Francie**.

Francesca *fem* the Italian form of **Frances**; a diminutive form is **Francheschina**.

Francesco *masc* the Italian form of **Francis**; a contracted form is **Franco**.

Francie *fem* a diminutive form of **Frances**.

Francine *fem* a diminutive form of **Frances, Françoise**.

Francis *masc* free (*Germanic*); diminutive forms are **Fra, Frank, Francie**.

Francisca *fem* the Spanish form of **Frances**.

Francisco *masc* the Spanish form of **Francis**.

Franco *masc* a contracted form of **Francesco**.

François *masc* the French form of **Francis**.

Françoise *fem* the French form of **Frances**.

Frank *masc* Frenchman (*Old French*) a diminutive form of **Francis**, **Franklin**; diminutive forms are **Frankie**, **Franky**.

Franklin, **Franklen**, **Franklyn** *masc* a surname, meaning freeholder, used as a first name (*Old French*); diminutive forms are **Frank**, **Frankie**, **Franky**.

Frans *masc* the Swedish form of **Francis**.

Franz, **Franziskus** *masc* German forms of **Francis**.

Franziska *masc* the German form of **Frances**.

Fraser, **Frasier** *masc* a Scottish surname, meaning from Frisselle or Fresel in France—possibly strawberry, used as a first name (*French*); variant forms are **Frazer**, **Frazier**.

Frayn, **Frayne** *masc* a surname, meaning ash tree, used as a surname (*Old French*); a variant form is **Fraine**.

Frazer, **Frazier** *masc* variant forms of **Fraser**.

Freda *fem* a diminutive form of **Winifred**; a variant form of **Frieda**.

Frédéric *masc* the French form of **Frederick**.

Frederica *fem* form of **Frederick**; diminutive forms are **Fred**, **Freddie**, **Freddy**, **Frieda**.

Frederick, **Frederic** *masc* abounding in peace; peaceful ruler (*Germanic*); diminutive forms are **Fred**, **Freddie**, **Freddy**.

Frédérique *fem* the French form of **Frederica**.

Fredrik *masc* the Swedish form of **Frederick**.

Freeman *masc* a surname, meaning free man, used as first name (*Old English*).

Frewin *masc* a surname, meaning generous friend, used as a first name (*Old English*).

Freya *fem* lady, the Norse goddess of love (*Norse*).

Frieda *fem* peace (*Germanic*); a diminutive form of **Frederica**.

Friede *fem* the German form of **Frieda**.

Friederike *fem* the German form of **Frederica**; a diminutive form is **Fritzi**.

Friedrich *masc* German forms of **Frederick**; a diminutive form is **Fritz**.

Fritz *masc* a diminutive form of **Friedrich**, also used independently.

Fritzi *fem* a diminutive form of **Friederike**.

Fulton *masc* a surname, meaning muddy place, used as a first name (*Old English*).

Fulvia *fem* yellow-haired (*Latin*).

Fyfe, Fyffe *masc* a surname, meaning from Fife, used as a first name.

G

Gabbie, Gabby *fem* diminutive forms of **Gabrielle**.

Gabe *masc* diminutive form of **Gabriel**.

Gabriel *masc* strength of God; man of God; in the Bible one of the archangels (*Hebrew*); a diminutive form is **Gabe**.

Gabrielle *fem* form of **Gabriel**; diminutive forms are **Gabbie, Gabby**.

Gad *masc* good luck, good fortune (*Hebrew*).

Gaea *fem* the Latin form of **Gaia**.

Gaia *fem* earth, in classical mythology the goddess of the earth (*Greek*); the Latin form is **Gaea**.

Gail *fem* a diminutive form of **Abigail**, now used independently; variant forms are **Gale, Gayle**.

Galatea *fem* white as milk, in Greek mythology a statue brought to life (*Greek*)

Gale *fem* a variant form of **Gail**; *masc* a surname,

meaning jail, used as a first name (*Old French*).

Galen *masc* the anglicized form of the Roman family name *Galenus*, calmer (*Latin*).

Galia *fem* wave (*Hebrew*).

Gallagher *masc* a surname, meaning foreign helper, used as a first name (*Irish Gaelic*).

Galloway *masc* a placename and surname, meaning stranger Gaels, used as a first name (*Old Welsh*).

Galton *masc* a surname, meaning rented farm, used as a first name (*Old English*).

Galvin *masc* bright, white (*Irish Gaelic*).

Gamaliel *masc* recompense of God (*Hebrew*).

Gardenia *fem* the name of a flowering plant with fragrant flowers, called after Dr Alexander Garden, used as a first name (*New Lat-*

in).

Gareth *masc* old man
(*Welsh*); diminutive forms
are **Gary, Garry**; a variant
form is **Garth**.

Garfield *masc* a surname,
meaning triangular piece of
open land, used as a first
name (*Old English*).

Garland *fem* the name for
a wreath or crown of flowers used as a first name
(*Old French*); *masc* a surname, meaning a maker of
metal garlands, used as a
first name (*Old English*).

Garnet *fem* the name of a
deep-red gemstone used as
a first name (*Old French*).

Garnet, Garnett *masc* a
surname, meaning pome-
granate, used as a first
name (*Old French*).

Garrard *masc* a variant
form of **Gerard**.

Garret, Garrett *masc* the
Irish Gaelic form of **Gerard**; a variant form of **Garrard**.

Garrison *masc* a surname,
meaning son of Garret,
used as a first name (*Old
English*).

Garry *masc* a variant form
of **Gary**; a placename,
meaning ——, used as a
first name (*Scots Gaelic*).

Garth *masc* a surname,
meaning garden or pad-
dock, used as a first name
(*Old Norse*); a variant form
of **Gareth**.

Garton *masc* a surname,
meaning fenced farm, used
as a first name (*Old Norse*).

Garve *masc* a placename,
meaning rough place, used
as a first name (*Scots Gaelic*).

Gary *masc* spear carrier
(*Germanic*); a diminutive
form of **Gareth**; a variant
form is **Garry**.

Gaspard *masc* the French
form of **Jasper**.

Gaston *masc* stranger,
guest (*Germanic*); from
Gascony (*Old French*).

Gautier, Gauthier *masc*
French forms of **Walter**.

Gavin *masc* an anglicized
form of **Gawain**.

Gawain *masc* white hawk
(*Welsh*).

Gay *fem* the quality of being joyous used as a first
name; *masc* an Irish diminutive form of **Gabriel**.

Gayle *fem* a variant form of
Gail.

Gaylord *masc* a surname,
meaning brisk noble man,

used as a first name (*Old French*).

Gaynor *fem* a medieval English form of **Guinevere**.

Gazella *fem* like a gazelle or antelope (*Latin*).

Gemma *fem* a gem (*Italian*); a variant form is **Jemma**.

Gene *masc* a diminutive form of **Eugene**, now used independently.

Geneva *fem* a variant form of **Genevieve**; the name of a Swiss city used as a first name.

Genevieve *fem* meaning uncertain, possibly tribe woman (*Celtic*).

Geneviève *fem* the French form of **Genevieve**.

Geoffrey *masc* a variant form of **Jeffrey**; a diminutive form is **Geoff**.

Georg *masc* the German form of **George**.

George *masc* a landholder; husbandman (*Germanic*); diminutive forms are **Geordie, Georgie, Georgy**.

Georges *masc* the French form of **George**.

Georgia, Georgiana,

Georgina *fem* forms of **George**; a diminutive form is **Georgie**.

Geraint *masc* old man (*Welsh*).

Gerald *masc* strong with the spear (*Germanic*); diminutive forms are **Gerrie, Gerry, Jerry**.

Geraldine *fem* form of **Gerald**.

Gerard *masc* firm spear (*Old German*); variant forms are **Garrard, Garratt, Gerrard**; diminutive forms are **Gerrie, Gerry, Jerry**.

Gérard *masc* the French form of **Gerard**.

Gerardo *masc* the Italian form of **Gerard**.

Géraud *masc* a French form of **Gerald**.

Gerhard *masc* the German form of **Gerard**.

Gerhold *masc* a German form of **Gerald**.

Germain *masc* brother (*Latin*).

Germaine *fem* form of **Germain**; a variant form is **Jermaine**.

Geronimo, Gerolamo *masc* Italian forms of **Jerome**.

Gerrie, Gerry *masc fem* diminutive forms of **Gerald, Geraldine, Gerard.**

Gershom *masc* an exile (*Hebrew*).

Gertrude *fem* spear maiden (*Germanic*); diminutive forms are **Gert, Gertie, Trudi, Trudy.**

Gervais *masc* the French form of **Gervase.**

Gervaise *masc* a variant form of **Gervase.**

Gervas *masc* the German form of **Gervase.**

Gervase, Gervaise *masc* spearman (*Germanic*); variant forms are **Gervaise, Jarvis, Jervis.**

Gervasio *masc* the Italian, Portuguese and Spanish form of **Gervase.**

Gethin *masc* dusky (*Welsh*).

Giacomo *masc* an Italian form of **James.**

Gian, Gianni *masc* diminutive forms of **Giovanni.**

Gibson *masc* a surname, meaning son of Gilbert, used as a first name (*Old English*).

Gideon *masc* a destroyer (*Hebrew*).

Giffard, Gifford *masc* a surname, meaning bloated (*Old French*) or gift (*Germanic*).

Gigi *fem* a French diminutive form of **Georgine, Virginie.**

Gil *masc* a diminutive form of **Gilbert, Gilchrist, Giles**; a Spanish form of **Giles.**

Gilbert *masc* yellow-bright; famous (*Germanic*); diminutive forms are **Gil.**

Gilberta, Gilberte *fem* forms of **Gilbert**; diminutive forms are **Gill, Gillie, Gilly.**

Gilchrist *masc* servant of Christ (*Scots Gaelic*); a diminutive form is **Gil.**

Gilda *fem* sacrifice (*Germanic*).

Giles *masc* a kid (*Greek*); a diminutive form is **Gil.**

Gill *fem* a diminutive form of **Gilberta, Gilberte, Gillian.**

Gilles *masc* the French form of **Giles.**

Gillespie *masc* a surname, meaning servant of a bishop, used as a first name (*Scots Gaelic*).

Gillian *fem* form of **Julian**; diminutive forms are **Gill, Gillie, Gilly.**

Gillie *fem* a diminutive form of **Gilberta, Gilberte, Gillian**.

Gillmore *masc* a variant form of **Gilmore**.

Gilly *fem* a diminutive form of **Gilberta, Gilberte, Gillian**.

Gilmore, Gilmour *masc* a surname, meaning servant of St Mary, used as a first name (*Scots Gaelic*); a variant form is **Gillmore**.

Gilroy *masc* a surname, meaning servant of the red haired one, used as a first name (*Gaelic*).

Gina *fem* a diminutive form of **Georgina**, also used independently.

Ginnie, Ginny *fem* a diminutive form of **Virginia**.

Gioacchino *masc* the Italian form of **Joachim**.

Giorgio *masc* the Italian form of **George**.

Giovanna *fem* the Italian form of **Jane**.

Giovanni *masc* the Italian form of **John**; diminutive forms are **Gian, Gianni**.

Gipsy *fem* a variant form of **Gypsy**.

Giraldo *masc* the Italian form of **Gerald**.

Giraud, Girauld *masc* French forms of **Gerald**.

Girolamo *masc* an Italian form of **Jerome**.

Girvan *masc* a placename, meaning short river, used as a first name (*Scots Gaelic*).

Gisela *fem* the Dutch and German form of **Giselle**.

Gisèle *fem* the French form of **Giselle**.

Giselle *fem* promise, pledge (*Germanic*)

Gitana *fem* gipsy (*Spanish*).

Giulio *masc* the Italian form of **Julius**.

Giuseppe *masc* the Italian form of **Joseph**; a diminutive form is **Beppe, Beppo**.

Gladwin *masc* a surname, meaning glad friend, used as a first name (*Old English*).

Gladys *fem* the anglicized Welsh form of **Claudia**.

Glanville *masc* Dweller on the oak tree estate (*French*); a diminutive form is **Glanvil**.

Gleda *fem* Old English version of Gladys (*Old English*).

Glen *masc* the surname, meaning a valley, used as a first name (*Scots Gaelic*); a variant form is **Glenn**.

Glenda *fem* clean and good (*Welsh*); a variant form is **Glenys**.

Glendon *masc* From the fortress in the Glen (*Celtic*).

Glenn *masc* a variant form of **Glen**, now also used as a feminine name.

Glenna *fem* form of **Glen**.

Glenys *fem* a variant form of **Glenda**; a variant form is **Glynis**.

Gloria *fem* glory (*Latin*).

Glyn *masc* valley (*Welsh*); a variant form is **Glynn**.

Glynis *fem* form of **Glyn**; a variant form of **Glenys**.

Glynn *masc* a variant form of **Glyn**.

Goddard *masc* pious; virtuous (*Old German*).

Godfrey *masc* at peace with God (*Germanic*).

Godiva *fem* gift of God (*Old English*)**u**.

Godwin *masc* God's friend (*Old English*).

Golda, Golde *fem* gold (*Yiddish*).

Goldie *fem* an anglized form of **Golda**; fair-haired (*English*).

Golding *masc* a surname, meaning son of gold, used as a first name (*Old English*).

Goldwin *masc* Golden friend (*Old English*).

Goliath *masc* mighty warrior (*Hebrew*).

Goodwin *masc* a surname, meaning good friend, used as a first name; (*Old English*).

Gordon *masc* a surname, meaning great hill, used as a first name (*Scots Gaelic*).

Gottfried *masc* the German form of **Godfrey**; a diminutive form is **Götz**.

Grace *fem* grace (*Latin*); a diminutive form is **Gracie**.

Grady *masc* a surname, meaning noble, used as a first name (*Irish Gaelic*).

Graham, Grahame, Graeme *masc* a Scottish surname, meaning gravelly homestead, used as a first name (*Old English*).

Gráinne *fem* love (*Irish Gaelic*).

Granger *masc* a surname, meaning farmer or bailiff, used as a first name (*Old English*).

Grant *masc* a surname, meaning large, used as a first name (*Norman French*).

Granville *masc* large town (*Old French*).

Gray *masc* a surname, meaning grey-haired, used as a first name (*Old English*); a variant form is **Grey**.

Greeley *masc* a surname, meaning pitted, used as a first name (*Old English*).

Greer *fem* form of the surname **Grier**.

Grégoire *masc* the French form of **Gregory**.

Gregor *masc* a Scots form of **Gregory**.

Gregorio *masc* the Italian and Spanish form of **Gregory**.

Gregory *masc* watchful; vigilant (*Greek*); a diminutive form is **Greg**.

Gresham *masc* a surname, meaning grazing meadow, used as a first name (*Old English*).

Greta *fem* a diminutive form of **Margaret**.

Gretchen *fem* a diminutive form of **Margaret, Margarete**.

Grete *fem* a diminutive form of **Margarete**.

Greville *masc* a surname, meaning from Gréville in France, used as a first name.

Grier *masc*, *fem* a surname, a contracted form of **Gregor**, used as a first name; a variant *fem* form is **Greer**.

Griff *masc* a diminutive form of **Griffin, Griffith**.

Griffin *masc* a Latinized form of **Griffith**; a diminutive form is **Griff**.

Griffith *masc* an anglicized form of **Gruffydd**; a diminutive form is **Griff**.

Griselda, Grizelda *fem* stone heroine (*Germanic*); diminutive forms are **Grissel, Grizel, Grizzel**.

Grover *masc* a surname, meaning from a grove of trees, used as a first name (*Old English*).

Gruffydd *masc* powerful chief (*Welsh*).

Gualterio *masc* the Spanish form of **Walter**.

Gualtieri *masc* the Italian form of **Walter**.

Gudrun *fem* God's secret (*Old Norse*)**a**.

Guglielmo *masc* the Italian form of **William**.

Guido *masc* the German, Italian, and Spanish forms of **Guy**.

Guilbert *masc* a French form of **Gilbert**.

Guillaume *masc* the French form of **William**.

Guillermo, Guillelmo *masc* Spanish forms of **William**.

Guinevere *fem* white and soft, the name of the wife of King Arthur (*Welsh*).

Gunhilda, Gunhilde *fem* warrior maid (*Old Norse*).

Gunnar *masc* the Scandinavian form of **Gunter**.

Gunter *masc* battle warrior (*Germanic*).

Günther *masc* the German form of **Gunter**.

Gus *masc* a diminutive form of **Angus, Augustus, Gustave**.

Gussie, Gusta *fem* diminutive forms of **Augusta**.

Gustaf *masc* the Swedish form of **Gustave**.

Gustave *masc* staff of the Goths (*Swedish*); a diminutive form is **Gus**.

Guthrie *masc* a surname, meaning windy, used as a first name (*Scots Gaelic*).

Guy *masc* a leader (*German-French*).

Guyon *masc* a French form of **Guy**.

Gwenda *fem* a diminutive form of **Gwendolen**, also used independently.

Gwendolen, Gwendolin, Gwendolyn *fem* white ring or bow (*Welsh*); diminutive forms are **Gwen, Gwenda, Gwennie**.

Gwillym, Gwilym *masc* Welsh forms of **William**.

Gwyn, Gwynn *masc* fair, blessed (*Welsh*); diminutive forms are **Gwyn, Guin**.

Gwyneth *fem* blessed (*Welsh*).

Gwynfor *masc* fair lord (*Welsh*).

Gypsy *fem* the name for a member of a people who live a nomadic life used as a first name; a variant form is **Gipsy**.

H

Haakon *masc* a variant form of **Hakon**.

Hackett *masc* a surname, meaning little woodcutter, used as a first name (*Old Norse*).

Haddan, Hadden, Haddon *masc* a surname, meaning heathery hill, used as a first name (*Old English*).

Hadley *masc* a surname, meaning heathery hill or heathery meadow, used as a first name (*Old English*).

Hadrian *masc* a variant form of **Adrian**.

Hagar *fem* flight (*Hebrew*).

Hagan, Hagan *masc* young Hugh (*Irish Gaelic*); thorn bush or thorn fence (*Germanic*).

Hagley *masc* a surname, meaning haw wood or clearing, used as a first name (*Old English*).

Haidee *fem* modest, honoured (*Greek*); a variant form of **Heidi**.

Haig *masc* a first name, meaning one who lives in an enclosure, used as a first name (*Old English*).

Hakon *masc* from the exalted race (*Old Norse*); a variant form is **Haakon**; a diminutive form is **Hako**.

Hal *masc* a diminutive form of **Halbert, Henry**.

Halbert *masc* brilliant hero (*Old English*); a diminutive form is **Hal**.

Halcyon, Halcyone *fem* variant forms of **Alcyone**.

Haldan, Haldane, Halden, Haldin *fem* a surname, meaning half Dane, used as a surname (*Old English*).

Hale *masc* a surname, meaning from the hall, used as a surname (*Old English*).

Haley *masc, fem* a variant form of **Hayley**.

Halford *masc* a surname, meaning from a ford in a hollow, used as a first

name (*Old English*).

Haliwell *masc* a variant form of **Halliwell**.

Hall *masc* a surname, meaning one who lives at a manor house, used as a first name (*Old English*).

Hallam *masc* a surname, meaning at the hollow (*Old English*), or a placename, meaning at the rocky place (*Old Norse*), used as a first name.

Halliwell *masc* a surname, meaning one who lives by the holy well, used as a first name (*Old English*); a variant form is **Haliwell**.

Halstead, Halsted *masc* a surname, meaning from the stronghold, used as a first name (*Old English*).

Halton *masc* a surname, meaning from the lookout hill, used as a first name (*Old English*).

Hamar *masc* strong man (*Old Norse*).

Hamilton *masc* a surname, meaning farm in broken country, used as a first name. (*Old English*).

Hamish *masc* a Scots Gaelic form of **James**.

Hamlet, Hamlett *masc* a surname, meaning little

home, used as a first name (*Germanic*).

Hammond *masc* a surname, meaning belonging to Hamon, used as a first name (*Old English*).

Hamon *masc* great protection (*Old English*).

Hanford *masc* a surname, meaning rocky ford or ford with cocks, used as a first name (*Old English*).

Hank *masc* a diminutive form of **Henry**.

Hanley *masc* a surname, meaning from the high meadow or hill, used as a first name (*Old English*).

Hannah *fem* grace (*Hebrew*); a variant form is **Ann**; a diminutive form is **Nana**.

Hannibal *masc* grace of Baal (*Punic*).

Hans *masc* a diminutive form of **Johann**.

Hansel *masc* gift from God (*Scandinavian*).

Happy *fem* an English adjective, meaning feeling, showing or expressing joy, now used as a first name (*Old English*).

Haralda *fem* form of **Harold**.

Harbert *masc* a variant form of **Herbert**.

Harcourt *masc* a surname, meaning from a fortified court (*Old French*), or falconer's cottage (*Old English*), used as a first name.

Harden *masc* a surname, meaning the valley of the hare, used as a first name (*Old English*).

Hardie, Hardey *masc* variant forms of **Hardy**.

Harding *masc* a surname, meaning brave warrior, used as a first name (*Old English*).

Hardy *masc* a surname, meaning bold and daring, used as a first name (*Germanic*); variant forms are **Hardey, Hardie**.

Harford *masc* a surname, meaning stags' ford, used as a first name (*Old English*).

Hargrave, Hargreave, Hargreaves *masc* a surname, meaning from the hare grove, used as a first name (*Old English*).

Harlan, Harland *masc* a surname, meaning rocky land, used as a first name (*Old English*).

Harley *masc* a surname, meaning from the hare meadow or hill, used as a first name (*Old English*).

Harlow *masc* a placename and surname, meaning fortified hill, used as a first name (*Old English*).

Harmony *fem* the word for the quality of concord used as a first name (*Greek*).

Harold *masc* a champion; general of an army (*Old English*).

Harper *masc* a surname, meaning harp player or maker, used as a first name (*Old English*).

Harriet, Harriot *fem* forms of **Harry**; diminutive forms are **Hattie, Hatty**.

Harris, Harrison *masc* surnames, meaning son of Harold or Harry, used as a first name (*Old English*)

Harry *masc* a diminutive form of **Henry**, also used independently.

Hart *masc* a surname, meaning hart deer, used as a first name (*Old English*).

Hartford *masc* a placename and surname, meaning ford of the deer, or army ford, used as a first name (*Old English*); a variant form is **Hertford**.

Hartley *masc* a surname,

meaning clearing with stags, used as a first name (*Old English*).

Hartmann, Hartman *masc* strong and brave (*Germanic*).

Hartwell *masc* a surname, meaning stags' stream, used as a first name (*Old English*).

Harvey, Harvie *masc* a surname, meaning battle worthy, used as a first name (*Breton Gaelic*); a variant form is **Hervey**.

Haslett, Hazlitt *masc* variant forms of **Hazlett**.

Hastings *masc* a placename and surname, meaning territory of the violent ones, used as a first name (*Old English*).

Hattie, Hatty *fem* a diminutive form of **Harriet**.

Havelock *masc* a surname, meaning sea battle, used as a first name (*Old Norse*).

Hawley *masc* a surname, meaning from a hedged meadow, used as a first name (*Old English*).

Hayden, Haydon *masc* a surname, meaning heather hill or hay hill, used as a first name (*Old English*).

Hayley *masc, fem* a surname, meaning hay clearing, used as a first name (*Old English*); a variant form is **Haley**.

Hayward *masc* a surname, meaning supervisor of enclosures, used as a first name (*Old English*); a variant form is **Heyward**.

Haywood *masc* a surname, meaning fenced forest, used as a first name (*Old English*); a variant form is **Heywood**.

Hazel *fem* the name of a tree used as a first name (*Old English*).

Hazlett, Hazlitt *masc* a surname, meaning hazel tree, used as a first name (*Old English*); variant forms are **Haslett, Hazlitt**.

Heath *masc* a surname, meaning heathland, used as a first name (*Old English*).

Heathcliff, Heathcliffe *masc* dweller by the heather cliff (*Old English*).

Heather *fem* the name of a purple or white-flowered plant of the heath family used as a first name.

Hebe *fem* young (*Greek*). In Greek mythology, the daughter of Zeus and goddess of youth and spring.

Hector *masc* holding fast (*Greek*).

Hedda *fem* war, strife (*Germanic*).

Hedwig, Hedvig *fem* strife (*Germanic*).

Hefin *masc* summery (*Welsh*).

Heidi *fem* diminutive of **Adelheid**; a variant form is **Haidee**.

Heinrich *masc* the German form of **Henry**; diminutive forms are **Heinz, Heinze**.

Helen, Helena *fem* light (*Greek*); diminutive forms are **Nell, Lena**.

Helene *fem* the German form of **Helen**.

Hélène *fem* the French form of **Helen**.

Helga *fem* healthy, happy, holy (*Old Norse*).

Helge *masc* form of **Helga**.

Helma *fem* protection (*Germanic*).

Héloïse *fem* a French variant form of **Éloise**.

Hendrik *masc* the Dutch form of **Henry**.

Henri *masc* the French form of **Henry**.

Henrietta *fem* form of

Henry; diminutive forms are **Hettie, Hetty, Netta, Nettie**.

Henriette *fem* the French form of **Henrietta**.

Henry *masc* the head or chief of a house (*Germanic*); diminutive forms are **Harry, Hal, Hank**.

Hephzibah *fem* my delight is in her (*Hebrew*); a diminutive form is **Hepsy**.

Hera *fem* queen of heaven; in Greek mythology, the sister and wife of Zeus (*Greek*). Her counterpart in Roman mythology is Juno.

Herakles *masc* the Greek counterpart of **Hercules**.

Herbert *masc* army bright (*Old English*); a variant form is **Harbert**; diminutive forms are **Herb, Herbie**.

Hercule *masc* the French form of **Hercules**.

Hercules *masc* glory of Hera (the Latin form of the name of Herakles, the Greek hero, son of Zeus and stepson of Hera).

Heribert *masc* the German form of **Herbert**.

Herman *masc* warrior (*Germanic*).

Hermann *masc* the German form of **Herman**.

Hermes *masc* in Greek mythology, the messenger of the gods, with winged feet. His counterpart in Roman mythology is Mercury.

Hermione *fem* a name derived from that of **Hermes**.

Hermosa *fem* beautiful (*Spanish*).

Hernando *masc* a Spanish form of **Ferdinand**.

Herrick *masc* a surname, meaning powerful army, used as a first name (*Old Norse*).

Herta *fem* of the earth (*Old English*); a variant form is **Hertha**.

Hertford *masc* a variant form of **Hartford**.

Hertha *fem* a variant form of **Herta**.

Hervé *masc* a French form of **Harvey**.

Hervey *masc* a variant form of **Harvey**.

Hesketh *masc* a surname, meaning horse track, used as a first name (*Old Norse*).

Hester, Hesther *fem* variant forms of **Esther**.

Hettie, Hetty *fem* diminutive forms of **Henrietta**.

Heulwen *fem* sunshine (*Welsh*).

Hew *masc* a Welsh form of **Hugh**.

Hewett, Hewit *masc* a surname, meaning little Hugh or cleared place, used as a first name (*Old English*).

Heyward *masc* a variant form of **Hayward**.

Heywood *masc* a variant form of **Haywood**.

Hezekiah *masc* strength of the Lord (*Hebrew*).

Hi *masc* a diminutive form of **Hiram, Hyram**.

Hibernia *fem* the Latin name for Ireland used as a first name.

Hibiscus *fem* marsh mallow, the name of a brightly flowering plant used as a first name (*Greek/Latin*).

Hieronymus *masc* the Latin and German forms of **Jerome**.

Hilaire *masc* the French form of **Hilary**.

Hilario *masc* the Spanish form of **Hilary**.

Hilary, Hillary *masc fem* cheerful; merry (*Latin*).

Hilda *fem* battle maid (*Germanic*); a variant form is **Hylda**.

Hildebrand *masc* battle sword (*Germanic*).

Hildegarde *fem* strong in battle (*Germanic*).

Hilton *masc* a surname, meaning from the hill farm, used as a first name (*Old English*); a variant form is **Hylton**.

Hiram *masc* brother of the exalted one (*Hebrew*); a variant form is **Hyram**; a diminutive form is **Hi**.

Hobart *masc* a variant form of **Hubert**.

Hogan *masc* youthful (*Irish Gaelic*).

Holbert, Holbird *masc* variant forms of **Hulbert**.

Holbrook *masc* a surname, meaning brook in the valley, used as a first name (*Old English*).

Holcomb, Holcombe *masc* a surname, meaning deep valley, used as a first name (*Old English*).

Holden *masc* a surname, meaning from the deep valley, used as a first name (*Old English*).

Holgate *masc* a surname, meaning road in a hollow, used as a first name (*Old English*).

Hollis *masc* a surname, meaning dweller near holly trees, used as a first name (*Old English*).

Holly, Hollie *fem* the name of the red-berried tree used as a first name (*English*).

Holmes *masc* a surname, meaning an island in a river, used as a first name (*Old English*).

Holt *masc* a surname, meaning a wood or forest, used as a first name (*Old English*).

Homer *masc* uncertain, possibly hostage (*Greek*); the name of the Greek epic poet of the first milennium BC.

Honey *fem* the word for a sweet substance used as a term of endearment and as a first name.

Honor, Honora *fem* variant forms of **Honour**.

Honoria *fem* honourable (*Latin*); diminutive forms are **Nora, Norah, Noreen**.

Honorius *masc* form of **Honoria**.

Honour *fem* the word for personal intregity used as a first name; variant forms are **Honor, Honora**.

Hope *fem* the word for the feeling of expectation used

as a first name (*English*).

Horace, Horatio *masc* origin uncertain, possibly a family name *Horatius* (*Latin*).

Horatia *fem* form of **Horace**.

Hortensia, Hortense *fem* of the garden (*Latin*).

Horton *masc* a surname, meaning muddy place, used as a first name (*Old English*).

Hosea *masc* salvation (*Hebrew*).

Houghton *masc* a surname, meaning place in an enclosure, used as a first name (*Old English*); a variant form is **Hutton**.

Houston, Houstun *masc* a surname, meaning Hugh's place, used as a first name (*Old English*).

Howard *masc* a surname, meaning mind strong, used as a first name (*Germanic*).

Howe *masc* a surname, meaning high one (*Germanic*) or hill (*Old English*) used as a first name.

Howel, Howell *masc* anglicized forms of **Hywel**.

Hubert *masc* mind bright (*Germanic*); a variant surname form is **Hobart**.

Huberta *fem* form of **Hubert**.

Hudson *masc* a surname, meaning son of little Hugh, used as a first name (*Old English*).

Hugh *masc* mind; spirit; soul (*Danish*).

Hugo *masc* the Latin, German, and Spanish form of **Hugh**.

Hugues *masc* the French form of **Hugh**.

Hulbert, Hulburd, Hulburt *masc* a surname, meaning brilliant, gracious, used as a first name (*Germanic*); variant forms are **Holbert, Holbird**.

Hulda, Huldah *fem* weasel (*Hebrew*).

Humbert *masc* bright warrior (*Germanic*).

Humphrey, Humphry *masc* giant peace (*Old English*); diminutive forms are **Hump, Humph**.

Hunt, Hunter *masc* surnames, meaning hunter, used as first names (*Old English*).

Huntingdon *masc* a placename and surname, meaning hunter's hill, used as a first name (*Old English*).

Huntington *masc* a surname, meaning hunter's farm, used as a first name (*Old English*).

Huntley, Huntly *masc* a surname, meaning hunter's meadow, used as a first name (*Old English*).

Hurley *masc* sea tide (*Gaelic*).

Hurst *masc* a surname, meaning wooded hill, used as a first name (*Old English*).

Hutton *masc* a variant form of **Houghton**.

Huw *masc* a Welsh variant form of **Hugh**.

Huxley *masc* a surname, meaning Hugh's meadow, used as a first name (*Old English*).

Hyacinth *fem* the name of the flower adapted from the name of the hero of Greek mythology whose blood after his killing by

Apollo caused a flower to spring up.

Hyam *masc* man of life (*Hebrew*); a variant form is **Hyman**; diminutive forms are **Hi, Hy**.

Hyde *masc* a surname, meaning a hide (a measurement unit) of land, used as a first name (*Old English*).

Hylda *fem* a variant form of **Hilda**.

Hylton *masc* a variant form of **Hilton**.

Hyman *masc* a variant form of **Hyam**.

Hypatia *fem* highest (*Greek*).

Hyram *masc* a variant form of **Hiram**; diminutive forms are **Hi, Hy**.

Hywel, Hywell *masc* sound; whole (*Welsh*); anglicized forms are **Howel, Howell**.

I

Iachimo *masc* an Italian form of **James**.

Iacovo *masc* an Italian form of **Jacob**.

Ian *masc* an anglicized form of **Iain**.

Iain *masc* the Scots Gaelic form of **John**.

Ianthe *fem* violet flower (*Greek*).

Ibby *fem* a diminutive form of **Isabel**.

Ichabod *masc* inglorious (*Hebrew*).

Ida *fem* god-like (*Germanic*).

Idabell *fem* god-like and fair.

Idris *masc* fiery lord (*Welsh*).

Idonia *fem* sufficient (*Latin*).

Idony, Idonie *fem* in Norse mythology, the keeper of the golden apples of youth (*Norse*).

Iestyn *masc* the Welsh form of **Justin**.

Ieuan, Ifan *masc* Welsh forms of **John**; a variant form is **Iwan**.

Ifor *masc* a Welsh form of **Ivor**.

Ignace *masc* the French form of **Ignatius**.

Ignacio *masc* a Spanish form of **Ignatius**.

Ignatia *fem* form of **Ignatius**.

Ignatius *masc* from *ignis*, fire (*Greek*).

Ignatz, Ignaz *masc* German forms of **Ignatius**.

Ignazio *masc* the Italian form of **Ignatius**.

Igor *masc* the Russian form of **Ivor**.

Ike *masc* a diminutive form of **Isaac**.

Ilario *masc* the Italian form of **Hilary**.

Ilona *fem* a Hungarian form of **Helen**; a diminutive form is **Ilka**.

Ilse *fem* a diminutive form of **Elisabeth**.

Immanuel *masc* a variant form of Emmanuel; a diminutive form is **Manny**.

Imogen *fem* from *innogen*, girl, maiden (*Celtic*), used by Shakespeare for one of his characters in *Cymbeline* and misspelled by him or his printer.

Imperial *fem* relating to an emperor (*Latin*).

Imre *masc* a Hungarian form of **Emeric**.

Ina *fem* a diminutive form of names ending in *-ina*, e.g. Georgina, Wilhelmina.

Inés, Inez *fem* Spanish forms of **Agnes**.

Inga *fem* a diminutive form of **Ingeborg, Ingrid**.

Inge *masc* a diminutive form of **Ingemar**; *fem* a diminutive form of **Ingeborg, Ingrid**.

Ingeborg *fem* fortification of Ing, the god of fertility (Frey) (*Old Norse*); diminutive forms are **Inga, Inge**.

Ingemar *masc* famous son of Ing (*Old Norse*); a variant form is **Ingmar**; a diminutive form is **Inge**.

Inger *fem* a variant form of **Ingrid**.

Ingmar *masc* a variant form of **Ingemar**.

Ingram *masc* a surname, meaning raven angel (*Germanic*) or river meadow (*Old English*), used as a first name.

Ingrid *fem* maiden of Ing, the god of fertility (Frey) (*Old Norse*); a variant form is **Inger**; diminutive forms are **Inga, Inge**.

Inigo *masc* a Spanish form of **Ignatius**, now used as an English-language form.

Innes, Inness *masc, fem* a surname, meaning island, used as a first name (*Scots Gaelic*).

Iola *fem* a variant form of **Iole**.

Iolanthe *fem* violet flower (*Greek*).

Iole *fem* violet (*Greek*); a variant form is **Iola**.

Iolo, Iolyn *masc* diminutive forms of **Iorwerth**.

Iona *fem* yew tree (*Celtic*), the name of the Scottish Hebridean island used as a first name.

Ione *fem* a violet (*Greek*)

Iorwerth *masc* handsome nobleman (*Welsh*); diminutive forms are **Iolo, Iolyn**.

Iphigenia *fem* strong (*Greek*).

Ira *masc* watchful (*Hebrew*).

Irene *fem* peace (*Greek*); a diminutive form is **Renie**.

Iris *fem* rainbow (*Greek*).

Irma *fem* noble one (*Germanic*).

Irvine, Irving *masc* a surname, meaning fresh or green river, used as a first name (*Celtic*).

Irwin *masc* a surname, meaning friend of boars, used as a first name (*Old English*).

Isa *fem* a diminutive form of **Isabel**.

Isaac *masc* laughter (*Hebrew*); a variant form is **Izaak**; a diminutive form is **Ike**.

Isabel, Isabella *fem* Spanish forms of **Elizabeth**, now used as separate English-language names; a variant form is **Isobel**; diminutive forms are **Ibby, Isa, Izzie, Izzy, Tib, Tibbie**.

Isabelle *fem* the French form of **Isabel**.

Isadora *fem* a variant form of **Isidora**.

Isaiah *masc* salvation of Jehovah(*Hebrew*).

Iseabail, Ishbel *fem* Scots forms of **Isabel**.

Iseult *fem* a French and Welsh form of **Isolde**.

Isham *masc* a surname, meaning home on the water, used as a first name (*Old English*).

Isidor *masc* the German form of **Isidore**.

Isidora *fem* form of **Isidore**; a variant form is **Isadora** .

Isidore *masc* gift of Isis (*Greek*).

Isidoro *masc* an Italian form of **Isidore**.

Isidro *masc* Spanish forms of **Isidore**.

Isla, Islay *fem* a Scottish island name used as a first name.

Isobel *fem* a variant form of **Isabel**.

Isola *fem* isolated, alone (*Latin*).

Isolde, Isolda, Isold *fem* beautiful aspect (*Welsh*).

Israel *masc* a soldier of God ruling with the Lord (*Hebrew*); a diminutive form is **Izzy**.

Istvan *masc* the Hungarian form of Stephen.

Ita, Ite *fem* thirst (for truth) (*Irish Gaelic*).

Ivan *masc* the Russian form of **John**.

Ivana *fem* form of **Ivan**.

Ives *masc* a surname, meaning son of Ive (yew), used as a first name (*Germanic*).

Ivo *masc* the Welsh form of **Yves**.

Ivor *masc* yew army (*Old Norse*).

Ivy *masc fem* the name of the plant used as a first name (*English*).

Iwan *masc* a variant form of **Ieuan**.

Izaak *masc* a variant form of **Isaac**.

Izzie, Izzy *masc fem* diminutive forms of **Isabel, Israel**.

J

Jabal *masc* guide (*Hebrew*).

Jabez *masc* causing pain (*Hebrew*).

Jacinta *fem* the Spanish form of **Hyacinth**.

Jacinth *fem* a variant form of **Hyacinth**.

Jack *masc* a diminutive form of **John**, now used independently; diminutive forms are **Jackie, Jacky**.

Jackie, Jacky *masc* a diminutive form of **Jack, John**; *fem* a diminutive form of **Jacqueline**.

Jackson *masc* a surname, meaning son of Jack, used as a first name.

Jacob *masc* supplanter (*Hebrew*); a diminutive form is **Jake**.

Jacoba *fem* fem form of **Jacob**.

Jacobo *masc* the Spanish form of **Jacob**.

Jacqueline *fem* a diminutive form of **Jacques**; a variant form is **Jaqueline**;

a diminutive form is **Jackie**.

Jacques *masc* the French form of **Jacob, James**.

Jacquetta *fem* form of **James**.

Jade *fem* the name of the light-green semi-precious stone used as a first name.

Jael *fem* wid she-goat (*Hebrew*).

Jagger *masc* a surname, meaning a carter, used as a first name (*Middle English*).

Jago *masc* a Cornish form of **James**.

Jaime *masc* a Spanish form of **James**; *fem* a variant form of **Jamie**.

Jairus *masc* he will enlighten (*Hebrew*).

Jake *masc* a diminutive form of **Jacob**, now used independently.

Jakob *masc* the German form of **Jacob, James**.

Jamal *masc fem* beauty (*Arabic*).

James *masc* a Christian form of **Jacob**; diminutive forms are **Jamie, Jem, Jim, Jimmy**.

Jamesina *fem* form of **James**; a diminutive form is **Ina**.

Jamie *masc* a diminutive form of **James**, now used independently, often as a girl's name.

Jan *masc* a diminutive form of **John**; the Dutch form of **John**; *fem* a diminutive form of **Jancis, Jane, Janet**, now used independently.

Jancis *fem* a combination of **Jan** and **Frances**; a diminutive form is **Jan**.

Jane *fem* form of **John**; variant forms are **Janet, Janeta, Janette, Janice, Janine, Jayne, Jean, Joan**; diminutive forms are **Jan, Janey, Janie**.

Janet, Janeta, Janette *fem* variant forms of **Jane**; a diminutive form is **Jan**.

Janice *fem* a variant form of **Jane**.

Janine *fem* a variant form of **Jane**y.

Japheth *masc* extension (*Hebrew*).

Jaqueline *fem* a variant

form of **Jacqueline**; a diminutive form is **Jaqui**.

Jared *masc* (servant (*Hebrew*).

Jarvis *masc* a surname form of **Gervase** used as a first name; a variant form is **Jervis**.

Jasmine, Jamsin *fem* the name of the flower used as a first name; variant forms are **Jessamine, Jessamyn, Yasmin, Yasmine**.

Jason *masc* healer (*Greek*); in Greek mythology, the hero who led the Argonauts.

Jasper *masc* treasure master (*Persian*).

Javan *masc* clay (*Hebrew*).

Javier *masc* a Portuguese and Spanish form of **Xavier**.

Jay *masc* a surname, meaning jay, the bird, used as a first name (*Old French*); *masc, fem* a diminutive form for names beginning with *J*.

Jayne *fem* a variant form of **Jane**.

Jean¹ *fem* a variant form of **Jane**; a diminutive form is **Jeanie**.

Jean² *masc* the French form of **John**.

Jeanette, Jeannette *fem* a diminutive form of **Jeanne**, now used independently as an English-language name.

Jeanne *fem* the French form of **Jane**; a diminutive form is **Jeanette**.

Jedidiah *masc* beloved of the Lord (*Hebrew*); a diminutive form is **Jed**.

Jefferson *masc* a surname, meaning son of Jeffrey or Geffrey, used as a first name (*Old English*).

Jeffrey, Jeffery *masc* district or traveller peace (*Germanic*); a variant form is **Geoffrey**; a diminutive form is **Jeff**.

Jehudi *masc* Jewish (*Hebrew*); a variant form is **Yehudi**.

Jehuda *fem* form of **Jehudi**; a variant form is **Yehuda**.

Jem, Jemmie, Jemmy *masc dimins.of* **James**.

Jemima, Jemimah *fem* dove (*Hebrew*); diminutive forms are **Mima, Mina**.

Jemma *fem* a variant form of **Gemma**.

Jenna, Jenni, Jennie *fem* diminutive forms of **Jane, Jennifer**, now used inde-pendently; a variant form is **Jenny**.

Jennifer, Jenifer *fem* the Cornish form of **Guinev-ere**; diminutive forms are **Jen, Jennie, Jenny**.

Jenny *fem* a diminutive form of **Jane, Jennifer**, now used independently; a variant form is **Jennie**.

Jeremia *fem* form of **Jere-miah**.

Jeremias *masc* a Spanish form of **Jeremy**.

Jeremy, Jeremiah *masc* Jehovah has appointed (*Hebrew*); a diminutive form is **Jerry**.

Jermaine *fem* a variant form of **Germaine**.

Jerome *masc* holy name (*Greek*); a diminutive form is **Jerry**.

Jérôme *masc* the French form of **Jerome**.

Jerónimo *masc* the Span-ish form of **Jerome**.

Jerry *masc* a diminutive form of **Gerald, Gerard, Jeremy, Jerome**, now used independently.

Jerusha *fem* possessed; married (*Hebrew*).

Jervis *masc* a variant form of **Jarvis**.

305

Jess *fem* a diminutive form of **Jessica, Jessie**.

Jessamine, Jessamyn *fem* variant forms of **Jasmine**.

Jesse *masc* wealth (*Hebrew*).

Jessica *fem* God is looking (*Hebrew*); a diminutive form is **Jess**.

Jessie, Jessy *fem* diminutive forms of **Janet**, now used as names in their own right.

Jethro *masc* (*Hebrew*) superiority.

Jewel *fem* the name for a precious stone or valuable ornament used as a first name.

Jezebel *fem* domination (*Hebrew*).

Jill *fem* a diminutive form of **Gillian, Jillian**, now used independently.

Jillian *fem* form of **Julian**; diminutive forms are **Jill, Jilly**.

Jim, Jimmie, Jimmy *masc* diminutive forms of **James**.

Jo *masc* a diminutive form of **Joab, Joachim, Joseph**; *fem* a diminutive form of **Joanna, Joseph, Josepha, Josephine**.

Joab *masc* Jehovah is Father (*Hebrew*).

Joachim *masc* God has established (*Hebrew*).

Joan, Joann, Joanna, Joanne *fem* forms of **John**; diminutive forms are **Joanie, Joni**.

Joaquin *masc* the Spanish form of **Joachim**.

Job *masc* one persecuted (*Hebrew*).

Jobina *fem* form of **Job**.

Jocelyn, Jocelin *masc, fem* little Goth (*Germanic*); diminutive forms are **Jos, Joss**.

Jock, Jockie *masc* a diminutive form of **John**.

Jodie, Jody *fem* diminutive forms of **Judith**, now used independently.

Joe, Joey *masc* diminutive forms of **Joseph**.

Joel *masc* Jehovah is God (*Hebrew*).

Johan *masc* a Swedish form of **John**.

Johann *masc* a German form of **John**; a diminutive form is **Hans**.

Johanna *fem* the Latin and German form of **Jane**.

Johannes *masc* a Latin

and German form of **John**.

John *masc* Jehovah has been gracious (*Hebrew*); diminutive forms are **Jack, Jackie, Jan, Jock, Johnnie, Johnny**.

Jolyon *masc* a variant form of **Julian**.

Jon *masc* a variant form of **John**; a diminutive form of **Jonathan**.

Jonah, Jonas *masc* dove (*Hebrew*).

Jonathan, Jonathon *masc* Jehovah gave (*Hebrew*); a diminutive form is **Jon**.

Joni *fem* a diminutive form of **Joan**.

Jordan *masc* flowing down (*Hebrew*); diminutive forms are **Jud, Judd**.

Jordana *fem* form of **Jordan**.

Jorge *masc* the Spanish form of **George**.

Jos *masc* a diminutive form of **Joseph, Joshua**; *masc, fem* a diminutive form of **Jocelyn, Jocelin**.

Joscelin *masc, fem* a French form of **Jocelyn**.

Josceline *fem* form of **Jocelyn**.

José *masc* the Spanish form of **Joseph**; diminutive

forms are **Pepe, Pepillo, Pepiro**.

Josef *masc* a German form of **Joseph**.

Josefa *fem* form of **Josef**.

Joseph *masc* God shall add (*Hebrew*); diminutive forms are **Jo, Joe, Joey, Jos**.

Josepha *fem* form of **Joseph**.

Josephine *fem* form of **Joseph**; diminutive forms are **Jo, Josie, Phenie**.

Josette *fem* a French diminutive form of **Josephine**, now used independently.

Josh *masc* a diminutive form of **Joshua**, now used independently.

Joshua *masc* Jehovah is salvation (*Hebrew*); a diminutive form is **Josh**.

Josiah, Josias *masc* Jehovah supports (*Hebrew*).

Josie *fem* a diminutive form of **Josephine**.

Joss *masc, fem* a diminutive form of **Jocelyn, Jocelin, Joscelin**.

Joy *fem* the name of the feeling of intense happiness used as a first name (*English*).

Joyce *fem* sportive (*Latin*).

Juan *masc* the Spanish form of **John**, now used as an English-language form.

Juana *fem* the Spanish form of **Jane**; a diminutive form is **Juanita**.

Judah *masc* confession (*Hebrew*); a diminutive form is **Jude**.

Jud, Judd *masc* diminutive forms of **Jordan**, also used independently.

Jude *masc* a diminutive form of **Judah**.

Judie, Judi *fem* diminutive forms of **Judith**, now used independently.

Judith *fem* of Judah (*Hebrew*); diminutive forms are **Jodie, Judy.**

Judy *fem* a diminutive form of **Judith**, now used independently.

Jules *masc* the French form of **Julius**; a diminutive form of **Julian, Julius**; *fem* a diminutive form of **Julia, Juliana**.

Julia *fem* forms of **Julius**; a variant form is **Juliana**; a diminutive form is **Julie**.

Julian *masc* sprung from or belonging to Julius (*Latin*); a variant form is **Jolyon**.

Juliana *fem* form of **Ju-**

lius.

Julie, Juliet *fem* diminutive forms of **Julia**, now used independently.

Julien *masc* the French form of **Julian**.

Julienne *fem* form of **Julien**.

Julieta *fem* a Spanish form of **Julia**.

Juliette *fem* the French form of **Julia**, now used as an English-language form.

Julio *masc* a Spanish form of **Julius**.

Julius *masc* downy-bearded (*Greek*).

June *fem* the name of the month used as a first name (*Latin*).

Juno *fem* queen of heaven, in Roman mythology the equivalent of **Hera** (*Latin*).

Justin *masc* the English form of *Justinus*, a Roman family name from **Justus** (*Latin*); a variant form is **Justinian**.

Justina, Justine *fem* forms of **Justin**.

Justinian, Justus *masc* variant forms of **Justin**.

Justus *masc* fair, just (*Latin*).

K

Kalantha, Kalanthe *fem* variant forms of **Calantha**.

Kalypso *fem* a variant form of **Calypso**.

Kane *masc* a surname, meaning warrior, used as a first name (*Irish Gaelic*).

Kara *fem* a variant form of **Cara**.

Karel *masc* the Czech and Dutch form of **Charles**.

Karen *fem* a Dutch and Scandinavian form of **Katherine**.

Karin *fem* a Scandinavian form of **Katherine**.

Karl *masc* a German form of **Charles**.

Karla *fem* form of **Karl**.

Karlotte *fem* a German form of **Charlotte**.

Karol *masc* the Polish form of **Charles**.

Karoline *fem* a German form of **Caroline**.

Karr *masc* a variant form of **Kerr**.

Kasimir *masc* peace (*Polish*).

Kaspar *masc* the German form of **Jasper**.

Kate *fem* a diminutive form of **Katherine**, also used independently.

Katerina *fem* a variant form of **Katherine**.

Kath, Kathie, Kathy *fem* diminutive forms of **Katherine**.

Katharina, Katharine *fem* German forms of **Katherine**; a diminutive form is **Katrine**.

Katherine *fem* pure (*Greek*); diminutive forms are **Kate, Kath, Katie, Katy, Kay, Kit, Kittie**.

Kathleen *fem* an Irish form of **Katherine**.

Kathryn *fem* an American form of **Katherine**.

Katie *fem* a diminutive form of **Katherine**, now used independently.

Katinka *fem* a Russian

form of **Katherine**.

Katrine *fem* a diminutive
form of **Katharina**; a variant form of **Katriona**; the
name of a Scottish loch,
meaning wood of Eriu, used
as a first name.

Katriona *fem* a variant
form of **Catriona**; a variant form is **Katrine**.

Katy *fem* a diminutive form
of **Katherine**, now used
independently.

Kavan *masc* a variant form
of **Cavan**.

Kay *masc* giant (*Scots
Gaelic*); *fem* a diminutive
form of **Katherine**, now
used independently; a variant form is **Kaye**.

Kayla, Kayleigh, Kayley
fem derivation uncertain,
possibly slender (*Irish
Gaelic*), a combination of
Kay and **Leigh**, or a variant form of **Kelly**.

Kean, Keane *masc* anglicized forms of **Cian**.

Kedar *masc* powerful (*Arabic*).

Keefe *masc* noble, admirable (*Irish Gaelic*).

Keegan *masc* a surname,
meaning son of Egan, used
as a first name (*Irish Gaelic*).

Keenan *masc* a surname,
meaning little ancient one,
used as a first name (*Irish
Gaelic*).

Keir *masc* a surname,
meaning swarthy, used as
a first name (*Scots Gaelic*).

Keira *fem* a variant spelling of **Ciara**.

Keith *masc* a placename
and surname, meaning
wood, used as a first name
(*Celtic*).

Keld *masc* a Danish form of
Keith.

Kelly *fem* a surname,
meaning descendant of
war, used as a first name
(*Irish Gaelic*).

Kelsey *masc* a surname,
meaning victory, used as a
first name (*Old English*).

Kelvin *masc* the name of a
Scottish river, meaning
narrow water, used as a
first name (*Scots Gaelic*).

Kemp *masc* a surname,
meaning warrior (*Old English*) or athlete (*Middle
English*), used as a first
name.

Ken *masc* a diminutive
form of **Kendall, Kend-
rick, Kenelm, Kennard,
Kennedy, Kenneth**.

Kendall, Kendal, Kendell

masc a surname, meaning valley of the holy river, used as a first name (*Celtic/Old English*); a diminutive form is **Ken**.

Kendra *fem* form of **Kendrick**.

Kendrick *masc* a surname, meaning hero, used as a first name (*Welsh*); a variant form is **Kenrick**; a diminutive form is **Ken**.

Kenelm *masc* royal helmet (*Germanic*) a diminutive form is **Ken**.

Kennard *masc* a surname, meaning strong royal, used as a first name (*Germanic*) a diminutive form is **Ken**.

Kennedy *masc* a surname, meaning helmeted or ugly head, used as a first name (*Gaelic*); a diminutive form is **Ken**.

Kennet *masc* a Scandinavian form of Kenneth; diminutive forms are **Ken, Kent**.

Kenneth *masc* fire-born; handsome (*Gaelic*); diminutive forms are **Ken, Kennie, Kenny**.

Kennie, Kenny *masc* diminutive forms of **Kenneth** and other names beginning with Ken-.

Kenrick *masc* a variant form of **Kendrick**.

Kent *masc* a surname, meaning from the county of Kent (meaning border), used as a first name (*Celtic*); a diminutive form of **Kennet, Kenton**.

Kenton *masc* a surname, meaning settlement on the river Kenn, or royal place, used as a first name (*Old English*); diminutive forms are **Ken, Kent**.

Kenyon *masc* white-haired (*Gaelic*); a surname, meaning mound of Ennion, used as a first name (*Welsh*).

Kermit *masc* son of Diarmid (*Irish Gaelic*).

Kern *masc* dark one (*Gaelic*).

Kerr *masc* a Scottish form of the surname **Carr**, used as a first name; a variant form is **Karr**.

Kerry *fem, masc* the name of the Irish county used as a first name.

Kester *masc* a diminutive form of **Christopher**.

Keturah *fem* incense (*Hebrew*).

Kevin, Kevan *masc* comely, loved (*Irish Gaelic*); a diminutive form is **Kev**.

Kezia, Keziah *fem* the cassia tree (*Hebrew*); diminutive forms are **Kizzie, Kiz-zy**.

Kieran *masc* an anglicized form of **Ciaran**.

Kiernan *masc* a variant form of **Tiernan**.

Kim *fem* a diminutive form of **Kimberley**, also used independently.

Kimberley *fem* a surname, meaning wood clearing, used as a first name (*Old English*); a diminutive form is **Kim**.

King *masc* the title of a monarch or a surname, meaning appearance, or serving in a royal household, used as a first name (*Old English*); a diminutive form of names beginning with King-.

Kingsley *masc* a surname, meaning king's meadow, used as a first name (*Old English*).

Kingston *masc* a pla-cename and surname, meaning king's farm, used as a first name (*Old English*).

Kinsey *masc* a surname, meaning royal victor, used as a first name (*Old English*).

Kirby *masc* a surname, meaning church village or

farm, used as a first name (*Old Norse*).

Kirk *masc* a surname, meaning one who lives near a church, used as a first name (*Old Norse*).

Kirkwood *masc* a sur-name, meaning church wood, used as a first name (*Old Norse/Old English*).

Kirsten *fem* a Scandinavi-an form of **Christine**.

Kirstie, Kirsty *fem* a di-minutive form of **Kirstin**, now used independently.

Kirstin *fem* a Scots form of **Christine**; a diminutive form is **Kirstie**.

Kish *masc* a gift (*Hebrew*).

Kit *masc* a diminutive form of **Christopher, Kristo-pher**; *fem* a diminutive form of **Katherine**.

Kittie, Kitty *fem* diminu-tive forms of **Katherine**.

Kizzie, Kizzy *fem* diminu-tive forms of **Kezia**.

Klara *fem* the German form of **Clara**.

Klaus *masc* a variant form of **Claus**.

Klemens *masc* a German form of **Clement**.

Knight *masc* a surname,

meaning bound to serve a feudal lord as a mounted soldier, used as a first name (*Old English*).

Knut *masc* a variant form of **Canute**.

Konrad *masc* a German and Swedish form of **Conrad**.

Konstanz *masc* the German form of **Constant**.

Konstanze *fem* the German form of **Constance**.

Kora *fem* a variant form of **Cora**.

Korah *masc* baldness (*Hebrew*).

Kris *masc* a diminutive form of **Kristoffer, Kristopher**.

Kristeen *fem* a variant form of **Christine**.

Kirstel *fem* a German form of **Christine**.

Kristen *masc* the Danish form of **Christian**, now also used in English as a girl's name.

Kristian *masc* a Swedish form of **Christian**.

Kristina *fem* the Swedish form of **Christina**.

Kristoffer *masc* a Scandinavian form of **Christopher**.

Kristopher *masc* a variant form of **Christopher**; diminutive forms are **Kit, Kris**.

Kurt *masc* a diminutive form of **Conrad**, now used independently; a variant form is **Curt**.

Kyle *masc* narrow (*Scots Gaelic*); the name of a region of southwest Scotland used as a surname.

Kylie *fem* a combination of **Kyle** and **Kelly**.

Kyrena *fem* a variant form of **Cyrena**.

L

Laban *masc* white (*Hebrew*).

Lachlan *masc* from the land of lakes (*Scots Gaelic*).

Lacey *masc, fem* a surname, meaning from Lassy in the Calvados region of Normandy, used as a first name (Old French).

Ladislao *masc* an Italian form of **Laszlo**.

Ladislas *masc* rule of glory (*Polish/Latin*).

Laszlo *masc* the Hungarian form of **Ladislas**.

Laetitia *fem* happiness (*Latin*); variant forms are **Latisha, Letitia**.

Laing *masc* a variant form of **Lang**.

Laird *masc* a Scots form of the surname Lord, meaning master, landowner (*Old English*), used as a first name.

Lalage *fem* chattering (*Greek-Latin*); a diminutive form is **Lallie, Lally**.

Lambert *masc* illustrious with landed possessions (*Germanic*).

Lamberto *masc* the Italian form of **Lambert**.

Lamond, Lamont *masc* a surname, meaning law giver, used as a first name (*Old Norse/Scots Gaelic*).

Lana *fem* a variant form of **Alana**.

Lance *masc* land (*Germanic*); a diminutive form of **Lancelot**.

Lancelot *masc* a little lance or warrior; or a servant (*French*); a diminutive form is **Lance**.

Lander, Landor *masc* variant forms of the surname **Lavender**.

Lane *masc* a surname, meaning narrow road, lane, used as a first name (*Old English*).

Lang *masc* a Scottish form of the surname Long, meaning tall or long, used as a first name (*Old Eng-*

lish); a variant form is **La-ing**.

Langford *masc* a surname, meaning long ford, used as a first name (*Old English*).

Langley *masc* a surname, meaning long meadow, used as a first name (*Old English*).

Lara *fem* a diminutive form of **Larissa** (*Latin*).

Laraine *fem* a variant form of **Lorraine**; the queen (*Old French*).

Larissa, Larisa *fem* meaning uncertain, possibly happy as a lark (*Greek/Russian*); diminutve forms are **Lara, Lissa**.

Lark *fem* the English word for a bird famed for rising early and for its song used as a first name.

Larry *masc* a diminutive form of **Laurence, Lawrence**.

Lars *masc* a Scandinavian form of **Laurence**.

Larsen, Larson *masc* son of Lars (*Scandinavian*).

Lascelles *masc* a surname, meaning hermitage or cell, used as a first name (*Old French*).

Latham, Lathom *masc* a surname, meaning barns,

used as a first name (*Old Norse*).

Latimer *masc* a surname, meaning interpreter, used as a first name (*Old French*).

Latisha *fem* a variant form of **Laetitia**.

Laura *fem* laurel, bay tree (*Latin*); a diminutive form is **Laurie**.

Laurabel *fem* a combination of **Laura** and **Mabel**.

Laurel *fem* a name for the evergreen bay tree used as a first name.

Lauren *fem* form of **Laurence**; a variant form is **Loren**; a diminutive form is **Laurie**.

Laurence *masc* from Laurentium in Italy, place of laurels (*Latin*); a variant form is **Lawrence**; diminutive forms are **Larry, Laurie**.

Laurens *masc* a Dutch form of **Lawrence**.

Laurent *masc* the French form of **Laurence**.

Laurette *fem* a French form of **Laura**; a variant form is **Lauretta**.

Laurie *masc* a diminutive form of **Laurence**; a surname form of this used as a

first name; variant forms
are **Lawrie, Lawry**; *fem* a
dimunitive form of **Laura,
Lauren**.

Lavender *fem* the English
name of the plant that
bears blue or mauve flow-
ers used as a first name;
masc a surname, meaning
launderer, used as a first
name (*Old French*); a variant form is **Lander**.

Laverne *fem* the alder tree
(*Old French*); diminutive
forms are **Verna, Verne**.

Lavinia, Lavina *fem* of
Latium in Italy (*Latin*).

Lawrence *masc* a variant
form of of **Laurence**; diminutive forms are **Larry,
Lawrie, Lawry**.

Lawrie, Lawry *masc* diminutive forms of **Law-
rence**; a variant form of
Laurie.

Lawson *masc* a surname,
meaning son of Lawrence,
used as a first name (*Old
English*).

Lawton *masc* a surname,
meaning from the place on
the hill, used as a first
name (*Old English*).

Layton *masc* a variant
form of **Leighton**.

Lazarus *masc* destitute of
help (*Hebrew*).

Lea *fem* a variant form of
Leah, Lee.

Leah *fem* languid, or wild
cow (*Hebrew*); variant
forms are **Lea, Lee**.

Leal, Leale *masc* a surname, meaning loyal, true,
used as a first name (*Old
French*).

Leander *masc* lion man
(*Greek*).

Leane *fem* a variant form
of **Leanne, Liane**.

Leandre *masc* a French
form of **Leander**.

Leandro *masc* an Italian
form of **Leander**.

Leanne *fem* a combination
of **Lee** and **Anne**; a variant
form is **Leane**.

Leanora, Leanore *fem*
German variant forms of
Eleanor.

Leda *fem* mother of beauty;
in Greek mythology, a
queen of Sparta who was
visited by Zeus (who ap-
peared to her in the form of
a swan) and gave birth to
Helen (*Greek*).

Lee *masc fem* a surname,
meaning field or meadow,
used as a first name (*Old
English*); a variant form is
Leigh; *fem* a variant form
of **Leah**.

Leif *masc* beloved one (*Old Norse*).

Leigh *masc* a variant form of **Lee**.

Leighton *masc* a surname, meaning herb garden, used as a first name (*Old English*); a variant form is **Layton**.

Leila *fem* night, dark (*Arabic*); variant forms are **Lela, Lila, Lilah**.

Leith *masc* a placename, meaning moist place (*Celtic*) or grey (*Scots Gaelic*), used as a first name.

Lela *fem* a variant form of **Leila**.

Leland *masc* a variant form of **Leyland**.

Lemuel *masc* devoted to God (*Hebrew*); a diminutive form is **Lem**.

Len *masc* a diminutive form of **Leonard, Lennox, Lionel**.

Lena *fem* a diminutive form of **Helena**, etc, also used independently.

Lennard *masc* a variant form of **Leonard**.

Lennie *masc* a diminutive form of **Leonard, Lennox, Lionel**.

Lennox *masc* a placename

and surname, meaning abounding in elm trees, used as a first name (*Scots Gaelic*).

Lenny *masc* a diminutive form of **Leonard, Lennox, Lionel**; a variant form is **Lonnie**.

Lenora *fem* a variant form of **Leonora**.

Leo *masc* lion (*Latin*); a variant form is **Leon**.

Leon *masc* a variant form of **Leo**.

Leona *fem* a variant form of **Leonie**.

Leonard *masc* lion strong (*Germanic*); a variant form is **Lennard**; diminutive forms are **Len, Lennie, Lenny**.

Leonarda *fem* form of **Leonard**.

Leonardo *masc* an Italian form of **Leonard**.

Leonhard *masc* a German form of **Leonard**.

Leonidas *masc* of a lion (*Greek*).

Leonie *fem* form of **Leo, Leon**; a variant form is **Leona**.

Leonora *fem* an Italian form of **Eleanor**; a variant form is **Lenora**; a diminutive form is **Nora**.

Leontine, Leontina *fem* form of **Leontius**.

Leontius *masc* of the lion (Latin).

Leontyne *fem* a variant form of Leontine.

Leopold *masc* bold for the people (*Germanic*).

Leopoldina, Leopoldine *fem* forms of Leopold.

Leopoldo *masc* an Italian and Spanish form of **Leopold**.

Leroy *masc* the king (*Old French*); a variant form is **Elroy**; diminutive forms are **Lee, Roy**.

Leslie *masc*, *fem* a surname, meaning garden by water, used as a first name (*Gaelic*).

Lesley *fem* form of Leslie.

Lester *masc* a surname, meaning from the Roman site (i.e. the present city of Leicester), used as a first name (*Old English*).

Leticia, Letitia *fem* variant forms of **Laetitia**.

Letizia *fem* an Italian form of **Laetitia**.

Lettice *fem* a variant form of **Laetitia**; diminutive forms are **Lettie, Letty**.

Lev *masc* a Russian form of **Leo**.

Levi *masc* joined (He*brew*).

Lewis *masc* bold warrior (*Germanic*); diminutive forms are **Lew, Lewie**.

Lex *masc* a diminutive form of **Alexander**.

Lexie, Lexy *fem* diminutive forms of **Alexandra**.

Leyland *masc* a surname, meaning fallow or untilled land, used as a first name (*Old English*); a variant form is **Leland**.

Liam *masc* the Irish form of **William**.

Liana, Liane, Lianna, Lianne *fem* sun (*Greek*); variant forms are **Leane, Leana, Leanna**.

Libby *fem* a diminutive form of **Elizabeth**.

Lidia *fem* an Italian and Spanish form of **Lydia**.

Liese *fem* a diminutive form of **Elisabeth**, now used independently.

Lil *fem* a diminutive form of **Lilian, Lily**.

Lila *fem* a variant form of **Leila**; a diminutive form of **Delilah**.

Lilac *fem* bluish (*Persian*),

the English name of the
syringa plant with fragrant
purple or white flowers
used as a first name.

Lilah *fem* a variant form of
Leila; a diminutive form of
Delilah.

Lili *fem* a variant form of
Lilie.

Lilian *fem* a diminutive
form of **Elizabeth**; a variant form of **Lily**; a variant
form is **Lillian**.

Lilias, Lillias *fem* Scottish
forms of **Lilian**.

Lilibet *fem* a diminutive
form of **Elizabeth**.

Lilie *fem* a German form of
Lily; a variant form is **Lili**.

Lilith *fem* of the night (*Hebrew*).

Lilli *fem* a variant form of
Lily.

Lillian *fem* a variant form
of **Lilian**.

Lily *fem* the name of the
flowering plant with showy
blossoms used as a first
name; a variant form is
Lilli; a diminutive form is
Lil.

Lin *fem* a diminutive form
of **Linda**.

Lina *fem* a diminutive form
of **Selina** and names ending in -lina, -line.

Lincoln *masc* a placename
and surname, meaning the
place by the pool, used as a
first name (*Celtic/Latin*).

Linda *fem* a diminutive
form of **Belinda, Ro-
salind**, etc, now used independently; a variant form
is **Lynda**; diminutive forms
are **Lin, Lindie, Lindy**.

Lindall, Lindell *masc* a
surname, meaning valley of
lime trees, used as a first
name (*Old English*).

Lindie *fem* a diminutive
form of **Linda**.

Lindley *masc* a placename
and surname, meaning
lime tree meadow or flax
field, used as a first name
(*Old English*); a variant
form is **Linley**.

Lindsay, Lindsey *masc*,
fem a surname, meaning
island of Lincoln, used as a
first name; variant forms
are **Linsay, Linsey, Linzi,
Lynsay, Lynsey**.

Lindy *fem* a diminutive
form of **Linda**.

Linford *masc* a surname,
meaning from the ford of
the lime tree or flax field,
used as a first name (*Old
English*).

Linley *masc* a variant form

of **Lindley**.

Linnette *fem* a variant form of **Lynette**.

Linsay, Linsey *masc, fem* variant forms of **Lindsay**.

Linton *masc* a surname, meaning flax place, used as a first name (*Old English*).

Linus *masc* flaxen-haired (*Greek*).

Linzi *fem* a variant form of **Lindsay**.

Lionel *masc* young lion (*Latin*); a diminutive form is **Len**.

Lis *fem* a diminutive form of **Elisabeth**.

Lisa *fem* a diminutive form of **Elizabeth**, now used independently; a variant form is **Liza**.

Lisbeth *fem* a diminutive form of **Elisabeth**.

Lisette *fem* a diminutive form of **Louise**.

Lisle *masc* a surname, meaning island, or from Lisle in Normandy, used as a first name (*Old French*); variant forms are **Lyall, Lyle**.

Lissa *fem* a diminutive form of **Larissa, Melissa**.

Lister *masc* a surname, meaning dyer, used as a

first name (*Old English*).

Litton *masc* a placename and surname, meaning loud torrent, used as a first name (*Old English*); a variant form is **Lytton**.

Livia *fem* a variant form of **Olivia**.

Liz *fem* a diminutive form of **Elizabeth**.

Liza *fem* a variant form of **Lisa**.

Lizbeth *fem* a diminutive form of **Elizabeth**.

Lizzie, Lizzy *fem* diminutive forms of **Elizabeth**.

Llewelyn *masc* lion-like (*Welsh*).

Lloyd *masc* a surname, meaning grey, used as a first name (*Welsh*).

Locke *masc* a surname, meaning enclosure, stronghold, used as a first name (*Old English*).

Logan *masc* a surname, meaning little hollow, used as a first name (*Scots Gaelic*).

Lois *fem* meaning uncertain, possibly good, desirable (*Greek*).

Lola *fem* a diminutive form of **Dolores, Carlotta**, now used independently.

Lombard *masc* a surname, meaning long beard, used as a first name (*Germanic*).

Lona *fem* a diminutive form of **Maelona**.

Lonnie *masc* a variant form of **Lenny**; a diminutive form of **Alonso**.

Lora *fem* a Welsh form of **Laura**.

Lorcan, Lorcán *masc* fierce (*Irish Gaelic*).

Lorelei *fem* the name of a rock in the River Rhine from where in German legend a siren lured boatmen.

Loren *fem* a variant form of **Lauren**.

Lorenz *masc* the German form of **Laurence**.

Lorenzo *masc* the Italian and Spanish form of **Laurence**.

Loretta *fem* a variant form of **Lauretta**.

Loring *masc* a surname, meaning man from Lorraine (bold and famous), used as a first name (*Germanic/Old French*).

Lorn *masc* a variant form of **Lorne**.

Lorna *fem* a name invented by R. D. Blackmore, possibly from **Lorne**, for the heroine of his novel *Lorna Doone*.

Lorne *masc* a Scottish placename (the northern area of Argyll), of uncertain meaning, used as a first name; a variant form is **Lorn**.

Lorraine *fem* a surname meaning man from Lorraine (bold and famous) used as a first name (*Old French*); a variant form is **Laraine**.

Lot *masc* a veil; a covering (*Hebrew*).

Lotario *masc* the Italian form of **Luther**.

Lothaire *masc* the French form of **Luther**.

Lottie, Lotty *fem* diminutive forms of **Charlotte**.

Lotus *fem* the English name of a fruit that in Greek mythology was said to induce langour and forgetfulness.

Lou *masc* a diminutive form of **Louis**; *fem* a diminutive form of **Louisa, Louise**.

Louella *fem* a combination of **Louise** and **Ella**.

Louis *masc* the French form of **Lewis**; diminutive forms are **Lou, Louie**.

Louisa *fem* form of **Louis**.

Louise *fem* the French form of **Louisa**, now used widely as an English-language form; diminutive forms are **Lisette, Lou**.

Lovel, Lovell *masc* a surname, meaning little wolf, used as a first name (*Old French*); a variant form is **Lowell**.

Lowell *masc* a variant form of **Lovel**.

Luc *masc* the French form of **Luke**.

Luca *masc* the Italian form of **Luke**.

Lucan *masc* a placename, meaning place of elms, used as a first name (*Irish Gaelic*).

Lucas *masc* a variant form of **Luke**.

Luce *fem* a diminutive form of **Lucy**.

Lucia *fem* form of **Lucian**.

Lucian *masc* belonging to or sprung from Lucius (*Latin*).

Lucien *masc* a French form of **Lucian**.

Luciano *masc* an Italian form of **Lucian**.

Lucienne *fem* form of **Lucien**.

Lucifer *masc* light bringer (*Latin*).

Lucilla *fem* a diminutive form of **Lucia**.

Lucille, Lucile *fem* French forms of **Lucia**, now used as English-language forms.

Lucinda *fem* a variant form of **Lucia**; a diminutive form is **Cindy**.

Lucio *masc* a Spanish form of **Luke**.

Lucius *masc* from lux, light (*Latin*).

Lucrèce *fem* a French form of **Lucretia**.

Lucretia, Lucrece *fem* from lucrum, gain (*Latin*).

Lucretius *masc* form of **Lucretia**.

Lucrezia *fem* an Italian form of **Lucretia**.

Lucy *fem* a popular form of **Lucia**; a diminutive form is **Luce**.

Ludlow *masc* a placename, meaning hill by the rapid river, used as a first name (*Old English*).

Ludmila, Ludmilla *fem* of the people (*Russian*).

Ludovic, Ludovick *masc* variant forms of of **Lewis**; a diminutive form is **Ludo**.

Ludvig *masc* a Swedish form of **Lewis**.

Ludwig *masc* the German form of **Lewis**.

Luella *fem* a variant form of **Louella**.

Luigi *masc* an Italian form of **Lewis**.

Luis *masc* a Spanish form of **Lewis**.

Luisa *fem* an Italian and Spanish form of **Louisa**.

Luise *fem* the German form of **Louisa**; a diminutive form is **Lulu**.

Lukas *masc* a Swedish form of **Luke, Lucas**.

Luke *masc* of Lucania in Italy (*Latin*).

Lulu *fem* a diminutive form of **Luise**.

Lundy *masc* a placename, meaning puffin island, used as a first name (Old Norse); born on Monday (*Old French*).

Lutero *masc* a Spanish form of **Luther**.

Luther *masc* illustrious warrior (*Germanic*).

Lyall *masc* a variant form of **Lisle**.

Lycurgus *masc* wolf driver (*Greek*).

Lydia *fem* of Lydia in Asia Minor (*Greek*).

Lyle *masc* a variant form of **Lisle**.

Lyn *fem* a diminutive form of **Lynette, Lynsay**.

Lynda *fem* a variant form of **Linda**; diminutive forms are **Lyn, Lynn, Lynne**.

Lynden, Lyndon *masc* a surname, meaning dweller by lime trees, used as a first name; a diminutive form is **Lyn**.

Lynette *fem* an English form of **Eluned**; variant forms are **Lynnette, Linnette**.

Lynn *fem* a diminutive form of **Lynda**, now used independently.

Lynn *masc* a surname, meaning pool or waterfall, used as a first name (*Celtic*); diminutive forms are **Lyn, Lin, Linn**.

Lynnette *fem* a variant form of **Lynette**.

Lynsay, Lynsey *masc, fem* variant forms of **Lindsay**.

Lyris *fem* She who plays the harp (*Greek*).

Lysander *masc* liberator (*Greek*); a diminutive form is **Sandy**.

Lysandra *fem* form of **Lysander**.

Lyss *masc* a diminutive form of **Ulysses**.

Lytton *masc* a variant form of **Litton**.

M

Maarten *masc* a Dutch form of **Martin**.

Mabel *fem* diminutive forms of **Amabel**, also used independently; a variant form is **Maybelle**.

Mabelle *fem* a French form of **Mabel**.

Madalena *fem* the Spanish form of **Madeleine**.

Maddalena *fem* the Italian form of **Madeleine**.

Maddie, Maddy *fem* diminutive forms of **Madeleine**.

Madeleine, Madeline *fem* from Magdala on the Sea of Galilee (*French*); a variant form is **Magdalene**; diminutive forms are **Maddie, Maddy, Mala**.

Madge *fem* diminutive forms of **Margaret, Marjory**.

Madison *masc* a surname, meaning son of Matthew or Maud, used as a first name (*Old English*).

Madoc *masc* good; beneficent (*Welsh*).

Madonna *fem* my lady, a title of the Virgin Mary (*Italian*).

Mae *fem* a variant form of **May**.

Maelona *fem* princess (Welsh); a diminutive form is **Lona**.

Maeve *fem* intoxicating (*Celtic*); variant forms are **Mave, Meave**.

Magda *fem* a German and Scandinavian form of **Magdalene**.

Magdalene, Magdalen *fem* variant forms of **Madeleine**.

Magee *masc* a surname, meaning son of Hugh, used a a first name (*Irish Gaelic*); a variant form is **McGee**.

Maggie *fem* diminutive forms of **Margaret**.

Magnolia *fem* the name of a tree with showy flowers, named after the French botanist Pierre Magnol, used as a first name.

Magnus *masc* great (*Latin*).

Mahalia *fem* tenderness (*Hebrew*).

Mai, Mair *fem* Welsh forms of **May**.

Maida *fem* the name of a place in Calabria in Spain, where a battle was fought in 1806, used as a first name; a diminutive form is **Maidie**.

Mairead *fem* an Irish form of **Margaret**.

Mairi *fem* Scots Gaelic form of **Mary**.

Maisie *fem* diminutive forms of **Margaret**, also used independently.

Maitland *masc* a surname, meaning unproductive land, used as a first name (*Old French*).

Makepeace *masc* a surname, meaning peacemaker, used as a first name (*Old English*).

Mala *fem* a diminutive form of **Madeleine**.

Malachi *masc* messenger of Jehovah (*Hebrew*).

Malcolm *masc* servant of Columba (*Scots Gaelic*); diminutive forms are **Ca-**

lum, **Mal**.

Malise *masc* servant of Jesus (*Scots Gaelic*).

Mallory *masc* a surname, meaning unfortunate, luckless, used as a first name (*Old French*).

Malone *masc* a surname, meaning follower of St John, used as a first name (*Irish Gaelic*).

Malvina *fem* smooth brow (*Scots Gaelic*).

Mame, Mamie *fem* diminutive forms of **Mary**, now used independently.

Manasseh *masc* one who causes to forget (*Hebrew*).

Manda *fem* a diminutive form of **Amanda**.

Mandy *fem* diminutive forms of **Amanda, Miranda**, now used independently; *masc* little man (*German*).

Manette *fem* a French form of **Mary**.

Manfred *masc* man of peace (*Germanic*); a diminutive form is **Manny**.

Manfredi *masc* the Italian form of **Manfred**.

Manfried *masc* a German form of **Manfred**.

Manley *masc* a surname,

meaning brave, upright, used as a first name (*Middle English*).

Manny *masc* diminutive forms of **Emmnauel, Immanuel, Manfred**.

Manuel *masc* the Spanish form of **Emmanuel**.

Manuela *fem* God with us (*Spanish*).

Marc *masc* a French form of **Mark**; a variant form of **Marcus**.

Marcel *masc* a French form of **Marcellus**.

Marcela *fem* a Spanish form of **Marcella**.

Marcella *fem* form of **Marcellus**.

Marcelle *fem* a French form of **Marcella**.

Marcello *masc* the Italian form of **Marcel**.

Marcellus *masc* the Latin and Scots Gaelic form of **Mark**.

Marcelo *masc* a Spanish form of **Marcel**.

Marcia *fem* form of **Marcius**; a variant form is **Marsha**; diminutive forms are **Marcie, Marcy**.

Marcius *masc* a variant form of **Mark**.

Marco *masc* the Italian form of **Mark**.

Marcos *masc* the Spanish form of **Mark**.

Marcus *masc* the Latin form of **Mark**, now used as an English variant form; a variant form is **Marc**.

Mared *fem* a Welsh form of **Margaret**.

Margaret *fem* a pearl (*Greek*); diminutive forms are **Greta, Madge, Maggie, Margie, May, Meg, Meggie, Meta, Peg**.

Margarete *fem* the Danish and German form of **Margaret**; diminutive forms are **Grete, Gretchen**.

Margaretha *fem* a Dutch form of **Margaret**.

Margarita *fem* the Spanish form of **Margaret**; a diminutive form is **Rita**.

Margaux *fem* a variant form of **Margot**.

Margery *fem* in the Middle Ages a diminutive form of **Margaret**, but now a name in its own right; a variant form is **Marjorie**; a diminutive form is **Madge, Marge**.

Margherita *fem* the Italian form of **Margaret**; a diminutive form is **Rita**.

Margie *fem* diminutive form of **Margaret**.

Margo, Margot *fem* diminutive forms of **Margaret, Marguerite**, now used independently; a variant form is **Margaux**.

Marguerite *fem* the French form of **Margaret**; diminutive forms are **Margo, Margot**.

Mari *fem* an Irish and Welsh form of **Mary**.

Maria *fem* the Latin, Italian, German, and Spanish forms of **Mary**; a diminutive form is **Ria**.

Mariam *fem* the Greek form of **Mary**.

Marian *fem* a French form of **Marion**.

Marianna *fem* an Italian form of **Marianne, Marion**.

Marianne *fem* a French and German form of **Marion**; a compound of **Mary** and **Ann**.

Maribella *fem* a compound of **Mary** and **Bella**.

Marie *fem* a French form of **Mary**; a diminutive form is **Marion**.

Marietta *fem* diminutive form of **Maria**, also used independently

Marigold *fem* the name of the golden flower used as a first name.

Marilyn *fem* diminutive form of **Mary**, also used independently.

Marina *fem* of the sea (*Latin*).

Mario *masc* an Italian form of **Marius**.

Marion *fem* a variant form of **Mary**; *masc* a French form of **Mary**, in compliment to the Virgin Mary.

Marisa *fem* summit (*Hebrew*).

Marius *masc* martial (*Latin*).

Marjorie, Marjory *fem* variant forms of **Margery**.

Mark *masc* a hammer; a male; sprung from Mars (*Latin*); a variant form is **Marcus**.

Markus *masc* the German and Sweidsh form of **Mark**.

Marland *masc* a surname, meaning lake land, used as a first name (*Old English*).

Marlene *fem* a contraction of **Maria Magdalena** (*German*).

Marlo *masc* a variant form of **Marlow**.

Marlon *masc* of uncertain

meaning, possibly hawk-like (*French*).

Marlow *masc* a placename and surname, meaning land of the former pool, used as a first name (*Old English*); variant forms are **Marlo, Marlowe**.

Marmaduke *masc* a mighty noble; Madoc's servant (*Celtic*); a diminutive form is **Duke**.

Marmion *masc* a surname, meaning brat, monkey, used as a first name (*Old French*).

Marsden *masc* a surname, meaning boundary valley, used as a first name (*Old English*).

Marsh *masc* a surname, meaning marsh, used as a first name (*Old English*).

Marsha *fem* a variant form of **Marcia**.

Marshall *masc* a surname, meaning horse servant, used as a first name (*Germanic*).

Marston *masc* a surname, meaning place by a marsh, used as a first name (*Old English*).

Marta *fem* the Italian, Spanish and Swedish form of **Martha**, now used as an English-language form; a

variant form is **Martita**.

Martha *fem* lady (Hebrew); diminutive forms are **Mat, Mattie**.

Marthe *fem* the French and German form of **Martha**.

Marti *fem* a diminutive form of **Martina, Martine**.

Martijn *masc* a Dutch form of **Martin**.

Martin *masc* of Mars; warlike (*Latin*); a variant form is **Martyn**; a diminutive form is **Marty**.

Martina *fem* forms of **Martin**; a diminutive form is **Marti**.

Martine *fem* the French form of **Martina**, now used as an English-language form; a diminutive form is **Marti**.

Martino *masc* an Italian and Spanish form of **Martin**.

Martita *fem* a variant form of **Marta**; a diminutive form is **Tita**.

Marty *masc* a diminutive form of **Martin**.

Martyn *masc* a variant form of **Martin**.

Marvin *masc* a variant form of **Mervin**.

Marwood *masc* a surname,

meaning bigger or boundary wood, used as a first name (*Old English*).

Mary *fem* bitter; their rebellion; star of the sea (*Hebrew*); variant forms are **Marion, Miriam**; diminutive forms are **Mamie, May, Minnie, Mollie, Polly**.

Maryann, Maryanne *fem* compounds of **Mary** and **Ann** or **Anne**.

Marylou *fem* a compound of **Mary** and **Louise**.

Massimiliano *masc* the Italian form of **Maximilian**.

Mat *masc* a diminutive form of **Matthew**; *fem* a diminutive form of **Martha, Mathilda**.

Mateo *masc* the Spanish form of **Matthew**.

Mather *masc* a surname, meaning mower, used as a first name (*Old English*).

Matheson, Mathieson *masc* a surname, meaning son of Matthew, used as a first name.

Mathias *masc* a variant form of **Matthias**.

Mathieu *masc* a French form of **Matthew**.

Mathilda *fem* a variant

form of **Matilda**.

Mathilde *fem* the French form of **Matilda**.

Matilda *fem* might war (Germanic); a variant form is **Mathilda**; diminutive forms are **Mat, Mattie, Tilda, Tilly**.

Matilde *fem* the Italian and Spanish form of **Matilda**.

Matt *masc* a diminutive form of **Matthew**.

Mattaeus *masc* a Danish form of **Matthew**.

Matteo *masc* the Italian form of **Matthew**.

Matthais *masc* a Greek form of **Matthew**.

Matthäus *masc* a German form of **Matthew**.

Mattheus *masc* a Dutch and Swedish form of **Matthew**.

Matthew *masc* gift of Jehovah (*Hebrew*); diminutive forms are **Mat, Matt, Mattie**.

Matthias *masc* a Latin form of **Matthew**; a variant form is **Mathias**.

Matthieu *masc* the French form of **Matthew**.

Mattie *fem* a diminutive form of **Matilda**; *masc* a

diminutive form of **Mat-thew**.

Maud, Maude *fem* a medieval form of **Matilda**.

Maura *fem* an Irish form of **Mary**.

Maureen *fem* an Irish diminutive form of **Mary**.

Maurice *masc* Moorish, dark-coloured (*Latin*); a diminutive form is **Mo**.

Mauricio *masc* a Spanish form of **Maurice**.

Maurits *masc* a Dutch form of **Maurice**.

Maurizio *masc* an Italian form of **Maurice**.

Mauro *masc* the Italian form of **Maurus**.

Maurus *masc* from Mauritania, Moorish (*Latin*).

Mave *fem* a variant form of **Maeve**; a diminutive form of **Mavis**.

Mavis *fem* an alternative name of the song thrush used as a first name (*English*); a diminutive form is **Mave**.

Max *masc* a diminutive form of **Maximilian, Maxwell**, also used independently; a diminutive form is **Maxie**.

Maxie *masc* a diminutive

form of **Max, Maximilian, Maxwell**; *fem* a diminutive form of **Maxine**.

Maximilian *masc* the greatest, a combination of *Maximus* and *Aemilianus* (*Latin*); diminutive forms are **Max, Maxie**.

Maximilien *masc* the French form of **Maximilian**.

Maxine *fem* form of **Max**.

Maxwell *masc* a surname, meaning spring of Magnus, used as a first name; a diminutive form is **Max**.

May *fem* diminutive form of **Margaret, Mary**; the name of the month used as a first name; a variant form is **Mae**; a diminutive form is **Minnie**.

Maybelle *fem* a compound of May and Belle; a variant form of **Mabel**.

Mayer *masc* a surname, meaning physician (*Old French*) or farmer (*Germanic*), used as a first name; variant forms are **Meyer, Myer**.

Maynard *masc* a surname, meaning strong, brave, used as a first name (*Germanic*).

Mayo *masc* a placename, meaning plain of the yew

tree, used as a first name (*Irish Gaelic*).

McGee *masc* a variant form of **Magee**.

Meave *fem* a variant form of **Maeve**.

Medea *fem* meditative; in Greek mythology the princess who helped Jason obtain the Golden Fleece from her father (*Greek*).

Medwin *masc* a surname, meaning mead friend, used as a first name (*ld English*).

Meg, Meggie *fem* diminutive forms of **Margaret**.

Megan *fem Welsh* diminutive form of **Meg**, now used independently.

Mehetabel, Mehitabel *fem* benefited of God (*Hebrew*).

Meironwen *fem* white dairymaid (*Welsh*).

Mel *masc* a diminutive form of **Melville, Melvin, Melvyn**.

Melanie *fem* black (*Greek*).

Melbourne *masc* a surname, meaning mill stream, used as a first name (*Old English*).

Melchior *masc* of uncertain meaning, possibly king of light; in the Bible, one of the three kings (*Hebrew*).

Melchiorre *masc* the Italian form of **Melchior**.

Melfyn *masc* from Carmarthen (*Welsh*).

Melinda *fem* honey (*Greek*) plus the suffix -inda.

Melisande *fem* the French form of **Millicent**.

Melissa *fem* a bee (*Greek*); a diminutive form is **Lissa**.

Melody *fem* a word for tune or tunefulness used as a first name.

Melville, Melvin, Melvyn *masc* a surname, meaning Amalo's place, used as a first name (*Old French*); a diminutive form is **Mel**.

Mercedes *fem* the Spanish form of **Mercy** (as a plural),

Mercer *masc* a surname, meaning merchant, used as a first name (*Old French*).

Mercy *fem* the quality of forgiveness used as a first name (*English*).

Meredith *masc*, *fem* a surname, meaning lord, used as a first name (*Welsh*).

Merfyn *masc* eminent matter (*Welsh*).

Meri *fem* a variant form of

Merry.

Meriel *fem* a Welsh form of **Muriel**; variant forms are **Merle, Meryl**.

Merle *masc* blackbird (*Old French*); a variant form of **Meriel**.

Merlin, Merlyn *masc* sea fort (*Welsh*).

Merri, Merrie *fem* variant forms of **Merry**.

Merrill *masc* a surname, meaning son of Muriel (*Celtic*) or pleasant place (*Old English*), used as a first name; variant forms are **Meryl, Merryll**.

Merry *fem* the adjective, meaning cheerful, mirthful, joyous, used as a first name (*Old English*); a diminutive form of **Meredith**; variant forms are **Meri, Merri, Merrie**.

Merryll *masc* a variant form of **Merrill**.

Merton *masc* a surname, meaning farmstead by the pool, used as a first name (*Old English*).

Mervin, Mervyn *masc* a surname, meaning famous friend, used as a first name (*Old English*); a variant form is **Marvin**; anglicized forms of **Merfyn**.

Meryl *fem* a variant form of **Meriel, Merrill**.

Meta *fem* a diminutive form of **Margaret**.

Meyer *masc* a variant form of **Mayer**.

Mia *fem* a diminutive form of **Maria**.

Micah *masc* who is like unto Jehovah? (*Hebrew*).

Michael *masc* who is like unto God? (*Hebrew*); diminutive forms are **Mick, Micky, Mike**.

Michaela *fem* form of **Michael**.

Michaella *fem* the Italian form of **Michaela**.

Michel *masc* the French form of **Michael**; a German diminutive of **Michael**.

Michele *masc* the Italian form of **Michael**.

Michèle, Michelle *fem* French forms of **Michaela**, now used as English-language forms.

Mick, Micky *masc* diminutive forms of **Michael**.

Mignon *fem* a word, meaning sweet, dainty, used as a first name (*French*); a diminutive form is **Mignonette**; a diminutive form is **Minette**.

Miguel *masc* the Spanish and Portuguese form of **Michael**.

Mikael *masc* the Swedish form of **Michael**.

Mike *masc* a diminutive form of **Michael**.

Mikhail *masc* a Russian form of **Michael**; a diminutive form is **Mischa**.

Mil *fem* a diminutive form of **Mildred, Millicent**.

Milcah *fem* queen (*Hebrew*).

Mildred *fem* gentle counsel (*Germanic*); diminutive forms are **Mil, Millie**.

Miles *masc* a soldier (*Germanic*); a variant form is **Myles**.

Milford *masc* a placename and surname, meaning mill ford, used as a first name (*Old English*).

Miller *masc* a surname, meaning miller, grinder, used as a first name (*Old English*); a variant form is **Milner**.

Millicent *fem* work and strength (*Germanic*); a diminutive form is **Millie**.

Millie *fem* diminutive form of **Amelia, Emilia, Mildred, Millicent**.

Millward *masc* a variant form of **Milward**.

Milne *masc* a surname, meaning at the mill, used as a first name (*Old English*).

Milner *masc* a variant form of **Miller**.

Milo *masc* the Greek samson (*Greek*).

Milton *masc* a surname, meaning middle farmstead or mill farm, used as a first name (*Old English*); a diminutive form is **Milt**.

Milward *masc* a surname, meaning mill keeper, used as a first name (*Old English*); a variant form is **Millward**.

Mima *fem* a diminutive form of **Jemima**.

Mimi *fem* an Italian diminutive form of **Maria**.

Mimosa *fem* the English name of a tropical shrub with yellow flowers used as a first name, from imitative (*Latin*).

Minerva *fem* wise one; in Roman mythology the counterpart of Athena, goddess of wisdom.

Minette *fem* a diminutive form of **Mignonette**..

Minna, Minne *fem* love (*Germanic*); diminutive forms of **Wilhelmina**.

Minnie *fem* a diminutive form of **Mary, May, Wilhelmina**.

Minta *fem* a diminutive form of **Araminta**.

Mira *fem* a diminutive form of **Mirabel, Miranda**.

Mirabel, Mirabelle *fem* wonderful (*Latin*); diminutive forms are **Mira, Myra**.

Miranda *fem* wonderful (*Latin*); diminutive forms are **Mira, Myra**.

Miriam *fem* variant form of **Mary**.

Mischa *masc* a diminutive form of **Mikhail**.

Mitchell *masc* a surname form of **Michael**; a surname, meaning big, great, used as a first name (*Old English*).

Mitzi *fem* a German diminutive form of **Maria**.

Mo *masc fem* diminutive form of **Maureen, Maurice, Morris**.

Modest *masc* the Russian form of *modestus*, obedient (*Latin*).

Modesty *fem* an English word from *modestus* (*Latin*) for the quality of being shy or humble used as a first name.

Modred *masc* counsellor; in Arthurian legend the knight who killed King Arthur (*Old English*).

Moira *fem* an anglicized Irish form of **Mary**; a variant form is **Moyra**.

Mollie, Molly *fem* diminutive forms of **Mary**, now used independently.

Mona *fem* noble (*Irish Gaelic*).

Monica *fem* of certain meaning, but possibly advising (*Latin*).

Monika *fem* the German form of **Monica**.

Monique *fem* the French form of **Monica**, now also used as an English form.

Monroe, Monro *masc* a surname, meaning mouth of the Roe river, used as a first name (*Irish Gaelic*); variant forms are **Munro, Munroe, Munrow**.

Montague, Montagu *masc* a surname, meaning pointed hill, used as a first name; a diminutive form is **Monty**.

Montgomery, Montgomerie *masc* a surname,

meaning hill of powerful man, used as a first name (*Old French/Germanic*); a diminutive form is **Monty**.

Monty *masc* a diminutive form of **Montague, Montgomery**.

Morag *fem* great (*Scots Gaelic*).

Moray *masc* a variant form of **Murray**.

Morgan *masc fem* sea-dweller (*Celtic*).

Morgana *fem* form of **Morgan**.

Moritz *masc* the German form of **Maurice**.

Morley *masc* a surname, meaning moor meadow, used as a first name (*Old English*).

Morna *fem* a Scots variant form of **Myrna**.

Morrice, Morris *masc* variant forms of **Maurice**; a diminutive form is **Mo**.

Mortimer *masc* a surname, meaning dead sea, used as a first name (*Old French*).

Morton *masc* a surname, meaning farmstead moor, used as a first name (*Old English*).

Morven *fem* a Scottish placename, meaning sea gap,

used as a first name (*Scots Gaelic*).

Mosè *masc* the Italian form of **Moses**.

Moses *masc* meaning uncertain, most probably an Egyptian name (*Hebrew*)..

Moyra *fem* a variant form of **Moira**.

Muir *masc* a Scottish form of the surname Moore, meaning moor (*Old French*), used as a surname.

Muirne *fem* beloved (*Irish Gaelic*).

Mungo *masc* amiable (*Gaelic*).

Munro, Munroe, Munrow *masc* variant forms of **Monroe**.

Murdo, Murdoch *masc* sea-warrior (*Scots Gaelic*).

Muriel *fem* sea bright (*Celtic*).

Murray *masc* a surname, meaning seaboard place, used as a first name; a variant form is **Moray**.

Myer *masc* a surname, meaning marsh (*Old Norse*), used a first name; a variant form of **Mayer**.

Myfanwy *fem* my fine one (*Welsh*).

Myles *masc* a variant form of **Miles**; devotee of Mary (*Irish Gaelic*).

Myra *fem* a name invented by the poet Fulke Greville, possibly as an anagram of **Mary**, or to mean she who weeps or laments (*Greek*); a diminutive form of **Mirabel, Miranda**.

Myrna *fem* beloved (*Irish Gaelic*); a variant form is **Morna**.

Myron *masc* fragrant oil (*Greek*).

Myrtle *fem* the name of the shrub used as a first name.

N

Naamah *fem* pretty, loved (*Hebrew*).

Naaman *masc* pleasant (*Hebrew*).

Nadezhda *fem* hope (*Russian*).

Nadia *fem* an English, French and Italian form of **Nadezhda**.

Nadine *fem* a French diminutive form of **Nadia**.

Nahum *masc* comforter (*Hebrew*).

Naida *fem* the water nymph (*Latin*); a diminutive form is **Naiada**.

Nairn *masc* dweller by the alder tree (*Celtic*).

Nairne *fem* from the river (*Gaelic*).

Nan *fem* a diminutive form of **Ann, Nancy, Nanette**.

Nana *fem* a diminutive form of **Hannah**.

Nancy *fem* a diminutive form of **Ann**, now used independently; diminutive forms are **Nan, Nina**.

Nanette *fem* a diminutive form of Ann, now used independently; a diminutive form is **Nan**.

Naomi *fem* pleasantness (*Hebrew*).

Napea *fem* girl of the valley (*Latin*); diminutive forms are **Napaea, Napia**.

Naphtali *masc* my wrestling (*Hebrew*).

Napier *masc* a surname, meaning linen keeper, used as a first name (*Old French*).

Napoleon *masc* lion of the forest dell (*Greek*); a diminutive form is **Nap**.

Nara *fem* nearest and dearest (*English*).

Narda *fem* fragrant perfume. The lingering essence (*Latin*).

Nash *masc* a surname, meaning ash tree, used as a first name (*Old English*).

Nat *masc* a diminutive

form of **Nathan, Nathaniel**.

Natal *masc* the Spanish form of **Noël**.

Natale *masc* the Italian form of **Noël**.

Natalie *fem* a French form of **Natalya** now used as an English-language form.

Natalia *fem* a Spanish form of **Natalya**.

Natalya *fem* Christmas (*Latin/Russian*).

Natasha *fem* a Russian diminutive form of **Natalya**.

Nathan *masc* gift (*Hebrew*); a diminutive form is **Nat**.

Nathania *fem* gift of God (*Hebrew*); diminutive forms are **Natene, Nathene, Nathane**.

Nathaniel, Nathanael *masc* God gave (Hebrew); a diminutive form is **Nat**.

Neal, Neale *masc* variant forms of **Neil**.

Nebula *fem* a cloud of mist (*Latin*).

Ned, Neddie, Neddy *masc* (contraction of "mine Ed") diminutive forms of **Edgar, Edmund, Edward, Edwin**.

Nehemiah *masc* Jehovah

comforts (*Hebrew*).

Neil *masc* champion (*Gaelic*); variant forms are **Neal, Neale, Nial, Niall**.

Nell, Nellie, Nelly *fem* diminutive forms of **Eleanor, Ellen, Helen**.

Nelson *masc* a surname, meaning son of Neil, used as a first name.

Nemo *masc* grove (*Greek*).

Nerice, Nerine, Nerissa *fem* from the sea (*Greek*).

Nero *masc* dark, black-haired (*Latin*).

Nerys *fem* lord (*Welsh*).

Nessa *fem* a diminutive form of **Agnes, Vanessa**.

Nessie *fem* a diminutive form of **Agnes**.

Nesta *fem* a Welsh diminutive form of **Agnes**.

Nestor *masc* coming home (*Greek*).

Netta, Nettie *fem* diminutive forms of **Henrietta**.

Neven *masc* a variant form of **Nevin**.

Neville *masc* a placename and surname, meaning new place, used as a first name (*Old French*).

Nevin *masc* a surname,

meaning little saint, used as a first name (*Irish Gaelic*); variant forms are **Nevin, Niven**.

Newell *masc* a surname, meaning new field, used as a first name (*Old English*).

Newland *masc* a surname, meaning new land, used as a first name (*Old English*).

Newlyn, Newlin *masc* a placename and surname, meaning pool for a fleet, used as a first name (*Cornish*).

Newman *masc* a surname, meaning newcomer, new settler, used as a first name (*Old English*).

Newton *masc* a surname, meaning new farmstead or village, used as a first name (*Old English*).

Nial *masc* variant forms of **Neil**.

Niamh *fem* bright (*Irish Gaelic*).

Niall *masc* a variant form of **Neil**.

Nickson *masc* a variant form of **Nixon**.

Niccolò *masc* an Italian form of **Nicholas**.

Nicholas *masc* victory of the people (*Greek*); a variant form is **Nicolas**; diminutive forms are **Nick, Nicky**.

Nick *masc* a diminutive form of **Nicholas, Nicol**.

Nicky *masc* a diminutive form of **Nicholas, Nicol**; *fem* a diminutive forme of **Nicole**.

Nicodemus *masc* conqueror of the people (*Greek*).

Nicol *masc* a Scottish surname form of **Nicholas** used as a first name.

Nicola *masc* an Italian form of **Nicholas**; *fem* a variant form of **Nicole**.

Nicolas *masc* a Spanish form of **Nicholas**.

Nicole *fem* form of **Nicholas**; variant forms are **Nicola, Nicolette, Colette**; diminutive forms are **Nicky, Nikkie**.

Nigel *masc* black (*Latin*).

Nikki *fem* a diminutive form of **Nicole**.

Nikolaus *masc* a German form of **Nicholas**.

Nils *masc* a Scandinavian form of **Neil**.

Nina *fem* a diminutive form of **Nancy**.

Ninette *fem French* a diminutive form of **Ann**.

Ninian *masc* meaning uncertain; the name of a 5th-century saint (*Celtic*).

Ninon *fem* a diminutive form of **Ann** (*French*).

Nita *fem* a diminutive form of **Anita, Juanita**.

Nixie *fem* Water sprite (*Germanic*); diminutive forms are **Nissie, Nissy**.

Nixon *masc* a surname, meaning son of Nicholas', used as a first name; a variant form is **Nickson**.

Noah *masc* rest (*Hebrew*).

Noble *masc* a surname, meaning noble, famous, used as a first name (*Old French*).

Noé *masc* the French and Spanish form of **Noah**.

Noè *masc* the Italian form of **Noah**.

Noël, Noel *masc .fem* Christmas (*French*)

Noëlle, Noelle *fem* form of **Noël**.

Nola *fem* famous (*Irish Gaelic*).

Nolan *masc* a surname, meaning son of the champion, used as a first name (*Irish Gaelic*)..

Noll, Nollie masc diminutive forms of **Oliver**.

Nona *fem* ninth (*Latin*).

Nora, Norah *fem* a diminutive form of **Eleanor, Honora, Leonora**, also used independently.

Norbert *masc* northern hero (*Germanic*).

Noreen *fem* an Irish form of **Nora**.

Norma *fem* a rule (*Latin*), but probably invented as the name of the heroine of Bellini's opera.

Norman *masc* northman (*Germanic*); a diminutive form is **Norrie**.

Northcliffe *masc* a surname, meaning north cliff, used as a first name (*Old English*).

Norton *masc* a surname, meaning northern farmstead or village, used as a surname (*Old English*).

Norville *masc* a surname, meaning north town, used as a first name (*Old French*).

Norvin *masc* northern friend (*Old English*).

Norward *masc* a surname, meaning northern guardian, used as a first name (*Old English*).

Norwell *masc* a surname, meaning northern stream,

used as a first name.

Norwood *masc* a surname, meaning north wood, used as a first name (*Old English*).

Nowell *masc* an English

form of **Noël**.

Nuala *fem* a diminutive form of **Fionnuala**, also used independently.

Nye *masc* a diminutive form of **Aneurin**.

O

Oakley *masc* a surname, meaning oak tree meadow, used as a first name (*Old English*).

Obadiah *masc* servant of Jehovah (*Hebrew*).

Obed *masc* serving God (*Hebrew*).

Oberon *masc* a variant form of **Auberon**.

Obert *masc* wealthy, brilliant (*Germanic*).

Octavia *fem* form of **Octavius**.

Octavie *fem* a French form of **Octavia**.

Octavius *masc* eighth (*Latin*).

Oda *masc* a French form of **Otto**.

Odd *masc* the Norwegian form of **Otto**.

Oddo, Oddone *masc* Italian forms of **Otto**.

Oded *masc* upholder (*Hebrew*).

Odelia, Odelie *fem* variant

forms of **Odile**.

Odette *fem* a diminutive form of **Oda**.

Odile, Odille *fem* rich, wealthy (*Germanic*); variant forms are **Odelia, Odelie, Ottilie, Otilie**.

Odoardo *masc* an Italian form of **Edward**.

Ofra *fem* a variant form of **Ophrah**.

Ogden *masc* a surname, meaning oak valley, used as first name (*Old English*).

Ogilvie, Ogilvy *masc* a surname, meaning high peak, used as a first name (*Celtic*).

Olaf, Olav *masc* divine remnant (*Old Norse*).

Oleg *masc* the Russian form of **Helge**.

Olga *fem* the Russian form of **Helga**.

Olimpia *fem* the Italian form of **Olympia**.

Olive *fem* an olive (*Latin*);

a variant form is **Olivia**.

Oliver *masc* an olive tree (*Latin*); diminutive forms are **Ollie, Olly, Noll, Nollie**.

Oliverio *masc* the spanish form of **Oliver**.

Olivia *fem* a variant form of **Olive**; a diminutive form is **Livia**.

Oliviero *masc* the Italian form of **Oliver**.

Ollie, Olly *masc* diminutive forms of **Oliver**.

Olwen *fem* white track (*Welsh*).

Olympe *fem* the French form of **Olympia**.

Olympia *fem* heavenly (*Greek*).

Omar *masc* first son (*Arabic*).

Ona *fem* a diminutive form of names ending -ona, e.g. Fiona.

Onefre *masc* a Spanish form of **Humphrey**.

Onefredo *masc* an Italian form of **Humphrey**.

Onfroi *masc* a French form of **Humphrey**.

Onofrio *masc* the Italian form of **Humphrey**.

Onorio *masc* the Italian form of **Honorius**.

Oona, Oonagh *fem* variant forms of **Una**.

Opal *fem* the name of the iridescent gemstone used as a first name, precious stone (*Sanskrit*).

Ophelia *fem* from *ophis*, serpent (*Greek*).

Ophélie *fem* the French form of **Ophelia**.

Ophrah, Ophra *fem* fawn (*Hebrew*); variant forms are **Ofra, Oprah**.

Oprah *fem* a modern variant of **Ophrah**.

Oran *masc* pale-skinned man (*Irish Gaelic*); variant forms are **Orin, Orrin**.

Orazio *masc* the Italian form of **Horace**.

Oren *masc* laurel (*Hebrew*).

Oreste *masc* the Italian form of **Orestes**.

Orestes *masc* mountain climber; in Greek mythology the son of Agnamemnon, who killed his mother and her lover in revenge for the death of his father. (*Greek*).

Orfeo *masc* the Italian form of **Orpheus**.

Oriana, Oriane *fem* golden

(*Latin*).

Oriel *fem* strife (*Germanic*).

Orin *masc* a variant form of **Oran**.

Orion *masc* son of light (*Greek*).

Orla *fem* golden girl (*Irish Gaelic*).

Orlanda *fem* form of **Orlando**.

Orlando *masc* the Italian form of **Roland**.

Ormond, Ormonde *masc* a surname, meaning from east Munster, used as a first name (*Irish Gaelic*).

Orna *fem* form or **Oran**.

Orpheus *masc* of undertain meaning; in Greek mythology, a poet who sought to retrieve his wife Eurydice from Hades.

Orrin *masc* a variant form of **Oran**.

Orso *masc* bear (*Latin/Italian*).

Orsola *fem* the Italian form of **Ursula**.

Orson *masc* little bear (*Latin/Old French*).

Ortensia *fem* the Italian form of **Hortense**.

Orville, Orvil *masc* golden place (*Old French*).

Orwin *masc* a variant form of **Erwin**.

Osbert *masc* god-bright (*Old English*); a diminutive form is **Ossie**.

Osborn, Osborne, Osbourne *masc* a surname, meaning divine bear, or warrior (*Germanic*) a diminutive form is **Ossie**.

Oscar *masc* divine spear (*Germanic*); a diminutive form is **Ossie**.

Oskar *masc* the German and Scandinavian form of **Oscar**.

Osmond, Osmund *masc* divine protection (*Germanic*); a diminutive form is **Ossie**.

Ossie *masc* a diminutive form of **Osbert, Osborn, Oscar, Osmond, Oswald**.

Osvaldo *masc* the Italian form of **Oswald**.

Oswald *masc* divine rule (*Germanic*).

Oswin *masc* god-friend (*Old English*).

Otis *masc* a surname, meaning son of Ote, used as a first name (*Germanic*).

Ottavia *fem* the Italian form of **Octavia**.

Ottavio *masc* the Italian form of **Octavius**.

Ottilie, Otilie *fem* variant forms of **Odile**.

Otto *masc* rich (*Germanic*).

Ottone *masc* an Italian form of **Otto**.

Owain *masc* a Welsh form of **Eugene**.

Owen *masc* a lamb; a young warrior (*Celtic*).

Oxford *masc* a placename, meaning ford for oxen, used as a first name (*Old English*).

Oxton *masc* a surname, meaning place for keeping oxen, used as a first name (*Old English*).

Oz, Ozzie, Ozzy *masc* diminutive forms of names beginning with *Os-*.

P

Pablo *masc* the Spanish form of **Paul**.

Paddy *masc* a diminutive form of **Patrick**; fem a diminutive form of **Patricia**.

Padraig *masc* the Irish Gaelic form of **Patrick**.

Paget, Pagett, Padget, Padgett *masc* a surname, meaning young page, used as a first name (*Old French*).

Paige, Page *fem* a surname, meaning page, used as a first name (*Old French*).

Palmiro *masc* palm (*Latin*).

Palmira *fem* form of **Palmiro**.

Paloma *fem* the Spanish word for dove used as a first name.

Pamela *fem* a name invented by the poet Sir Philip Sidney derived from the Greek work for honey; a diminutive form is **Pam**.

Pancho *masc* a diminutive form of **Francisco**.

Pandora *fem* gifted (*Greek*); in Greek mythology, the first woman on earth.

Pansy *fem* thought (*French*); the name of the garden flower used as a first name.

Paola *fem* the Italian form of **Paula**.

Paolo *masc* the Italian form of **Paul**.

Pascal *masc* of the passover (*Latin/French*).

Pasquale *masc* the Italian form of **Pascal**.

Pat *masc* a diminutive form of **Patrick**; fem a diminutive form of **Patricia**.

Patience *fem* patience (*Latin*).

Patric *masc* a variant form of **Patrick**.

Patrice *masc* the French form of **Patrick**; fem the French form of **Patricia**.

Patricia *fem* form of
Patrick; diminutive forms
are **Paddy, Pat, Patsy,
Pattie, Patty, Tricia**.

Patricio *masc* the Spanish
form of **Patrick**.

Patricius *masc* a variant
form of **Patrick**.

Patrick *masc* noble; a pa-
trician (*Latin*); variant
forms are **Patric, Patricius**; diminutive forms are
Paddy, Pat.

Patrizia *fem* the Italian
form of **Patricia**.

Patrizio *masc* the Italian
form of **Patrick**.

Patrizius *masc* the German form of **Patrick**.

Patsy *fem* a diminutive
form of **Patricia**.

Pattie, Patty *fem* diminutive forms of **Martha, Patience, Patricia**.

Paul *masc* little (*Latin*).

Paula *fem* form of **Paul**.

Paulette *fem* a French
form of **Paula**.

Paulina, Pauline *fem* diminutive forms of **Paula**.

Payne, Payn *masc* a surname, meaning country-
man, used as a first name
(*Old French*).

Peace *fem* the word for the
condition of tranquillity or
calm used as a first name
(*Latin*).

Pearl *fem* the name of the
lustrous white gem used as
a first name.

Pedaiah *masc* Jehovah
ransoms (*Hebrew*).

Pedro *masc* the Portuguese
and Spanish form of **Peter**.

Peer *masc* a Norwegian
form of **Peter**.

Peg, Peggie, Peggy *fem*
diminutive forms of **Margaret**.

Peleg *masc* division (*Hebrew*).

Penelope *fem* duck
(*Greek*); diminutive forms
are **Pen, Penny**.

Penny *fem* diminutive form
of **Penelope**, now used
independently.

Peony *fem* healing (*Greek*),
the name of a plant with
pink, red, white or yellow
flowers used as a first
name.

Pepe *masc* a diminutive
form of **José**.

Pepin *masc* enduring (*Germanic*).

Pepillo, Pepito *masc* diminutive forms of **José**.

Per *masc* a Scandinavian form of **Peter**.

Percival, Perceval *masc* pierce valley (*Old French*).

Percy *masc* a surname, meaning from Perci-en-Auge in Normandy, used as a first name (*Old French*).

Perdita *fem* lost (*Latin*), invented by Shakespeare for a character in *The Winter's Tale*.

Peregrine *masc* wanderer (*Latin*); a diminutive form is **Perry**.

Peronel *fem* a contraction of **Petronel**.

Perry *masc* diminutive form of **Peregrine**, now used in its own right; a surname, meaning pear tree, used as a first name (*Old English*).

Persephone *fem* of uncertain meaning; in Greek mythology, goddess of the underworld (*Greek*).

Persis *fem* a Persian woman (*Greek*).

Peter *masc* stone (*Latin*); diminutive forms are **Pete, Peterkin**.

Petra *fem* form of **Peter**.

Petrina *fem* a diminutive form of **Petra**.

Petronel, Petronella *fem* form of Petronius, a Roman family name (*Latin*).

Petrus *masc* a German form of Peter.

Petula *fem* asking (*Latin*); a diminutive form is **Pet**.

Petunia *fem* the name of a plant with white, blue or purple flowers used as a first name.

Phebe *fem* a variant form of **Phoebe**.

Phedra *fem* bright (*Greek*).

Phèdre *fem* the French form of **Phedra**.

Phelim *masc* always good (*Irish*).

Phemie, Phamie *fem* diminutive forms of **Euphemia**.

Phenie *fem* a diminutive form of **Josephine**.

Phil *masc* a diminutive form of **Philip, Phillip**; *fem* a diminutive form of **Philippa**.

Philbert *masc* very bright (*Germanic*).

Philemon *masc* friendly (*Greek*).

Philip *masc* lover of horses (*Greek*); a variant form is **Phillip**; diminutive forms are **Phil, Pip**.

Philipp *masc* the German form of **Philip**.

Philippa *fem* form of **Philip**; diminutive forms are **Phil, Pippa**.

Philippe *masc* the French form of **Philip**.

Phillip *masc* a a variant form of **Philip**; diminutive forms are **Phil, Pip**.

Philomena *fem* love and strength (*Greek*).

Phineas, Phinehas *masc* serpent's mouth (*Hebrew*).

Phoebe *fem* moon (*Greek*); a variant form is **Phebe**.

Phyllida *fem* a variant form of **Phyllis**.

Phyllis *fem* a green bough (*Greek*).

Pia *fem* form of **Pio**.

Pierce *masc* a surname form of Piers used as a first name.

Pierre *masc* the French form of **Peter**.

Piers *masc* a variant form of **Peter**.

Pierse *masc* a surname form of Piers used as a first name.

Pieter *masc* a Dutch form of **Peter**.

Pietro *masc* the Italian form of **Peter**.

Pilar *fem* pillar (*Spanish*), an allusion to the Virgin Mary who appeared to St James the Greater standing on a pillar.

Pio *masc* the Italian form of **Pius**.

Pip *masc*. a diminutive form of **Philip, Phillip**; *fem* a diminutive form of **Philippa**.

Pippa *fem* a diminutive form of **Philippa**.

Pius *masc* holy (*Latin*).

Placido *masc* peaceful (*Latin/Spanish*).

Plato *masc* broad (*Greek*).

Polly *fem* diminutive form of **Mary**, now used independently.

Pollyanna *fem* a compound of **Polly** and **Anna**.

Pomona *fem* fruitful (*Latin*).

Poppy *fem* the name of the plant that has bright red flower used as a first name.

Portia *fem* gift (*Latin*).

Presley *masc* a surname, meaning priests' meadow, used as a first name.

Prima *fem* form of **Primo**.

Primo *masc* first born (*Latin*).

Primrose *fem* the name of the yellow spring flower used as a first name.

Priscilla *fem* from *prisca*, ancient (*Latin*); diminutive forms are **Cilla, Prissie**.

Prosper *masc* favourable, fortunate (*Latin*).

Pròspero *masc* the Italian form of **Prosper**.

Prudence *fem* the word for the quality of caution or circumspection used as a first name (*Latin*); diminutive forms are **Prue, Prudie**.

Prue *fem* a diminutive form of **Prudence, Prunella**.

Prunella *fem* plum (*Latin*); a diminutive form is **Prue**.

Psyche *fem* of the soul(*Greek*).

Pugh *masc* a surname, meaning son of Hugh, used as a first name (*Welsh*).

Q

Queenie *fem* a diminutive form of the word queen, the supreme woman, used as a first name (*Old English*).

Quenby *fem* a surname, meaning queen's manor, used as a first name (*Old English*).

Quentin *masc* fifth (*Latin*); a variant form is **Quinton**.

Querida *fem* beloved, a Spanish term of endearment used as a first name.

Quinta *fem* form of **Quinto**.

Quinto *masc* the Italian form of **Quintus**.

Quintus *masc* fifth (*Latin*).

Quenel, Quennel *masc* a surname, meaning queen war, used as a first name (*Old English*).

Quigley, Quigly *masc* a surname, meaning untidy, used as a first name (*Irish Gaelic*).

Quinby *masc* a variant form of **Quenby**.

Quincy, Quincey *masc* a surname, meaning fifth place, used as a first name (*Latin/French*).

Quinlan *masc* well formed (*Irish Gaelic*).

Quinn *masc* a surname, meaning wise, used as a first name (*Irish Gaelic*).

Quinton *masc* a variant form of **Quentin**.

R

Rab, Rabbie *masc* diminutive forms of **Robert**.

Raban *masc* raven (*Germanic*).

Rachel *fem* lamb (Hebrew); a variant form is **Rachelle**; diminutive forms are **Rae, Ray**.

Rachele *fem* the Italian form of **Rachel**.

Rachelle *fem* a variant form of **Rachel**.

Radcliffe *masc* a surname, meaning red cliff, used as a first name (*Old English*).

Radley *masc* a surname, meaning red meadow, used as a first name (*Old English*).

Radnor *masc* a placename and surname, meaning red slopes, used as a first name (*Old English*).

Rae *fem* a diminutive form of **Rachel**.

Rafe *masc* a variant form of **Ralph**.

Raffaele, Raffaello *masc*

Italian forms of **Raphael**.

Rafferty *masc* a surname, meaning prosperous, used as a first name (*Irish Gaelic*).

Rahel *fem* a German form of **Rachel**.

Raimondo *masc* the Italian form of **Raymond**.

Raimund *masc* the German form of **Raymond**.

Raimundo *masc* a Spanish form of **Raymond**.

Rainaldo *masc* an Italian form of **Reginald**.

Rainier *masc* a French form of **Rayner**.

Raisa *fem* tolerant (*Greek*).

Raleigh *masc* a surname, meaning red or deer meadow, used as a first name (*Old English*); variant forms are **Rawley, Rayleigh**.

Ralph *masc* famous wolf or hero (*Germanic*); variant forms are **Rafe, Rolph**.

Ram *masc* height (*Hebrew*).

Ramón *masc* a Spanish form of **Raymond**.

Ramona *fem* form of **Ramón**.

Ramsden *masc* Ram's valley (*Old English*).

Ramsay, Ramsey *masc* a placename and surname, meaning wild garlic river island, used as a first name (*Old Norse*).

Ranald *masc* a variant form of **Reginald**.

Rand *masc* a diminutive form of **Randal, Randolf**.

Randal, Randall *masc* a surname diminutive form of **Randolph** used as a first name (*Old English*); a variant form is **Ranulf**.

Randolf, Randolph *masc* shield-wolf (*Germanic*); a variant form is **Ranulf**; diminutive forms are **Rand, Randy**.

Randy *masc* a diminutive form of **Randolf**, also used independently.

Ranee, Rani *fem* queen (*Hindi*).

Rankin, Rankine *masc* a diminutive surname form of **Randolph** used as a first name.

Ransom *masc* a surname, meaning son of Rand, used

as a first name.

Ranulf *masc* a variant form of **Randolf**.

Raoul *masc* the French form of **Ralph**.

Raphael *masc* the healing of God (*Hebrew*).

Raphaela *fem* form of **Raphael**.

Raquel *fem* the Spanish form of **Rachel**.

Ras *masc* a diminutive form of **Erasmus, Erastus**.

Rasmus *masc* a diminutive form of **Erasmus**.

Rastus *masc* a diminutive form of **Erastus**.

Rawley *masc* a variant form of **Raleigh**.

Rawnsley *masc* a surname, meaning Raven's meadow, used as a first name (*Old English*).

Ray *masc* a diminutive form of **Raymond**, now used independently; *fem* a diminutive form of **Rachel**; a variant form is **Rae**.

Rayleigh *masc* a variant form of **Raleigh**.

Raymond, Raymund *masc* wise protection (*Germanic*); a diminutive form is **Ray**.

Rayne *masc*, *fem* a surname, meaning mighty army, used as a first name; variant forms are **Raine** (*fem*), **Rayner** (*masc*).

Rayner *masc* a variant form of **Rayne** (*Germanic*).

Rea *fem* a variant form of **Rhea**.

Read, Reade *masc* a surname, meaning red headed, used as a first name(*Old English*); variant forms are **Reed, Reede**.

Reading *masc* a placename and surname, meaning people of the red one, used as a first name; a variant form is **Redding**.

Reagan *masc* a variant form of **Regan**.

Reardon *masc* a variant form of **Riordan**.

Rebecca, Rebekah *fem* noose (Hebrew); diminutive forms are Beckie, **Becky**.

Redding *masc* a variant form of **Reading**.

Redman *masc* a surname, meaning red cairn or thatcher, used as a first name (*Old English*); a variant form of **Redmond**.

Redmond *masc* counsel profection (*Germanic*); a

variant form is **Redman**.

Reece *masc* a surname form of **Rhys** used as a first name.

Reed, Reede *masc* variant forms of **Read**.

Rees *masc* the English form of **Rhys**.

Reeve, Reeves *masc* steward, bailiff (*Old English*).

Regan *masc*, *fem* a surname, meaning little king, used as a first name (*Irish Gaelic*); variant forms are **Reagan, Rogan**.

Regina *fem* queen (*Latin*).

Reginald *masc* counsel rule (*Germanic*); diminutive forms are **Reg, Reggie**.

Reilly *masc* a surname, meaning valiant, used as a first name (*Irish Gaelic*); a variant form is **Riley**

Reinald *masc* an early English form of **Reginald**.

Reine *fem* queen (*French*).

Reinhard *masc* a German form of **Reynard**.

Reinhold *masc* a Scandinavian form of **Reginald**.

Reinold *masc* a Dutch form of **Reginald**.

Remus *masc* power (*Latin*).

Renaldo *masc* a Spanish form of **Reginald**.

Renata *fem* a diminutive form of **Renée**.

Renato *masc* an Italian and Spanish form of **Reginald**.

Renatus *masc* the Latin form of **René**.

Renault *masc* a French form of **Reginald**.

René *masc* born again (*French*).

Renée *fem* form of **René**.

Renfrew *masc* a placename and surname, meaning point of the torrent, used as a first name (*Celtic*).

Rennie, Renny *masc* a diminutive surname form of Reynold used as a first name.

Renton *masc* a surname, meaning farmstead of Power, used as a first name (*Old English*).

Reuben *masc* behold a son (*Hebrew*); a diminutive form is **Rube**.

Reuel *masc* friend of God.

Reva *fem* form of **Reeve**.

Rex *masc* king (*Latin*).

Rexanne *fem* a compound of **Rex** and **Anne**; a variant form of **Roxanne**.

Reynard *masc* brave advice (*Germanic*); fox (*French*).

Reynold *masc* strong rule (*Germanic*).

Rhea, Rheia *fem* of uncertain origin and meaning; in Roman mythology she was the mother of Remus and Romulus; in Greek mythology she was the mother of several gods, including Zeus; a variant form is **Rea**.

Rhiain *fem* maiden (*Welsh*).

Rhiannon *fem* goddess (*Welsh*).

Rhoda *fem* rose (*Greek*).

Rhodri *masc* circle ruler (*Welsh*).

Rhona *fem* a variant form of **Rona**.

Rhys *masc* ardour (*Welsh*).

Ria *fem* a German diminutive form of **Maria**.

Rica *fem* a diminutive form of **Roderica**.

Ricardo *masc* a Spanish form of **Richard**.

Riccardo *masc* an Italian form of **Richard**.

Rich masc a diminutive form of **Richard, Richmond**.

Richard masc a strong king; powerful (*Germanic*); diminutive forms are **Dick, Rich, Richey, Richie, Rick, Rickie, Ricky, Ritchie**.

Richey, Richie masc diminutive forms of **Richard, Richmond**.

Richmond masc a surname, meaning strong hill, used as a first name (*Old French*); diminutive forms are **Rich, Richey, Richie**.

Rider masc a surname, meaning knight, rider, used as a first name (*Old English*).

Ridley masc a surname, meaning cleared meadow, used as a first name (*Old English*).

Rigby masc a surname, meaning farm on a ridge, used as first name (*Old English*).

Rigg masc a surname, meaning at the ridge, used as a first name (*Old English*).

Riley masc a variant form of **Reilly**.

Rina fem a diminutive form of names ending -rina.

Rinaldo masc an Italian form of **Reginald**.

Ring masc a surname, meaning wearing a ring, used as a first name (*Old English*).

Riordan masc a surname, meaning bard, used as a first name (*Irish Gaelic*); a variant form is **Reardon**.

Ripley masc a placename and surname, meaning strip-shaped clearing, used as a first name (*Old English*).

Rita fem a diminutive form of **Margarita, Margherita**, used independently.

Ritchie masc a diminutive and surname form of **Richard**.

Ritter masc knight or rider (*Germanic*).

Roald masc famous ruler (*Old Norse*).

Robert masc bright in fame (*Germanic*); diminutive forms are **Bob, Bobby, Rab, Rob, Robbie, Robby, Robin**.

Roberta fem form of **Robert**.

Roberto masc the Italian and Spanish form of **Robert**.

Robin masc, fem a diminu-

tive form of **Robert**, now
used independently; a variant form is **Robyn**.

Robina *fem* form of **Robin**.

Robinson *masc* a surname,
meaning son of Robert,
used as a first name (*Old
English*).

Robyn *masc, fem* a variant
form of **Robin**.

Rocco *masc* of uncertain
meaning, possibly crow
(*Germanic*).

Rochelle *fem* little rock
(*French*).

Rochester *masc* a placename, and surname,
meaning Roman fort at the
bridges, used as a surname
(*Old English*).

Rock *masc* stone or oak
(*Old English*).

Rocky *masc* an English
form of **Rocco**.

Rod *masc* a diminutive
form of **Roderick, Rod-
ney**.

Rodden *masc* a surname,
meaning valley of deer,
used as a first name (*Old
English*).

Roddy *masc* a diminutive
form of **Roderick, Rod-
ney**.

Roderica *fem* form of Rod-

erick; a variant form is
Rodericka; a diminutive
form is **Rica**.

Roderich *masc* the German form of **Roderick**.

Roderick, Roderic *masc*
fame powerful (*Germanic*);
diminutive forms are **Rod,
Roddy, Rurik**.

Roderico *masc* an Italian
form of **Roderick**.

Rodger *masc* a variant
form of **Roger**.

Rodney *masc fem* a surname and placename, used
as a first name; a diminutive form is **Rod**.

Rodolf *masc* an Italian and
Spanish form of **Rudolph**.

Rodolphe *masc* a French
form of **Rudolph**.

Rodrigo *masc* an Italian
and Spanish form of **Roderick**.

Rodrigue *masc* the French
form of **Roderick**.

Rogan *masc* a variant form
of **Regan**.

Roger *masc* famous with
the spear (*Germanic*); a
variant form is **Rodger**.

Rogerio *masc* the Spanish
form of **Roger**.

Rohan *masc* healing, incense (*Sanskrit*).

Rohanna *fem* form of **Rohan**.

Róisín, Roisin *fem* an Irish form of **Rose**.

Roland *masc* fame of the land (*Germanic*); variant forms are **Rolland, Rowland**; a diminutive form is **Roly**.

Rolanda, Rolande *fem* forms of **Roland**.

Roldán, Rolando *masc* Spanish forms of **Roland**.

Rolf *masc* a contraction of **Rudolf**; a variant form is **Rollo**.

Rolland *masc* a variant form of **Roland**.

Rollo *masc* a variant form of **Rolf**.

Rolph *masc* a variant form of **Ralph**.

Roly *masc* a diminutive form of **Roland**.

Roma *fem* a Roman (*Latin*).

Romeo *masc* a Roman (*Latin*).

Romilly *masc* a surname, meaning broad clearing (*Old English*) or place of Romilius (*Old French*), used as a first name

Romney *masc* a placename, meaning at the broad river, used as a first

name (*Old English*).

Ròmolo *masc* the Italian form of Romulus, of Etruscan origin and unknown meaning; in Roman legend, Romulus and his brother Remus founded Rome.

Romy *fem* a diminutive form of **Rosemary**.

Ron *masc* a diminutive form of **Ronald**.

Rona *fem* the name of a Scottish island, meaning rough rocky island, used as a first name (*Old Norse*); a variant form is **Rhona**.

Ronald *masc* a variant form of **Reginald**; diminutive forms are **Ron, Ronnie, Ronny**.

Ronalda *fem* form of **Ronald**; diminutive forms are **Ronnie, Ronny**.

Ronan *masc* little seal (*Irish Gaelic*).

Ronnie, Ronny *masc* diminutive forms of **Ronald**; *fem* diminutive forms of **Ronalda, Veronica**.

Rooney *masc* red, red-complexioned (*Gaelic*).

Rory *masc* red (*Irish and Scots Gaelic*).

Rosa *fem* a rose (*Latin*); diminutive forms are **Rosetta, Rosie**.

Rosabel, Rosabella, Rosabelle *fem* a compound of **Rosa** and **Bella**.

Rosalie, Rosalia *fem* little and blooming rose.

Rosalind, Rosaline *fem* beautiful as a rose (*Latin*); a diminutive form is **Linda**.

Rosamund, Rosamond *fem* horse protection; famous protection (*Germanic*); rose of the world (*Latin*).

Rosanne, Rosanna *fem* compounds of **Rose** and **Anne**; variant forms are **Roseanne, Roseanna**.

Roscoe *masc* a surname, meaning deer wood, used as a first name (*Old Norse*).

Rose *fem* the English form of **Rosa**; the name of the flower used as a first name; diminutive forms are **Rosette, Rosie**.

Roseanne, Roseanna *fem* variant forms of **Rosanne, Rosanna**.

Rosemarie *fem* a combination of **Rose** and **Marie**.

Rosemary *fem* the name of the plant associated with remembrance used as a first name; diminutive forms are **Romy, Rosie**.

Rosemonde *fem* a French form of **Rosamund**.

Rosetta *fem* a diminutive form of **Rosa**.

Rosette *fem* a diminutive form of **Rose**.

Rosh *masc* head (*Hebrew*).

Rosie *fem* a diminutive form of **Rosa, Rose, Rosemary**, now also used independently.

Roslin, Roslyn *masc, fem* a placename, meaning unploughable land by the pool, used as first name (*Scots Gaelic*); a variant form is **Rosslyn**.

Rosmunda *fem* the Italian form of **Rosamund**.

Ross *masc* a placename and surname, meaning promontory or moorland, used as a first name (*Scots Gaelic*).

Rosslyn *masc, fem* a variant form of **Roslin**.

Rowan *masc* red (*Irish Gaelic*).

Rowe *masc* a surname, meaning hedgerow, used as a first name (*Old English*).

Rowell *masc* a surname, meaning rough hill, used as a first name (*Old English*).

Rowena *fem* fame and joy

(*Germanic*).

Rowland *masc* a variant form of **Roland**.

Rowley *masc* a surname, meaning rough meadow, used as a first name (*Old English*).

Roxanne, Roxane *fem* dawn of day (*Persian*); a variant form is **Rexanne**; a diminutive form is **Roxie**.

Roxburgh *masc* a placename and surname, meaning Rook's fortress, used as a first name (*Old English*).

Roy *masc* red (*Gaelic*); king (*Old French*).

Royal *masc* a variant form of **Royle**; *fem* the adjective meaning befitting a monarch, regal, used as a first name.

Royce *masc* a surname form of **Rose** used as a first name.

Royle *masc* a surname, meaning rye hill, used as a first name (*Old English*); a variant form is **Royal**.

Royston *masc* a surname, meaning place of Royce, used as a first name (*Germanic/Old English*).

Rube *masc* a diminutive form of **Reuben**.

Rubén *masc* a Spanish form of **Reuben**.

Ruby *fem* the name of the red gemstone used as a first name.

Rudi *masc* German diminutive form of **Rüdiger, Rudolf**.

Rüdiger *masc* the German form of **Roger**.

Rudolf, Rudolph *masc* famous wolf; hero (*Germanic*).

Rudyard *masc* reed enclosure (*Old English*).

Rufe *masc* a diminutive form of Rufus.

Rufus *masc* red-haired (*Latin*); a diminutive form is **Rufe**.

Rugby *masc* a placename and surname, meaning Hroca's stronghold, used as a first name (*Old English*).

Ruggiero, Ruggero *masc* Italian forms of **Roger**.

Rupert *masc* an anglicized Germanic form of **Robert**.

Ruprecht *masc* the German form of **Robert**.

Rurik *masc* a diminutive form of **Roderick, Roderic**.

Russell *masc* a surname meaning, red hair, used as

a first name (Old French);
a diminutive form is **Russ**.

Rutger *masc* a Dutch form
of **Roger**.

Ruth *fem* friend (*Hebrew*).

Rutherford *masc* a surname, meaning cattle ford,
used as a first name (*Old
English*).

Rutland *masc* a pla-
cename, meaning Rota's
estate, used as a first name

(*Old English*).

Ruy *masc* a Spanish form
of **Roderick**.

Ryan *masc* the Irish surname of uncertain meaning
used as a first name.

Rye *masc* From the river-
bank (*French*).

Rylan, Ryland *masc* a
surname, meaning where
rye grows, used as a first
name (*Old English*).

S

Sabin *masc* a shortened form of **Sabinus**.

Sabina *fem* Sabine woman (*Latin*).

Sabine *fem* a French and German form of **Sabina**.

Sabino *masc* an Italian form of **Sabinus**.

Sabinus *masc* Sabine man (*Latin*); a shortened form is **Sabin**.

Sabra *fem* restful (*Hebrew*).

Sabrina *fem* of uncertain meaning, linked to the name of the River Severn (*pre-Celtic*); a variant form is **Zabrina**.

Sadie *fem* a diminutive form of **Sara**.

Sal *fem* a diminutive form of **Sally, Sarah**.

Salina *fem* From the salty place (*Greek*).

Sally, Sallie *fem* diminutive forms of **Sara**, now used independently.

Salome *fem* peaceful (*Hebrew*).

Salomon *masc* the French form of **Solomon**.

Salomo *masc* a Dutch and German form of **Solomon**.

Salomone *masc* the Italian form of **Solomon**.

Salvador *masc* Christ the saviour (*Latin/Spanish*).

Salvatore *masc* the Italian form of **Salvador**.

Salvia *fem* sage (*Latin*).

Sam *masc* a diminutive form of **Samuel**, now used independently; *fem* a diminutive form of **Samantha**.

Samantha *fem* meaning obscure, possibly listener (*Aramic*) or a compound of **Sam** and **Anthea**; a diminutive form is **Sam**.

Sammy *masc* a diminutive form of **Samuel**.

Samson, Sampson *masc* like the sun (*Hebrew*).

Samuel *masc* name of God, or heard by God (*Hebrew*); diminutive forms are **Sam,**

Sammy.

Samuele *masc* the Italian form of **Samuel**.

Samuela *fem* form of **Samuel**.

Sancha, Sanchia *fem* variant forms of **Sancia**.

Sancho *masc* holy (*Spanish*).

Sancia *fem* form of **Sancho**; variant form are **Sancha, Sanchia**.

Sanders *masc* from Alexander (*Old English*); a diminutive form is **Sandy**.

Sandie *fem* a diminutive form of **Alexandra**.

Sandra *fem* a diminutive form of **Alessandra, Alexandra**, now used independently.

Sandy *masc* a diminutive form of **Alexander, Lysander, Sanders**; *fem* a diminutive form of **Alexandra**.

Sanford *masc* a surname, meaning sandy ford, used as a first name (*Old English*).

Sanson *masc* the German form of **Samson**.

Sansón *masc* the Spanish form of **Samson**.

Sansone *masc* the Italian

form of **Samson**.

Santo *masc* saint (*Italian*).

Sapphire *fem* from *saphir*, beautiful (*Hebrew*); the name of the blue precious stone used as a first name.

Sarah, Sara *fem* princess (*Hebrew*); diminutive forms are **Sadie, Sal, Sally**.

Saul *masc* asked for by God (*Hebrew*).

Savanna *fem* a form of the word for an open grassland used as a first name (*Spanish*).

Saveur *masc* the French form of **Salvador**.

Saxon *masc* people of the short swords (*Germanic*).

Scarlett *fem* a variation of the word scarlet, a bright red colour, used as a first name by Margaret Mitchell in her novel *Gone with the Wind*.

Scott *masc* a surname, meaning of Scotland, used as a first name.

Sealey *masc* a variant form of **Seeley**.

Seamas, Seamus *masc* Irish Gaelic forms of **James**.

Sean *masc* an Irish Gaelic form of **John**.

Searle *masc* a surname, meaning armed warrior, used as a surname (*Germanic*).

Seaton *masc* a placename and surname, meaning farmstead at the sea, used as a first name (*Old English*); a variant form is **Seton**.

Sebastian *masc* august, majestic (*Greek*).

Sebastiano *masc* the Italian form of **Sebastian**.

Sébastien *masc* the French form of **Sebastian**.

Secondo *masc* the Italian form of **Secundus**.

Secundus *masc* second born (*Latin*).

Seeley *masc* a first name, meaning blessed and happy, used as a first name (*Old English*); a variant form is **Sealey**.

Seigneur *masc* a variant form of **Senior**.

Selby *masc* a placename and surname, meaning place by the willow trees, used as a first name (*Old English*).

Selden *masc* From the valley of the willow tree (*Old English*).

Selig *masc* blessed, happy

one (*Yiddish*); a variant form is **Zelig**.

Selina, Selena *fem* parsley; heavenly (*Greek*); a diminutive form is **Lina**.

Selma *fem* form of **Anselm**.

Selwyn, Selwin *masc* wild (Old French) (*Germanic*).

Semele *fem* single (*Latin*).

Senga *fem* slender (*Gaelic*); backward spelling of **Agnes**.

Senior *masc* a surname, meaning lord, used as a first name (*Old French*); a variant form is **Seigneur**.

Seonaid *fem* a Gaelic form of **Janet**.

Septima *fem* form of **Septimus**.

Septimus *masc* seventh (*Latin*).

Seraphina, Serafina *fem* of the seraphim, of burning faith (*Hebrew*).

Serena *fem* calm; peaceful (*Latin*).

Serge *masc* the French form of **Sergius**.

Sergei *masc* the Russian form of **Sergius**.

Sergio *masc* the Italian form of **Sergius**.

Sergius *masc* a Roman family name of Etruscan origin and unknown meaning.

Sesto *masc* the Italian form of **Sextus**.

Seth *masc* appointed (*Hebrew*).

Seton *masc* a variant form of **Seaton**..

Seumas *masc* a Gaelic form of **James**.

Sewald, Sewall, Sewell, *masc* a surname, meaning sea powerful, used as a first name (*Old English*); a variant form is **Siwald**.

Sexton *masc* a surname, meaning sacristan, used as a first name (*Old French*).

Sextus *masc* sixth (*Latin*).

Seymour *masc* a surname, meaning from Saint-Maur in France, used as a first name (*Old French*).

Shalom *masc* peace (*Hebrew*).

Shamus *masc* an anglicized form of **Seamus**.

Shane *masc* an anglicized form of **Sean**.

Shanley *masc* a surname, meaning son of the hero, used as a first name (*Irish Gaelic*).

Shannon *fem* the name of the Irish river, meaning the old one, used as a first name.

Shari *fem* a diminutive form of **Sharon**.

Sharon *fem* a Biblical placename mentioned in the Song of Solomon used as a first name (*Hebrew*); a diminutive form is **Shari**.

Shaw *masc* a surname, meaning small wood or grove, used as a first name (*Old English*).

Shawn, Shaun *masc* anglicized forms of **Sean**.

Shea *masc* a surname, meaning stately, dauntless, used as a first name (*Irish Gaelic*).

Sheelagh *fem* a variant form of **Sheila**.

Sheelah *fem* petition (*Hebrew*); a variant form of **Sheila**.

Sheena *fem* an anglicized form of **Sine**.

Sheffield *masc* a placename, meaning open land by the Sheaf river, used as a first name (*Old English*).

Sheila, Shelagh *fem* anglicized forms of **Sile**; variant forms are **Sheelagh, Sheelah**.

Sheldon *masc* a surname, meaning heathery hill with a shed, flat-topped hill, or steep valley, used as a first name (*Old English*).

Shelley *fem* a surname, meaning clearing on a bank, used as a firrst name (*Old English*).

Shepard *masc* a surname, meaning sheep herder, shepherd, used as a first name (*Old English*).

Sherborne, Sherbourne *masc* a surname, meaning clear stream, used as a first name (*Old English*).

Sheree, Sheri *fem* variant forms of **Chérie**.

Sheridan *masc* a surname, meaning seeking, used as a first name (*Irish Gaelic*).

Sherlock *masc* fair-haired (*Old English*).

Sherman *masc* a surname, meaning shearman, used as a first name (*Old English*).

Sherwin *masc* a surname, meaning loyal friend or fast-footed, used as a first name (*Old English*).

Sherwood *masc* a placename and surname, meaning shore wood, used as a first name (*Old English*).

Sheryl *fem* a variant form of **Cheryl**.

Shirley *fem* a surname and placename, meaning thin clearing, used as a first name; a diminutive form is **Shirl**.

Sholto *masc* sower, seed-bearing (*Scots Gaelic*).

Shona *fem* the anglicized form of **Seonaid**.

Sian *fem* the Welsh form of **Jane**.

Sibeal *fem* an Irish form of **Sybyl**.

Sibyl, Sibylla *fem* soothsayer (*Greek*); variant forms are **Sybyl, Sybylla**; a diminutive form is **Sib**.

Siddall, Siddell *masc* a surname, meaning broad slope, used as a first name (*Old English*).

Sidney *masc fem* a surname, meaning wide island, used as a first name; a variant form is **Sydney**; a diminutive form is **Sid**.

Sidonia, Sidonie, Sydony *fem* of Sidon (*Latin*).

Siegfried *masc* victory peace (*Germanic*).

Siegmund *masc* the German form of **Sigmund**.

Sierra *fem* the name for a

mountain range used as a
first name (*Spanish*).

Sigismond *masc* the
French form of **Sigmund**.

Sigismondo *masc* the Italian form of **Sigmund**.

Sigiswald *masc* victorious
ruler (*Germanic*).

Sigmund *masc* victory protection (*Germanic*); a diminutive form is **Sig**.

Sigrid *fem* fair and victorious (*Old Norse*); a diminutive form is **Siri**.

Sigurd *masc* victorious
guardian (*Old Norse*).

Silas *masc* a shortened
form of **Silvanus**.

Sile *fem* the Gaelic form of
Celia, Cecily, often ren-
dered in English as **Sheila,
Shelagh**, etc.

Silvain *masc* a French
form of **Silvanus**.

Silvana *fem* form of **Silvano**.

Silvano *masc* the Italian
form of **Silvanus**.

Silvanus *masc* of a wood
(*Latin*); a variant form is
Sylvanus.

Silvester *masc* of a wood
(*Latin*); a variant form is
Sylvester; a diminutive
form is **Sly**.

Silvestre *masc* a French
and Spanish form of **Silvester**.

Silvestro *masc* an Italian
form of **Silvester**.

Silvia *fem* of a wood (*Latin*); a variant form is **Sylvia**.

Silvie *fem* the French form
of **Silvia**.

Silvio *masc* the Italian and
Spanish forms of **Silvanus**.

Sim *masc* a diminutive
form of **Simon, Simeon**;
fem a diminutive form of
Simone.

Simon, Simeon *masc* hear-
ing with acceptance (*He-
brew*); diminutive forms are
Sim, Simmy.

Simona *fem* form of **Simon**; a diminutive form is
Sim.

Simone *fem* the French
form of **Simona**.

Sinclair *masc* a surname,
meaning from St Clair in
France, used as a first
name (*Old French*); a variant form is **St Clair**.

Sine *fem* a Gaelic form of
Jane, often rendered in
English as **Sheena**.

Sinead *fem* an Irish Gaelic
form of **Janet**.

Siobhan *fem* an Irish Gaelic form of **Jane**.

Sioned *fem* a Welsh form of **Janet**.

Sisley *fem* a variant form of **Cecily**; diminutive forms are **Sis, Sissie, Sissy**.

Siwald *masc* a variant form of **Sewald**.

Skelton *masc* a surname, meaning farmstead on a hill, used as first name (*Old English*).

Skerry *masc* sea rock (*Old Norse*).

Skipper *masc* a nickname and surname, meaning jumping (Middle English) or ship's captain (*Dutch*), used as a first name; a diminutive form is **Skip**.

Skipton *masc* a placename and surname, meaning sheep farm, used as a first name (*Old English*).

Slade *masc* a surname, meaning valley, used as a first name (*Old English*).

Sly *masc* a diminutive form of **Silvester, Sylvester**.

Smith *masc* a surname, meaning blacksmith, used as a first name (*Old English*).

Snowden, Snowdon *masc* a surname, meaning snowy hill, used as a first name (*Old English*).

Sofie *fem* the French form of **Sophie**.

Sol *masc* the sun (*Latin*); a diminutive form of **Solomon**.

Solly *masc* a diminutive form of **Solomon**.

Solomon *masc* peaceable (*Hebrew*); diminutive forms are **Sol, Solly**.

Solveig *fem* house strong (*Old Norse*).

Somerled *masc* summer traveller (*Old Norse*).

Somerset *masc* a placename, meaning settlers around the summer farmstead, used as a first name (*Old English*).

Somerton *masc* a placename, meaning summer farmstead, used as a first name (*Old English*).

Somhairle *masc* an Irish and Scots Gaelic form of **Somerled**.

Sonya, Sonia *fem* a Russian diminutive form of **Sophia**.

Sophia *fem* wisdom (*Greek*).

Sophie, Sophy *fem* diminutive forms of **Sophia**, now

used independently.

Sophronia *fem* of a sound mind (*Greek*).

Sorcha *fem* bright one (*Irish Gaelic*).

Sorley *masc* an anglicized form of **Somhairle**.

Sorrel *masc* sour (*Germanic*), the name of a salad plant used as a first name.

Spencer *masc* a surname, meaning steward or dispenser, used as a first name (*Old French*).

Spring *fem* desire (*Sanskrit*), the name of the season between winter and summer used as a first name.

Squire *masc* a surname, meaning shield bearer, used as a first name (*Old French*).

Stacey *masc* a diminutive form of **Eustace**, now used independently; *fem* a diminutive form of **Eustacia, Anastasia**, now used independently.

Stacy, Stacie *fem* diminutive forms of **Eustacia, Anastasia**, now used independently.

Stafford *masc* a surname, meaning ford by a landing place, used as a first name

(*Old English*).

Stamford *masc* a variant form of **Stanford**.

Standish *masc* a surname, meaning stony pasture, used as a first name (*Old English*).

Stanford *masc* a surname, meaning stone ford, used as a first name (*Old English*); a variant form is **Stamford**.

Stanhope *masc* a surname, meaning stony hollow, used as a first name (*Old English*).

Stanislas, Stanislaus *masc* government and glory (*Slavonic*).

Stanley *masc* a surname and placename meaning stony field, used as a first name (*Old English*).

Stanton *masc* a surname, meaning stony farmstead, used as first name (*Old English*).

Star, Starr *fem* an English form of **Stella**.

Stasia *fem* a diminutive form of **Anastasia**.

Stefan *masc* a German form of **Stephen**.

Stefano *masc* the Italian form of **Stephen**.

Steffi, Steffie *fem* diminutive forms of **Stephanie**.

Stella *fem* star (*Latin*).

Stephan *masc* a German form of **Stephen**.

Stephanie *fem* form of **Stephen**; a diminutive form is **Stevie**.

Stephen, Steven *masc* crown (*Greek*); diminutive forms are **Steve, Stevie**.

Sterling *masc* a surname, meaning little star, used as a first name (*Old English*); a variant form is **Stirling**.

Stewart *masc* a variant and surname form of **Stuart**.

Stirling *masc* a variant form of **Sterling**; a placename, meaning enclosed land by the stream, used as a first name (*Scottish Gaelic*).

St John *masc* Saint John (pronounced *sinjon*).

Stockland *masc* a surname, meaning land of a religious house, used as a first name (*Old English*).

Stockley *masc* a surname, meaning cleared meadow of a religious house, used as a first name (*Old English*).

Stockton *masc* a placename and surname, meaning outlying farmstead, used as a first name (*Old English*).

Stoddard *masc* a surname, meaning horse keeper, used as a first name (*Old English*).

Stoke *masc* a placename and surname, meaning outlying farmstead, used as a first name (*Old English*).

Storm *masc, fem* the word for a meteorological condition of violent winds and rain, hail or snow used as a first name (*Old English*).

Stowe *masc* a surname, meaning holy place, used as a first name (*Old English*).

Strachan, Strahan *masc* a surname, meaning littl valley, used as a first name (*Scots Gaelic*).

Stratford *masc* a placename, meaning ford on a Roman road, used as a first name (*Old English*).

Stuart, Stewart, Steuart *masc* the surname meaning "steward" used as a first name (*Old English*).

Sukey, Sukie *fem* diminutive forms of **Susan**.

Sullivan *masc* a surname, meaning black-eyed, used as a surname (*Irish Gaelic*).

Summer *fem* season (*Sanskrit*), the name of the season between spring and autumn used as a personal name.

Sumner *masc* a surname, meaning one who summons, used as a first name (*Old French*).

Susan *fem* the English form of **Susanna**; diminutive forms are **Sue, Sukey, Sukie, Susie, Susy**.

Susanna, Susannah *fem* lily (*Hebrew*); a variant form is **Suzanna**.

Susanne *fem* a German form of **Susanna**.

Sutherland *masc* a placename and surname, meaning southern land, used as a first name (*Old Norse*).

Sutton *masc* a placename and surname, meaning southern farmstead, used as a first name (*Old English*).

Suzanna *fem* a variant form of **Susanna**.

Suzanne *fem* a French and German form of **Susan**.

Sven *masc* lad (*Old Norse*).

Sybille *fem* the French form of **Sybyl**.

Sybyl, Sybilla *fem* variant forms of **Sibyl, Sibylla**; a diminutive form is **Syb**.

Sydney *masc* a variant form of **Sidney**.

Sylvain *masc* a French form of **Silvanus**.

Sylvanus *masc* a variant form of **Silvanus**.

Sylvester *masc* a variant form of **Silvester**; a diminutive form is **Sly**.

Sylvia *fem* a variant form of **Silvia**.

Sylvie *fem* the French form of **Silvia**.

T

Tabitha *fem* gazelle (*Aramaic*); diminutive forms are **Tab, Tabby**.

Tad *masc* a diminutive form of **Thaddeus**, also used independently.

Taddeo *masc* the Italian form of **Thaddeus**.

Tadhg *masc* an Irish Gaelic form of **Thaddeus**; a variant form is **Teague**.

Taffy *masc* Welsh form of David (*Celtic*).

Taggart *masc* a surname, meaning priest, used as a surname (*Scots Gaelic*).

Tate *masc* a surname, meaning cheerful, used as a first name (*Old Norse*); variant forms are **Tait**, **Teyte**.

Talbot *masc* a surname, meaning command of the valley, used as a first name (*Germanic*).

Talitha *fem* maiden (*Aramaic*).

Tallulah *fem* a placename, meaning spring water,

used as a first name (*North American Indian*).

Tam *masc* (*Scots*) a diminutive form of **Thomas**.

Tamar *fem* palm tree (*Hebrew*); diminutive forms are **Tammie, Tammy**.

Tamara *fem* the Russian form of **Tamar**.

Tammie, Tammy *fem* diminutive forms of **Tamar**, **Tamsin**; *masc* a diminutive form of **Thomas**.

Tamsin *fem* a Cornish contraction of **Thomasina**, now used independently; a diminutive form is **Tammie**.

Tancredi, Tancredo *masc* Italian forms of **Tancred**.

Tancred*masc* thought strong (*Germanic*).

Tania, Tanya *fem* diminutive forms of **Tatiana, Titania**, now used independently.

Tanisha *fem* born on Monday (*Hausa*).

Tansy *fem* immortal (*Greek*), the name of a medicinal plant bearing yellow flowers used as a first name.

Tara *fem* a placename, meaning rocky assembly place, used as a first name; in Irish history, the site of ancient royal power (*Irish Gaelic*).

Tate *masc* a variant form of **Tait**.

Tatiana *fem* form of a Roman family name of unknown meaning (*Latin*); diminutive forms are **Tania, Tanya**.

Taylor *masc* a surname, meaning tailor, used as a first name (*Old French*).

Teague *masc* a variant form of **Tadhg**.

Tebaldo *masc* an Italian form of **Theobold**.

Ted, Teddie, Teddy *masc* diminutive forms of **Edward, Theodore, Theodoric**.

Tempest *fem* the word for a violent storm used as a first name (*Latin*).

Tennison, Tennyson *masc* variant forms of **Dennison**.

Teobaldo *masc* an Italian and Spanish form of **Theobald**.

Teodorico *masc* an Italian form of **Theodoric**.

Teodoro *masc* an Italian and Spanish form of **Theodore**.

Teodora *fem* an Italian and Spanish form of **Theodora**.

Teodosia *fem* an Italian form of **Theodosia**.

Terence *masc* from a Roman family name of unknown origin (*Latin*); variant forms are **Terrance, Terrence**; diminutive forms are **Tel, Terry**.

Terencio *masc* a Spanish form of **Terence**.

Teresa *fem* the Italian and Spanish forms of **Theresa**.

Terese *fem* a variant form of **Theresa**.

Teri *fem* a diminutive form of **Theresa**.

Terrance, Terrence *masc* variant forms of **Terence**.

Terri *fem* a diminutive form of **Teresa, Theresa**, now used independently.

Terris, Terriss *masc* a surname, meaning son of Terence, used as a first name.

Terry *fem* a diminutive form of **Teresa**; *masc* a diminutive form of **Terence**.

Tertius *masc* third (*Latin*).

Tess, Tessa, Tessie *fem* diminutive forms of **Esther, Teresa, Theresa**.

Teyte *masc* a variant form of **Tait**.

Thaddeus *masc* gift of God (*Greek-Aramaic*); diminutive forms are **Tad, Thad, Thaddy**.

Thaine *masc* a surname, meaning holder of land in return for military service, used as a first name (*Old English*); a variant form is **Thane**.

Thalia *fem* flourishing blossom (*Greek*).

Thane *masc* a variant form of **Thaine**.

Thea *fem* a diminutive form of **Althea, Dorothea**, now used independently.

Thecla *fem* god glory (*Greek*).

Thelma *fem* will (*Greek*).

Theda *fem* a diminutive form of **Theodora, Theodosia**.

Thelma *fem* a name coined in the 19th century by

Marie Corelli for her novel *Thelma*, perhaps from wish (*Greek*).

Theo *masc fem* diminutive forms of **Theobald, Theodore, Theodora**.

Theobald *masc* bold for the people (*Germanic*); a diminutive form is **Theo**.

Theodor *masc* a Scandinavian and German form of **Theodore**.

Theodora *fem* form of **Theodore**; diminutive forms are **Dora, Theo**.

Theodore *masc* the gift of God (*Greek*); diminutive forms are **Ted, Teddie, Teddy, Theo**.

Theodoric, Theodorick *masc* people powerful (*Germanic*); diminutive forms are **Derek, Derrick, Dirk, Ted, Teddie, Teddy**.

Theodorus *masc* a Dutch form of **Theodore**.

Theodosia *fem* gift of God (*Greek*).

Theodosius *masc* form of **Theodosia**.

Theophila *fem* form of **Theophilus**.

Theophilus *masc* lover of God (*Greek*).

Theresa *fem* carrying ears

of corn (*Greek*); diminutive forms are **Teri, Terri, Terry, Tess, Tessa, Tessie, Tracey, Tracie, Tracy**.

Thérèse *fem* the French form of **Theresa**.

Theresia, Therese *fem* German forms of **Theresa**.

Theron *masc* hero (*Greek*).

Thewlis *masc* a surname, meaning ill-mannered, used as a first name (*Old English*).

Thibaut *masc* a French form of **Theobald**.

Thierry *masc* a French form of **Theodoric**.

Thirza *fem* pleasantness (*Hebrew*); variant forms are **Thyrza, Tirza**.

Thomas *masc* twin (*Aramaic*); diminutive forms are **Tam, Thom, Tom, Tommy**.

Thomasina, Thomasine *fem* forms of **Thomas**.

Thor *masc* thunder (Old Norse), in Norse mythology, the god of thunder; a variant form is **Tor**.

Thora *fem* form of **Thor**.

Thorburn *masc* a surname, meaning Thor's warrior or bear, used as a first name (*Old Norse*).

Thordis *fem* a variant form of **Tordis**.

Thorndike, Thorndyke *masc* a surname, meaning thorny ditch, used as a first name (*Old English*).

Thorne *masc* a surname, meaning thorn tree or hawthorn, used as a first name (*Old English*).

Thorold *masc* Thor rule (Old Norse); a variant form is **Torold**.

Thorp, Thorpe *masc* a surname, meaning farm village, used as a first name (*Old English*).

Thorwald *masc* ruled by Thor (*Old Norse*); a variant form is **Torvald**.

Thurstan, Thurston *masc* a surname, meaning Thor stone, used as a first name (*Old Norse*).

Thyrza *fem* a variant form of **Thirza**.

Tib, Tibbie *fem* Scots diminutive forms of **Isabel, Isabella**.

Tibold *masc* a German form of **Theobald**.

Tiebout *masc* a Dutch form of **Theobald**.

Tiernan, Tierney *masc* a surname, meaning lord,

used as a first name (*Irish Gaelic*); a variant form is **Kier-nan**.

Tiffany *fem* the manifestation of God, the festival of Epiphany (*Greek*).

Tilda, Tilde *fem* diminutive forms of **Matilda**.

Till *masc* a German diminutive form of Dietrich.

Tilly *fem* a diminutive form of **Matilda**.

Tim *masc* a diminutive form of **Timon, Timothy**.

Timon *masc* reward (*Greek*).

Timothea *fem* form of **Timothy**.

Timothy *masc* honouring God (*Greek*); diminutive forms are **Tim, Timmie, Timmy**.

Tina *fem* a diminutive form of **Christina, Christine**, etc, also used independently.

Tiphaine *fem* a French form of **Tiffany**.

Tiree *fem* the name of an island, meaning land of corn, used as a first name (*Scots Gaelic*).

Tirza, Tirzah *fem* variant forms of **Thirza**.

Tita *fem* form of **Titus**; a

diminutive form of **Martita**.

Titania *fem* giant, in medieval folklore wife of Oberon and queen of fairies (*Greek*); diminutive forms are **Tania, Tanya**.

Titian *masc* an English form of **Titianus**.

Titianus *masc* a Roman name derived from **Titus**.

Tito *masc* the Italian and Spanish form of **Titus**.

Titus *masc* protected (*Latin*)

Tiziano *masc* the Italian form of **Titianus**.

Tobey *fem* form of **Toby**; a variant form is **Tobi**.

Tobi *masc* a variant form of **Toby**; *fem* a variant form of **Tobey**.

Tobias, Tobiah *masc* Jehovah is good (*Hebrew*); a diminutive form is **Toby**.

Toby *masc* a diminutive form of **Tobias**, now used independently; a variant form is **Tobi**.

Todd *masc* a surname, meaning fox, used as a first name (*Old Norse*).

Todhunter *masc* a surname, meaning foxhunter, used as a first name (*Old*

Norse/Old English).

Tom *masc* a diminutive
form of **Thomas**, now used
independently.

Tomas *masc* the Spanish
form of **Thomas**.

Tomasina, Tomina *fem*
forms of **Thomas**.

Tomás *masc* a Spanish
form of **Thomas**.

Tomaso, Tommaso *masc*
Italian forms of **Thomas**.

Tommaso *masc* an Italian
form of **Thomas**.

Tommie, Tommy *masc*
diminutive forms of **Thomas**.

Toni *fem* diminutive forms
of **Annette, Antoinette,
Antonia**, now used inde-
pendently.

Tonia *fem* a diminutive
form of **Antonia**.

Tonie *fem* diminutive
forms of **Annette, Antoinette, Antonia**, now used
independently.

Tony *masc* a diminutive
form of **Antony**; *fem* a diminutive form of **Annette,
Antoinette, Antonia**.

Topaz *fem* the name of a
white gemstone used as a
first name topaz gem.

Tordis *fem* Thor's goddess

(Old Norse); a variant form
is **Thordis**.

Tormod *masc* Thor's spirit
(Old Norse).

Torold *masc* a variant form
of **Thorold**.

Torquil *masc* God's cauldron *(Old Norse)*.

Tor *masc* a variant form of
Thor.

Torr *masc* a surname,
meaning tower *(Old Eng-
lish)* or bull *(Old French)*
used as a first name.

Torvald *masc* a variant
form of **Thorwald**.

Tory *fem* a diminutive form
of **Victoria**.

Townsend, Townshend
masc a surname, meaning
end of the village, used as a
first name *(Old English)*.

Tracey *masc* a variant
form of **Tracy**; *fem* a diminutive form of **Teresa,
Theresa**.

Tracie *fem* a diminutive
form of **Teresa, Theresa**,
now used independently.

Tracy *masc* a surname,
meaning Thracian, used as
a first name *(Old French)*;
a variant form is **Tracey**;
fem a diminutive form of
Teresa, Theresa, now
used independently.

Traherne *masc* a surname, meaning iron strength, used as a first name (*Welsh*).

Travers *masc* a surname, meaning crossing, crossroads, used as a first name (*Old French*); a variant form is **Travis**.

Traviata *fem* lead astray, the title of Verdi's opera used as a first name (*Italian*).

Travis *masc* a variant form of **Travers**.

Tremaine, Tremayne *masc* a surname, meaning homestead on the rock, used as a first name (*Cornish*).

Trent *masc* a river name, meaning liable to flood, used as a first name (*Celtic*).

Trev *masc* a diminutive form of **Trevor**.

Trevelyan *masc* a surname, meaning mill farm, used as a first name (*Cornish*).

Trevor *masc* a surname, meaning big river, used as a first name (*Welsh*); a diminutive form is **Trev**.

Tricia *fem* a diminutive form of **Patricia**.

Trilby *fem* a name coined by George du Maurier in the 19th century for the heroine of his novel *Trilby*.

Trisha *fem* a diminutive form of **Patricia**.

Tristram, Tristam, Tristan *masc* grave; pensive (*Latin*); tumult (*Celtic*).

Trix, Trixie *fem* diminutive forms of **Beatrice**.

Troy *masc* a surname, meaning of Troyes, used as a first name (*Old French*); the name of the city in Asia Minor besieged by the Greeks used as a first name.

Truda, Trudie, Trudy *fem* diminutive forms of **Gertrude**.

True *masc* the adjective for the quality of being faithful and loyal used as a first name.

Truelove *masc* a surname, meaning faithful sweetheart, used as a first name (*Old English*).

Trueman, Truman *masc* a surname, meaning faithful servant, used as a first name (*Old English*).

Trystan *masc* a Welsh form of **Tristan**.

Tudor *masc* a Welsh form

of **Theodore**.

Tuesday *fem* day of Mars
(Old English), the name of
the second day of the week
used as a first name (*Old
English*).

Tullio *masc* the Italian
form of **Tullius**.

Tullius *masc* a Roman family name of Etruscan origin
and uncertain meaning.

Tully *masc* a surname,
meaning flood, used as a
first name (*Irish Gaelic*);
an English form of **Tullius**.

Turner *masc* a surname,
meaning worker on a lathe,
used as a first name (*Old
French*).

Turpin *masc* a surname,
meaning Thor the Finn,
used as a first name (*Old
Norse*).

Twyford *masc* a surname,
meaning double ford, used

as a first name (*Old English*).

Ty *masc* a diminutive form
of **Tybalt, Tyler, Tyrone,
Tyson**.

Tybalt *masc* a variant form
of **Theobald**; a diminutive
form is **Ty**.

Tye *masc* a surname,
meaning enclosure, used as
a first name (*Old English*).

Tyler *masc* a surname,
meaning tile-maker, used
as a first name (*Old English*); a diminutive form is
Ty.

Tyrone *masc* a placename
and surname, meaning
land of Owen, used as a
first name (*Irish Gaelic*); a
diminutive form is **Ty**.

Tyson *masc* a surname,
meaning firebrand, used as
a first name (*Old French*);
a diminutive form is **Ty**.

U

Uberto *masc* an Italian form of **Hubert**.

Uda *fem* form of **Udo**.

Udo *masc* prosperous (*Germanic*).

Udall, Udell *masc* a surname, meaning yew-tree valley, used as a first name (*Old English*).

Ugo, Ugolino, Ugone *masc* Italian forms of **Hugh**.

Ulises *masc* a Spanish form of **Ulysses**.

Ulisse *masc* an Italian form of **Ulysses**.

Ulmar, Ulmer *masc* wolf (*Old English*).

Ulric, Ulrick *masc* wolf power (*Old English*); the English form of **Ulrich**.

Ulrica *fem* English form of **Ulrike**.

Ulrich *masc* fortune and power (*Germanic*).

Ulrike *fem* form of **Ulrich**.

Ulysses *masc* wrathful (*Greek*)—*dimin* **Lyss**.

Umberto *masc* the Italian form of **Humbert**.

Una *fem* a lamb; hunger (*Irish Gaelic*); *fem* form of one (*Latin*) used by Edmund Spenser in *The Faerie Queene*.

Unity *fem* the quality of harmony or concord used as a first name.

Unwin *masc* a surname, meaning not a friend, used as a surname (*Old English*).

Upton *masc* a surname, meaning upper farmstead, used as a first name (*Old English*).

Urania *fem* heavenly—the name of one of the muses (*Greek*).

Urbaine *masc* the French form of **Urban**.

Urban *masc* towm-dweller (*Latin*).

Urbano *masc* the Italian form of **Urban**.

Uri *masc* light (*Hebrew*).

Uriah *masc* fire of the Lord
(*Hebrew*).

Urian *masc* a husbandman
(*Danish*).

Uriel *masc* light of God
(*Hebrew*).

Ursula *fem* she-bear (*Latin*).

Ursule *fem* the French
form of **Ursula**.

Uzziah *masc* Jehovah is
strength (*Hebrew*).

Uzziel *masc* God is
strength (*Hebrew*).

V

Vachel *masc* little calf (*Old French*).

Vail *masc* a surname, meaning valley, used as a first name (*Old English*).

Val *masc* a diminutive form of **Valentine**; *fem* a diminutive form of **Valentina, Valerie**.

Valborga *fem* Protecting ruler (*Germanic*); diminutive forms are **Walburga, Walborga, Valburga**.

Valdemar *masc* a variant form of **Waldemar**.

Valdemaro *masc* an Italian form of **Waldemar**.

Valentin *masc* a French, German and Scandinavian form of **Valentine**.

Valentina *fem* form of **Valentine**; a diminutive form is **Val**.

Valentine *masc fem* strong; healthy; powerful (*Latin*); a diminutive form is **Val**.

Valentino *masc* an Italian form of **Valentine**.

Valerian *masc* form of **Valerie**.

Valeriano *masc* an Italian form of **Valerian**.

Valerie *fem* strong (*Latin*); a diminutive form is **Val**.

Valerio *masc* an Italian form of **Valerian**.

Valéry *masc* foreign power (*Germanic*).

Van *masc* from, of, a prefix in Dutch surnames now used independently as an English-language first name.

Vance *masc* young (*Old English*).

Vanessa *fem* a name invented by Jonathan Swift for his friend Esther Vanhomrigh, created from the prefix of her surname plus the suffix *essa*; a diminutive form is **Nessa**.

Vasili, Vassily *masc* Russian forms of **Basil**.

Vaughan, Vaughn *masc* a surname, meaning small one, used as a first name

(*Welsh*).

Velvet *fem* the English name of a rich, soft cloth used as a first name .

Venetia *fem* the name of the region around Venice in northern Italy used as a first name (*Latin*).

Vera *fem* faith (*Russian*); true (*Latin*).

Vere *masc* a surname, meaning from Ver in France, used as a first name (*Old French*).

Vergil *masc* a variant form of **Virgil**.

Verity *fem* truth (*Latin*).

Verne, Verna *fem* diminutive forms of **Laverne**.

Vernon *masc* a surname, meaning alder tree, used as a first name (*Old French*).

Verona *fem* a variant form of **Veronica**.

Veronica *fem* true image (*Latin*); a variant form is **Verona**; diminutive forms are **Ronnie, Ronny**.

Veronika *fem* a Scandinavian form of **Veronica**.

Veronike *fem* a German form of **Veronica**.

Véronique *fem* a French form of **Veronica**.

Vesta *fem* of uncertain meaning; in Roman mythology, the goddess of the hearth (*Latin*).

Vi *fem* a diminutive form of **Viola, Violet**.

Vicente *masc* a Spanish form of **Vincent**.

Vicki, Vickie, Vicky *fem* a diminutive form of **Victoria**, now used independently.

Victoire *fem* a French form of **Victoria**.

Victor *masc* conqueror (*Latin*); a diminutive form is **Vic**.

Victoria *fem* victory (*Latin*); diminutive forms are **Tory, Vickie, Vita**.

Vidal *masc* a Spanish form of *vitalis* (*Latin*), living vital.

Vilhelm *masc* a Swedish form of **William**.

Vilhelmina *fem* a Swedish form of **Wilhelmina**.

Vilma *fem* a diminutive form of **Vilhelmina**.

Vincent *masc* conquering; victorious (*Latin*); diminutive forms are **Vince, Vinnie, Vinny**.

Vincente *masc* an Italian form of **Vincent**.

Vincentia *fem* form of **Vincent**.

Vincenz *masc* a German form of **Vincent**.

Vinnie, Vinny *masc* diminutive forms of **Vincent**.

Vinson *masc* a surname form of **Vincent** used as a first name (*Old English*).

Viola, Violet *fem* a violet (*Latin*); a diminutive form is **Vi**.

Violetta *fem* the Italian form of **Viola, Violet**.

Virgil *masc* staff bearer (*Latin*), the name of the Roman poet of the first century BC; a variant form is **Vergil**.

Virgilio *masc* the Italian and Spanish form of **Virgil**.

Virginia *fem* virginal (*Latin*); a diminutive form is **Ginnie**.

Virginie *fem* a Dutch and French form of **Virginia**.

Vita *fem* form of **Vito**; a diminutive form of **Victoria**.

Vitale *masc* an Italian form of *vitalis* (*Latin*), living, vital.

Vito *masc* the Italian form of **Vitus**.

Vitore *masc* an Italian form of **Victor**.

Vitoria *fem* a Spanish form of **Victoria**.

Vitorio *masc* the Spanish form of **Victor**.

Vittorio *masc* an Italian form of **Victor**.

Vitus *masc* life (*Latin*).

Viv *fem* a diminutive form of **Vivien**.

Vivian, Vyvian *masc* full of life (Latin); a variant form is **Vyvian**.

Vivien, Vivienne *fem* form of **Vivian**; a diminutive form is **Viv**.

Vladimir *masc* Royally famous. A renowned monarch (*Slavic*).

Vladislav *masc* great ruler (*Slavonic*).

Vyvian *masc* a variant form of **Vivian**.

W

Wade *masc* a surname, meaning to go, or at the ford, used as a first name (*Old English*).

Wadsworth *masc* a surname, meaning Wade's homestead, used as a first name (*Old English*); a variant form is **Wordsworth**.

Wainwright *masc* a surname, meaning maker of carts, used as a first name (*Old English*).

Wake *masc* a surname, meaning alert, watchful, used as a first name (*Old English*).

Waldo *masc* ruler (*Germanic*).

Waldemar *masc* noted ruler (*Germanic*); a variant form is **Valdemar**.

Walker *masc* a surname, meaning a fuller, used as a first name (*Old English*).

Wallace *masc* a Scots variant form of **Wallis**; a diminutive form is **Wally**.

Wallis *masc fem* a surname, meaning foreigner, used as a first name (*Old French*); a variant form is **Wallace**; a diminutive form is **Wally**.

Wally *masc* a diminutive form of **Wallace, Wallis**.

Walt *masc* a diminutive form of **Walter, Walton**.

Walter *masc* ruler of army, people (*Germanic*); diminutive forms are **Walt, Wat, Watty**.

Walther *masc* a German form of **Walter**.

Walton *masc* a surname, meaning farmstead of the Britons, used as a first name (*Old English*); a diminutive form is **Walt**.

Wanda *fem* a variant form of **Wenda**.

Ward *masc* a surname, meaning watchman; guard, used as a first name (*Old English*).

Warfield *masc* a surname, meaning field of the stream of the wrens, used as a first

name (*Old English*).

Warne *masc* a surname, meaning alder wood, used as a first name (*Cornish*).

Warner *masc* a surname, meaning protecting army, used as a first name (*Germanic*).

Warren *masc* a surname, meaning wasteland or game park, used as a first name (*Old French*).

Warwick *masc* a placename and surname, meaning dwellings by the weir, used as a first name (*Old English*).

Washington *masc* a placename and surname, meaning Wassa's estate, used as a first name (*Old English*).

Wat, Watty *masc* a diminutive form of **Walter**.

Waverley *masc* a placename, meaning meadow or clearing by the swampy ground, used as a first name (*Old English*).

Wayne *masc* a surname, meaning a carter, used as a first name.

Webb *masc* a surname, meaning weaver, used as a first name (*Old English*).

Webster *masc* a surname,

meaning woman weaver, used as a first name (*Old English*).

Wellington *masc* a placename and surname, meaning Weola's farmstead, used as a first name (*Old English*).

Wenceslaus, Wenceslas *masc* wreathed with glory (*Slavonic*).

Wenda *fem* form of **Wendel**; a variant form is **Wanda**.

Wendel, Wendell *masc* of the Wend people (*Germanic*); a variant form is **Wendel**.

Wendy *fem* invented by J. M. Barrie for the main female character in his play *Peter Pan*.

Wentworth *masc* a surname, meaning winter enclosure, used as a first name (*Old English*).

Werner *masc* a German form of **Warner**.

Wesley *masc* a surname, meaning west wood, made famous by the Methodists John and Charles Wesley, used as a first name (*Old English*); a diminutive form is **Wes**.

Whitaker *masc* a surname, meaning white acre, used as a first name (*Old Eng-

lish); a variant form is
Whittaker.

Whitman *masc* a surname,
meaning white- or fair-
haired, used as a first
name (*Old English*).

Whitney *masc*, *fem* a surname and placename,
meaning white island or
Witta's island, used as a
first name (*Old English*).

Whittaker *masc* a variant
form of **Whitaker**.

Wilbert *masc* well-born
(*Old English*).

Wilbur *masc* wild boar (*Old
English*).

Wilfrida, Wilfreda *fem*
form of **Wilfrid**.

Wilfrid, Wilfred *masc* will
peace (*Germanic*); a diminutive form is **Wilf**.

Wilhelm *masc* the German
form of **William**; a diminutive form is **Wim**.

Wilhelmina, Wilhelmine
fem form of **Wilhelm**; diminutive forms are **Elma,
Minna, Minnie, Wilma**.

Will, Willie, Willy *masc*
diminutive forms of **William**.

Willa *fem* form of **Will,
William**.

Willard *masc* a surname,

meaning bold resolve, used
as a first name (*Old English*).

Willemot *masc* resolute in
spirit (*Germanic*).

William *masc* resolute helmet (*Germanic*); diminutive
forms are Bill, Will.

Williamina *fem* form of
William.

Willoughby *masc* a surname, meaning farm by the
willows, used as a first name
(*Old Norse/Old English*).

Willson *masc* a variant
form of **Wilson**.

Wilma *fem* a diminutive
form of **Wilhelmina**; *fem*
form of **William**.

Wilmer *masc* famous will
or desire (*Old English*);
masc form of **Wilma**.

Wilmot *masc* a diminutive
surname form of **William**
used as a first name.

Wilson *masc* a surname,
meaning son of Will, used
as a first name (*Old English*); a variant form is
Willson.

Wilton *masc* a placename
and surname, meaning
floodable place, used as a
first name (*Old English*).

Wim *masc* a contraction of
Wilhelm.

Windham *masc* a variant form of **Wyndham**.

Windsor *masc* a placename and surname, meaning slope with a windlass, used as a first name (*Old English*).

Winifred *fem* joy and peace (*Old English*); diminutive forms are **Freda, Win, Winnie, Wynn, Wynne**.

Winslow *masc* a placename and surname, meaning Wine's burial mound, used as a first name (*Old English*).

Winston *masc* a placename and surname, meaning friend's place or farm, used as a first name (*Old English*).

Winter *masc* the name for the cold season of the year used as a first name (*Old English*).

Winthrop *masc* a surname, meaning friend's farm village, used as a first name(*Old English*).

Winton *masc* a surname, meaning friend's farm, used as a first name (*Old English*).

Wolf, Wolfe *masc* wolf (*Old English*).

Wolfgang *masc* bold wolf (*Germanic*).

Wolfram *masc* wolf raven (*Germanic*).

Woodrow *masc* a surname, meaning row (of houses) in a wood, used as a first name; a diminutive form is **Woody**.

Woodward *masc* a surname, meaning forest guardian, used as a first name (*Old English*).

Woody *masc* a diminutive form of **Woodrow**, now used independently.

Wordsworth *masc* a variant form of **Wadsworth**.

Worth *masc* a surname, meaning farmstead, used as a first name (*Old English*).

Wyman *masc* a surname, meaning battle protector, used as a first name (*Old English*).

Wyn *masc* white (*Welsh*); a variant form is **Wynn**.

Wyndham *masc* a surname, meaning homestead of Wyman, used as a first name (*Old English*); a variant form is **Windham**.

Wynn, Wynne *masc, fem* a surname, meaning friend, used as a first name; *masc* a variant form of **Wyn**; *fem* a diminutive form of **Winifred**.

XYZ

Xanthe *fem* yellow (*Greek*).

Xavier *masc* a placename, meaning new house owner, used as a first name (*Spanish/Basque*).

Xaviera *fem* form of **Xavier**.

Xena, Xene, Xenia *fem* hospitality (*Greek*).

Xenos *masc* stranger (*Greek*).

Xerxes *masc* royal (*Persian*).

Yale *masc* a surname, meaning fertile upland (*Welsh*).

Yasmin, Yasmine *fem* variant forms of **Jasmine**.

Yehuda *fem* a variant form of **Jehuda**.

Yehudi *masc* a Jew (*Hebrew*).

Yolanda, Yolande *fem* a variant form of **Viola**.

York, Yorke *masc* a placename and surname, meaning estate of Eburos or of the yew trees, used as a first name (*Celtic/Latin/Old English*).

Yseult *fem* an old French form of **Isolde**.

Yuri *masc* a Russian form of **George**.

Yves *masc* yew tree (*French-Germanic*).

Yvette *fem* a diminutive form of Yves.

Yvonne *fem* form of **Yves**.

Zabdiel *masc* gift of God (*Hebrew*).

Zabrina *fem* a variant form of **Sabrina**.

Zaccheus *masc* innocent; pure (*Hebrew*).

Zachary, Zachariah, Zacharias, Zecheriah*masc* Jehovah has remembered (*Hebrew*); diminutive forms are **Zach, Zack, Zak**.

Zadok *masc* righteous (*Hebrew*).

Zara *fem* flower (*Arabic*).

Zeb *masc* a diminutive form of **Zebadiah, Zebe-**

dee, **Zebulun**.

Zebadiah, Zebedee *masc* gift of the Lord (*Hebrew*).

Zebulon, Zebulun *masc* elevation (*Hebrew*); diminutive forms are **Lonny, Zeb**.

Zedekiah *masc* justice of the Lord (*Hebrew*); a diminutive form is **Zed**.

Zeke *masc* a diminutive form of **Ezekiel**.

Zelig *masc* a variant form of **Selig**.

Zelma *fem* a variant form of **Selma**.

Zenas *masc* gift of Zeus (*Greek*).

Zenobia *fem* having life from Zeus (*Greek*).

Zephaniah *masc* hid of the Lord (*Hebrew*); a diminutive form is **Zeph**.

Zinnia *fem* the name of a plant with brightly coloured flowers used as a first name, named after the German botanist J. G. Zinn.

Zoë, Zoe *fem* life (*Greek*).

A Listing of Girls' Names

A

Abbie, Abby
Aberah
Abigail
Abra
Acacia
Acantha
Ada
Adabelle
Adah
Adalia
Adamina
Adar
Addie
Addie, Addy,
 Mina
Adela
Adelaide
Adèle, Adele
Adelheid
Adeline, Adelina
Adelphia
Adina
Adolpha
Adonia
Adora
Adorabella
Adorna
Adrianne,
 Adrienne
Aefa
Afra
Africa
Agatha

Agave
Aggie, Aggy
Agnes
Agnès
Agnese
Ailean
Aileen
Ailsa
Aimée
Áine
Aisleen, Aisling
Alana, Alanna,
 Alannah
Alarice
Alberta
Albina
Alcina
Alcyone
Alda
Aldora
Aleria
Alethea
Alexa
Alexandra,
 Alexandrina
Alexia
Alexina
Alfonsine
Alfreda
Alice, Alicia
Alida
Aliénor
Alima
Aline

Alison
Alix
Allegra
Allie, Ally
Allison
Allison, Al, Allie
Alloula, Allula,
 Aloula
Alma
Almira
Aloha
Alta
Althea
Alula
Alura
Alva
Alvina, Alvine
Alys, Alyssa
Alyth
Alzena
Amabel
Amadea
Amalia
Amanda
Amber
Ambrosine
Amelia
Amélie
Amelinda
Amena
Amethyst
Amy
Anastasia
Anatholia,

Anatola
Anatolia
Andrea
Andrina,
 Andrine
Anemone
Angel
Angela, Angelina
Angelica
Angharad
Anita
Ann
Anna
Annabel,
 Annabelle, An
Anne
Anneka
Annette
Annika
Annis, Annice
Annona
Annunciata
Anona
Anora
Anselma
Anthea
Antoinette
Antonia
Anwen
Aoife
Aphra
April
Ara
Arabella,
 Arabela
Araminta
Ardath
Ardella, Ardelle,
 Ardel
Areta, Aretha
Argenta,

Argente, Arge
Aretta, Arette
Aria
Ariadne
Arianna
Arianne
Ariella, Arielle
Arlene
Armelle
Armilla
Armina, Armine
Arnalda
Arselma
Artemis
Arva
Arwenna
Asphodel
Astra
Astrid
Atalanta,
 Atalante
Atalya
Athena,
 Ahthene, Athen
Atlante
Audrey
Augusta
Aura, Aure,
 Aurea
Aurelia
Auria
Aurora
Autumn
Ava
Avera
Averil, Averill
Avice, Avis
Avril
Azaliea, Azalia,
 Azalee
Azaria

Azura, Azure

B

Bab, Babs
Bambi
Baptista
Barbara, Barbra
Basilia
Bathilda
Bathilde
Bathsheba
Bea
Beata
Beatrice, Beatrix
Beckie, Becky
Beda
Bee
Belinda
Bella, Belle
Bena
Benedicta
Benita
Berenice
Bernadette
Bernice
Berta
Bertha
Berthe
Berthilda,
 Berthilde,
 Bertilda,
 Bertilde
Beryl
Bess, Bessie
Beth
Bethan
Bethany
Betsy, Bette,
 Bettina, Betty
Beulah
Beverley,

Beverly	Calandre	Cass
Bianca	Calandria	Cassandra
Biddy	Calantha	Cassie
Bina, Binah,	Calanthe	Catalina
Bine	Caledonia	Caterina
Binnie	Calla	Catharina,
Birgit	Callie	Catharine,
Blanca	Calliope	Catherina
Blanche	Callista	Catherine
Blodwen	Cally	Catrin
Blossom	Calumina	Catriona
Bonita	Calvina	Cecile
Bonnie	Calypso	Cecily, Cecilia
Branwen	Camila	Ceinwen
Brenda	Camilla	Celandine
Brenna	Candie	Celeste,
Bridget	Candice,	Celestine
Brigid	Candace	Celia
Brigide	Candida	Cendrillon
Brigitte	Candy	Cerian
Briony	Cara	Cerys
Britt	Caridad	Chandra
Brittany	Carina	Chanel
Bronwen	Carissa	Charis
Brunella	Carla	Charity
Brunhilda,	Carlie	Charlene
Brunhilde	Carlin	Charlotte
Brynmor	Carlotta	Charmaine
Bryony	Carly	Charmian
Buena	Carmel	Chelsea
Bunty	Carmela	Cher, Chérie
Buona	Carmelita	Cherry
	Carmen	Cheryl
C	Carnation	Chiara
Caddie	Carola	Chiquita
Cadence	Carole	Chloë, Chloe
Cadenza	Carolina	Chloris
Cáit	Caroline,	Chrissie
Caitlín, Caitrín	Carolyn	Christabel
Cal	Carrie	Christiana
Calandra	Carys	Christina

Christine
Chrystal
Ciara
Cicely
Cilla
Cinderella
Cindy
Cinzia
Claire
Clara
Clarabel,
 Clarabella,
 Clarabelle
Clare
Claribel
Clarice
Clarinda
Clarissa
Clarrie
Claudia
Clem
Clematis
Clemency
Clementine,
 Clementina
Cleo
Cleopatra
Cliantha
Clio
Clorinda
Clothilde,
 Clotilde
Clover
Colette
Colleen
Collette
Columbine
Comfort
Concepcion
Concepta
Concetta

Concha, Conchita
Consolata
Consolation
Constance
Constanta
Constanza
Consuela
Cora
Corabella,
 Corabelle
Coral
Coralie
Corazón
Cordelia
Corinna, Corinne
Cornelia
Corona
Cosima
Costanza
Cressida
Cristal
Cristina
Crystal
Cynthia
Cyrene, Cyrena
Cytherea
Cytereia

D

Daffodil
Dagmar
Dahlia
Daisy
Dalilah, Dalila
Danaë
Danielle
Daphne
Dara
Darcie
Daria
Darlene, Darleen

Darrelle
Darryl
Daryl
Davina
Dawn
Deana, Deane
Deanna
Deborah, Debra
Decima
Dee
Deirdre
Delfine
Delia
Delicia
Delight
Delilah, Delila
Delma
Delores
Delphine
Delyth
Demetria
Dena, Dene
Denice
Denise
Desdemona
Desirée
Devona
Di
Diana
Diane, Dianne
Dido
Dilys
Dina
Dinah
Dione, Dionne
Dixie
Dodie, Dodo
Dolina
Dolly
Dolores
Donalda

Donata	Eileen	Emerald
Donna	Eilidh	Emilia
Dora	Eira	Emilie
Dorcas	Eirlys	Émilie
Doreen	Eithne	Emily
Dorinda	Elaine	Emma
Doris	Eldora	Emmeline
Dorothea	Eldrida	Ena
Dorothée	Eleanor,	Enda
Dorothy	Eleanore	Enfys
Dorrie, Dorry	Eleanora	Engelberta,
Drusilla	Electra	Engelbertha,
Dulcie	Elen	Engelbert
Dyan	Elena	Enid
Dymphna	Eleonora	Enrica
	Eleonore	Enrichetta
E	Eléonore	Enriqueta
Éanna	Elfleda	Eranthe
Earlene, Earline	Elfreda	Erda
Eartha	Elga	Erica
Easter	Elin	Erika
Ebba	Elinor	Erin
Ebony	Elisa	Erlene, Erline
Echo	Elisabeth	Erma
Eda	Elisabetta	Erna
Edana	Élise	Ernesta
Edie	Elizabeth	Ernestine
Edina	Ella	Esmeralda
Edith	Ellen	Esta
Edlyn	Ellice	Estelle, Estella
Edmonda	Ellie	Ester
Edna	Elma	Esther
Edrea	Éloise, Eloisa	Estrella
Edwardina	Elsa	Ethel
Edwige	Elsie	Ethna
Edwina	Elspeth, Elspet	Etta, Ettie
Edy	Eluned	Eudora
Edyth, Edythe	Elva	Eufem
Effie	Elvina	Eugenia
Egberta	Elvira	Eugénie
Eglantine	Emeline	Eulaliefem

Eunice
Euphemia
Eustacia
Eva
Evadne
Evangeline
Eve
Eveline
Evita
Evodia

F

Fabia
Fabienne
Fabiola
Faith
Fanchon
Fanny
Faustina,
 Faustine
Fatima
Favor, Favour
Fawn
Fay, Faye
Felicia
Felicidad
Felicie
Felicity
Fenella
Fern
Fernanda
Ffion
Fid
Fidelia
Fidelma
Fifi
Filippa
Finola
Fiona
Fionnuala
Flanna

Flavia
Fleur
Fleurette
Flo
Flora
Florence
Florrie, Flossie
Flower
Floy
Fortune
Fran
Franca
Frances
Francesca
Francie
Francine
Francisca
Françoise
Freda
Frederica
Frédérique
Freya
Frieda
Friede
Friederike
Fritzi
Fulvia

G

Gabbie, Gabby
Gabrielle
Gaea
Gaia
Gail
Galatea
Gale
Galia
Gardenia
Garland
Garnet
Gay

Gayle
Gaynor
Gazella
Gemma
Geneva
Genevieve
Geneviève
Georgia,
 Georgiana,
 Georgina
Geraldine
Germaine
Gertrude
Gigi
Gilberta,
 Gilberte
Gilda
Gill
Gillie
Gillian
Gilly
Gina
Ginnie, Ginny
Giovanna
Gipsy
Giselle
Gisela
Gisèle
Gitana
Gladys
Gleda
Glenda
Glenna
Glenys
Gloria
Glynis
Godiva
Golda, Golde
Goldie
Grace
Gráinne

Greer
Greta
Gretchen
Grete
Griselda, Grizelda
Gudrun
Guinevere
Gunhilda, Gunhilde
Gussie, Gusta
Gwenda
Gwendolen, Gwendolin, Gwendolyn
Gwyneth, Gwynneth
Gypsy

H

Hagar
Haidee
Halcyon, Halcyone
Hannah
Happy
Haralda
Harmony
Harriet, Harriot
Hazel
Heather
Hebe
Hedda
Hedwig, Hedvig
Heidi
Helen, Helena
Helene
Hélène
Helga
Helma
Héloïse

Henrietta
Henriette
Hephzibah
Hera
Hermione
Hermosa
Herta
Hertha
Hester, Hesther
Hettie, Hetty
Heulwen
Hibernia
Hibiscus
Hilda
Hildegarde
Holly, Hollie
Honey
Honor, Honora
Honoria
Honour
Hope
Horatia
Hortensia, Hortense
Huberta
Hulda, Huldah
Hylda
Hypatia

I

Ianthe
Ibby
Ida
Idabell
Idonia
Idony, Idonie
Ignatia
Ilona
Ilse
Imogen
Imperial

Ina
Inés, Inez
Inga
Ingeborg
Inger
Ingrid
Iola
Iolanthe
Iole
Iona
Ionefem
Iphigenia
Irene
Iris
Irma
Isa
Isabel, Isabella
Isabelle
Isadora
Iseabail, Ishbel
Iseult
Isidora
Isla, Islay
Isobel
Isola
Isolde, Isolda, Isold
Ita, Ite
Ivana

J

Jacinta
Jacinth
Jacoba
Jacqueline
Jacquetta
Jade
Jael
Jamesina
Jancis
Jane

Janet, Janeta,
 Janette
Janice
Janine
Jaqueline
Jasmine, Jamsin
Jayne
Jean
Jeanette,
 Jeannette
Jeanne
Jehuda
Jemima,
 Jemimah
Jemma
Jenna, Jenni,
 Jennie
Jennifer, Jenifer
Jenny
Jeremia
Jermaine
Jerusha
Jess
Jessamine,
 Jessamyn
Jessica
Jessie, Jessy
Jewel
Jezebel
Jill
Jillian
Joan, Joann,
 Joanna, Joanne
Jobina
Jodie, Jody
Johanna
Joni
Jordana
Josceline
Josefa
Josepha

Josephine
Josette
Josie
Joy
Joyce
Juana
Judie, Judi
Judith
Judy
Julia
Juliana
Julie, Juliet
Julienne
Julieta
Juliette
June
Juno
Justina, Justine

K

Kalantha,
 Kalanthe
Kalypso
Kara
Karen
Karin
Karla
Karlotte
Karoline
Kate
Katerina
Kath, Kathie,
 Kathy
Katharina,
 Katharine
Katherine
Kathleen
Kathryn
Katie
Katinka
Katrine

Katriona
Katy
Kayla, Kayleigh,
 Kayley
Keira
Kelly
Kendra
Kerry
Keturah
Kezia, Keziah
Kim
Kimberley
Kirsten
Kirstie, Kirsty
Kirstin
Kittie, Kitty
Kizzie, Kizzy
Klara
Konstanze
Kora
Kristeen
Kirstel
Kristina
Kylie
Kyrena

L

Laetitia
Lalage
Lana
Lara
Laraine
Larissa, Larisa
Lark
Latisha
Laura
Laurabel
Laurel
Lauren
Laurette
Lavender

Laverne
Lavinia, Lavina
Lea
Leah
Leane
Leanne
Leanora,
 Leanore
Leda
Leila
Lela
Lena
Lenora
Leona
Leonarda
Leonie
Leonora
Leontine,
 Leontina
Leontyne
Leopoldina,
 Leopoldine
Lesley
Leticia, Letitia
Letizia
Lettice
Lexie, Lexy
Liana, Liane,
 Lianna, Lianne
Libby
Lidia
Liese
Lil
Lila
Lilac
Lilah
Lili
Lilian
Lilias, Lillias
Lilibet
Lilie

Lilith
Lilli
Lillian
Lily
Lin
Lina
Linda
Lindie
Lindy
Linnette
Linzi
Lis
Lisa
Lisbeth
Lisette
Lissa
Livia
Liz
Liza
Lizbeth
Lizzie, Lizzy
Lois
Lola
Lona
Lora
Lorelei
Loren
Loretta
Lorna
Lorraine
Lottie, Lotty
Lotus
Louella
Louisa
Louise
Luce
Lucia
Lucienne
Lucilla
Lucille, Lucile
Lucinda

Lucrèce
Lucretia, Lucrece
Lucrezia
Lucy
Ludmila,
 Ludmilla
Luella
Luisa
Luise
Lulu
Lydia
Lyn
Lynda
Lynette
Lynn
Lynnette
Lyris
Lysandra

M

Mabel
Mabelle
Madalena
Maddalena
Maddie, Maddy
Madeleine,
 Madeline
Madge
Madonna
Mae
Maelona
Maeve
Magda
Magdalene,
 Magdalen
Maggie
Magnolia
Mahalia
Mai, Mair
Maida
Mairead

Mairi
Maisie
Mala
Malvina
Mame, Mamie
Manda
Mandy
Manette
Manuela
Marcela
Marcella
Marcelle
Marcia
Mared
Margaret
Margarete
Margaretha
Margarita
Margaux
Margery
Margherita
Margie
Margo, Margot
Marguerite
Mari
Maria
Mariam
Marian
Marianna
Marianne
Maribella
Marie
Marietta
Marigold
Marilyn
Marina
Marion
Marisa
Marjorie,
 Marjory
Marlene

Marsha
Marta
Martha
Marthe
Marti
Martina
Martine
Martita
Mary
Maryann,
 Maryanne
Marylou
Mathilda
Mathilde
Matilda
Matilde
Mattie
Maud, Maude
Maura
Maureen
Mave
Mavis
Maxine
May
Maybelle
Meave
Medea
Meg, Meggie
Megan
Mehetabel,
 Mehitabel
Meironwen
Melanie
Melinda
Melisande
Melissa
Melody
Mercedes
Mercy
Meri
Meriel

Merri, Merrie
Merry
Meryl
Meta
Mia
Michaela
Michaella
Michèle, Michelle
Mignon
Mil
Milcah
Mildred
Millicent
Millie
Mima
Mimi
Mimosa
Minerva
Minette
Minna, Minne
Minnie
Minta
Mira
Mirabel,
 Mirabelle
Miranda
Miriam
Mitzi
Modesty
Moira
Mollie, Molly
Mona
Monica
Monika
Monique
Morag
Morgana
Morna
Morven
Moyra
Muirne

Muriel
Myfanwy
Myra
Myrna
Myrtle

N

Naamah
Nadezhda
Nadia
Nadine
Naida
Nairne
Nan
Nana
Nancy
Nanette
Naomi
Napea
Nara
Narda
Natalie
Natalia
Natalya
Natasha
Nathania
Nebula
Nell, Nellie, Nelly
Nerice, Nerine, Nerissa
Nerys
Nessa
Nessie
Nesta
Netta, Nettie
Niamh
Nicole
Nikki
Nina
Ninette

Ninon
Nita
Nixie
Noëlle, Noelle
Nola
Nona
Nora, Norah
Noreen
Norma
Nuala

O

Octavia
Octavie
Odelia, Odelie
Odette
Odile, Odille
Ofra
Olga
Olimpia
Olive
Olivia
Olwen
Olympe
Olympia
Ona
Oona, Oonagh
Opal
Ophelia
Ophélie
Ophrah, Ophra
Oprah
Oriana, Oriane
Oriel
Orla
Orlanda
Orna
Orsola
Ortensia
Ottavia
Ottilie, Otilie

P

Paige, Page
Palmira
Paloma
Pamela
Pandora
Pansy
Paola
Patience
Patricia
Patrizia
Patsy
Pattie, Patty
Paula
Paulette
Paulina, Pauline
Peace
Pearl
Peg, Peggie, Peggy
Penelope
Penny
Peony
Perdita
Peronel
Persephone
Persis
Petra
Petrina
Petronel, Petronella
Petula
Petunia
Phebe
Phedra
Phèdre
Phemie, Phamie
Phenie
Philippa
Philomena
Phoebe

Phyllida
Phyllis
Pia
Pilar
Pippa
Polly
Pollyanna
Pomona
Poppy
Portia
Prima
Primrose
Priscilla
Prudence
Prue
Prunella
Psyche

Q

Queenie
Quenby
Querida
Quinta

R

Rachel
Rachele
Rachelle
Rae
Rahel
Raisa
Ramona
Ranee, Rani
Raphaela
Raquel
Rea
Rebecca,
  Rebekah
Regina
Reine
Renata

Renée
Reva
Rexanne
Rhea, Rheia
Rhiain
Rhiannon
Rhoda
Rhona
Ria
Rica
Rina
Rita
Roberta
Robina
Rochelle
Roderica
Rohanna
Róisín, Roisin
Rolanda,
  Rolande
Roma
Romy
Rona
Ronalda
Rosa
Rosabel,
  Rosabella,
  Rosabelle fem
Rosalie, Rosalia
Rosalind,
  Rosaline
Rosamund,
  Rosamond
Rosanne,
  Rosanna
Rose
Roseanne,
  Roseanna
Rosemarie
Rosemary
Rosemonde

Rosetta
Rosette
Rosie
Rosmunda
Rowena
Roxanne, Roxane
Ruby
Ruth

S

Sabina
Sabine
Sabra
Sabrina
Sadie
Sal
Salina
Sally, Sallie
Salome
Salvia
Samantha
Samuela
Sancha, Sanchia
Sancia
Sandie
Sandra
Sapphire
Sarah, Sara
Savanna
Scarlett
Selina, Selena
Selma
Semele
Senga
Seonaid
Septima
Seraphina,
  Serafina
Serena
Shannon
Shari

Sharon
Sheelagh
Sheelah
Sheena
Sheila, Shelagh
Shelley
Sheree, Sheri
Sheryl
Shirley
Shona
Sian
Sibeal
Sibyl, Sibylla
Sidonia, Sidonie,
 Sydony
Sierra
Sigrid
Sile
Silvana
Silvia
Silvie
Simona
Simone
Sine
Sinead
Siobhan
Sioned
Sisley
Sofie
Solveig
Sonya, Sonia
Sophia
Sophie, Sophy
Sophronia
Sorcha
Spring
Stacy, Stacie
Star, Starr
Stasia
Steffi, Steffie
Stella

Stephanie
Sukey, Sukie
Summer
Susan
Susanna,
 Susannah
Susanne
Suzanna
Suzanne
Sybille
Sybyl, Sybilla
Sylvia
Sylvie

T

Tabitha
Talitha
Tallulah
Tamar
Tamara
Tammie, Tammy
Tamsin
Tania, Tanya
Tanisha
Tansy
Tara
Tatiana
Tempest
Teodora
Teodosia
Teresa
Terese
Teri
Terri
Terry
Tess, Tessa,
 Tessie
Thalia
Thea
Thecla
Thelma

Theda
Thelma
Theodora
Theodosia
Theophila
Theresa
Thérèse
Theresia,
 Therese
Thirza
Thomasina,
 Thomasine
Thora
Thordis
Thyrza
Tib, Tibbie
Tiffany
Tilda, Tilde
Tilly
Timothea
Tina
Tiphaine
Tiree
Tirza, Tirzah
Tita
Titania
Tobey
Tomasina,
 Tomina
Toni
Tonia
Tonie
Topaz
Tordis
Tory
Tracie
Traviata
Tricia
Trilby
Trisha
Trix, Trixie

405

Truda, Trudie,
 Trudy
Tuesday

U

Uda
Ulrica
Ulrike
Una
Unity
Urania
Ursula
Ursule

V

Valborga
Valentina
Valerie
Vanessa
Velvet
Venetia
Vera
Verity
Verne, Verna
Verona
Veronica
Veronika

Veronike
Véronique
Vesta
Vi
Vicki, Vickie,
 Vicky
Victoire
Victoria
Vilhelmina
Vilma
Vincentia
Viola, Violet
Violetta
Virginia
Virginie
Vita
Vitoria
Viv
Vivien, Vivienne

W

Wallis
Wanda
Wenda
Wendy
Wilfrida,
 Wilfreda

Wilhelmina,
 Wilhelmine
Willa
Williamina
Wilma
Winifred
Wynn, Wynne

XYZ

Xanthe
Xaviera
Xena, Xene,
 Xenia
Yasmin, Yasmine
Yehuda
Yolanda, Yolande
Yseult
Yvette
Yvonne
Zabrina
Zara
Zelma
Zenobia
Zinnia
Zoë, Zoe

A Listing of Boys' Names

Aaron
Abbott
Abel
Abe
Abelard
Abiathar
Abiel
Abihu
Abijah
Abner
Abner
Abraham
Abraham
Abraham
Ace
Ackley
Adair
Adalard
Adam
Addison
Adin
Adlai
Adler
Adney
Adolf
Adolph,
 Adolphus
Adolphe
Adon,, Adonai
Adoniram
Adrian
Adriel
Aeneas
Afonso

Agostino
Agustin
Ahern
Ahren
Aidan
Aiken
Ainsley
Ainslie
Al
Alain
Alan
Alard
Alaric
Alarice
Alasdair,
 Alastair
Alban
Albern
Albert
Albrecht
Alcott
Alden
Alder
Aldis
Aldo, Aldous
Aldrich
Aldwin
Alec, Aleck
Aled
Aleron
Alex
Alexis
Alf, Aldie
Alfonso

Alford
Alfred
Alger
Algernon
Alick
Alister
Allan, Allen
Allard
Almo
Alonso
Aloysius
Alpha
Alpheus
Alphonso,
 Alphonsus
Alpin
Alroy
Alston
Altman
Alton
Alun
Alvah
Alvin, Alwin
Amadeus
Amado
Amariah
Amasa
Ambert
Ambrogio
Ambrose
Amédée
Amerigo
Amery
Ammon

Amory	Armel	Atwell
Amos	Armin	Auberon
Anastasius	Armstrong	Aubin
Anatole	Arn	Aubrey
Andie	Arnall	August
André	Arnaud, Arnaut	Auguste
Andreas	Arnatt, Arnett	Augustin
Andrés	Arne	Augustine
Andrew	Arno	Augustus
Aneirin, Aneurin	Anrold	Aurelius
Angelo	Arnott	Austin
Angus	Arnulf	Avery
Annan	Arphad	Awen
Anscom	Artemas	Axel
Ansley	Arthur	Axton
Anson	Arthuro	Aylmer
Anstice	Arundel	Aylward
Anthony	Arvad	Azarias
Antoine	Arval, Arvel	
Anton	Arvid	**B**
Antonio	Arvin	Bailey, Baillie
Antony	Arwel	Bainbridge
Antwan	Arwyn	Baird
Anwell	Asahel	Baldemar
Anwen	Asaph	Baldovin
Anyon	Ascot, Ascot	Baldric, BAldrick
Aonghas	Ashburn	Baldwin
Archard	Ashby	Balfour
Archer	Asher	Ballard
Archibald	Ashford	Balthasar,
Ardal	Ashley, Ashleigh	Balthazar
Arden	Ashlin	Bancroft
Ardley	Ashton	Baptist
Ardolph	Ashur	Baptiste
Argus	Asphodel	Barclay
Argyle, Argyll	Athanasius	Bard
Aric	Atherton	Bardolph
Ariel	Athol, Atholl	Barlow
Aries	Atlee, Atley	Barnaby,
Arlen	Atwater,	Barnabus
Armand	Atwatter	Barnard

Barnet, Barnett
Barnum
Baron
Barret, Barrett
Barron
Barry
Bart
Barthold
Bartholomew
Bartley
Barton
Bartram
Barzillai
Basil
Basile
Basilio
Bat
Batiste
Battista
Baudouin
Baudric
Bautista
Baxter
Bayley
Beal, Beale, Beall
Beaman
Beau
Beaufort
Beaumont
Beavan, Beaven
Bellamy
Ben
Benedetto
Benedict, Benedick
Benedikt
Beniamino
Benito
Benjamin
Benjie

Bennet
Bennie, Benny
Benoît
Benson
Bentley
Beppe, Beppo
Berkeley, Berkley
Bernard
Bernardino
Bernardo
Bernhard, Bernhardt
Bernie
Bert
Berthold
Bertie
Bertram
Bertrand
Bevan
Bevin
Bevis
Bije
Bill
Billie
Bing
Birch
Birk
Bishop
Björn
Black
Blair
Blaise
Blake
Bleddyn
Bliss
Blyth, Blythe
Boas, Boaz
Bob, Bobbie, Bobby
Bonar

Boniface
Bonnar
Booth
Boris
Botolf, Botolph
Bourn, Bourne
Bowen
Bowie
Boyce
Boyd
Boyne
Brad
Bradford
Bradley
Brady
Braham
Bram
Bramwell
Bran
Brand
Brandon
Brendon
Brent
Brewster
Brian
Brice
Brigham
Brock
Broderic, Broderick
Brodie, Brody
Bron
Bronwen
Brook, Brooke
Brooks
Bruce
Bruno
Bryan
Bryce
Bryn
Buck

Buckley
Budd, Buddy
Burchard
Burdon
Burford
Burgess
Burk, Burke
Burkhard
Burl
Burley
Burn, Burne
Burnett
Burt
Burton
Buster
Byrne
Byron

C

Caddick,
 Caddock
Cadell
Cadmus
Cadwallader
Caesar
Cain
Calder
Caldwell
Caleb
Caley
Calhoun
Callisto
Calum, Callum
Calvert
Calvin
Calvino
Cameron
Camille
Campbell
Canice
Canute

Caradoc,
 Caradog
Cardew
Carey
Carl
Carleton
Carlo
Carlos
Carlton
Carmichael
Carol
Carr
Carrick
Carroll
Carson
Carter
Carver
Carwyn
Cary
Casey
Cashel
Casimir
Caspar, Casper
Cassidy
Cassian, Cassius
Castor
Cathal
Cato
Cavan
Cecil
Cécile
Cedric
Cemlyn
Cephas
Ceri
César
Cesare
Chad
Chiam
Chance
Chancellor

Chancey
Chandler
Chapman
Charles
Chase
Chauncey,
 Chaunce
Chester
Chilton
Chris
Christian
Christie
Christmas
Christoph
Christopher
Christy
Churchill
Cian
Ciarán
Claiborne
Clarence
Clark, Clarke
Claud
Claude
Claudio
Claudius
Claus
Clay
Clayborne
Clayton
Clement
Cleveland
Cliff
Clifford
Clifton
Clint
Clinton
Clive
Clovis
Clyde
Cnut

Cody	Creighton	Danby
Colby	Crépin	Dandie
Col	Crispin, Crispian	Dane
Cole	Crispus	Daniel
Coleman	Cristiano	Dante
Coin	Cristóbal	Darby
Collier, Collyer	Cristoforo	Darcy, D'Arcy
Colm	Cromwell	Darell
Colman, Colmán	Crosbie, Crosby	Darien
Colombe	Cullan, Cullen	Dario
Columba	Culley	Darius
Columbine	Curran	Darnell
Colyer	Curt	Darrell, Darrel
Comyn	Curtis	Darren, Darin
Con	Cuthbert	Darton
Conan, Cónán	Cy	David
Conn	Cyprian	Davidde
Connall	Cyrano	Davide
Connor	Cyril	Davie
Conrad	Cyrill	Davin
Conroy	Cyrille	Davis
Constant	Cyrillus	Davy
Constantine	Cyrus	Dean
Consuelo		Dearborn
Conway	**D**	Decimus
Cooper	Dafydd	Declan
Corbet, Corbet	Dag	Dedrick
Corcoran	Dagan	Deinol
Corey	Dai	Dell
Cornelius	Dale	Delmar
Cornell	Daley	Demetre
Corona	Dallas	Demetrio
Corrado	Dalton	Demetrius
Corwin	Daly	Dempsey
Cosimo	Dalziel	Dempster
Cosmo	Damian	Den
Courtney	Damiano	Denby
Cradoc	Damien	Denis, Dennis
Craig	Damon	Denison
Cranley	Dan	Denley
Crawford	Dana	Denman

411

Dennison
Denton
Denver
Deon
Derek
Dermot
Derrick, Derrik
Derry
Derwent
Desmond
Deverell,
 Deverill
Devin, Devinn
Devlin
Devon
Dewey
Dewi
De Witt
Dexter
Diamond
Diarmid
Diarmuid
Dick, Dickie,
 Dickson
Dickson
Dicky
Dido
Diego
Dietrich
Digby
Dillon
Dino
Dion
Dirk
Dixon
Dolan
Dilph
Domenico
Domingo
Dominic,
 Dominick

Dominique
Don
Dónal
Donal
Donald
Donall
Donato
Doolan
Doran
Dorian
Dorward
Dougal, Dougall
Douglas
Dow
Doyle
D'Oyley
Drake
Drew
Driscoll, Driscol
Druce
Drummond
Drury
Dryden
Duane
Dudley
Duff
Dugal, Dugald
Duggie
Duke
Duncan
Dunlop
Dunn, Dunne
Dunstan
Durand, Durant
Durward
Durwin
Dustin
Dwane, Dwayne
Dwight
Dyan
Dyfan

Dylan

___E___

Eachan,
 Eachann,
 Eacheann
Eamon, Eamonn
Earl, Earle
Eaton
Eben
Ebenezer
Eberhard, Ebert
Ed
Edan
Edbert
Eddie, Eddy
Edel
Edelmar
Eden
Edgar
Edmond
Edmund
Edoardo
Édouard
Edric
Edryd
Edsel
Eduardo
Edwald
Edward
Edwin
Egan
Egbert
Egidio
Ehren
Eilir
Einar
Elder
Eldon
Eldred
Eldrid, Eldridge

Eleazer	Eoin	Ezekeil
Elfed	Ephraim	Ezra
Elgan	Erasmus	
Eli	Reastus	**F**
Elias	Erastus	Fabian
Eliezer	Ercole	Fabián
Elijah	Eric	Fabiano
Eliot	Erich	Fabien
Elis	Erik	Fabio
Elisha	Erland	Faber, Fabre
Elliot	Erle	Fabrice
Ellis	Ern	Fabrizio
Elmer	Ernest	Fairfax
Elmo	Ernesto	Fairley, Fairlie
Elmore	Ernst	Fane
Elroy	Erskine	Farnall, farnell
Elton	Erwin	Farquar
Elvey	Eryl	Farr
Elvin	Esau	Farrel
Elvis	Esmé	Federico
Elvy	Esmond	Felice
Elwin	Este	Felipe
Emanuel	Estéban	Felix
Emery	Ethan	Felton
Emil	Etienne	Fenton
Émile	Ettore	Ferdinand
Emilio	Euan	Fredinando
Emlyn	Eugen	Fergal
Emery	Eugene	Fergie
Emory	Eugène	Fergus
Emrys	Eurig, Euros	Fergy
Emyr	Eusebio	Fernand
Eneas	Eustace	Fernando
Enée	Eustache	Fidel
Engelbert	Eustachio	Fidèle
Ennis	Eustachio	Fidelio
Enoch	Eustaquio	Fidelis
Enos	Evan	Fielding
Enrico	Evelyn	Filippo
Enrique	Everard	Findlay
Eoghan	Everley	Fingal
	Ewart	

413

Finn
Fionn
Fiske
Fitch
Fitz
Fitzgerald
Fitzhugh
Fitzpatrick
Fitzroy
Flann
Flannan
Flavian, Flavius
Fleming
Fletcher
Flinn
Flint
Florian
Floyd
Flynn
Forbes
Ford
Forrest, Forrestt
Forrester,
 Forster
Foster
Fra
Fraine
Francesco
Francis
Francisco
Franco
François
Frank
Franklin,
 Franklen,
 Franklyn
Frans
Franz,
 Franziskus
Franziska
Fraser, Frasier

Frayn, Frayne
Frazer, Frazier
Frédéric
Frederick,
 Frederic
Fredrik
Freeman
Frewin
Friedrich
Fritz
Fulton
Fyfe, Fyffe

G

Gabe
Gabriel
Galen
Gallagher
Galloway
Galton
Galvin
Gamaliel
Gareth
Garfield
Garnet, Garnett
Garret, Garrett
Garrad
Garrison
Garry
Garth
Garton
Garve
Gary
Gaspard
Gaston
Gautier,
 Gauthier
Gavin
Gawain
Gaylord
Gene

Geoffrey
Georg
George
Georges
Geraint
Gerald
Gerard
Gérard
Gerardo
Geeraud
Gerhard
Gerhold
Germain
Gerrie, Gerry
Gershom
Gervas
Gervais
Gervaise
Gervasio
Gethin
Giacomo
Gian, Gianni
Gibson
Gideon
Giffard, Gifford
Gil
Gilbert
Gilchrist
Giles
Gilles
Gillespie
Gillmore
Gilmore, Gilmour
Gilroy
Giocchino
Giorgio
Giovanna
Giraldo
Girauld
Girolamo
Girvan

Giulio
Giuseppe
Gladwin
Glanville
Glen
Glendon
Glenn
Glyn
Glynn
Goddard
Godfrey
Godwin
Golding
Goldwin
Goodwin
Gordon
Gottfried
Grady
Graham,
 Grahame,
 Graeme
Granger
Grant
Granville
Gray
Greeley
Grégoire
Gregor
Gregorio
Gregory
Grasham
Greville
Grier
Griff
Griffin
Griffith
Grover
Gruffydd
Gualterio
Gualtieri
Guglielmo

Guido
Guilbert
Guillaume
Guillermo,
 Guillelmo
Gunnar
Gunter
Günther
Gus
Gustaf
Gustave,
 Gustavus
Guthrie
Guy
Guyon
Gwynfor

H

Haakon
Hackett
Hadley
Hadrian
Hagan
Hagley
Haig
Hakon
Hal
Halbert
Hale
Haley
Halford
Haliwell
Hall
Hallam
Halliwell
Halstead,
 Halsted
Halston
Hamar
Hamilton
Hamish

Hamlet, Hamlett
Hammond
Hamon
Hanford
Hank
Hanley
Hannibal
Hans
Hansel
Harbert
Harcourt
Harden
Hardie, Hardey
Harding
Hardy
Harford
Hargrave,
 Hargreave,
 Hargeaves
Harlan, Harland
Harley
Harlow
Harold
Harper
Harris, Harrison
Harry
Hart
Hartford
Hartley
Hartmann,
 Hartman
Hartwell
Harvey, Harvie
Haslett, hazlitt
Hastings
Havelock
Hawley
Hayden, Haydon
Hayley
Hayward
Haywood

415

Hazel
Hazlett, Hazlitt
Heath
Heathcliff,
 Heathecliffe
Hector
Hefin
Heinrich
Helge
hendrik
Henri
Henry
Heakles
Herbert
Hercule
Hercules
Heribert
Herman
Hermann
Hermes
Hernando
Herrick
Hertford
Hervé
Hervey
Hesketh
Hew
Hewett, Hewit
Heyward
Heywood
Hezekiah
Hi
Hieronymus
Hilaire
Hilario
Hilary, Hillary
Hildebrand
Hilton
Hiram
Hobart
Hogan

Holbert, Holbird
Holbrook
Holcomb,
 Holcombe
Holden
Holgate
Hollis
Holmes
Holt
Homer
Honorius
Horace, Horatio
Horton
Hosea
Houghton
Houston,
 Houstun
Howard
Howe
Howel, Howell
Hubert
Hudson
Hugh
Hugo
Hugues
Hulbert,
 Hulburd,
 Hulburt
Humbert
Humphrey,
 Humphry
Hunt, Hunter
Huntingdon
Huntington
Huntley, Huntly
Hurley
Hurst
Hutton
Huw
Huxley
Hyam

Hyde
Hylda
Hylton
Hyman
Hyram
Hywel, Hywell

I

Iachimo
Iacovo
Ian
Iain
Ichabod
Idris
Iestyn
Ieuan, Ifan
Ifor
Ignace
Ignacio
Ignatius
Ignatz, Ignaz
Ignazio
Igor
Ike
Ilario
Immanuel
Imre
Inge
Ingemar
Ingmar
Ingram
Inigo
Innes, Inness
Iolo, Iolyn
Iorwerth
Ira
Irvine, Irving
Irwin
Isaac
Isaiah
Isham

416

Isidor
Isidore
Isidoro
Isidro
Israel
Istvan
Ivan
Ives
Ivo
Ivor
Ivy
Iwan
Izaak
Izzie, Izzy

J

Jabal
Jabez
Jack
Jackie, Jacky
Jackson
Jacob
Jacobo
Jacques
Jagger
Jago
Jaime
Jairus
Jake
Jacob
Jamal
James
Jamie
Jan
Japheth
Jared
Jarvis
Jason
Jasper
Javan
Javier

Jay
Jean
Jedidiah
Jefferson
Jeffrey, Jeffery
Jehudi
Jeremias
Jeremy,
 Jeremiah
Jerome
Jérôme
Jerônimo
jerry
Jervis
Jesse
Jethro
Jo
Joab
Joachim
Joaquin
Job
Jocelyn, Jocelin
Jock, Jockie
Joe, Joey
Joel
Johan
Johann
Johannes
John
Jolyon
Jon
Jonah, Jonas
Jonathan,
 Jonthon
Jordan
Jorge
Jos
Joscelin
José
Josef
Joseph

Josh
Joshua
Joss
Juan
Judah
Jud, Judd
Jude
Jules
Julian
Julien
Julio
Julius
Justin
Justinian
Justus

K

Kane
Karel
Karl
Karlotte
Karol
Karr
Kasimir
Kaspar
Kavan
Kay
Kean, Keane
Keadr
Keefe
Keegan
Keir
Keith
Keld
Kelsey
Kelvin
Kemp
Ken
Kendrick
Kenelm
Kennard

	L	Leland
Kennedy		Lemuel
Kennet	Laban	Len
Kenneth	Lachlan	Lennard
Kennie, Kenny	Lacey	Lennie
Kenrick	Ladislao	Lennox
Kent	Ladislas	Lenny
Kenton	Laszlo	Leo
Kenyon	Laing	Leon
Kermit	Laird	Leonard
Kern	Lamvert	Leonardo
Kerr	Lamberto	Leaonhard
Kerry	Lamond, Lamont	Leonidas
Kester	Lance	Leontius
Kevin, kevan	Lancelot	Leopold
Kieran	Lander, Landor	Leopoldo
Kiernan	Lane	Leroy
Kiernan	Lang	Leslie
King	Langley	Lester
Kingsley	Larry	Lev
Kingston	Lars	Levi
Kinsey	Larsen, Larson	Lewis
Kirby	Lascelles	Lex
Kirk	Latimer	Lewis
Kirkwood	Laurence	Leyland
Kish	Laurens	Liam
Kit	Laurent	Libby
Klaus	Laurie	Lidia
Klemens	Lawrence	Liese
Knight	lawson	Lil
Knut	Lawton	Lila
Konrad	Layton	Lincoln
Konstanz	Lazarus	Lindall, Lindell
Korah	Leal, Leale	Lindley
Kris	Leander	Lindsay, Lindsey
Kristen	Leandre	Linford
Kristian	Leandro	Linley
Kristoffer	Lee	Linsay, Linsey
Kristopher	Leif	Linton
Kurt	Leigh	Linus
Kyle	Leighton	Lionel
	Leith	

Lisle	Lukas	Marco
Lister	Luke	Marcos
Litton	Lundy	Marcus
Llewelyn	Lutero	Mario
Lloyd	Luther	Marius
Locke	Lyall	Mark
Logan	Lycurgus	Markus
Lombard	Lyle	Marland
Lonnie	Lynden, Lyndon	Marlo
Lorcan, Lorcán	Lynn	Marlon
Lorenz	Lynsay, Lynsey	Marlow
Lorenzo	Lysander	Marmaduke
Loring	Lyss	Marmion
Lorn	Lytton	Marsden
Lorne		Marsh
Lot	M	Marshall
Lotario	Maarten	Marston
Lothaire	Madison	Martijn
Lou	Madoc	Martin
Louis	Magee	Martino
Lovel, Lovell	Magnus	Marty
Lowell	Maitland	Martyn
Luc	Makepeace	Marvin
Luca	Malachi	Marwood
Luca	Malcolm	Massimiliano
Lucan	Malise	Mat
Lucas	Mallory	Mateo
Lucian	Malone	Mather
Lucien	Manasseh	Matheson,
Luciano	Manfred	Mathieson
Lucifer	Manfredi	Mathias
Lucio	Manfried	Mathieu
Lucius	Manley	Matt
Lucretius	Manny	Mattaeus
Ludlow	Manuel	Matteo
Ludovic,	Marc	Matthais
Ludovick	Marcel	Matthäus
Ludvig	Marcello	Mattheus
Ludwig	Marcellus	Matthew
Luigi	Marcelo	Matthias
Luis	Marcius	Matthieu

419

Maurice
Mauricio
Maurits
Maurizio
Mauro
Maurus
Max
Maxie
Maximilian
Maximilien
Maxwell
Mayer
Maynard
Mayo
McGee
Medwin
Mel
Melbourne
Melchior
Melchiorre
Melfyn
Melville, Melvin,
 Melvyn
Mercer
Meredith
Merfyn
Merle
Merlin, Merlyn
Merrill
Merryll
Merton
Mervin, Mervyn
Meyer
Micah
Michael
Michel
Michele
Mick, Micky
Miguel
Mikael
Mike

Mikhail
Miles
Milford
Miller
Millward
Milne
Milner
Milo
Milton
Milward
Mischa
Mitchell
Mo
Modest
Modred
Monroe, Monro
Montague,
 Montagu
Montgomery,
 Montgomer
Monty
Moray
Morgan
Moritz
Morley
Morrice, Morris
Mortimer
Morton
Mosè
Moses
Muir
Mungo
Munro, Munroe,
 Munrow
Murdo, Murdoch
Murray
Myer
Myles
Myron

N

Naaman
Nahum
Nairn
Naphtali
Napier
Napoleon
Nash
Nat
Natal
Natale
Nathan
Nathaniel,
 Nathanael
Neal, Neale
Ned, Neddie,
 Neddy
Nehemiah
Neil
Nelson
Nemo
Nero
Nestor
Neven
Neville
Nevin
Newell
Newland
Newlyn, Newlin
Newman
Newton
Nial
Niall
Nickson
Niccolò
Nicholas
Nick
Nicky
Nicodemus
Nicol
Nicola

420

Nicolas
Nigel
Nikolaus
Nils
Ninian
Nixon
Noah
Noble
Noé
Noè
Noël, Noel
Nolan
Noll, Nollie
Norbert
Norman
Northcliffe
Norton
Norville
Norvin
Norward
Norwell
Norwood
Nowell
Nye

O

Oakley
Obadiah
Obed
Oberon
Obert
Octavius
Oda
Odd
Oddo, Oddone
Oded
Odoardo
Ogden
Ogilvie, Ogilvy
Olaf, Olav
Oleg

Oliver
Oliverio
Oliviero
Ollie, Olly
Omar
Onefre
Onefredo
Onfroi
Onofrio
Onorio
Oran
Orazio
Oren
Oreste
Orestes
Orfeo
Orin
Orion
Orlando
Ormond,
 Ormonde
Orpheus
Orrin
Orso
Orson
Orville, Orvil
Orwin
Osbert
Osborn, Osborne,
 Osbourne
Oscar
Oskar
Osmond,
 Osmund
Ossie
Osvaldo
Oswald
Oswin
Otis
Ottavio
Otto

Ottone
Owain
Owen
Oxford
Oxton
Oz, Ozzie, Ozzy

P

Pablo
Paddy
Padraig
Paget, Pagett,
 Padget, Padgett
Palmiro
Pancho
Paolo
Pascal
Pasquale
Pat
Patric
Patrice
Patricio
Patricius
Patrick
Patrizio
Patrizius
Paul
Payne, Payn
Pedaiah
Pedro
Peer
Peleg
Pepe
Pepin
Pepillo, Pepito
Per
Percival,
 Perceval
Percy
Peregrine
Perry

421

A Listing of Boys' Names

Peter
Petrus
Phelim
Phil
Philbert
Philemon
Philip
Philipp
Philippe
Phillip
Phineas,
 Phinehas
Pierce
Pierre
Piers
Pierse
Pieter
Pietro
Pio
Pip
Pius
Placido
Plato
Presley
Primo
Prosper
Pròspero
Pugh

Q

Quentin
Quinto
Quintus
Quenel, Quennel
Quigley, Quigly
Quinby
Quincy, Quincey
Quinlan
Quinn
Quinton

R

Rab, Rabbie
Raban
Radcliffe
Radley
Radnor
Rafe
Raffaele,
 Raffaello
Rafferty
Raimondo
Raimund
Raimundo
Rainaldo
Rainier
Raleigh
Ralph
Ram
Ramón
Ramsden
Ramsay, Ramsey
Ranald
Rand
Randal, Randall
Randolf,
 Randolph
Randy
Rankin, Rankine
Ransom
Ranulf
Raoul
Raphael
Ras
Rasmus
Rastus
Rawley
Rawnsley
Ray
Rayleigh
Raymond,

Raymund
Rayner
Read, Reade
Reading
Reagan
Reardon
Redding
Redman
Redmond
Reece
Reed, Reede
Rees
Reeve, Reeves
Regan
Reginald
Reilly
Reinald
Reinhard
Reinhold
Reinold
Remus
Renaldo
Renato
Renatus
Renault
René
Renfrew
Rennie, Renny
Renton
Reuben
Reuel
Rex
Reynard
Reynold
Rhodri
Rhys
Ricardo
Riccardo
Rich
Richard
Richey, Richie

Richmond
Rider
Ridley
Rigby
Rigg
Riley
Rinaldo
Ring
Riordan
Ripley
Ritchie
Ritter
Roald
Robert
Roberto
Robin
Robinson
Robyn
Rocco
Rochester
Rock
Rocky
Rod
Rodden
Roddy
Roderich
Roderick, Roderic
Roderico
Rodger
Rodney
Rodolf
Rodolphe
Rodrigo
Rodrigue
Rogan
Roger
Rogerio
Rohan
Roland
Roldán, Rolando

Rolf
Rolland
Rollo
Rolph
Roly
Romeo
Romilly
Romney
Ròmolo
Ron
Ronald
Ronan
Ronnie, Ronny
Rooney
Rory
Roscoe
Rosh
Roslin, RoslynRoss Rosslyn masc,
Rowan
Rowe
Rowell
Rowland
Rowley
Roxburgh
Roy
Royal
Royce
Royle
Royston
Rube
Rubén
Rudi
Rüdiger
Rudolf, Rudolph
Rudyard
Rufe
Rufus
Rugby
Ruggiero,

Ruggero
Rupert
Ruprecht
Rurik
Russell
Rutger
Rutherford
Rutland
Ruy
Ryan
Rye
Rylan, Ryland

S

Sabin
Sabino
Sabinus
Salomon
Salomo
Salomone
Salvador
Salvatore
Sam
Sammy
Samson, Sampson
Samuel
Samuele
Sancho
Sanders
Sandy
Sanford
Sanson
Sansón
Sansone
Santo
Saul
Saveur
Saxon
Scott
Sealey

Seamas, Seamus	Sherbourne	Somerset
Sean	Sheridan	Somerton
Searle	Sherlock	Somhairle
Seaton	Sherman	Sorley
Sebastian	Sherwin	Sorrel
Sebastiano	Sherwood	Spencer
Sébastien	Sholto	Squire
Secondo	Siddall, Siddell	Stacey
Secundus	Sidney	Stafford
Seeley	Siegfried	Stamford
Seigneur	Siegmund	Standish
Selby	Sigismond	Stanford
Selden	Sigismondo	Stanhope
Selig	Sigiswald	Stanislas,
Selwyn, Selwin	Sigmund	Stanislaus
Senior	Sigurd	Stanley
Septimus	Silas	Stanton
Serge	Silvain	Stefan
Sergei	Silvano	Stefano
Sergio	Silvanus	Stephan
Sergius	Silvester	Stephen, Steven
Sesto	Silvestre	Sterling
Seth	Silvestro	Stewart
Seton	Silvio	Stirling
Seumas	Sim	St John
Sewald, Sewall,	Simon, Simeon	Stockland
Sewell,	Sinclair	Stockley
Sexton	Siwald	Stockton
Sextus	Skelton	Stoddard
Seymour	Skerry	Stoke
Shalom	Skipper	Storm
Shamus	Skipton	Stowe
Shane	Slade	Strachan,
Shanley	Sly	Strahan
Shaw	Smith	Stratford
Shawn, Shaun	Snowden,	Stuart, Stewart,
Shea	Snowdon	Steuart
Sheffield	Sol	Sullivan
Sheldon	Solly	Sumner
Shepard	Solomon	Sutherland
Sherborne,	Somerled	Sutton

Sven
Sydney
Sylvain
Sylvanus
Sylvester

T

Tad
Taddeo
Tadhg
Taffy
Taggart
Tate
Talbot
Tam
Tancredi,
  Tancredo
Tancredmasc
Tate
Taylor
Teague
Tebaldo
Ted, Teddie,
  Teddy
Tennison,
  Tennyson
Teobaldo
Teodorico
Teodoro
Terence
Terencio
Terrance,
  Terrence
Terris, Terriss
Tertius
Teyte
Thaddeus
Thaine
Thane
Theo
Theobald

Theodor
Theodore
Theodoric,
  Theodorick
Theodorus
Theodosius
Theophilus
Theron
Thewlis
Thibaut
Thierry
Thomas
Thor
Thorburn
Thorndike,
  Thorndyke
Thorne
Thorold
Thorp, Thorpe
Thorwald
Thurstan,
  Thurston
Tibold
Tiebout
Tiernan, Tierney
Till
Tim
Timon
Timothy
Titian
Titianus
Tito
Titus
Tiziano
Tobi
Tobias, Tobiah
Toby
Todd
Todhunter
Tom
Tomas

Tomás
Tomaso,
  Tommaso
Tommaso
Tommie, Tommy
Tony
Tormod
Torold
Torquil
Tor
Torr
Torvald
Townsend,
  Townshend
Tracey
Tracy
Traherne
Travers
Travis
Tremaine,
  Tremayne
Trent
Trev
Trevelyan
Trevor
Tristram,
  Tristam, Tristan
Troy
True
Truelove
Trueman,
  Truman
Trystan
Tudor
Tullio
Tullius
Tully
Turner
Turpin
Twyford
Ty

Tybalt
Tye
Tyler
Tyrone
Tyson

U

Uberto
Udo
Udall, Udell
Ugo, Ugolino,
 Ugone
Ulises
Ulisse
Ulmar, Ulmer
Ulric, Ulrick
Ulrich
Ulysses
Umberto
Unwin
Upton
Urbaine
Urban
Urbano
Uri
Uriah
Urian
Uriel
Uzziah
Uzziel

V

Vachel
Vail
Val
Valdemar
Valdemaro
Valentin
Valentine
Valentino
Valerian

Valeriano
Valerio
Valéry
Van
Vance
Vasili, Vassily
Vaughan,
 Vaughn
Vere
Vergil
Vernon
Vicente
Victor
Vidal
Vilhelm
Vincent
Vincente
Vincenz
Vinnie, Vinny
Vinson
Virgil
Virgilio
Vitale
Vito
Vitore
Vitorio
Vittorio
Vitus
Vivian, Vyvian
Vladimir
Vladislav
Vyvian

W

Wade
Wadsworth
Wainwright
Wake
Waldo
Waldemar
Walker

Wallace
Wallis
Wally
Walt
Walter
Walther
Walton
Ward
Warfield
Warne
Warner
Warren
Warwick
Washington
Wat, Watty
Waverley
Wayne
Webb
Webster
Wellington
Wenceslaus,
 Wenceslas
Wendel, Wendell
Wentworth
Werner
Wesley
Whitaker
Whitman
Whitney
Whittaker
Wilbert
Wilbur
Wilfrid, Wilfred
Wilhelm
Will, Willie,
 Willy
Willard
Willemot
William
Willoughby
Willson

A Listing of Boys' Names

Wilmer
Wilmot
Wilson
Wilton
Wim
Windham
Windsor
Winslow
Winston
Winter
Winthrop
Winton
Wolf, Wolfe
Wolfgang
Wolfram
Woodrow
Woodward

Woody
Wordsworth
Worth
Wyman
Wyn
Wyndham
Wynn, Wynne

XYZ

Xavier
Xenos
Xerxes
Yale
Yehudi
York, Yorke
Yuri
Yves

Zabdiel
Zaccheus
Zachary,
 Zachariah,
 Zacharias,
 Zecheriah
Zadok
Zeb
Zebadiah,
 Zebedee
Zebulon, Zebulun
Zedekiah
Zeke
Zelig
Zenas
Zephaniah

Index to Weekley Text

INDEX

Acknowledgement

Grateful acknowledgment is made to John Murray for permission to reproduce the text of *Jack and Jill* by Professor Ernest Weekley.